Entrepreneurship

Development & Management

Dr. VASANT DESAI
Director,
Visvesvaraya Institute of
Socio-economic Research (VISER),
Mumbai.

Dr. KULVEEN KAUR
M.Com., M.Phil., Ph.D.
Visiting Faculty
Department of Business Administration
Utkal University
Bhubaneswar, Odisha.

Himalaya Publishing House
ISO 9001:2015 CERTIFIED

First Edition : 2013
Reprint : 2017
Reprint : 2022
Reprint : 2023

Published by : Mrs. Meena Pandey
for **HIMALAYA PUBLISHING HOUSE PVT. LTD.,**
"Ramdoot", Dr. Bhalerao Marg, Girgaon, Mumbai - 400 004.
Phone: 022-23860170, 23863863; **Fax:** 022-23877178
E-mail: himpub@bharatmail.co.in; **Website:** www.himpub.com

Branch Offices :

New Delhi : "Pooja Apartments", 4-B, Murari Lal Street, Ansari Road, Darya Ganj, New Delhi - 110 002. Phone: 011-23270392, 23278631; Fax: 011-23256286

Nagpur : Kundanlal Chandak Industrial Estate, Ghat Road, Nagpur - 440 018. Phone: 0712-2721215, 2721216

Bengaluru : Plot No. 91-33, 2nd Main Road, Seshadripuram, Behind Nataraja Theatre, Bengaluru - 560 020. Phone: 080-41138821; Mobile: 09379847017, 09379847005

Hyderabad : No. 3-4-184, Lingampally, Besides Raghavendra Swamy Matham, Kachiguda, Hyderabad - 500 027. Phone: 040-27560041, 27550139

Chennai : No. 34/44, Motilal Street, T. Nagar, Chennai - 600 017. Mobile: 09380460419

Pune : "Laksha" Apartment, First Floor, No. 527, Mehunpura, Shaniwarpeth (Near Prabhat Theatre), Pune - 411 030. Phone: 020-24496323, 24496333; Mobile: 09370579333

Cuttack : Plot No. 5F-755/4, Sector-9, CDA Markat Nagar, Cuttack - 753 014, Odisha. Mobile: 09338746007

Kolkata : 3, S.M. Bose Road, Near Gate No. 5, Agarpara Railway Station, North 24 Parganas, West Bengal - 700 109. Mobile: 09674536325

DTP : Sri Siddhi Softtek, Bengaluru.

Printed by : Geetanjali Press Pvt. Ltd., Nagpur. On behalf of HPH.

Preface

In the 21st century, entrepreneurship has assumed great importance. The waves of economic liberalization and globalization have opened up several opportunities to the potential entrepreneurs in the industrial, service and agricultural sectors. The new millennium is the age of entrepreneurship. Entrepreneurship is the outlook of mind to seek opportunities, take calculated risks and receive benefits by setting up a venture. It includes several activities involved in conception, creation and running of an enterprise.

Entrepreneurial development and management has come to be recognised globally as the key to rapid and sustainable economic development. Indeed, the entrepreneur with their vision, passion, ability and innovative qualities lay down a strong foundation for sustainable growth.

Entrepreneurship management is basically concerned with the development, and coordination of entrepreneurial functions. An effective organisation, sound planning, proper coordination of business activities and rational decision-making are the important aspects of entrepreneurship management. The foundation of effective management needs both policy and strategy to be determined and made known.

Literature on entrepreneur development and management has been growing in recent years. Though there have been numerous articles in various journals on entrepreneurial development, especially in India and quite a few edited books containing articles on different aspects of the subject by different authors. This book is intended to help furnish the much needed information on this subject.

The purpose of the book is to describe the essential features of an entrepreneur and entrepreneurship to provide a sense of direction for planners and policy-makers, on the one end, and the emerging crop of young entrepreneurs, both men and women, educated, uneducated, professional and non-professional, to reap immense benefits and decide the future course of action, on the other. In fact, this book is not a fresh beginning nor is it the last word. Subsequent studies will elaborate on many of the issues raised here.

Outline of the Book

However the presentation of the subject is our own creation.

The study consists of 16 chapters grouped into 6 units:

Unit 1: Entrepreneur

Chapter 1: Concept of Entrepreneur

Chapter 2: Types of Entrepreneur

Chapter 3: Nature and Importance

Chapter 4: Entrepreneurial Traits and Skills

Unit 2: Entrepreneurship

Chapter 5: Concept of Entrepreneurship

Chapter 6: Entrepreneurial Motivation and Achievement

We do not make any claim to originality or comprehensiveness. Rather we have sincerely attempted to bring together the scattered literature on the subject. However, the presentation of the subject is my own creation.

In the preparation of this book, we have drawn heavily from the published works in the sphere of entrepreneurial development and management.

We hope that the students, teachers, the policy makers, entrepreneurs and others interested in the subject will find the study quite useful. We look forward to receive suggestions from them for improving the contents and presentation of this study.

Authors

Contents

1 CHAPTER

THE ENTREPRENEUR: DEFINITION AND CONCEPT

"A good entrepreneur is one who is capable of inspiring confidence in people, and has the ability to motivate them to work with him in fulfilling the economic goals set by him."

Leadership is Laddership

Managewment is efficiency in climbing the ladder of success; leadership determines whether the ladder is leaning against the right wall.

— Stephen Covey, Management Guru

INTRODUCTION

The entrepreneur is an important input of economic development. He is a catalyst of development; with him we prosper, without him we are poor. In this chapter, we discuss the definitions and structure of entrepreneur.

The entrepreneur of the world are the wisest minds who leave an indelible mark in the history of mankind. They make it possible through their action, and not through words. They do things in a completely new way. They think beyond the obvious. They go deeper. They think from different perspectives and angles.

You give them any job, they do it with perfection. Nothing is impossible for them. They respond positively to the situation and tell, "Certainly I can do this". Then they get busy and find out how to do it.

The entrepreneur of the world do have a larger quest quotient than the intelligence quotient. They have always something to learn. They keep learning because they enjoy challenges. They believe, "who so neglects learning in his youth, loses the past and is dead for the future". They know, "Learning is not compulsory ... neither the survival". Agreeably, the whole world is a laboratory to the inquiring mind of entrepreneurs of the world.

Definition of an Entrepreneur

The term "entrepreneur" is defined in a variety of ways. Yet no consensus has been arrived at on the precise skills and abilities that make a person a successful entrepreneur.

The concept of entrepreneur varies from country-to-country as well as from period-to-period and the level of economic development thoughts and perceptions. A review of research done in different disciplines over the years would improve our understanding of the concept of entrepreneur.

> The word entrepreneur is derived from the French word 'Entreprendre' which means to 'undertake', i.e., the person who undertakes the risk of new enterprise.

The word entrepreneur, therefore, first appeared in the French language in the beginning of the sixteenth century. The word was also applied to the leaders of military expedition. But it was **Richard Cantillon** an Irishman, living in France who first used the term ***entrepreneur*** to refer to economic activities. According to Cantilon: "An entrepreneur is a person who buys factor services at certain prices with a view to selling its product at uncertain prices." Thus, to Cantilon, an entrepreneur is a bearer of risk which is non-insurable. Around 1700 A.D., the term was used for architects and contractors of public works.

Bernard Belidor applied it to the function of buying labour and material and uncertain prices and selling the resultant product at contracted price.

In many countries, the entrepreneur is often associated with a person who starts his own new and small business. Business encompasses manufacturing, transport, trade and all other self-employed vocations in the service sector. But not every new small business is entrepreneurial or represents entrepreneurship.

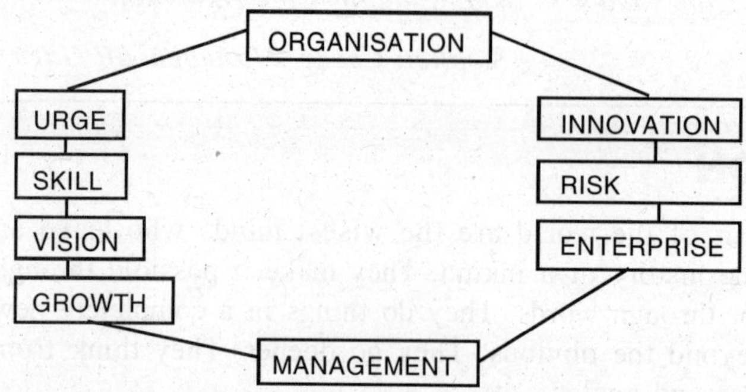

Fig. 1.1: Basics of an Entrepreneur

Another Frenchman, J.B. Say, expanded Cantillon's ideas and conceptualised the entrepreneur as an organiser of a business firm, central to its distributive and production functions. Beyond stressing the entrepreneur's importance to the business, Say did little with his entrepreneurial analysis.

According to **Jean Baptiste** say, an entrepreneur is the economic agent who unties all means of production, the labour force of the one and the capital or land of the others and who finds in the value of the products his results from their employment, the reconstitution of the entire capital that he utilises and the value of the wages, the interest and the rent which he pays as well as profit belonging to himself. He emphasised the functions of coordination, organisation and supervision. Further, it can be said that the entrepreneur is an organiser and speculator of a business enterprise. The entrepreneur lifts economic resources out of an area of lower into an area of higher productivity and greater yield.

The New Encyclopaedia Britannica considers an entrepreneur as "an individual who bears the risk of operating a business in the face of uncertainty about the future conditions". Leading economists of all schools, including Karl Marx have emphasised the contribution of the entrepreneurs to the development of economies, but Joseph Schumpeter who argues that the rate of growth in an economy depends to a great extent on the activities of entrepreneurs, has probably put greater emphasis on the entrepreneurial function than any other economist.

As Professor **Jan Tinbergen** points out: "The best entrepreneur in any developing country is not necessarily the man who uses much capital, but rather the man who knows how to organise the employment and training of his employees. Whoever concentrates on this is rendering a much more important service to his country than the man who uses huge capital."

Adam Smith, the father of classical economics, did not use the term ***entrepreneur*** anywhere. Instead, he used the words like ***employer***, the ***merchant***, the ***undertaker*** and the ***master***.

Alfred Marshall wrote about the capitalists and management but he was silent about their difference. As such, the classical economists ignored the term ***entrepreneur*** entirely.

According to **A.P. Usher:** "Specialization or division of labour necessitates an entrepreneurial function the crux of which is to co-ordinate different economic activities. This view on entrepreneurship was very narrow and it reduced the entrepreneurship activities to no more than a managerial function."

F.H. Knight, in his article on *Risk, Uncertainty and Profit* propounded the maxim that "entrepreneur are a specialized group of persons who bear risks and deal with uncertainty." He also identified social, psychological and economic factors which govern the supply of entrepreneurship.

According to **David Ricardo,** a contemporary of **J.B. Say:** "The foremost motive of a risk taker is to amass capital and capital accumulation is the *sine qua non* of economic development."

J.S. Mill viewed the word ***entrepreneur*** as organizer who was paid for his non-manual type of work. According to him: "Extraordinary skills acted as the bedrock in production process that ought to be possessed by the entrepreneur."

Leon Walrus, in his papers, *The Theory of Social Wealth* (Allen and Unwin, London, 1954) pointed out that entrepreneur is the coordinator of basic factors of production. He treated **'*entrepreneur*'** as the fourth factor of production who combines other factors such as land, labour and capital.

Table 1.1 The Entrepreneur: Other Definitions

Adam Smith described entrepreneur as a person who only provides capital without taking active part in the leading role in enterprise.

Richard Cantillon considered all persons engaged in economic activity as entrepreneurs.

Jean Baptiste Say opined that the entrepreneur was a person endowed with the qualities of judgement, perseverance and a knowledge of the world as well as of business. The entrepreneur shifts economic resources out of an area of lower and into an area of higher productivity and greater yield. The definition included the concept of bringing together the factors of production.

French tradition regard an entrepreneur as a person translating a profitable idea into a productive activity.

Karl Marx regarded entrepreneur as a social parasite.

Joseph A. Schumpeter recognised that a person who introduces innovation changes is an entrepreneur. He treated entrepreneur as an integral part of economic growth. The fundamental source of equilibrium was the entrepreneur.

Frank Young describes entrepreneur as a change agent.

Noah Webster thinks entrepreneur is one who assumes the responsibility of the risk and management of business.

***Francis A.* Walker** observes that the true entrepreneur is one who is endowed with more than average capacities in the risk of organising and coordinating the various other factors of production.

Peter F. Drucker defines an entrepreneur as one who always searches for change, respond to it and exploits it as an opportunity. Innovation is the specific tool of entrepreneurs, the means by which they exploit change as an opportunity for a different business or service.

Arthur Dewing conceptualised the function of the entrepreneur as one that promotes ideas into business.

Clarence H. Danof considers entrepreneur as a person who makes decision under alternative courses of action.

Entrepreneur has become the focal point in economic activities. He is viewed as an initiator of action, a stimulant of socio-economic change and development.

Robert D. Hisrich says, "The person who is going to establish a successful new business venture must also be a visionary leader — a person who dreams great dreams. Although there are many definitions of leadership, the one that best describes the needed intrapreneurial leadership is: A leader is like a gardener. When you want a tomato, you take a seed, put it in fertile soil, and carefully water under tender care. You don't manufacture tomatoes, you grow them."

Martin Luther King said, "I have a dream, and thousands followed in spite of overwhelming obstacles. In order to establish a successful new business venture the intrapreneurial leader must have a dream and work against all obstacles to achieve it."

Entrepreneur is one who distinguishes as a person who undertakes to organise, manage and assume the risk of running a factory and/or a business or an enterprise.

Entrepreneurship is neither a science nor an art. It is a practice. It has a knowledge base. Knowledge in entrepreneurship is a mean to an end. Indeed, what constitutes knowledge in practice is largely defined by the ends, that is by practice.

According to ***Everett E. Haggen***, an entrepreneur is an economic man who tries to maximise his profits by innovations. Innovations involve problem-solving and the entrepreneur gets satisfaction from using his capabilities in attacking problems.

According to ***David McClelland***: "An entrepreneur is someone who exercises some control over the means of production and produces more than what he can consume in order to sell (or exchange) it for individual (or household) income."

An entrepreneur, as defined by ***Robert E. Nelson***, is a person who is able to look at environment, identify opportunities to improve the environment, marshall resources and implement action to maximize those opportunities.

According to ***J.K. Galbraith***: "An entrepreneur must accept the challenge and should be willing hard to achieve something."

Akhouri, M.M.P. describes entrepreneur as a character who contributes innovativeness, readiness to take risk, sensing opportunities, identifying and mobilising potential resources concern for excellence, and who is persistent in achieving the goal. The term entrepreneur contain notions of newness, innovation, vision, organising, creating wealth, mobilising resources, risk taking and achievement a driving force of economic development.

Not every new small business is entrepreneurial or represents entrepreneurship. To be entrepreneurial, an enterprise has to have special characteristics over and above being new and small. Indeed, entrepreneurs create something new, something different, they change or transmute value.

Laura Parkin: Entrepreneurs are both born and made. While some people are born with natural talent and risk tolerance. Entrepreneurship is a discipline and entrepreneurship skills can be learned by everyone.

Albert Shapero observes that the entrepreneur takes initiative, organises some social and economic mechanisms, and accepts risks of failure.

Karl Vesper affirms that the entrepreneur is seen differently by economists, psychologists, business persons and politicians.

Robert C. Ronstadt considers that the wealth is created by individuals who assume the major risks in terms of equity, time, commitment, and value for some product or service.

According to ***David Ricardo***, the foremost motive of a risk taker is to a mass capital and capital accumulation is the *sine qua non* of economic development.

John Stuart Mill viewed the world entrepreneur as organiser who is paid for his non-manual type of work.

Leon Walrus pointed out that entrepreneur is the coordinator of basic factors of production. He treated 'entrepreneur' as the fourth factor of production who combines other factors such as land, labour and capital.

Carl Menger considers the entrepreneur as the change agent who transforms resources into useful goods and services, often creating the circumstances that lead to industrial growth.

Frank H.Knight points out that entrepreneurs are a specialised group of persons who bear risk and deals with uncertainty.

Mark Cassons opines that an entrepreneur is a person who specialises in taking judgemental decision about the coordination of scarce resources.

Max Weber states that the entrepreneurs are a product of particular social condition in which they are brought up and it is the society which shapes individuals as entrepreneurs.

A.David Silver described the entrepreneur as 'energetic, single minded, and having "a mission and clear vision; he or she intends to create out of this vision a product or service in a field many have determined is important to improve the lives of millions."

Henry Ford who created the manufacturing miracle that launched a modern era in industry, said that, entrepreneur can do anything with passion and enthusiasm. Enthusiasm is the yeast that makes his hopes rise to the stars. Enthusiasm is the spark in his eye, the swing in his gait, the grip of his hand, the irresistible surge of his will and his energy to execute his ideas. Enthusiasts are fighters, they have fortitude, they have strong qualities. Enthusiasm is at the bottom of all progress. With it there is accomplishment. Without it there are only alibis.

2

CHAPTER

TYPES OF ENTREPRENEURS

> *"Entrepreneur is a person who discovers new ideas and business opportunities, brings together funds to establish a business, organises and manages its operations in order to provide economic goods and services, for the public. Entrepreneurs have strong convictions, self-motivation, the will to grow and prosper tremendously and also the courage to go bankrupt if they fail in their venture. But in majority of cases they start with nothing but entrepreneurial ability and end with positive results."*

INTRODUCTION

In the previous chapter, we have analysed the concept of entrepreneur and its understanding over the centuries, particularly in the post industrial revaluation. In modern times stress has been laid on the entrepreneur. Entrepreneurial development is the thrust area of development planners, economic thinkers and policymakers. What is more, the entrepreneur has emerged as *a kingpin* of development.

"Entrepreneur is a person who discovers new ideas and business opportunities, brings together funds to establish a business, organises and manages its operations in order to provide economic goods and services, for the public. Entrepreneurs have strong convictions, self-motivation, the will to grow and prosper tremendously and also the courage to go bankrupt if they fail in their venture. But in majority of the cases, they start with nothing but entrepreneurial ability and end with positive results."

By and large, entrepreneurs are found in every economic system and in every form of economic activity as well as in other social and cultural activities. They are found amongst artisans, labourers, artists, importers, exporters, engineers, supervisors, bankers, industry, professionals, etc. They are also found among farmers, fishermen, forest workers, tribals and so on. Some writers have also identified entrepreneurs among politicians, theologists, philosophers and bureaucrats.

Broadly, entrepreneurs are classified into business community and others. This chapter attempts to analyse different types of entrepreneurs in business as well as in different faculties of understanding. On the basis of his study of American agriculture, Clarence Danhof classified entrepreneurs into four categories, namely, Innovative Entrepreneur, etc. The other classification is based on technology, economic activity and market economy.

Box 2.1 **A Fair Success Path**

Sunita Ramnathkar, a chemistry graduate and housewife, set up a factory in Andheri, a distant suburb of Mumbai with a net capital of ₹ one lakh in 1982. In a span of 12 years, the compnay, Fem Care Pharma Pvt. Ltd., has come a long way and has crossed ₹ 33.5 crore turnover mark with its key products. Its first product was 'Fem Instoblcach'. Today the company has broadened its product base. Fem has succeeded in carving a niche for itself in all its product-lines. While the distribution of the other products in the Fem range are handled by 450 stockists, sales and marketing for the Pharma range is via medical representatives and is restricted to Karnataka, Maharashtra and Madhya Pradesh and Fem has been developing its expertise in niche marketing developing into a fine art.

After all, whatever the generic name of the product, success of a brand depends on how the consumer values it.

Economists View

In economic analysis, entrepreneurial functions are supposed to be directed towards the materialistic objective of maximisation though its foundations may be of a high order such as spiritual, patriotic, social, psychological or ethnic. Entrepreneurial activity is a form-giving, activity-giving form to the wishes of the society, to ideas, to the efforts of factors and to the raw material to be processed through.

According to **Jean Baptiste** entrepreneurial functions.

1. **Direction**
2. **Superintendence**
3. **Control**

Direction: He is a goal-oriented person; he has to keep the organisation constantly on the path of his objective. His is an activity of producing in the present what the future will demand. John Stuart also emphasised managerial and administrative functions of an entrepreneur according to Marshall. Organisation building capacity is the most critical skill expected of an entrepreneur according to Alfred. Organisation building capacity is the most critical skill expected of an entrepreneur. He assigns to the entrepreneur the functions of risk-bearing, innovation and management. To Cantillion, an entrepreneur is an uncertainty-bearer buying at a fixed price and selling at an uncertain one.

Israle, M. viewed the entrepreneur as a disequilibrating force. It is the alertness to unnoticed opportunities which creates a tendency of the ever-circular flow of equilibrium. Harvey Leibenstenin states, "Entrepreneur is an individual or group of individuals with four major characteristics. He connects different markets; he is capable of making up market deficiencies (gap-filling); he is input complete and he creates or expands time-binding, input-transforming entities (firms)."

To Joseph, A., innovation is the sole function of an entrepreneur. It covers the introduction of new goods, a new method of production, a new market, a new source of supply of raw materials or half-manufactured goods and a new organisation of any industry for the creation of a monopoly position or breaking it. The function of the entrepreneur is to reform or revise the pattern of production. So, Schumpeter has given a social context to the activity, a psychological objective to be attained and a functionality spearheading development of the community. Lazarfeld as also Meier and Baldwin concur with Schumpeter.

Bert F. Hoselitz reports, "The primary function of entrepreneurship is the investment of time, capital and energy in economically significant pursuit; the emphasis is on decision-making in its various aspects."

Frederick Fritz enumerates four functions : the undertaking or managing of risks and handling of economic uncertainty; planning and innovation; coordination, administration and control and routine supervision. Ability to build an organisation is, perhaps, Harbinson adds, the most precious of all entrepreneurial skills. Redlich's three-fold division of function is: (i) capitalist — employing the factors and buying raw material, setting up the organisation; (ii) managerial — innovation, supervision and coordination of productive activities, and (iii) entrepreneurial — decision-making. Benjamin Higgins lists seeing opportunities for introduction of new techniques, new products and exploitation of new resources and organising factors of production into an enterprise to take advantage of these opportunities as essential for economic development.

B.C.Tandon discusses the function of an entrepreneur in a developing economy in the context of economic, legal, political and cultural environment. Accordingly, the entrepreneur must possess: (a) capacity to assume risk and self-confidence; (b) technological knowledge, alertness to know opportunities, willingness to accept change and ability to initiate; (c) ability to marshal resources, and (d) ability of organisation and administration. He has to have tact, patience, sagacity, power of observation and ability of discrimination. He should have the capacity to pick and choose associates and subordinates and wisely delegate authority to inspire loyalty. He must be able to multiply 'himself' effectively. Tandon describes the entrepreneur as an 'ideal-type' rather than as 'social-type.' Frank, H. identifies entrepreneurship with control and responsibility.

Economic functions described above isolate the entrepreneur from the economic environs, social milieu and political ethos in which he functions. Maximization is taken as the pole star in his voyage. It seems to be conveniently assumed that he is abundantly provided with all the resources and the market readily absorbs what he put into it. Reality is, however, full of bottlenecks and hurdles which are ignored in the above-mentioned works. Small industry is a natural habitat of the entrepreneur where his role is like that of a stoker who keeps the fire burning. Economic functioning takes no notice of this.

Sociologists View

Sociologists consider the entrepreneur as a role performer corresponding to the role expected by the society. Wishes of the society are exhibited through customs and taboos, rewards and restraints, ethnic values and child-rearing practices, nationalistic attitude and patriotic inculcations and protestant ethics. He is conditioned by the social milieu to which he belongs. According to Peter Marris, to assemble or reassemble from what is available, very concrete kind of imagination, to see what others have missed, sensitivity to business and social environment, zest in industrial development and entrepreneurial courage are the factors that make an entrepreneur. According to Flavia Derossi, coordination at every stage — inception, maintenance and expansion — is the function of an entrepreneur. She feels an entrepreneur needs two qualities: (i) Optimistic outlook that there is a possibility of change, the environment can be mastered and he himself can introduce the required change. He finds difficulties challenging and stimulating; he thrives on them. And (ii) In a share as in the dynamic industry, new problems are seized upon as opportunities for testing one's own capabilities.

According to T.C. Cochran, the entrepreneur represents society's model personality. His performance depends upon his own attitudes towards his occupation, the role expectations of sanctioning groups and the occupational requirements of the job. Society's values are the most important determinant of attitudes and role expectations.

Arthur, H.Cole, states that entrepreneurship should not be studied by focusing on individual entrepreneur but rather than by looking at the enterprise. Special attention was often paid to the social relations within the enterprise and to the relations between the enterprise and its surroundings.

Everett, E. Hagen also concluded that entrepreneurs have emerged from certain communities and castes.

Thus, Hagen disregard the complicated institutional environment that surrounds the entrepreneur.

Psychologists View

Among psychologists, Frank Young describes an entrepreneur as a change-agent. K.L.Sharma maintains that entrepreneurs are men who exhibit qualities of leadership is solving persistent professional problems; but those persons likewise demonstrate eagerness to seize unusual opportunities. They have a business gambler's itch. T.V. Rao and Udai Pareek describe entrepreneurship as a creative and innovative response to the environment. The entrepreneur is goal-oriented rather than means-oriented. He must not only have a high capacity of risk-taking but must also have a high capacity of risk-sustaining which is a function of a high degree of self-confidence.

Joseph Schumpeter states that the entrepreneur is mainly motivated and driven by three things:

(i) 'the dream and the will to found a private kingdom';

(ii) 'the will to conquer';

(iii) 'the joy of creating.'

J. Schumpeter's formulation can be translated as:

(i) the desire for power and independence;

(ii) the will to succeed;

(iii) the satisfaction of getting things done.

According to him, money is not what ultimately motivates the entrepreneur 'Entrepreneurs', according to Schumpeter, 'are certainly not economic men in the theoretical sense.'

According to David McClelland, entrepreneurship has to do with an individual's so-called need for achievement (referred to n-Achievement). He identified three features of entrepreneurs that were related to their need for achievement: (1) desire to accept responsibility for solving problems, setting goals and reaching the goals; (2) a willingness to accept moderate risks; (3) a desire to know the outcomes of their decisions. It was widely believed that a high achievement motivation has a strong likelihood of predicting entrepreneurial behaviour. Individuals with high achievement motive tend to take keen interest in situations of high risk, desire for responsibility and a desire for a concrete measure of task performance.

According to Fredrik Barth, entrepreneurship has essentially to do with connecting two spheres in the society, between which there exists a difference in value. Something which is cheap in one sphere, may be expensive in another sphere. Barth, one of the leading anthropologists of the world, states that entrepreneurial behaviour means to connect two different spheres in the society, between which there is a huge discrepancy in value.

In sum, the foregoing description of the functions of an entrepreneur presents the profile of a functionary. Economists present him as a perceiver of otherwise unnoticed opportunity, organisation builder, adaptor of new profitable activity and beneficiary thereof. Sociologists present him as a personality moulded by various practices of social enforcement and values imbibed in him. Psychologically, entrepreneurship is a vigorous application of the person's energies towards the long-cherished goals.

CLASSIFICATION OF ENTREPRENEURS

The entrepreneurs in business are broadly classified according to the types of business, use of professional skill, motivation, growth and stages of development. Clarence Danhof Classifies entrepreneurs on the basis of stage of economic development: some others have classified on the basis of their functions and characteristics. The former reflects the role played by the entrepreneurs in the economic development, and later type reflects the degree of their involvement. The various types of entrepreneurs have been shown in Table 2.1.

The above classification of entrepreneurs is not exhaustive, for it aims at highlighting the broad range of entrepreneurs found in various businesses and professions. We shall now discuss in brief, each type of entrepreneur.

According to the Type of Business

Entrepreneurs are found in various types of businesses occupation of varying size. We may broadly classify them as follows:

***Business Entrepreneurs*:** They are individuals who conceive an idea for a new product or service and then create a business to materialise their idea into reality. They tap both production and marketing resources in their search to develop a new business opportunity. They may set up a big establishment or a small business unit. They are called *small business entrepreneurs* when found in small business units such as printing press, textile processing house, advertising agency, readymade garments or confectionery. In a majority of cases, entrepreneurs are found in small trading and manufacturing business and entrepreneurship flourishes when the size of the business is small.

Trading Entrepreneur: He undertakes trading activities and is not concerned with the manufacturing work. He identifies potential markets, stimulates demand for his product-line and

Table 2.1 Classification of Entrepreneurs

According to the types of business

1. Business entrepreneurs
2. Trading entrepreneurs
   - (i) Wholesale trade
   - (ii) Retail trade
   - (iii) Mall trading
   - (iv) Exporters
   - (v) Importers
   - (vi) Stock trading
   - (vii) Real estate
3. Industrial entrepreneurs
   - (i) Large
   - (ii) Medium
   - (iii) Small and
   - (iv) Tiny Sector
4. Corporate entrepreneurs
5. Agricultural entrepreneurs
   - (i) Plantation
   - (ii) Horticulture
   - (iii) Dairy
   - (iv) Forestry
   - (v) Floriculture
   - (vi) Animal Husbandry
   - (vii) Poultry
   - (viii) Seeds
6. Retail entrepreneurs
7. Service entrepreneurs
   - (i) Repairs
   - (ii) Engineering
   - (iii) Beauty Parlours
   - (iv) Others
8. Re-engineering entrepreneurs
9. Health entrepreneurs

According to the use of technology

1. Technical entrepreneurs
2. Non-technical entrepreneurs
3. Professional entrepreneurs
4. High-tech entrepreneurs
5. Low-tech entrepreneurs
6. Business process outsourcing
7. Knowledge process outsourcing
8. IT entrepreneurs
9. E-entrepreneurs
10. Legal processing outsourcing

According to the motivation

1. Pure entrepreneurs
2. Induced entrepreneurs
3. Motivated entrepreneurs
4. Spontaneous entrepreneurs
5. Forced entrepreneurs
6. Accidental entrepreneurs
7. Achieving entrepreneurs
8. Successful entrepreneurs

According to the growth

1. Growth entrepreneurs
2. Super-growth entrepreneurs
3. Aspiring entrepreneurs
4. Lifestyle entrepreneurs

According to the stages of development

1. First generation entrepreneurs
2. Modern entrepreneurs
3. Classical entrepreneurs
4. Generation-next entrepreneurs
5. Inherited entrepreneurs

According to area

1. Urban entrepreneurs
2. Rural entrepreneurs
   (i) Artisans
   (ii) Handlooms
   (iii) Sericulture
   (iv) Agri
   (v) Khadi
   (vi) Village industries
   (vii) Handicrafts and
   (viii) Rural service
3. Global entrepreneurs
4. Local entrepreneurs

According to organisation

1. Individual entrepreneurs
2. Group entrepreneurs
3. Institutional entrepreneurs
4. Private entrepreneurs
5. Public entrepreneurs
6. Government entrepreneurs

According to gender and age

1. Men entrepreneurs
2. Women entrepreneurs
   (i) Young entrepreneurs
   (ii) Old entrepreneurs
   (iii) Middle-aged entrepreneurs

Unclassified

1. Professional entrepreneurs
2. Non-professional entrepreneurs
3. New Modern entrepreneurs
4. Trading entrepreneurs
5. Skilled entrepreneurs
6. Non-skilled entrepreneurs
7. Imitating entrepreneurs
8. Serial entrepreneurs
9. Social entrepreneurs
10. National entrepreneurs
11. International entrepreneurs
12. Bureaucratic entrepreneurs
13. Orthodox entrepreneurs
14. Immigrant entrepreneurs
15. Innovative entrepreneurs
16. Philonthropreneurs
17. Entertainment entrepreneurs
18. Creative entrepreneurs

- 19. Knowledge entrepreneurs
- 20. Education entrepreneurs
- 21. Intrapreneurs
- 22. Ultrapreneurs
- 23. Mompreneurs
- 24. Alterpreneurs
- 25. Artapreneurs
- 26. Joint entrepreneurs
- 27. Generous entrepreneurs
- 28. Promoter entrepreneurs
- 29. Multifaced entrepreneurs
- 30. Entrepreneur employees
- 31. Accidental entrepreneurs

creates a desire and interest among buyers to go in for his product. He is engaged in both domestic and overseas trade. Britain, due to geographical limitations, has developed trade through trading entrepreneurs. These entrepreneurs demonstrated their ability in pushing many ideas ahead which promoted their business.

***Industrial Entrepreneur*:** Industrial entrepreneur is essentially a manufacture who identifies the potential needs of customers and tailors products or services to meet the marketing needs. He is a product-oriented man who starts in an industrial unit because of the possibility of making some new product. The entrepreneur has the ability to convert economic resources and technology into a considerably profitable venture. He is found in any industrial units such as the electronic industry, textile unit, machine tools or video cassette making and the like.

***Corporate Entrepreneur*:** This entrepreneur is a person who demonstrates his innovative skill in organising and managing a corporate undertaking. A corporate undertaking is a form of business organisation which is registered under some statute or Act which gives it a separate legal entity. A trust registered under the Trust Act, or a company registered under the Companies Act are examples of corporate undertakings. He is thus an individual who plans, develops and manages a corporate body.

***Agricultural Entrepreneur*:** Agricultural entrepreneurs are those who undertake such agricultural activities as raising and marketing of crops, fertilisers and other inputs of agriculture. They are motivated to raise the productivity of agriculture through mechanisation, irrigation and application of technologies for dry land agriculture. They cover a broad spectrum of the agricultural sector and include agriculture and allied occupations.

Social Entrepreneur

Ashoka-Innovators for the Public, a global non-profit organisation committed to nurturing social entrepreneurship, says a social entrepreneur is one who recognises the part of society which is stuck and provides new ways to get it unstuck. Be it dedicated efforts for child upliftment, fighting for the conservation of Assam's rainforests, working for the betterment of the blind or initiatives to empower women, the entrepreneur's passion is so strong that he can't let "the opportunity to make a difference" go by.

Ashoka was the idea of one man, William Drayton. His key insight was that there exist people in all countries who, like business entrepreneurs, have vision, creativity and tenacity, but who are possessed with a need to make a difference, to change society. He dubbed these people "social entrepreneurs." Social entrepreneurs, he explained, were "rare men and women who possess the vision, creativity and extraordinary determination of the business entrepreneur but who devote these qualities to introducing new solutions to societal problems." He also realized that a little investment in such people would go farther in terms of their social impact than simply giving money for projects would. "It is arrogant to think that well-meaning outsiders can make a dent in the horrendous social problems besetting every country in the world .... We empower social entrepreneurs from the communities and get out of their way. It is amazing how effective they become in finding their own solutions."

Like the visionary social entrepreneurs, Verghese Kurien of Amul, Rippan Kapur of CRY, Jeroo Billimoria of Childline (where children in trouble in numerous Indian cities can pick up a phone ad make a toll-free call for help) and many others, a social entrepreneur approach to implement ideas in creative, innovative and unconventional. It's their sensitivity and the ability to voice and take a stand which differentiates them from others.

David Bornstein

David Bornstein, the exponent of social innovations and entrepreneurship believes that the future belongs to social entrepreneurs. They are news worthy and pose serious threats to the *status quo*.

In essence they are both the same. However, while the former is concerned about profits, the latter is fanatical about a cause. So much so, that he or she is not happy solving an idea in one village or two villages. Yet at the same time, social entrepreneurs have got to be very systematic, are basically really good people, with a high streak of integrity. And finally, they are really self-effacing — always passing on the credit of their work to the team.

Most of these social entrepreneurs start with a higher base of education with greater access to information, and are more aware of problems around them in this era of the internet. Between 1970 and 1985, adult literacy rates have increased in the developed world from 43 per cent to 60 per cent and there has been a proliferation of the dot orgs too. Finally, there is more opportunity both politically and financially now, than ever before in history. Per capita incomes in free market economies have risen by more than 700 per cent in the 20th century. So essentially, freedom, wealth, exposure, social mobility and greater individual confidence are driving this huge wave of social innovation and entrepreneurship. After all people are tired with the inefficiency of governments and the indifference of corporates, and want to make a change and this is the case everywhere.

According to the Use of Technology

The application of new technology in various sectors of the national economy is essential for the future growth of business. We may broadly classify these entrepreneurs on the basis of the use of technology as follows:

Technical entrepreneur: A technical entrepreneur is essentially an entrepreneur of 'craftsman type.' He develops new and improved quality of goods because of his craftsmanship. He concentrates more on production rather than marketing. He does not care much to generate sales by applying various sales promotional techniques. He demonstrates his innovative capabilities in matters of production of goods and rendering services. The greatest strength which the technical entrepreneur has is his skill in introduction techniques.

Non-technical entrepreneur: Non-technical entrepreneurs are those who are not concerned with the technical aspects of the product in which they deal. They are concerned only with developing alternative marketing and distribution strategies to promote their business.

Professional entrepreneur: Professional entrepreneur is a person who is interested in establishing a business but does not have interest in managing or operating it once it is established. A professional entrepreneur sells out the running business and starts another venture with the sales proceeds. Such an entrepreneur is dynamic and he conceives new ideas to develop alternative projects.

According to Motivation

Motivation is the force that influences the efforts of the entrepreneur to achieve his objectives. An entrepreneur is motivated to achieve or prove his excellence in job performance. He is also motivated to influence others by demonstrating his power, thus satisfying his ego.

Pure entrepreneur: A pure entrepreneur is an individual who is motivated by psychological and economical rewards. He undertakes an entrepreneurial activity for his personal satisfaction in work, ego or status.

Induced entrepreneur: This entrepreneur is one who is induced to take up an entrepreneurial task due to the policy measures of the government that provides assistance, incentives, concessions and necessary overhead facilities to start a venture. Most of the entrepreneurs belong to this category and enter business due to financial, technical and several other facilities provided to them by the state agencies to promote entrepreneurship. A person with a sound project is provided package assistance to his project. Today, import restrictions and allocation of production quotas to small units have induced many people to start a small-scale industry.

Motivated entrepreneur: New entrepreneurs are motivated by the desire for self-fulfilment. They come into being because of the possibility of making and marketing some new products for the use of consumers. If the product is developed to a saleable stage, the entrepreneur is further motivated by reward in terms of profit.

Spontaneous entrepreneurs: These entrepreneurs start their business out of their natural talents. They are persons with initiative, boldness and confidence in their ability which motivate them to undertake entrepreneurial activity. Such entrepreneurs have a strong conviction and confidence in their ability.

According to Growth

The development of a new venture has a greater chance of success. The entrepreneur enters a new and open field of business. The customer's approval to the new product gives them psychological satisfaction and enormous profit. The industrial units are identified as high growth, medium growth and low growth industries and as such we have 'Growth Entrepreneur' and 'Super Growth Entrepreneur.'

Growth Entrepreneur: He necessarily takes up a high growth industry and chooses an industry which has sustained growth prospects.

Super Growth Entrepreneur: This category of entrepreneurs are those who have shown enormous growth of performance in their venture. The growth performance is identified by the liquidity of funds, profitability and gearing.

According to Stages of Development

Entrepreneurs may also be classified as the first generation entrepreneur, modern entrepreneur and classical entrepreneur, depending upon the stage of development.

First-generation Entrepreneur: A first-generation entrepreneur is one who starts an industrial unit by means of an innovative skill. He is essentially an innovator, combining different technologies to produce a marketable product or service.

Modern Entrepreneur: A modern entrepreneur is one who undertakes those ventures which go well along with the changing demand in the market. They undertake those ventures which suit the current marketing needs.

Classical Entrepreneur: A classical entrepreneur is one who is concerned with the customers and marketing needs through the development of self-supporting ventures. He is a stereotype entrepreneur whose aims to maximise his economic returns at a level consistent with the survival of the firm with or without an element of growth.

Women Entrepreneurs' Enterprises

In 1988, for the first time, the definition of Women Entrepreneurs' Enterprise was evolved that termed an SSI unit/industry-related service or business enterprise, managed by one or more women entrepreneurs in proprietary concerns, or in which she/they individually or jointly have a share capital of not less than 51 per cent as partners/shareholders/directors of a private limited company/members of a cooperative society, as a Woman Enterprise.

Women entrepreneurs have been on the Indian business scene for quite sometime now and have achieved remarkable success. However, their number in relation to the overall number of small-scale enterprises is still very small. One of the reasons for this is the initial hesitation and inhibition, both familial and social, due to the traditional perception of the women's role. Moreover, like any other entrepreneur, any first generation woman entrepreneur has to compete in the business against those already well established.

Woman entrepreneurs, as a group, came into prominence in the late 1970s. The information contained in the Second All India SSI Census 1987-88 shows that about 7.7 per cent of the small enterprises were owned by women. Industry group-wise, the most popular activity of women entrepreneurs was food processing followed by garment making. Realising the great untapped potential, the Government has been making concerted efforts to channelise the skills and talent of women towards economic and business generating activities.

Table 2.2 Comparison between Male and Female Entrepreneurs

Characteristics	*Male Entrepreneurs*	*Female Entrepreneurs*
Motivation	Achievement — strive to make things happen Personal independence — self-image as it relates to status through their role in the corporation is unimportant Job satisfaction arising from the desire to be in control	Achievement — accomplishment of a goal Independence — to do it alone
Departure point	Dissatisfaction with present job Sideline in college, sideline to present job, or outgrowth of present job Discharge or layoff Opportunity for acquisition	Job frustration Interest in and recognition of opportunity in the area Change in personal circumstances
Sources of funds	Personal assets and savings Bank financing Investors Loans from friends and family	Personal assets and savings Personal loans
Occuptional background	Experience in line of work Recognized specialist or one who has gained a high level of achievement in the field Competent in a variety of business functions	Experience in area of business Middle-management or administrative level experience in field Service-related occupational background
Personality characteristics	Opinionated and persuasive Goal-oriented Innovative and idealistic High level of self-confidence Enthusiastic and energetic Must be own boss	Flexible and tolerant Goal oriented Creative and realistic Medium level of self-confidence Enthusiastic and energetic Ability to deal with the social and economic environment
Background	Age when starting venture: 25-35 Father was self-employed College education — degree in business or technical area (usually engineering) Firstborn child	Age when starting venture 35-45 Father was self-employed College educated — degree in liberal arts Firstborn child
Support groups	Friends, professional acquaintances (lawyers, accountants) Business associates Spouse	Close friends Spouse Family Women's professional groups Trade associations
Type of business started	Manufacturing or construction	Service related — educational services, consulting, or public relation

Others

Innovative Entrepreneurs: Innovative entrereneurship is characterised by aggressive assemblage of information and analysis of results, deriving from a novel combination of factors. Men/women in this group are generally aggressive in experimentation who exhibit cleverness in putting attractive possibilities into practice. One need not invent but convert even old established products or services, by changing their utility, their value, their economic characteristics into something new, attractive and utilitarian. Therein lies the key to their phenomenal success. Such an entrepreneur is one who sees the opportunity for introducing a new technique of production process, a new commodity, a new market, a new service or even reorganisation of an existing enterprise.

Adoptive or Imitative Entrepreneurs: Imitative entrepreneurship is characterised by readiness to adopt successful innovation inaugurated by innovating entrepreneurs. In other words, imitators follow the innovators later after observing how the latter fare. These groups are also revolutionary entrepreneurs with the difference that they do not innovate the changes themselves. They just imitate techniques and technology innovated by others. Such entrepreneurs are particularly important in developing countries because they contribute significantly to the development of such economies. Imitative entrepreneurs are most suitable for the developing regions because in such countries people prefer to imitate the technololgy, knowledge and skill already available in more advanced countries.

The reason for the backwardness of the underdeveloped countries lies in the fact that they are deficient in innovating and imitating entrepreneurs when they are found in abundance in developed countries. Men are needed who can imitate the technologies and products to the particular conditions prevailing in such countries. And at times there is a need of changing and adjusting the new technologies to their special conditions. Such countries, primarily need imitators who are responsible for transforming the system with the limited resources they possess.

Fabian Entrepreneurs: Fabian entrepreneurship is characterised by great caution and scepticism in practising any change. Such entrepreneurs have neither will to introduce new changes nor desire to adopt new methods innovated by the most enterprising entrepreneurs. Such entrepreneurs are shy and lazy. Their dealings are determined by customs, religion, tradition and past practices. They are not much interested in taking risk and they try to follow the footsteps of their predecessors.

Drone Entrepreneurship: Drone entrepreneurship is characterised by a refusal to adopt and use opportunities to make changes in production. Such entrepreneurs may even suffer losses but they do not make changes in production methods. They are laggards because they continue in their traditional way and in fields their product loses, its marketability or their operation becomes uneconomical — they are pushed out of the market.

Aspiring Entrepreneurs: Aspiring entrepreneurs dream of starting a bussiness; they hope for the chance to be their own bosses, but they have not yet made the leap from their current employment into the uncertainty of a start up.

Lifestyle Entrepreneurs: Lifestyle entrepreneurs have developed an enterprise that fits their individual circumstances and style of life. Their basic intention is to earn an income for themselves and their families.

Growth Entrepreneurs: Growth entrepreneurs have both the desire and ability to grow as fast as large as possible.

Opportunist Entrepreneurs: Opportunist entrepreneurs are those who have grabbed an opportunity which has come in their way.

E-entrepreneurs: The new electronic or e-entrepreneur is mostly concerned with "click-through schemes and capturing eye-balls." The e-entrepreneur comes in many modes. Young and ambitious, older and corporate based, international and risk taking.

Mompreneurs: Homemaker entrepreneur is a mompreneur. Entrepreneurship is one way for women to get around corporate glass ceiling (not everyone can do an Indra Nooyi). It also gives them the flexibility to care for the home while avoiding barriers — and bosses — who come with traditional jobs, although there are bound to be other hurdles. For the 21st century women, there's no business like own business.

The New Kingmakers Entrepreneurs: The Indian economy is blooming and spreading its wings beyond its borders. To fulfill their growth aspirations there is need for corporate leaders to lead. With India Inc. in the throes of a top-level talent crunch, headhunters hold the keys to the corner office. A new breed of new kingmaker (headhunters) entrepreneurs have emerged.

Professor Entrepreneurs: It requires guts, motivation, inspiration, business sense, financial backing, among other traits to be an entrepreneur. A few characteristics are in-born and a few, taught. But somewhere down the line, the professors who play a vital role in the lives of the budding visionaries fade away and get lost in history books. What remains etched in our minds are the names of the people who stormed the world to set up vast empires of businesses. Ever thought of the people responsible behind the success of these entrepreneurs? Meet Prof. Radha Iyer, Prof. Suresh Rao and Prof. Arya Kumar who left their illustrious corporate careers and turned to academics to give direction to budding entrepreneurs. They are the pioneers in creating 'entrepreneurship' courses in their respective institutes thereby giving the visionaries a platform to hone and learn the skills to make the perfect kill!

IT Entrepreneurs

The new breed of IT entrepreneurs are creating a new business model that takes them straight to the top of the value chain. The empirical study suggests that they have two things in common — a narrowly defined niche and a skew towards products. They are confident, ambitious, innovative and acquired creativity in the competitive global environment. They are the brave new bunch of entrepreneurs who are raring to take on the world of information technology. They need to be encouraged and respected.

Intrapreneur

Tempted to point out a spelling error above? Wait a second! This exciting word is young but full of potential. Introduced by Gifford and Elizabeth Pinchot in 1973 as "intra-corporate entrepreneur" and later re-coined, the term "intrapreneur" was officially recognised in 1992 with this definition in American Heritage Dictionary: "A person within a large corporation who takes direct responsibility for turning an idea into a profitable finished product through assertive risk-taking and innovation."

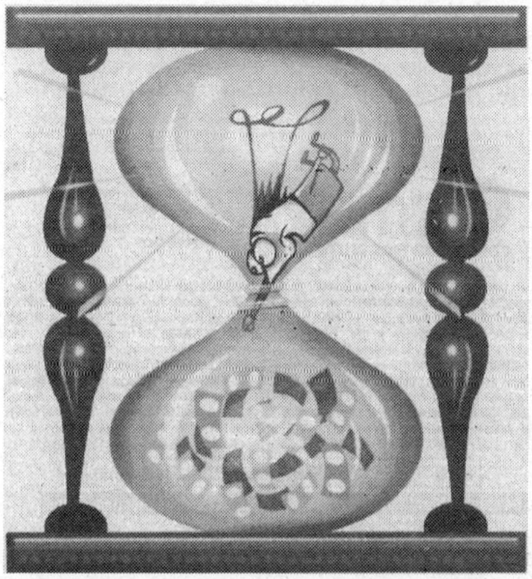

Blend of the two terms intra+entrepreneur, intrapreneur embodies the same characteristics as the entrepreneur, conviction, passion, and drive. If the company is supportive, the intrapreneur succeeds. If it's not, the intrapreneur usually fails or leaves to start a new company. An intrapreneur thinks like an entrepreneur seeking out opportunities, which benefit the corporation. But there are, of course, a few things that are different between intrapreneurship and entrepreneurship. For starters, the intrapreneur acts within the confines of an existing organisation. The dictates of most organisations would be that the intrapreneur should ask for permission before attempting to create a desired future — in practice, the intrapreneur is more inclined to act first and ask for forgiveness than to ask for permission before acting.

The intrapreneur is also typically the intra-organisational revolutionary — challenging the *status quo* and fighting to change the system from within. This obviously creates a certain amount of organisational friction. A healthy dose of mutual respect is required in order to ensure that such friction can be positively channelled. One advantage of intrapreneurship over entrepreneurship is that intrapreneur typically finds a ready source of "free" resources within the organisation that can be applied to the opportunity being exploited.

To sum up the basic differences we could say firstly, entrepreneurship involves huge amount of risk while there is no personal risk involved in case of an intrapreneurship. Secondly, an intrapreneur is dependent on the organization in which he is working while an entrepreneur doesn't work in any confines, hence independent in every task he undertakes. While companies admire an intrapreneur who is an independent thinker, being too independent could cause problems. The biggest difference between intrapreneurship and entrepreneurship, according to Pinchot, is that an intrapreneur has to deal with authority figures. "So if you absolutely cannot stand to be told what to do by others, you may not do well as an intrapreneur," he says.

Intrapreneurship is more important now than ever before. No one needs to be told that the world is changing now faster than ever before. Organisations are finding it harder and harder to survive by merely competing. They are, therefore, increasingly looking towards their intrapreneurs to take them beyond competition to create new businesses in new markets.

INFORMATION: STRATEGIC CATALYST OF ENTREPRENEURIAL TRANSFORMATION

With all the recent attention paid to information as a strategic entrepreneurial resource, it is possible to overlook that which is simple and obvious: that information is a commodity that enterprises are run by people. Businesses do not make decisions, people do. The right information coming at the right time and place in an appropriate context leads to an informed decision, and an informed decision is always better than a blind one.

This in itself is not a new phenomenon. What is new is the requirement that entrepreneurs in every enterprise, intrapreneurs in every major corporation, government body or large institutions responsibly navigate their organisations through a more rapidly changing and complex environment, with more uncertainty, more viability, a greater number of stakeholders and wider range of choices than has ever been the case.

This kind of environment demands a leadership that can anticipate the future impact of relevant trends, current decisions and evolving possibilities. It requires that both leaders and followers be prepared to redirect and mobilise an organisation in quick response to the opportunities presented by shifting markets, diversifying needs, evolving technology and changing social norms.

In the past, we tended to think of human resources as only arms and legs. More recently and more importantly, we have begun to realise the tremendous potential represented by minds and their capacity to grow, adapt, learn and innovate. If we are to capitalise on the full capacity of people to think and create, then we must begin to view information, communication and the technology on which they are based as another critical human resource.

Another emerging aspect of the potential of human resources is the recognition that our employees are not the only human resources available to us. Instead, we should be viewing an expanded set of stakeholders and their human potential as well. It is a simple and obvious fact that our shareholders, customers, suppliers and the communities in which we operate are made up of people too. We tend to overlook the obvious potential role information can play in the development of mutually beneficial relationships with each of these stakeholder groups. All we have said about the value and potential of information and communications as human resource can be applied as well to our relationships with other organisations, public and the marketplace.

In the past few years, we have all seen numerous articles focussing on the concept of competitive advantage, but only a few have envisioned the power of using information as a competitive weapon. There seem to be two overriding strategies: one is to bundle information or technology with the company's products, electronically connecting with suppliers or with customers to place orders, invoice, pay bills and the like. This is the area where a number of well known successes have been documented. A second way to achieve competitive advantage through information is by delivering information capacity that allows the business to lead, manage and utilise its resources in a manner superior to others in the industry.

Distinctiveness in the future will come from leveraging and creatively bringing to bear value-adding forms of information, communication and technology to achieve excellence in:

- Strategic market intelligence, by combining factual, databased trends with human judgement and learning;
- Personal excellence as a result of leveraging the uniquely human qualities of judgements, experience, insight and creativity to our internal and external relationships;
- Product and service excellence, by adding information components to the product or service bundles we offer in the marketplace;
- Functioning excellence, by creating fluid networks unbounded by the constraints of time, technology, structure or geography, and
- Stakeholder excellence, due to the extension of organisational boundaries to connect with external stakeholders in new ways, so as to add mutual value and influence.

The power of information to make an impact upon people, on an individual and collective basis is real. It is our challenge to apply new thinking to the extended uses of information as a catalyst for excellence. After all, it is thinking that drives behaviour, and behavior in turn drives on results; and it is information that moulds thinking towards new, higher results. We are all convinced that this in an integrated and escalating process that gains substance through time and that our challenge as leaders is to make this gain a reality.

CONCLUSION

It should be noted that private entrepreneurship has to harmonise economic opportunities with social and moral responsibility. As our wise people have said, unless the pursuit of wealth is integrated with the pursuit of *Dharma*, there could be no lasting prosperity and peace, whether within a country or among nations. The highly developed countries have realised that aggressive entrepreneurship without an ethical base can produce more harm than good, more misery than happiness and more destruction than creation. *Harmonised planning of economic and moral values is a long drawn-out process, but the goal has to be kept in mind constantly*. One should remain optimistic that entrepreneurship in India will develop on these lines, to promote India's economic development on a sound basis, as an integral part of the world economy. The burst of creativity and innovation in emerging technological industries holds tremendous promise for economic development and technological business growth. When talent is linked with technology, people recognise and then push viable ideas and the entrepreneurial process is under way.

Liberalisation and the new economic policy have thrown open the doors for every entrepreneur to seek its own fortunes and thus contribute his mite to the growth of the economy. In a way, the new economic policy has been fostering the spirit of entrepreneurship. The human capital and infrastructure provide the two major assets in a global economy. The states are striving to provide a framework that will improve investment, infrastructure, agriculture and industry. They have endeavoured to dovetail industrial growth with creation of employment and balanced development. The country has a vast pool of skilled manpower and there is no dearth of entrepreneurs.

In this time of rapid economic development and technological change, entrepreneurial spirit can be unique and of important advantage, but only if we learn to use it. The entrepreneurs are the agents of change and our hope for the future. In fact, the entrepreneur always searches for change, responds to it and exploits it as an opportunity.

3 CHAPTER NATURE AND IMPORTANCE OF ENTREPRENEURS

> *"Excellence doesn't happen miraculously but springs from pace setting levels of personal effectiveness and efficiency. Great business, government and non-profit organisations owe their greatness to a few individuals who mastered leadership skills and passed those skills on to others."*
>
> — *John Gardner*

INTRODUCTION

The world is rapidly changing; we should be able to change our attitudes and approaches to prevent a country of India's size and potential to exist on the periphery of the world's economy. The process of development includes creation of appropriate infrastructure and setting up and management of public utilities. Non-conventional energy sources have to be developed on a commercial scale. Similarly, application of modern scientific techniques in agriculture and horticulture has become imperative for providing a sound base for a more rapid growth of employment and incomes. There is also a need for rapid growth of distributed industries in a multi-directional way. Apart from land, labour and capital, there is greater need for entrepreneurs to strive for growth on an ongoing basis. In this context an attempt has been made in this chapter to analyse the nature and importance of entrepreneurs.

Entrepreneurial Qualities

The entrepreneurial qualities are to some extent innate. But not all of them are entirely innate. Some can be enhanced by training, or simply by experience. For example, analytical ability and computational skill can be enhanced by education at school and university, while practical knowledge and foresight skills can be enhanced by the general experience of everyday life. Entrepreneurial careers will be strongly influenced by the desire to enhance qualities which are scarce, yet difficult to obtain through delegation because of the problems involved in screening

Quality - An inherent/ distinguishing characteristics. A personal trait especially a character trait

for them. Of the two indispensable qualities of the entrepreneur, imagination is almost entirely innate, while foresight, can be enhanced by a varied experience. Imagination and foresight are the scarce qualities which are difficult to analyse and quantify. Delegation skill and organisational skill, though not essential, are highly desirable whenever large-scale decision making is involved. These are qualities which can be enhanced through experience.

Entrepreneurial Functions

A successful entrepreneur recognises the commercial potential of a product or service, design operating policies in marketing, production, product development and the organisational structure. He carries out the whole set of activities of the business. He has a high capacity for taking calculated risks and has faith in his own capabilities.

According to some economists, the functions of an entrepreneur incorporate co-ordination of the business management of the enterprise, risk-taking, controlling the enterprise, innovation for change, motivation and other related activities. In reality, an entrepreneur has to carryout a combination of these in keeping with time and environment. Truly, he has to consider new ideas, demands and exploit the opportunities, and thereby contribute to technical progress. He is thus a nucleus of high growth of the enterprise.

An entrepreneur is expected to perform the following functions:

1. *Assumption of Risk:* The entrepreneur assumes all possible risks of business, which emerge due to the possibility of changes in the tastes of consumers, techniques of production and inventions. Such risks are not insurable. If they meterialise, the entrepreneur has to bear the loss himself. Thus, risk-bearing or uncertainty-bearing still remains the most important function of an entrepreneur which he tries to reduce by his initiative, skill and good judgement.

2. *Business Decisions:* The entrepreneur has to decide the nature and type of goods to be produced. He enters the particular industry which offers him the best prospects and produces whatever commodities he thinks will pay him the most and employs those methods of production which seem to him the most profitable. He effects suitable changes in the size of the business, its location, techniques of production and does everything that is needed for the development of his business.

3. *Managerial Functions:* The entrepreneur performs the managerial function though they are different from entrepreneurial functions. He formulates production plans, sees to the finance, deals with purchase of raw materials, provides production facilities, organises sales including management. In a large establishment, these management functions are delegated to the paid managerial personnel.

The entrepreneurial functions can be performed by different categories of people under different economic systems. In principle, the entrepreneur could be a planner in a socialist economy, or even a priest or king in a traditional society. In practice, entrepreneurship is closely identified with private enterprise in a market economy.

An entrepreneur performs many useful functions. He undertakes a venture, assumes risk and earns profit. He is the man having a strong motivation to achieve success. He is self-confident in his entrepreneurial abilities. He exploits opportunities wherever and whenever they arise.

The entrepreneur can identify opportunities to start a business either as a manufacturer or as a distributor, for entrepreneurship exists in every field of economic endeavour. Manufacturing activities require a relatively high capital investment and a greater degree of entrepreneurial abilities than distribution activities. Entrepreneurship has also been developed in the trading sector. Britain, for example, has developed trading entrepreneurship while Germany and Japan have developed industrial entrepreneurship. A manufacturing entrepreneur demonstrates his entrepreneurial talents by bringing out new products while a trading entrepreneur performs his entrepreneurial functions in creating demand for the business in which he deals.

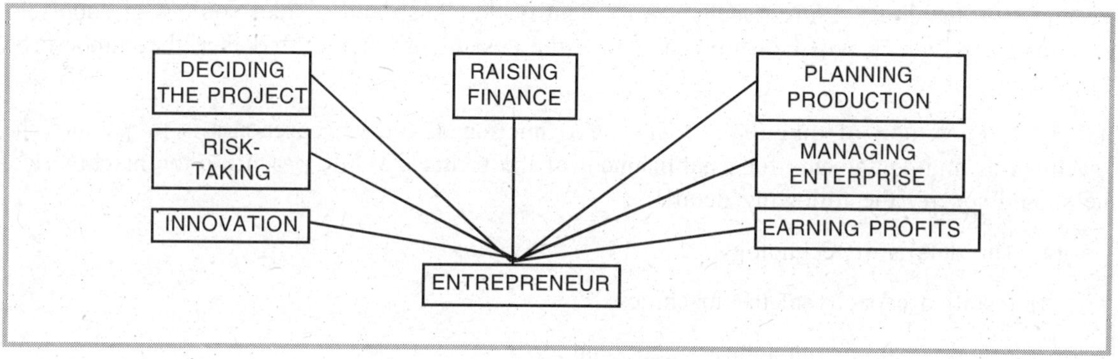

Fig. 3.1: Entrepreneurial Functions

Functions of Entrepreneurs

Entrepreneurs is an opportunity seeker. He is also the organiser and coordinator of the agents of production. He has to execute many a good functions while establishing a small-scale enterprise. He not only perceives the business opportunities but also mobilizes the other resources like **5 Ms** — man, money, machine, materials and methods. However, the main functions of the entrepreneurs are discussed further.

1. Idea generation: This is the most important function of the entrepreneur. Idea generation can be possible through the vision, insight, observation, experience, education, training and exposure of the entrepreneur. Idea generation precisely implies product selection and project identification. Ideas can be generated through environmental scanning and market survey. It is the function of the entrepreneurs to generate as many ideas as he can for the purpose of selecting the best business opportunities which can subsequently be taken up by him as a commercially-viable business venture.

2. Determination of objectives: The next function of the entrepreneur is to determine and lay down the objectives of the business, which should be spelt out on clear terms. In other words, entrepreneur should be very much clear about the following things:

(i) The nature of business

(ii) The type of business

This implies whether the enterprise belongs to the category of a manufacturing concern or a service-oriented unit or a trading business, so that the entrepreneurs can very well carry on the venture in accordance with the objectives determined by him.

3. Raising of funds: Fund raising is the most important function of an entrepreneur. All the activities of a business depend upon the finance and its proper management. It is the responsibility of the entrepreneur to raise funds internally as well as externally. In this matter, he should be aware of the different sources of funds and the formalities to raise funds. He should have the full knowledge of different government sponsored schemes such as PMRY, SGSY, REGP, etc., by which he can get Government assistance in the form of seed capital, fixed and working capital for his business.

4. Procurement of raw materials: Another important function of the entrepreneur is to procure raw materials. Entrepreneur has to identify the cheap and regular sources of supply of raw materials, which will help him to reduce the cost of production and face the competition boldly.

5. Procurement of machinery: The next function of the entrepreneurs is to procure the machineries and equipments for establishment of the venture. While procuring the machineries, he should specify the following details:

(a) The details of technology

(b) Installed capacity of the machines

(c) Names of the manufacturers and suppliers

(d) Whether the machines are indigenously made or foreign made

(e) After-sales service facilities

(f) Warranty period of the machineries.

All these details are to be minutely observed by the entrepreneurs.

6. Market research: The next important function of the entrepreneur is market research and product analysis. Market research is the systematic collection of data regarding the product which the entrepreneur wants to manufacture. Entrepreneur has to undertake market research persistently in order to know the details of the intending product, i.e., the demand for the product, the supply of the product, the price of the product, the size of the customers, etc., while starting an enterprise.

7. Determination of form of enterprise: The function of an entrepreneur in determining the form of enterprise is also important. Entrepreneur has to decide the form of enterprise based upon the nature of the product, volume of investment, nature of activities, types of product, quality of product, quality of human resources, etc. The chief forms of ownership organizations are sole proprietorship, partnership, joint stock company and cooperative society. Determination of ownership right is essential on the part of the entrepreneur to acquire legal title to assets.

8. Recruitment of manpower: Entrepreneur has to perform the following activities while undertaking this function:

(a) Estimating manpower need of the organization.

(b) Laying down of selection procedure.

(c) Devising scheme of compensation.

(d) Laying down the rules of training and development.

9. Implementation of the project: Entrepreneur has to work on the implementation schedule or the action plan of the project. The identified project is to be implemented in a time-bound manner. All the activities from the conception stage to the commissioning stage are to be accomplished by him in accordance with the implementation schedule to avoid cost and time overrun, as well as competition. Thus, implementation of the project is an important function of the entrepreneur.

To conclude with, all these functions of the entrepreneur can precisely be put into the following categories:

(i) Innovation

(ii) Risk bearing

(iii) Organization and management.

Decision Maker

Arther H. Cole described an entrepreneur as a decision maker and attributed the following functions to him:

1. The determination of those objectives of the enterprise and the change of those objectives as conditions required or made advantageous;
2. The development of an organisation, including efficient relations with subordinates and all employees;
3. Securing adequate financial resources, and maintaining good relations with the existing and potential investors;
4. The requisition of efficient technological equipment and the revision of it as new machinery appeared;
5. The development of a market for the products and the devising of new products to meet or anticipate consumer's demand; and
6. The maintenance of good relations with public authorities and with the society at large.

Modern writers on this subject have outlined the following three broad functions of an entrepreneur:

1. Innovation,
2. Risk-taking, and
3. Organisation and management of business so as to have leadership and control over it.

ENTERPRISE AND SOCIETY

Entrepreneurs play a significant role in economic development of a society and country. According to Harbison, entrepreneurs are prime movers of innovation, growth and as such, entrepreneurship is a dynamic force. The important roles that an entrepreneur plays are as follows:

1. Generation of Employment Opportunities

Entrepreneurs play a significant role in generation of employment opportunities by:

(i) establishing new units in manufacturing, trading and service sectors.

(ii) laying emphasis on village and cottage industries.

(iii) utilising the surplus labour force in varied industrial and/or service activities.

(iv) upholding self-employment as a core objective.

2. Complementing and Supplementing Economic Growth

The role of entrepreneurs not only complements but also supplements the economic growth of the country in the following manner:

(i) Generation of employment

(ii) Capital formation

(iii) Increasing per capita income

(iv) Improvement in physical quality of life

(v) Improvement in standard of living

(vi) Growth of infrastructural facilities

(vii) Initiating change in the economy

(viii) Forward and backward linkages

(ix) Development of backward areas

(x) Economic independence.

3. Bringing about Social Stability and Balanced Regional Development of Industries

Entrepreneurs play a crucial and unique role in bringing about social stability and balanced regional development.

(i) Absorption of workforce in industries

(ii) Alleviation of poverty

(iii) Improving health and education

(iv) Glorification of self-help

(v) Checking monopolies

(vi) Equitable distribution of income

(vii) Creation of social infrastructures

(viii) Empowering women and weaker sections of the society

(ix) Supply of qualitative goods and services.

ENTREPRENEURIAL PROCESS

Definitions

Bygrave and Hofer (1891) defined the entrepreneurial process as 'involving all the functions, activities, and actions associated with perceiving of opportunities and creation of organizations to pursue them.

Churchill and Lewis (1983) defined the entrepreneurial process similar to a product life cycle by listing in turn: birth, early growth stage, maturity and decline/death.

Baron's (2004) states that 'willingness to start enterprise', 'identifying opportunities' and 'success of the enterprise' are the three stages of the process.

Wickham (2001) proposed that the following characteristics of the entrepreneurial process which is supported by Bygrave (1993) are:

- Initiated by human decision
- Takes place on the level of individual enterprise
- Discontinous
- Holistic approach
- Dynamic approach
- Unique approach
- Includes various antecedents and variables

Elements of the Entrepreneurial Process

Bull *et.al.,* (1995) identified the following components of entrepreneurship:

- Creating (recognising) and developing an opportunity
- Evaluating the opportunity's desirability:
  - its economic potential
  - the financial risks involved
  - the personal risks involved
- Marshalling the resources to exploit it:
  - Financial
  - Managerial
  - Technical
  - Physical

- Possessing the will or tenacity to "do it"
- Managing the launch including:
  - Competitive and co-operative relationships
  - Networks
- Managing the downstream opportunity capture and realisation:
  - Creation of value for the entrepreneur and society
  - Realisation of value for the entrepreneur and his/her family.

Wickham (2001) focused on a model of the process by which entrepreneurs create new wealth. The process consists of four elements, namely the entrepreneur, the opportunity, resources and organisation.

Steps in Enterpreneurial Process

Entrepreneurial process is a leadership function which centres round the dynamics of entrepreneurial growth and change. It is a process comprising several distinct stages.

The *first* stage in the entrepreneurial process is some change in the socio-economic environment leading to changes in the every aspect of life in the country. *Inter alia,* the change creates needs for new goods and services.

The *second* stage is by starting a new venture.

The *third* process is intrapreneurship. It is the process of extending the enterprises domain of competence by exploiting new opportunities through new combinations of its available resources.

The *fourth* process is to coordinating the varied activities to achieve the entreprenerial goal.

According to Barringer and Ireland (2010) there are four steps in entrepreneurial process. *i.e.,*

1. **Decision to become an entrepreneur** Many people opt for entrepreneurship as their career because of many reasons. Some delve into the industry because they want to run their own business, answering to no one and setting all the rules and protocols by themselves. Others jump into entrepreneurship because they have seen that most successful people in the world own a successful business. There are also others that make entrepreneurship as a second career because their current jobs are not earning enough for them.

2. **Developing successful business idea** Many enterprises have succeeded in their venture because they were able to develop business ideas. Choosing an idea is quite difficult and the entrepreneur has to weigh objectively his intrinsic capabilities in finalising an idea. One can take help of different sources and methods to develop wide range of ideas like creativity, brainstroming, observing market, etc. Successful business idea includes opportunity recognition by analysing environment (macro and micro), feasibility planning, business plan and models.

3. **Moving idea to entrepreneurial firm** Once an idea has been developed the next step is the conversion of idea into reality. This stage includes selecting an appropriate form of

ownership, location of enterprise, type of products to be dealt with, sources of finance and materials, searching for appropriate human resource who will support him in his venture, etc.

4. Managing and growing entrepreneurial firm - The journey of an entrepreneur doesn't end with just deciding, developing and moving towards entrepreneurial venture. Growth includes new challenges and requirements. It has been found that many of the ventures die out in just three because of their inability to manage and grow their firms. In order to grow one has to take into consideration many factors like target market, brand buiding, evaluating challenges and preparing strategies.

Mind Vs. Money in Commencing A New Buisness

A business organisation requires the 5Ms i.e., Men, Money, Material, Machines and Management (Mind) for its initiation and functioning. Men, Material and Machines can be bought with the help of Money. So, basically Money and Management are required to keep a business going on.

A good mind alone without any money cannot run a business. It will not be able to purchase or borrow land and building to set up the business or the furniture for the office. Neither will it be able to get machnies to work with or hire human resources to carry-out its work. Without money it would not be possible to purchase raw material and other goods. Very often we find that even if a person wants to start his business or expand the existing one, he/she is unable to do so due to lack of finance.

Similarly, money alone cannot take a business far. Without proper use and control of money, a business cannot survive. And to do so, management (mind) is required. Money without mind is soon lost. Therefore, money and mind are like the two tyres of a bicycle. If anyone of them is not present or is deflated, the cycle will not be able to run. But the question arises, between the two-money and mind, which is more important? Let us take an example. Suppose a person has lots of money and has started a business but lacks calrity of vision, planning, organising, directing and controlling his business, he/she will not be able to hold on for long. He/she will suffer at the hands of competitors, suppliers, customers as well as the employees. Soon even the existing money will be lost. We have heard of people acquiring big business houses or inheriting large amount of money but due to their lack of ability they could not sustin their position.

If a person has the ability and the requisite management skills to start a business, he can take his small business to great heights. Classic examples are Bata, T-Series, Hero Cycles and the like. They have shown that with the right kind of attitude and management skills one can steer one's business in the right direction and grow. Moreover, if one works with zeal and passion and has feasible ideas, one can collect resources also. TV channels like CNBC Awaaz and CNBC TV 18 had started programmes like "Entrepreneur" and "Starting Up" respectively. Here the entrepreneurs were invited to present their business ideas and the judges, who themselves were corporate heads, judged their presentation. The idea which was the best and the most feasible was funded by the judges themselves. Here the mind fetched money for the entrepreneurs.

So, although both money and mind are required to start a business, the mind is more important to make the most of your money.

What Leads to a Successful Small Business?

1) A Feasible Business Plan

A plan helps the entrepreneur to decide the future course of action. If the plan is good one then it will help the entrepreneur to spend his money wisely and avoid costly mistakes. Hence, a good business planning is essential for the success of small business men.

2) Market Research

The process of gathering, analyzing and interpreting information about a market, about a product or service to be offered for sale in that market, and about the past, present and potential customers for the product or service; research into the characteristics, spending habits, location and needs of your business's target market, the industry as a whole, and the particular competitors you face.

3) Information about Industry and Market Trends

An understanding of industry and market trends helps the entrepreneur to decide about his products, services and price. It helps the entrepreneur to stay competitive and meet the customer needs.

4) Good Quality HR

It is the people involved in a business that make or break it. Therefore, it is very essential to hire and retain the right kind of people for the job. It has been rightly said that right person, in right place and at right time is one of the key factor for success of any organization.

5) Understanding Government Regulations

An entrepreneur should have a good understanding of government regulations and should follow them accordingly. This will help him to work within the limits of law and avoid making mistakes.

6) Time Management

As specialization is difficult in small business, the entrepreneur himself has to look into all the functions. As such, effective time management will help him to do work better and faster. It will also reduce stress and fatigue.

7) Hard Working

There is no substitute to hard work. As it has been rightly said that, "the only substitute to hard work is harder work". An entrepreneur who goes an extra mile to satisfy his customers will never be out of business. Hard work, driven with passion and talent go a long way on the road of success.

ENTREPRENEURIAL FAILURE

Many of the small businesses fail during their teething stage. Business failure means the firm's inability to exist due to loss of capital or insufficient return on investments. Most business failure can range from poor planning, inability of business to adapt and meet new demands.

Some of the reasons that leads to business failure are:

1. Lack of proper financing

Finance is one of the most important resource needed for starting up and carrying on a business. Many a times entrepreneurs fail to get adequate finance to start a business or even if they start an enterprise they cannot carry it for long. Finance is required to meet the day-to-day activities of the enterprise. Inadequate funds, incorrect combination of funds, overconfidence on trade credit, overoptimistic projections or overtrading, often results in failure of business.

2. Lack of entrepreneurial skills

Lack of entrepreneurial skills during the initial stages of start up of an enterprise can be one of the causes for the failure of the business. An entreprereneur should be a good planner and organizer. He should have the skills to put his resources together and manage them efficiently. But all entrepreneurs do not possess these skills to run their enterprise. Even though they manage to get the resources they are not able to utilize them properly and this results in failure of their business.

3. Inventory blockage

A fast moving inventory results in proft and prosperity of the enterprise. If due to any reason there is inventory blockage, i.e., goods are not being sold out then business will be in danger. Until and unless, the goods are sold out, the money invested in these goods is blocked and because of this the business will not be able to earn any profits and will fail to survive.

4. Poor business plan

A good business plan is vital for the success of any business. A plan shows the entrepreneur how things are to be done. A poor plan will not be able to guide the entrepreneur to do right things at right time. This will result in commitment of costly mistakes which will ultimately prove to be fatal for the enterprise.

5. Failing to adapt

Today, in this fast changing world where everyday and everywhere new technologies and inventions are coming up, no business can afford to carry on their business activities with old methods. It has to change and adapt itself with the changing environment. Any business which fails to do so will perish within a short span of time.

6. Improper location

Location of a business plays a very important role in determining the success of a business. Nearness to raw material and market, access to transportation, etc., all help the business to carry on its work efficiently. Improper location results in increased cost and reduced profits. Hence, a business which is not located properly cannot survive for long.

7. Ineffective marketing

Due to lack of marketing skills, sometimes the entrepreneurs fail to sell their products. Besides, due to inadequate finance they are not in a position to spend huge amount on advertisement and sales promotion. Underestimating the strength of competitors, misreading customer requirements, lack of promotion and customer awareness, may lead to business failures.

8. Lack of management skills

Management skills like planning, organising, staffing, directing and controlling, etc., help the entrepreneur to manage the business efficiently. If the entrepreneur lacks these management skills then he will not be able to run his business successfully. Lack of relevant sectoral experience, ineffective financial and managerial control systems, unresolved differences of opinion, unreal expectations, no formal or clear structures often results, etc., may ruin the business.

9. Poor product quality

In order to survive in this competitive world, an entrepreneur has to offer good quality products and services to attract the customers. if the entrepreneur is unable to provide good quality products at competitive prices and if it continues for long then chances are there for business failure.

10. Insufficient operational activities

Underinvestment in equipments, excessive overheads, high operational costs and/or low productivity, poor capacity utilization, inadequate physical distribution, etc., may contribute to the business failures.

4 CHAPTER

Entrepreneurial Traits and Skills

"The five essential entrepreneurial skills for success are concentration, discrimination, organisation, innovation and communication."

— ***Henry Reed***

"To manage a business successfully requires as much courage as that possessed by the soldier who goes to war. Business courage is the more natural because all the benefits which the public has in material wealth come from it."

— ***Charles Abbott***

INTRODUCTION

Entrepreneurial traits and motivation are an indispensible function of management. Entrepreneur is human being who has his dignity, self-respect, values, sentiments, aspirations, dreams apart from economic status. Indeed, economic betterment and social upliftment motivates a person to distinguish from others. The entrepreneurs have some basic values and responsibilities.

In this chapter, we shall examine the entrepreneurial traits and motivation.

The right attitude is a winning combination of taking initiative, taking right decisions at right time, being passionate about one's work, being innovative, analytical, focused, be professional and intelligent with impeccable behaviour, be a positive thinker, perseverance, hard working as well as creative.

On the other hand, one may have talent in abundance, but if the right mental attitude is missing, it will never allow him to reach his ultimate potential. Attitude is what separates excellence from mediocrity. I also believe that personal integrity is crucial and an employee should tell nothing but the truth. For me, an employee's secret of success is passion. Thinking big can ensure that he emerges a winner in his chosen field. In short, the entrepreneur is the ambassador of his enterprise.

Whenever we are looking around, we find certain entrepreneurs doing exceedingly well. They are managing their enterprises very well and are out to make them grand success. The various questions that normally arise are — who are they? what they possess? and various other questions related with their style of functioning. In their case there is a judicious mixture of knowledge, skill and personality. All these are called entrepreneurial traits or competencies. Knowledge refers to the collection and retention of information about any job or activity. Knowledge forms the basis for any action. Only knowledge cannot ensure success. Success depends upon the ability or skill of using the acquired knowledge for achieving desired results. Skill refers to practical application or use of the knowledge. Thus performance depends upon both knowledge and skill. Motivation is an inner urge in an individual which calls for action. According to Steneir: "A motive is an inner-state that energizes, activates or moves and directs or channels behaviour goals". It is this inner urge in an individual to achieve his/her goal which David McClelland has termed as 'Achievement Motivation'. It is this urge to achieve goal which prompts the individual to perform better and better. Thus, in order to achieve success in any venture a person must possess a judicious combination of knowledge, skill and motive.

Entrepreneurial Competencies

According to a recent study, it was found out that possession of certain competencies or abilities result in superior performance. An entrepreneur may possess certain competencies and at the same time it is possible to develop these through training, experience and guidance. Various competencies required for superior performance were identified during the study and are as under:

1. Initiative: It is an inner urge in an individual to do or initiate something. There is popular saying: 'Well begun is half done'. It is the entrepreneur who takes or initiates the first move towards setting up of an enterprise. Most of the innovators have got this urge to do something different. Entrepreneur basically is an innovator who carries out new combinations to initiate and accelerate the process of economic development.

2. Looking for Opportunity: An entrepreneur is always on the look out or searching for opportunity and is ready to exploit it in the best interests of the organisation.

3. Persistence: An entrepreneur is never disheartened by failures. He believes in the Japanese proverb: 'Fall seven times, stand up at eight'. He follows Try Try Again for overcoming the obstacles that come in the way of achieving goals.

4. Information Seeker: A successful entrepreneur always keep his eyes and ear open and is receptive to new ideas which can help him in realising his goals. He is ready to consult expert for getting their expert advise.

5. Quality Consciousness: Successful entrepreneur do not believe in moderate or average performance. They set high quality standards for themselves and then put in their best for achieving these standards. They believe in excellence, which is reflected in everything they do.

6. Commitment to Work: Successful entrepreneurs are prepared to make all sacrifices for honouring the commitments they have made. Whatever they commit, they take it as a moral binding for honouring their commitments, irrespective of the costs involved.

7. Commitment to Efficiency: Top performers are always keen to devise new methods aimed at promoting efficiency. They are keen to evolve and try new methods aimed at making working easier, simpler, better and economical.

8. Proper Planning: Successful entrepreneurs develop or evolve future course of action keeping in mind the goals to be realised. They believe in developing relevant and realistic plans and ensure proper execution of the same in their pursuit of attaining their goals.

9. Problem Solver: Successful entrepreneurs take problem as a challenge and put in their best for finding out the most appropriate solution for the same. They will first of all understand the problem and then evolve appropriate strategy for overcoming the problem.

10. Self confidence: Top performers are not cowed down by difficulties as they believe in their own abilities and strengths. They have full faith on their knowledge, skill and competence and are not worried about future uncertainties.

11. Assertive: An assertive person knows what to say, when to say, how to say and whom to say. He believes in his abilities and ensures that others fall in line with his thinking, aimed at promoting the interests of the organisation.

12. Persuasive: A successful entrepreneur through his sound arguments and logical reasoning is in a position to convince others to do the works the way he wants them to do. It is not physical but intellectual force he will use for convincing others.

13. Effective Monitoring: Top performers ensure that everything is carried out in their organisations as per their wishes. They ensure regular monitoring of the working so that the goals of the organisation are achieved in best possible manner.

14. Employees Welfare: Future of the organisation depends on its employees. If the employees are dedicated, committed and loyal, the organisation is bound to perform well. A successful entrepreneur tries to promote organisation's interests through promotion of interests of the workers. He takes personal interest in solving problems confronting workers and generates the feeling that there is interpendence of the interests of workers and the management.

15. Effective Strategist: A successful entrepreneur possesses the ability to evolve relevant strategy, aimed at safeguarding or promoting organisation's interests. Strategy may be with respect to facing future uncertainties or challenges posed by competitors.

Characteristics of Entrepreneurs

The characteristics of an entrepreneur that contribute to success are the result of his achievement motivation. The characteristics of achievement motivated persons as identified by McClelland have been discussed in the chapter on "Future of Entrepreneurship in India". A successful entrepreneur must be a person with technical competence, initiative, good judgement, intelligence, leadership qualities, self-confidence, energy, attitude, creativeness, fairness, honesty, tactfulness and emotional stability.

1. Mental ability: Mental ability consists of intelligence and creative thinking. An entrepreneur must be reasonably intelligent, and should have creative thinking and must be able to engage in the analysis of various problems and situations in order to deal with them. The entrepreneur should anticipate changes and must be able to study the various situations under which decisions have to be made.

2. Clear objectives: An entrepreneur should have a clear objective as to the exact nature of the business, the nature of the goods to be produced and subsidiary activities to be undertaken. A successful entrepreneur may have the objective to establish the product, to make profit or to render social service.

3. ***Business secrecy*:** An entrepreneur must be able to guard business secrets. Leakage of business secrets to trade competitions is a serious matter which should be carefully guarded against by an entrepreneur. An entrepreneur should be able to make a proper selection of his assistants.

4. ***Human relation ability*:** The most important personality factors contributing to the success of an entrepreneur are emotional stability, personal relations, consideration and tactfulness. An entrepreneur must maintain good relation with his customers if he is to establish relations that will encourage them to continue to patronise his business. He must also maintain good relations with his employees if he is to motivate them to perform their jobs at a high level of efficiency. An entrepreneur who maintains good relations with customers, employees, suppliers, creditors and the community is much more likely to succeed in his business than the individual who does not invest in maintaining these relations.

5. ***Communication ability*:** This ability pertains to communicate effectively. Good communication also means that both the sender and the receiver understand each other and are being understood. An entrepreneur who can effectively communicate with customers, employees, suppliers and creditors will be more likely to succeed than the entrepreneur who does not.

6. ***Technical knowledge*:** An entrepreneur must have a reasonable level of technical knowledge. This is the one ability that most people are able to acquire if they try hard enough.

An entrepreneur who has a high level of administrative ability, mental ability, human relations ability, communication ability and technical knowledge stands a much better chance of success than his counterpart who possesses low levels of these basic qualities. Brilliant men with first class degrees from university hesitate becoming entrepreneurs because the one thing they cannot be taught is coping with human emotions.

Robert D. Hisrich has identified a few more capabilities or personal characteristics that an entrepreneur should possess. According to him, the entrepreneur must have an adequate commitment, motivation and skills to start and build a business. The entrepreneur must determine if the management team has the necessary complementary skills to succeed. Some key characteristics of a successful entrepreneur are:

Motivator: An entrepreneur must build a team, keep it motivated and provide an environment for individual growth and career development.

Self-confidence: Entrepreneurs must have belief in themselves and the ability to achieve their goals.

Long-term involvement: An entrepreneur must be committed to the project with a time horizon of five to seven years. No ninety-day wonders are allowed.

High energy level: Success of an entrepreneur demands the ability to work long hours for sustained periods of time.

Persistent problem-solver: An entrepreneur must have an intense desire to complete a task or solve a problem. Creativity is an essential ingredient.

Initiative: An entrepreneur must be able to set challenging but realistic goals.

Moderate risk-taker: An entrepreneur must be a moderate risk-taker and learn from failures.

These personal traits go a long way in making an entrepreneur successful. However, no entrepreneur possesses total strength. In such cases, he acquires and/or associates and thus strengthens his enterprise.

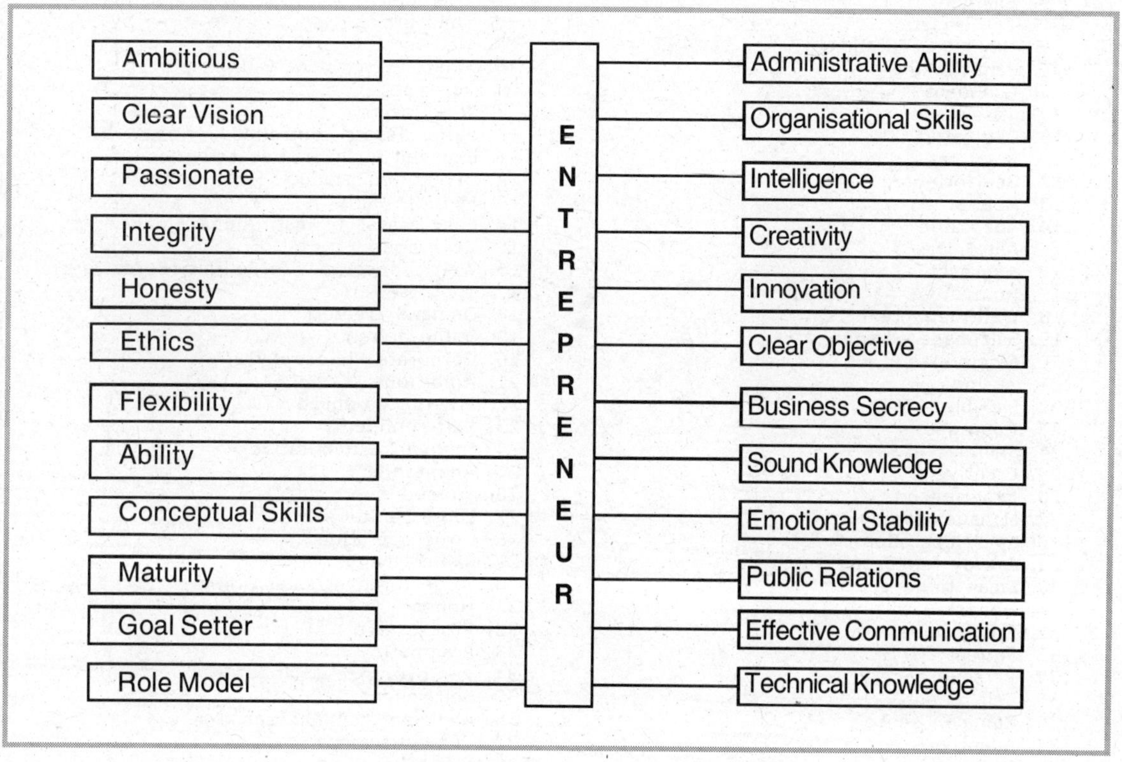

Fig. 4.1: Characteristics of an Entrepreneur

Qualities of an Entrepreneur

A true entrepreneur besides possessing functional qualities, must also possess a broad personality which help in developing initiative and drive to accomplish great tasks and face challenges squarely.

James J. Berne has stressed the following qualities of a good entrepreneur:

1. He is an enterprising individual, is energetic, hard working, resourceful, aware of new opportunities and able to adjust himself to changing conditions with ease and willing to assume risks involved in change.
2. He is interested in advancing technologically and in improving the quality of his product or service.
3. He is interested in expanding the scale of his operations by reinvesting his earnings.
4. He visualizes changes and adapts to changing conditions.
5. He is a firm believer in planning and systematic work.

Table 4.1 Characteristics of Entrepreneurs

Small-scale Entrepreneurs	*Large-scale Entrepreneurs*
1. Young men	1. Middle aged Professionals
2. Ambitious	2. Professional Specialists
3. Intelligent	3. Shareholders contribute venture capital
4. Energetic	4. Energetic
5. Enthusiastic	5. Outsourcing
6. Minimum education	6. Net-workers
7. Hard working	7. Ability to get along with people
8. Confident	8. Tolerant
9. Passionate	9. Risk Takers
10. Dedicated	10. Large Assets controlled
11. Practical	11. Engaged in diversified activities
12. Goal-oriented	12. Diversified products
13. Mobile	13. Multiple activities
14. Adaptable	14. Easy assess to institutional finance
15. Able	15. Leverages
16. Aggressive	16. Well connected with Politics, Bureacrats
17. Innovative	17. Trend setters
18. Well-mannered	18. Demand creators
19. Self-made person	19. Value-driven
20. Disciplined	20. Corporate Philosophy
21. Zealous	21. Ambitious
22. Flexible	22. Drive to go ahead
23. Courageous	23. Self-confident
24. Skilful	24. Innovative/immitative
25. Creative	25. Adaptable
26. Experienced	26. Trained
27. Manager capital	27. Large capital
28. Small operation	28. Large operation
29. Employ few people	29. Skilled manpower
30. Small turnover	30. Large turnover/sales/profit
31. Honest	31. Honest
32. Progressive	32. Progressive
33. Patient	33. Pragmatic
34. Perseverance	34. Perseverance
35. Self-reliant	35. Self-reliant
36. Common sense	36. Abundant common sense
37. Adaptive	37. Competitive
38. Ability to strive	38. Versatile
39. Compassionate	39. Quality conscious
40. Dreamer	40. Visionaries
41. Conscious	41. Focussed
42. Intuitive	42. Singleness of purpose
43. Practical	43. Ability to change
44. Imaginative	44. Educated
45. Achiever	45. A strong need to achieve
46. Hopefull	46. Passionate
47. Independent	47. Analytical
48. Self-starter	48. Optimistic
49. Individualist	49. Organisational man
50. Sensitive	50. Loyal
51. Perceptive	51. Pleasing personality
52. Quality-conscious	52. Dynamic
53. Desire to share experience	53. Tolerant
54. Ability to change	54. Active
55. Money-oriented	55. Contributor
56. Driven by values	56. Knowledgeable
57. Intrapreneurial	57. Motivator
58. Facilitator	58. Strategist
59. Learner	59. Goal conscious
60. Opportunist	60. Compassionate
61. Ability to strive	61. Leader
62. Task master	62. Scanner — Looking for opportunities
63. Striving Richness	63. Planner
64. Gut-Feeler	64. Thinker
65. Dictator	65. People Manager

6. He works for the society at large and for the good of his fellow-beings.

These qualities sum up, what is usually implied from the phrase, the "spirit of enterprise". It is difficult to conceivers of a first-rate industrial entrepreneur who is not adaptable to change, anxious to grow large and improve technologically.

Entrepreneurship appears as a personal quality which enables certain individuals to make decision with far-reaching consequences. The personal qualities that contribute to the success of an entrepreneur are as follows:

***1. Motivation Towards Achievement*:** A successful entrepreneur should be a good administrator. He should know the art of getting things done by other people without hurting their feelings or self-respect. He should have a strong motivation towards the achievement of a task and must be able to exert considerable efforts in getting things done by others.

***2. Creativity*:** Mental ability consists of intelligence, an analytical approach and creative things. An entrepreneur should have creative thinking and be able to engage in the analysis of various problems and situations in order to deal with them. The entrepreneur should anticipate changes and must be able to study various situations in which decisions may have to be made.

***3. Clarity*:** An entrepreneur should have clear objective as to the exact nature of the business, the nature of the goods to be produced and the subsidiary activities to be undertaken.

The qualities of an entrepreneur are given in Fig.7.2.

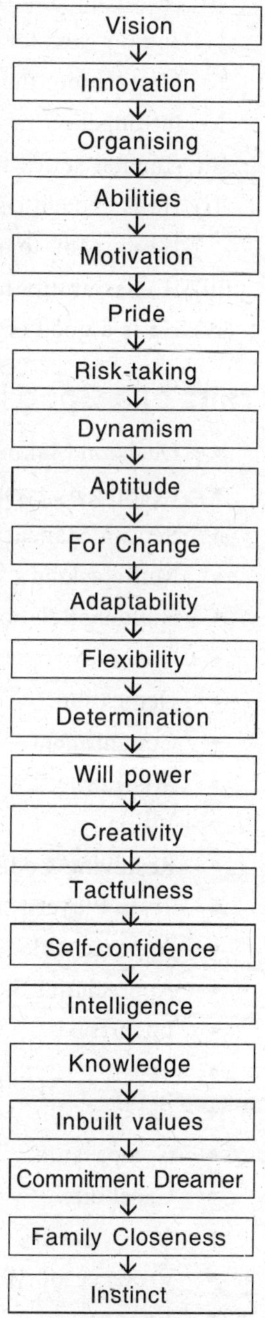

Fig. 4.2: Qualities of a Successful Entrepreneur

Kilby has rightly enumerated the following activities for a successful entrepreneur in an underdeveloped economy:

1. Perception of market opportunities (novel or imitative).
2. Gaining command over scarce resources.
3. Purchasing of inputs.
4. Marketing of the product and responding effectively to competition.
5. Dealing with public bureaucracy as regards concessions, licences, taxes, etc., provided through the various fiscal policies of the government.
6. Management of the human relations within the enterprise.
7. Management of customer and supplier relations.
8. Financial management.
9. Production management, including control through written records, supervision, coordinating input flows with orders, maintenance.

10. Acquiring and overseeing assembly of the plant.
11. Taking care for minimising inputs for a given production process.
12. Maintaining the production process and improving the quality of the product.
13. Introduction of new production techniques and product-lines.

B.C.Tandon states that successful entrepreneurs possess following four qualities:

(i) He is enough risk-bearer.
(ii) He is ready to adopt change, if the situations warrant.
(iii) He has ability to Marshall resources at his command.
(iv) He is a good organiser as well as a good manager.

Traits of a Good Leader

- Decision Making
- Leading by Example
- Setting Standards
- Multi tasking
- Building Relationship
- Creativity
- Dedication
- Commitment
- Mission
- Vision
- Resolving Conflicts
- Team Player
- Approachable
- Appreciating Skills
- Integrity
- Trust
- Passion
- Compassion
- Capability
- Involvement
- Presence of Mind
- Energy
- Clarity of Thought
- Patience
- Daring to Dream
- Sincerity

- Trust
- Honesty

United States Agency for International Development states the following competencies of successful entrepreneur:

Proactivity	
1. Initiative	Does things before being asked or forced by events.
2. Assertiveness	Confronts problems with others directly. Tells others what they have to do.
Achievement Orientation	
3. Sees and acts on opportunities	Seizes unusual opportunities, to start a new business, obtain financing, land, work space, or assistance.
4. Efficiency Orientation.	Looks for and finds ways to do things faster or at less cost.
5. Concern for high quality work.	States a desire to produce or sell a top or better quality product or service.
6. Systematic Planning.	Breaks a large task down into subtasks or subgoals. Anticipates obstacles. Evaluates alternatives.
7. Monitoring.	Develops or uses procedures to ensure that work is completed or that work meets standards.
Commitment to Others	
8. Commitment to Work Contract.	Makes a personal sacrifice or expands extraordinary efforts to complete a job. Pitches in with workers or works in their place to get job done.
9. Recognizing the importance of Business Relationships.	Acts to build rapport or friendly relationships with customers. Sees interpersonal relationships as a fundamental business resource. Places long-term goodwill over short-term gain.

From the above discussion and definitions, it can be stated that entrepreneurial activities encompass those factors right from the perception of the profitable opportunity to its translation into reality through establishing a successful enterprise and further leading to its growth and development. Especially in an underdeveloped economy, the expectations from entrepreneurial units are much more varied and related to many dimensions, including socio-economic objectives. This is because this type of economy is characterised by a majority of low income strata than the developed economy characterised by high income.

Entrepreneurial Skills

To deal with entrepreneurial skills is to concern oneself with a wide coverage of aspects of setting up an enterprise and its management. It is not confined to visualization, planning, setting-up and risk-taking. The skills which an entrepreneur includes are his ability to deal with situations, organisations and social and economic forces as they emerge from time-to-time. The skills to deal with a situation fore-visualised or suddenly emerging must be an essential characteristic of an entrepreneur.

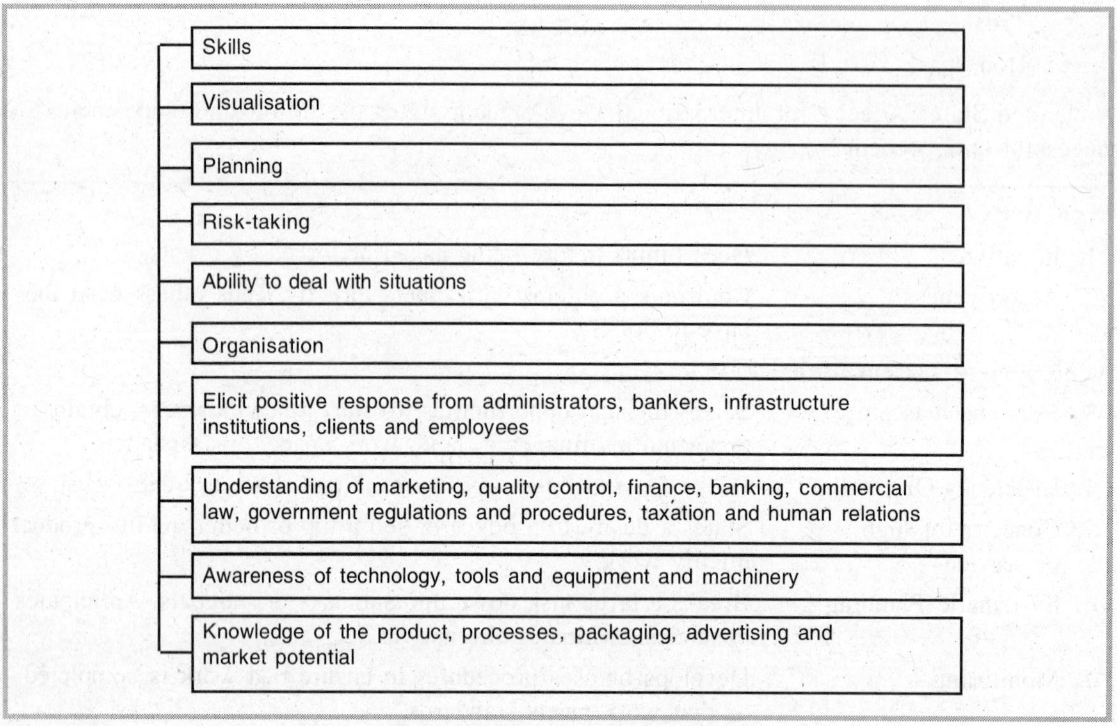

Fig. 4.3: Entrepreneurial Skills

The small entrepreneur must have skills to positive response from administrators, bankers, infrastructure institutions, clients and employees.

The entrepreneur is rarely a master of the management skills, and yet is usually directly responsible for all aspects of business. Often he or she has to be the general manager, production manager, purchasing manager, personnel manager, controller and research organiser for the business all rolled into at least during its early years. The entrepreneur therefore has to have an understanding of marketing, quality control, finance, banking, commercial law, government regulations and procedures, and human relation as each of them has a vital bearing on the health of the enterprise.

Need for Skills

We often talk of transfer of technology. As a matter of fact, the whole world is talking about it. There is hardly any international event at the global and regional level where this subject does not come up for discussion. The poor nations demand technology and resources from industrialised and rich countries and rightly so. The developing countries would rather export semi-finished and finished products which are value-added than export raw materials. The development of entrepreneurial skill must precede transfer of technology if we do not desire to keep such technologies and equipment serving such technologies idle. One has also to realise that technologies are developing very fast and the skills are to match with this dynamic growth. The entrepreneur has to be made aware of the imperative needs of updated technologies, modern tools and equipments, processes and system and skills. In this task his whole organisation, however small it may be has to join the exercise.

Box 4.1 The Wealth of Knowledge

Skills and knowledge have become the only source of sustainable long-term competitive advantage. Knowledge, which used to be tertiary — after raw materials and capital — in determining economic success, is now primary. With this comes the need for more differentiated systems of determining who owns what intellectual property, better protection for whatever is owned and faster systems of dispute resolution when disputes arise.

Clear, easily enforceable, sellable ownership rights to intellectual property have to be established. Reverse engineering (the politically correct phrase for copying) is a way of life in the corporate world. But where should the limits be? Whatever the answer, it's not to be found in a patent system more than a century old.

It is not so clear, however, what it means to own knowledge or how those ownership rights can be enforced. What part of their knowledge can employees take with them when they move to a new employer? How do employers stop employees from taking the employer's intellectual property when they go? Where is the dividing line between knowledge in the public domain and knowledge in the private domain? Without stronger systems of protection, companies will defend their economic positions by keeping their knowledge secret, but a recent study found that 73 per cent of private patents were based on knowledge generated by public sources such as universities and non-profit or government laboratories. *– Lester C.Thurow*

Chart 4.1

Examples of three types of essential capabilities that help enterprises create capabilities desired/appreciated by customers and also reduce cost of creating and delivering such benefits.

1. **Product specific capabilities visible to customers**

- Quality of the total product and also that of the individual components of the same
- Performance features/attributes
- Range/variety
- New products/upgrades

2. **Process specific capabilities — visible to customers (Transaction related)**

- Order fulfillment process
- Pre and post-sales services
- Tendering process
- Dealer management process
- Order tracking process
- Meeting special or emergency requirements (product/quality/volume/packing
- Complaint handling process and for resolving customer's problem
- Documentation

3. Process-specific capabilities — invisible to customers (leading to creating product or transaction-specific benefits (Ref.in (1) and (2) or helping in reducing the cost)

- Creation and management of database on low cost and right quality inputs
- Value engineering process
- Selection process for sub-contractors/vendors
- Purchase process
- Material movement process (from suppliers to manufacturers to customers)
- PPC process
- Production process/set up process/methods
- New product development process
- Quality assurance process
- Support services process (e.g., Bill processing, credit not issued, etc.)

Willingness to Change

Adding value requires willingness to change. Adding something innovative springs from nurturing attitudes. And as research and development build a critical mass, new products and services increasingly happen.

The journey of change is not without its obstacles. But it is also a journey that is full of rewards. The key to reaping the rewards and minimixing the breakdowns is to lead with your heart, not your head. Your heart is where you will find your willingness. Your head is where you will find resistance and fear.

When we begin to feel resistance and fear that it can be easy to lose touch with the willingness that we had at the beginning of the process. When this happens, we need to focus on reconnecting with the part of us that originally wanted to make the change — the part that is excited about learning new things, facing new challenges, and bringing more joy and fulfillment to our life.

Adding value is not simply a matter of doing good — rather it is a synergistic process. It is a collaborative process of problem-solving and of designing robust systems that produce goods and services that meet customer needs and specifications. It is a process of making thousands of moments of truth happy experiences for those involved.

Adding value is easier when we use the right tool for the job. Adding something new can come from the tool of stretch goals. Cutting waste, reducing failure costs, and delivery problems comes from tools of substraction, from employing the tool of simplicity. Intensification of effort can come from incentive tools, and from the tool of division — from focus of effort upon specific tasks. Adding value can come from teaming up to do a job, from enlisting others in a pyramid of effort.

Adding value goes beyond customer-satisfaction to customer-confidence. Trust is generated from honest relationships that are built into goods and services. It means being able to depend upon those who have earned that trust.

Add value to your life by self-improvement. The Japanese have a term for the kind of attitude and action they want their employees to nurture; it is kaizen. Kaizen means to continuously find small ways of improving yourself in whatever you do. It is an attitude that manifests itself in action. How does one do that? It is a matter of improving one's character, one's personality, one's relationships, and by increasing one's skill level.

At the company level, less rather than more, means finding ways to cut waste, cut costs, and to make one's product and service better fit one's customers: more durable, easier to use, more beautiful, and more accessible. Some gurus of quality refer to this as cutting failure costs — the aggregate cost of failure to do things right. Not doing it right costs in inspection, complaints, loss of customers, and rework. Less waste is more profit.

Chart 4.2

The Skills Needed

- Individual skills
- Functional skills specific to jobs
- Knowledge skills
- Analytical skills
- Problem-solving skills
- Negotiation skill
- Out of the box thinking skills
- Interpersonal skills/communication skills
- Business skills
- Management skills
- Behavioural skills
- Learning skills
- Planning and implementation skills
- Ability to relate/understand desparate information/technology to develop new product/ process service ideas
- Flexibility to work under unstructured/fast changing environment
- Risk management

Group Skills

- Ability to work together
- Ability to learn together
- Ability to use task forces/project teams
- Ability to work in unstructured situation
- Ability to work with "tight" resource base

Technical Skills

- Writing
- Oral communication
- Monitoring environment
- Technical business management
- Technology
- Interpersonal
- Listening
- Ability to organise
- Network building
- Management style
- Coaching
- Being a team player

Business Management Skills

- Planning and goal setting
- Decision making
- Human relations
- Marketing
- Finance
- Accounting
- Management
- Control
- Negotiation
- Venture launch
- Managing growth

Personal Entrepreneurial Skills

- Inner control/disciplined
- Risk-taker
- Innovative
- Change-oriented
- Persistent
- Visionary leader
- Ability to manage change

Enterprise Skills

- Identify value creating processes and capabilities that leads to either differentiation or cost or both

- Market sensing skill
- Creating/setting new direction/vision
- Pulling in place a right organisational structure/systems/physical infrastructure
- Selecting the right people
- Inculcating ethics/principle centred management
- Encouraging subsidiaries/departments/functions to innovate
- Establishing networks and alliance
- Set clearly defined goals
- Never waiver in your belief that you can achieve them
- Manage your attitude and discipline
- Persevere when adversity strikes
- Learn to take risks and embrace change
- Love and be loved
- Make a difference whenever, wherever, and however, you can

Behaviourial Skills

- Motivation
- Judgement
- Resilience
- Initiative
- Team working
- Self-management
- Self-confidence
- Improvement Reorientation
- Trust yourself
- Initiative taking

Call it a premonition, an instinct, a feeling — whatever you label it, it's your intuition talking. Intuition by definition is quick and ready insight. The more you practice identifying, listening to, and acting on your intuition, the more you'll trust your instincts in the future, which is the first step to building the life you truly want. Once you know where you want to go, intuition will show you how to get there. So, tune into your intuition and go with your gut.

Communication Skills

- Be flexible
- Able to identify an opportunity to communicate
- Don't blow your own trumpet
- Put your intelligence into words
- Emphasise on the issue
- Communicate well
- Communicate with illustrations
- Interact effectively

(i) self-awareness
(ii) empathy
(iii) responsiveness
(iv) alertness
(v) timeliness
(vi) proficiency
(vii) clarity
(viii) focus
(ix) compassionation
(x) positive attitude
(xi) dissemination
(xii) presentation
(xiii) listen willingly

Listening Skills

- Listen without the intervention of any thoughts
- Pay more attention to others
- Establish rapport
- Actively listen

Soft Skills

- Using your knowledge effectively
- Clarity in expressions
- Read a lot
- Rapport building
- Be alive and alert
- Good knowledge of English
- Step out of the box, physically and mentally
- Take the lead

A Learning Organisation

- Is an active philosophy; not merely an organisational system
- Believes that its only competitive advantage is learning
- Encourages people to learn to produce the results they desire
- Nurtures creative and innovative patterns of collective learning
- Develops fresh organisational capabilities all the time

Never underestimate the power of belief when it comes to fulfilling your dreams.

Belief fuels enthusiasm. Ride the wave of passion and manage your attitude. Continue to dream big dreams, but realise that short-term goals that take you to the next plateau are the real keys to success. Goals are dreams with deadlines.

Tap your creative soul — imagine. Imagination is seeing things, not as they are, but as they could be. Have heroes. Failure is a big part of life, but it is how we react to failing that will determine our destiny. If we learn from it and move on, it can help to make us all we can be.

To get what you have never had, you must do what you have never done. When you face adversity, be focused but patient, and the right answers will usually surface before you know it. Exercise to energise. Exercise is a small price.

The World Health Organisation defines life skills as the abilities for adaptive and positive behaviour that enable individuals to deal effectively with the demands and challenges of everyday life.

WHO categorises life skills into three components:

- *Thinking skills:* Self-awareness, social-awareness, goal-setting, problem-solving and decision-making. To be able to think critically, information must be provided to make informed decisions and choices. Skills to think critically can be developed if teenagers are given the opportunity to look at different perspectives of an issue, the pros and the cons of making a decision over the other and making them realise the negative consequences of making hasty, unplanned decisions.
- *Social skills:* Appreciating/validating others; working with others; understanding their roles; building positive relationships with friends and family; listening and communicating effectively; taking responsibility and coping with stress. These enable adolescents to be accepted in society and accept social norms which provide the foundation for adult social behaviour.
- *Negotiation skills* mean not only negotiating with others but with oneself. To negotiate with others, one needs to know what one wants in life; is firm on one's values and beliefs and can, therefore, say 'no' to harmful behaviour and risky temptations.

The Global Leader of the Future

- Thinks globally
- Anticipates opportunity
- Creates a shared vision
- Develops and empowers people
- Appreciates cultural diversity
- Builds teamwork and partnerships
- Embraces change
- Shows technological savvy
- Encourages constructive challenge
- Ensures customer satisfaction
- Achieves a competitive advantage
- Demonstrates personal mastery
- Shares leadership
- Lives the values

It is observed that in many least developed countries, sophisticated equipment and machinery imported at heavy cost, often under pressure of international financial institutions or aid agreements are lying unutilised for want of trained hands. It is obvious that the accelerated development of human resources and appropriate training of manpower must be concurrent with the transfer of technologies which are relevant to the needs of each developing country. This will call for an inventory of existing manpower, degree of their present skills, arrangements for proper imparting and skills needed. This should have a relation to natural endowment and resources and their optimum utilisation.

Types of Skills

Types of skills vary according to location, products, clientele, etc. In rural areas, a small enterprise making goods for local consumption based on local raw materials would need relatively simpler skills. In urban areas, the product, processes, packaging, advertising have to match with the growing sophistication of consumer goods, preference of needs, etc. They call for an intensification of effort to develop matched skills in all areas of entrepreneurial activity.

Skills for New Class of Entrepreneurs

As stated earlier, entrepreneurship till recently in most of the developing countries has been confined to persons coming from the traditionally trade-oriented families. Now there is emphasis on new classes of entrepreneurs. These would include women, tribals and young men from non-traditional families. For women entrepreneurs, special training facilities have to be provided owing to the special difficulties faced by them as compared to men. For tribal entrepreneurs, care will have to be taken that their basic culture, crafts and skills are not materially affected.

Soft Skill Appraisal

Fourteen soft skills to turnout the perfect executive needed by almost every organisation today.

Executives who can communicate, organise, present, sell, create, initiate, be team players and who add to the organisation's bottom line; because corporates need to survive with competition, new technology and recession in the new world.

Given below is a performance appraisal of an executive after training.

		Rating*
1.	Technical knowledge regarding the industry and the job he/she was involved	Good
2.	Communications skills	
	(a) Oral	Good
	(b) Written	Good
	(c) Listening skills	Good
3.	Ability to work in a team	Excellent
4.	Ability to take initiative	Excellent
5.	Ability to develop a healthy long-term relationship with clients	Good
6.	Ability to relate theoretical learning to the practical training	Good

7.	Creativity and ability to innovate with respect to work methods and procedures	Good
8.	Ability to grasp new ideas and knowledge	Good
9.	Presentation skills	Excellent
10.	Documentation skills	Excellent
11.	Sense of Responsibility	Excellent
12.	Acceptability (patience, pleasing manners, the ability to instil trust, etc.)	Good
13.	His/her ability and willingness to put in hard work	Good
14.	In what ways do you consider the student to be valuable to the organisation? Consider the student's value in terms of: (a) Qualification (b) Skills and abilities (c) Activities/Roles performed	Yes

Additionally, the following soft skills add to broaden entrepreneurial capabilities and improve decision making.

Soft Skills

P – Problem-solving (judgement, logic, conflict resolution)

E – Ethics (courtesy, honesty, professionalism)

O – Open-mindedness (flexibility, open to new ideas, positive outlook)

P – Persuasiveness (diplomacy, communication, listening skills)

L – Leadership (accountability, management, motivational skills)

E – Educational interests (continual thirst for knowledge and skill development)

Source: Infotech Enterprise

1. Competency Recognition: An individual's behaviour or performance depends upon the competencies he possesses. Therefore, in order to get desired behaviour we should be in a position to know as to what are the competencies required in the individuals to perform in a particular manner. Under this step an effort is made to recognise the competencies.

2. Self-assessment: After getting clear-cut idea about the competencies required for a particular type of behaviour, it is for the entrepreneur to see as to what extent he possesses these competencies and to what extent he is employing these competencies for achieving the desired goal.

3. Comparison of Competencies: The next step is to compare individual competencies with the competencies required for the desired performance. Wherever we find deficiencies an earnest attempt is made to find out the reasons for the same.

4. Developing Competencies and Feedback: Once it is realised that an individual does not possess a particular competency required for a particular type of behaviour, the next step will be to develop this competency. Assistance from various behavioural scientists may be taken for devising out ways and means for developing the required competency. In order to ensure that the required competency becomes part of the individual's behaviour, he is asked to practise the needed competency repeatedly. Lastly an attempt is made to know as to what extent change in individual behaviour has taken place due to acquiring of the requisite competency and to what extent it has been useful. It is through continuous application that one can ensure that the desired competency becomes part of his habit or personality.

5. Motivation: If the entrepreneur is to succeed and build an effective organisation to excell in global competitiveness he should be motivated as well as motivate the team. "The ability to keep yourself and your team motivated is very important because it has a direct impact on individual and organisational productivity", says Edsil Coutinho who runs a logistical supply company and manages about 1,000 people. "For example, there are times when you need people to put in long hours, often without the promise of a reward. During such times, it is important to keep them motivated. Even if the situation is bleak, the leader should take it upon oneself to motivate others and see the bright side of the problem." There are several motivational practices available at the hands of entrepreneurs.

- Most powerful motivators are rewards which in themselves include four types: membership and seniority, job status, competency and performance.
- Job design — the process of assigning tasks to a job — can be an effective tool to motivate employees. There are six approaches to job design: job rotation, job enlargement, job enrichment, social technical systems and ergonomics.
- OB Mod is based on the principle of law of effect. The principle states that repetition of a behaviour depends upon its earlier consequences.
- If consequences of the previous action are positive, the behaviour tends to get repeated. Being based on the principle of law of effect, OB Mod acts as a powerful motivator.
- Empowerment is another motivational practice. Empowerment makes employees believe that they own the jobs.
- Goal setting too is a powerful motivational practice. Performance goals, if properly set, will motivate employees considerably.
- Problem employees need to be given one more chance, probably by shifting them to a new work environment. If they fail to respond, suspension of workers and firing of managers need to be resorted to.
- Flexi time, MBO, flexible benefits and other such practices also help motivate employees.

5 CHAPTER

THE CONCEPT OF ENTREPRENEURSHIP

> *"The Essence of Entrepreneurship: The only effective antidote to poverty and deprivation lies in encouragement to entrepreneurship.*
>
> *Entrepreneurship is the dynamic process of creating incremental wealth. The wealth is created by individuals who assume the major risks in terms of equity, time, and/or career commitment or provide value for some product or service. The product or service may or may not be new or unique, but value must somehow be infused by the entrepreneur by receiving and locating the necessary skills and resources."*

INTRODUCTION

Entrepereneurship introduces a critical element of dynamism into an economic system. It is no coincidence that the world's leading economy, the USA, is believed to be the most entrepreneurial society in the world. The process of globalisation and liberalisation has introduced two sets of changes — the first is the obvious introduction of dynamism into the system through the process of globalisation. While new opportunities have opened up in international markets, the bar has been raised in the domestic market through international products and services being available to Indian consumers. The domestic market will no longer be lower-risk. It will force Indian entrepreneurs to regain their spirit of innovation.

The more subtle change is social: increase in literacy levels, greater consumer awareness, enhanced media penetration, and basic changes in family structure. These changes are bound to result in a higher level of entrepreneurial activity in future.

In keeping with the demands for greater innovation in Indian enterprises, several have fundamentally redesigned structures. There are no easy answers to how the rate of change in entrepreneurial activity can be increased. The solutions to eliminate some of the structural constraints to entrepreneurship are really no different from the solutions to driving higher economic growth rates. Entrepreneurship extends beyond a conventional business and economic perspective. Creativity, innovation, and bringing a vision to life are as much entrepreneurial activities in a social sphere — and have the same impact on society as does business entrepreneurship to the economy.

Indians have always been entrepreneurs: we have all heard about businesses growing from father to son or the rags-to-riches story in conventional industry. But recently there has been a shift in the nature of Indian entrepreneurship. It has come to stand for something that is out of the box and globally oriented. It began with the infotech revolution a decade ago. Now all the signs point to another industry joining this new wave of Indian enterprise. Venture capitalists and economic forecasters believe biotechnology is India's next big thing, its new IT.

A COMPLEX PHENOMENON

The concept of entrepreneurship is a complex phenomenon. Broadly, it relates to the entrepreneur, his vision and its implementation. The key player is the entrepreneur. Entrepreneurship refers to a process of action an entrepreneur (person) undertakes to establish his/her enterprise. It is a creative and innovative response to the environment.

Entrepreneurship is thus a cycle of actions to further the interests of the entrepreneur. In this chapter, the concept of entrepreneurship and the related issues are analysed, discussed, and deliberated.

One of the qualities of entrepreneurship is the ability to discover an investment opportunity and to organise an enterprise, thereby contributing to real economic growth. It involves taking of risks and making the necessary investments under conditions of uncertainty and innovating, planning and taking decisions so as to increase production in agriculture, business, industry, etc.

Entrepreneurship is a composite skill, the resultant of a mix of many qualities and traits. These include imagination, readiness to take risks, ability to bring together and put to user other factors of production, capital, labour, land, as also intangible factors such as the ability to mobilise scientific and technological advances.

A hard practical approach is necessary to be able to implement and manage a project by securing the required licences, approvals and finance from governmental and financial agencies. The personal incentive is to make profits from the successful management of the project. A sense of cost-consciousness is even more necessary for the long-term success of the enterprise. However, both are different sides of the same coin. Entrepreneurship lies perhaps more in the ability to minimise the use of resources and to put them to maximum advantages. Without an awareness of quality and desire for excellence, consumer acceptance cannot be achieved and sustained. Above all enterpreneurship today is the product of teamwork and the ability to create, build and work as a team. The entrepreneur is the maestro of the business orchestra, wielding his baton to which the band is played.

What is Enterpreneurship

Entrepreneurship is the propensity of mind to take calculated risks with confidence to achieve a pre-determined business or industrial objective. In substance, it is the risk-taking ability of the individual, broadly coupled with correct decision-making. When one witnesses a relatively larger number of individuals and that too generation-after-generation in a particular community, who engage themselves in the industrial or commercial pursuits and appear to take risks and show enterprise, it is acknowledged to be a commercial class. The commercial class is a myth just like that of the so-called martial race. There are neither, for all-time, martial races nor commercial classes. Communities, which in the course of history once appeared to be martial in spirit have, in later periods, emerged as mercantile societies. Those who were once more concerned with and relished in trade, later in history, seem to have taken to the profession of the sword. Today, it is quite evident to anyone that national communities which have developed world wide industrial and consequent commercial interests are militarily powerful: nay, great industrial powers have today become super-military powers as well. Enterprise finds manifestation in different ways. The capacity to take risk independently and individually, with a view to making profits and seizing an opportunity to make more earning in the market-oriented economy, is the dominant characteristic of modern entrepreneurship. Enterprise, ready for the pursuit of business and responsive to profit by way of producing and or marketing goods and commodities, to meet the expanding and diversifying actual and potential needs and demands of the customers, is what constitutes *entrepreneurial stuff*. But this kind of sensitivity of enterprising citizens throws up a species of entrepreneurs, who are mostly mercantile in outlook and performance. In underdeveloped countries like India, a new species of entrepreneurs is desirable, because here the economic progress has to be brought about along with social justice. Entrepreneurship in India, therefore, has to subserve the national objective. There is an apparent conflict between social objectives and economic imperatives. This conflict has to be resolved first by the individual entrepreneur in his own mind and make economic growth, which induces industrial development, as one of the instruments of attaining the social objective. A high sense of responsibility is thus an essential attribute of emergent entrepreneurship in India.

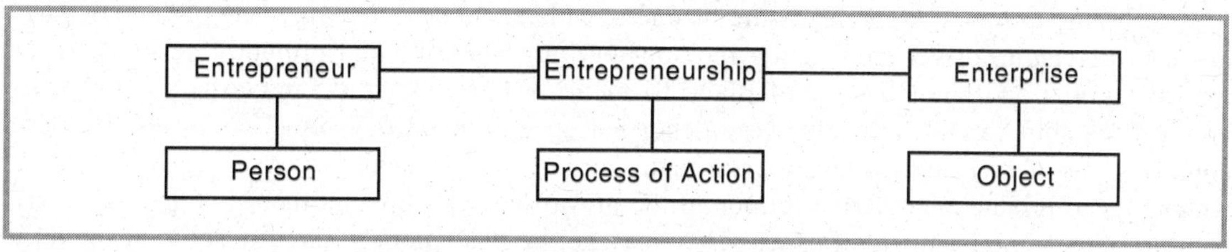

Fig. 5.1: Concept of Entrepreneurship

Stimulation of Entrepreneurship

Entrepreneurship development is probably one of the most elusive, complicated and perplexing issues in the promotion and growth of small enterprises. Recently, a number of development agencies have been involved. However, in spite of all these efforts, there have been only a few partially successful programmes and many colossal failures in the field.

The stimulation of entrepreneurship is a function of both internal and external variables. The presence of certain personal qualities in an individual is a requisite. Some of the findings about entrepreneurs in Nepal are as follows:

(a) Mainly there are two types of entrepreneurs: the government and private individuals.

(b) In a family-run business, the entrepreneur is owner as well as manager. Entrepreneurs are frequently found to have parents who were engaged in business-related occupations. Membership in certain types of communities (Mewass, Marwadies, Gurung, etc.), is highly correlated with entrepreneurship.

(c) Many people who migrated from the hills to the southern part of the country (Terai), and returned have become entrepreneurs, and

(d) In the family, a change is taking place. Now the educated young members are becoming entrepreneurs rather than the head of the family who is generally old.

Definition

Entrepreneurship is a multi-dimensional task defined differently by different authorities. Cantilon was the first to use the term 'entrepreneur'. He portrayed an entrepreneur as one discharging the faction of direction and speculation. J.B. Say, moving along in the French (Cantillion) tradition, was the first to assign the entrepreneur a position in the economic process. According to him, an entrepreneur's function is to combine the factors of production into a producing organism, but to Adam Smith, thc father of political economy, the entrepreneur was a proprietary capitalist, a supplier of capital and at the same time, working as manager, intervening between thc labour and the consumer. Adam Smith also treated him with the capitalist. Schumpeter was decidedly the first economic thinker to have assigned the entrepreneur a key role in the process of economic development. In Schumpeter's system, entrepreneurship is essentially a creative activity. The entrepreneur is the innovator who introduces something new into the economy. The innovation may be a method of production not yet tested by experience in the branch of manufacture concerned or a product with which consumers are not yet familiar, or a new source of raw material or of a market hitherto unexploited or other innovations in the strict sense of the term.

According to him, entrepreneurs are business leaders and not simple owners of capital. They are men of vision, drive and talent, who spot out opportunities and promptly seize them for exploitation. It will not be out of place to mention here that the innovator's concept of entrepreneurship cannot be exclusively depended upon in underdeveloped countries. In these countries, business leaders who promote many large and small enterprises and adapt Western techniques of production and distribution to the prevailing conditions in their own industries are entrepreneurs of no mean significance. They may not be innovators in the true sense of the term but they are men of great vision and effective industial leaders who transform the economic landscape of their countries. People like Jamsetji Nusserwanji Tata, M. Visvesvaraya, G.D. Birla, Jamnalal Bajaj, Laxmanrao Kirloskar and other visionaries, builders and thinkers laid the foundation for a modern industrialised India. Professor Bert F. Hoselitz calls them imitative entrepreneurs, and regards their existence as quite purposeful in a mixed economy. "Coupled with all historical experiences of Western Europe, it appears to be safe to assume", he writes, that "small and medium-scale entrepreneurs are likely to play an important role in developing countries for several decades, provided these developing nations permit a private sector of enterprise in the industrial, commercial and financial field at all".

This definition stresses four basic aspects of being an entrepreneur regardless of the field. First, entrepreneurship involves the creation process — creating something new of value. The creation has to have value to the entrepreneur and value to the audience for which it is developed. This audience can be: (1) the market of buyers in the case of a business innovation, (2) the hospital's administration in the case of a new admitting procedure and software, (3) prospective students in the case of a new course or even college of entrepreneurship, or (4) the constituency for a new service provided by a non-profit agency. Second, entrepreneurship requires the devotion of the necessary time and effort. Only those going through the entrepreneurial process appreciate the significant amount of time and effort it takes to create something new and make it operational. Assuming the necessary risks is the third aspect of entrepreneurship. These risks take a variety of forms, depending on the field of effort of the entrepreneur, but usually centre around financial, psychological, and social areas. The final part of the definition involves the rewards of being an entrepreneur. The most important of these rewards is independence, followed by personal satisfaction. For profit entrepreneurs, the monetary reward also comes into play. For some of these entrepreneurs, money becomes the indicator of the degree of success.

For the person who actually starts his or her own business, the experience is filled with enthusiasm, frustration, anxiety, and hard work. There is a high failure rate due to such things as poor sales, intense competition, lack of capital, or lack of managerial ability. The financial and emotional risk can also be very high. What, then, causes a person to make this difficult decision? The question can be best explored by looking at the decision process involved in becoming an entrepreneur.

Besides, in South-East Asian countries, at the pre-take-off stage, the need is for more promoters, risk-takers and business organisers than fair innovators. In the emerging countries, employment creation is a far more immediate goal for the entrepreneurs than technological innovation. As Professor Jan Tinbergen points out: "The best entrepreneur to any developing country is not necessarily the man who use much capital, but rather the man who knows how to organise the employment and training of his employees. Whoever concentrates on this is rendering a much more important service to this country than the man who uses huge capital."

Concept of Entrepreneurship

From classical economics to the post-Keynesian analysts, the topic of the entrepreneur has been surveyed and observations, theories and pronouncements advanced. Not only were pure economists involved in this endeavour, but also prominent social theorists such as Marx, Weber, Sombard and Veblen.

In general, contemporary economists agree that the entrepreneur is a business leader and that his role in fostering economic growth and development is a pivotal one. At present, however, there is no consensus at to what constitutes the essential activity which makes the entrepreneur a crucial figure, while some economists have identified the basic entrepreneurial requirements of production resources, the provision of capital or the introduction of innovations. Professor James R. Omps of the International Institute of Entreprenology, Honolulu, Hawaii, in his paper entitled "*Entreprenology, the Critical Factor in Nation Development*", has this to say:

"In all crisis situations, there is one critical factor. There is one factor in each situation that can be cited as being the straw that broke the camel's back! In listing some of today's possible critical factors, such familiar words and phrases as limited natural resources... food... energy all would emerge. A question may be phrased thus:

"What is the critical factor?"

Over-population?

Food shortages?

Energy shortages?

Lack of technology? And

All of the above?

"Many factors have been proposed ... and yet is it possible that the most critical factor has not been recognised? What is this factor that has either been stifled or totally ignored? It is a relatively untapped source... that of qualified individuals with peculiarly unique aptitudes for innovation ... for change, aptitudes, in other words, for using present-day technology in ways yet unheard for perhaps even unthought of. The critical factor is a dire shortage of the appropriate economic innovator and implement... the entreprenologists."

In the words of **A.H. Cole**, entrepreneurship is the purposeful activity of an individual or a group of associated individuals, undertaken to initiate, maintain or organise a profit-oriented business unit for the production or distribution of economic goods and services.

Frank H. Knight seriously questioned the unimportance of entrepreneurship in his publication '*Risk, Uncertainty and Profit*' (1921) and expressed views similar to those of Cantilon. Knight emphasised that many uncertainties of economic life can be insured but some uncertainties are such which can never be reduced to objective measurement because they involve unprecendented situations. Knight remarked that "The only 'risk' which leads to profits is a unique uncertainty resulting from an exercise of ultimate responsibility which in its very nature cann't be insured not capitalised nor salaried". Thus, he draws a distinction between the ordinary risk and uncertainty. A risk can be insured whereas uncertainty is a risk which can't be calculated and can't be insured. *He showed that the man who earns positive profits in this "uncertainty" about the future and guesses the price at which will he sell the output is an entrepreneur*. In spite of some criticism, Knight could provide with a satisfactory explanation of entrepreneurship.

McClelland described the innovative characteristics of entrepreneurial role. Entrepreneurial role, by definition, involves doing things in a new and better way. A businessman who simply behaves in a traditional way is not an entrepreneur. Moreover, entrepreneurial role calls for decision making under uncertainty. If there is no significant uncertainty and the action involves applying known and predictable results, then entrepreneurship is not at all involved.

McClelland, like others, identified two characteristic of entrepreneurship. First, doing things in a 'new and better way'. This is synonymous with the innovative characteristics given by Schumpeter and secondly, decision-making under uncertainty, i.e., risk as identified by Cantilon. McClelland more explicitly emphasised the need for achievement or achievement-orientation as the most directly relevant factor for explaining economic behaviour. This motive is defined as tendency to strive for success in situations involved and of one's performance in relation to the same standard of excellence.

As per **Casson** entrepreneurship consists of an eccentric evaluation of economic events which other people are unwilling to support. As per **Janil and Stevenson**, "Entrepreneurship is a process by which individuals — either on their own or inside organisation — persue opportunities without regard to the sources they currently control". Although English classical economists failed to recognise entrepreneurship as a moving force towards the development of an economy but some of them like Israel Kirzner and Mark Casson did have their strong views about entrepreneurship. As **Kirzner** puts it, "Entrepreneurship means alertness towards profit opportunities".

Friedrich Von Hayek (1899-1922) **Ludwig Von Mises** (1881-1973), Keynes defined entrepreneurship and assigned a role played by entrepreneurship. Thus, entrepreneurship came up as a theory which has ability to mobilise the resources and combine them to initiate change in production.

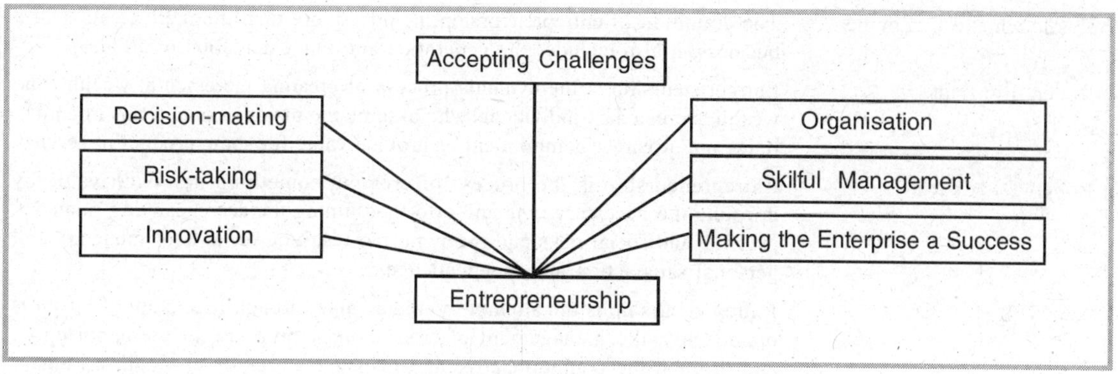

Fig. 5.2: Characteristics of Entrepreneurship

Box 5.1 Entrepreneurship: Some Important Definitions

Joseph Alois Schumpeter: (1883-1950)	Schumpeter described entrepreneurship as a process to shatter the *status quo* through new combinations of resources and new methods of commerce.
Richard Cantilon:	Entrepreneurship is a matter of foresight and willingness to assume risks, which is not necessarily connected with the employment of labour in some productive process.
Leon Walrus:	Entrepreneurship is not itself a factor of production, but rather a function that can be carried on by an agent.
William Diamond:	Entrepreneurship is equivalent to 'enterprise' which involves the willingness to assume risks in undertaking an economic activity particularly a new one.
Jaffrey A.Timmons:	Entrepreneurship is the ability to create and build something from practically nothing. A human creative activity.
Janil and Howard Stevenson:	Entrepreneurship is a process by which individuals — either on their own or inside organisation — persue opportunities without regard to the sources they currently control.
Israel Kirzner:	Entrepreneurship means alertness towards profit opportunities.
Arthur H. Cole:	Entrepreneurship is the purposeful activity of an individual or a group of associated individuals, undertaken to initiate, maintain or aggrandise profit by production or distribution of goods and services.
Everett E. Heggins:	Entrepreneurship is meant the function of seeking investment and production opportunity, organising an enterprise to undertake a new production process, raising capital, hiring labour, arranging the supply of raw materials, finding site, introducing a new technique and commodities, discovering new sources of raw materials and selecting top managers of day-to-day operations of the enterprise.
Peter F. Drucker: (1909-2005)	Entrepreneurship is neither a science nor an art. It is a practice. It has knowledge base. Knowledge in entrepreneurship is a means to an end. It is not just about making money. It is about imagination, flexibility, creativity, willingness to think conceptually, readiness to take risks, ability to mobilise agents of production and capacity to see change as an opportunity. It is also about marrying passion and process with a good dose of perseverance.
M. Low and J. MacMillan:	Entrepreneurship is the creation of a privative economic organisation (or network of organisations) for the purpose of gain or growth under conditions of risk and uncertainty.

H. Aldrich and C. Zimmer:	The definition of entrepreneurship includes more than the mere creation of a business, it also includes the generation and implementation of an idea.
Robert Ronstadt:	Entrepreneurship is the dynamic process of creating incremental wealth. The wealth is created by individuals who assume the major risks in terms of equity, time, and/or career commitment or provide value for some product or service.
Robert D. Hisrich:	Entrepreneurship is the process of creating something new with value by devoting the necessary time and effort, assuming the accompanying financial, psychic, and social risks and receiving the resulting rewards of monetary and personal satisfaction and independence.
John J. Kao:	Entrepreneurship is the attempt to create value through regulation of business opportunity, the management of risk-taking appropriate to the opportunity, and through the communicative and management skills to mobilise human, financial, and material resources necessary to bring a project to fruitition.
Robert K. Lamb:	Entrepreneurship is that form of social decision which is performed by economic innovators.
V. R. Gaikwad:	Entrepreneurship connotes innovativeness, an urge to take risk in face of uncertainties and an intuition.
Musscleman and Jackson:	Entrepreneurship is the investing and risking of time, money and effort to start a business and make it successful.
H. N. Pathak:	Entrepreneurship involves (i) perception of an opportunity (ii) organising an industrial unit, and (iii) running the industrial unit as a profitable, going and growing concern.
The Global Entrepreneurship Monitor:	Entrepreneurship, the process of planning, organising, operating and assuming the risk of a business venture, is now a mainstream activity.

The culture of entrepreneurship is deeply rooted: Entrepreneurs are celebrated role models, failure is seen as a learning experience, and the entrepreneurial career option is regarded as attractive. In today's economic environment, entrepreneurship is a key component of globalisation.

In other words, entrepreneurship means the function of creating something new, organising and coordinating and undertaking risk and handling economic uncertainty. **Higgins** defines the term as, "Entrepreneurship is meant the function of seeing investment and production opportunity, organising an enterprise to undertake a new production process, raising capital, hiring labour, arranging for the supply of raw materials and selecting top managers for day-to-day operation of the enterprise".

According to **Peter Drucker**, "Entrepreneurship is neither a science nor an art. It is a practice. It has a knowledge base. Knowledge in entrepreneurship is a means to an end. Indeed what constitutes knowledge in practice is largely defined by the ends, that is, by the practice." Entrepreneurship is considerably less risky, if the entrepreneur is methodical and does not violate elementary and well known rules.

Innovation and entrepreneurship are thus needed in society as much as in the economy, in public service institutes as much as in business. It is precisely because innovation and entrepreneurship are not 'root and branch' but 'one step at a time', a product here, a policy there, a public service yonder; because they are not planned but focussed on this opportunity and that need; because they are tentative and will disappear if they do not produce the expected and needed results; because, in other words, they are pragmatic rather than dogmatic and modest rather than grandiose — that they promise to keep any society, economy, industry, public service or business flexible and self-renewing.

Thus, entrepreneurship is a complex phenomenon. "Some think of entrepreneurs primarily as innovators, some chiefly as managers of enterprise, some as bearers of risks and others place major emphasis on their function as mobilisers and allocators of capital". In the Indian context, however, an entrepreneur may at best be defined as a person (or a group of persons) responsible for existence of new business enterprises.

Phases of Entrepreneurship Development

Broadly, entrepreneurship development consists of the three following phases:

(a) ***Initial Phase:*** Creation of awareness about the entrepreneurial opportunities based on survey.

(b) ***Development Phase:*** Implementation of training programmes to develop motivation and management skill.

(c) ***Support Phase:*** Infrastructure support of counselling and assisting to establish a new enterprise and to develop existing units.

Entrepreneurship Stimulants

A variety of social, economic, political and cultural factors are stimulating entrepreneurial activity and thus generating more robust economic development. These stimulants are as follows:

- An increasing focus on capital formation. Availability of capital is a stimulant to an entrepreneur to start a new firm and/or give birth to a new idea.
- The ability to transform scientific and technical developments through new institutional development is a second stimulant.
- A third stimulant is the supportive government programmes.
- Availability of required training and input is ranked fourth.
- A collaborative relationship between business and research and their direct attempts to transfer technology to the market, place may provide stimulus to a number of entrepreneurs who seek the opportunity to commercialise their ideas, and
- Finally, an endeavour to create an environment conducive to innovation will provide a much needed stimulant to entrepreneurial activities.

The innovation centre provides technological evaluation, entrepreneurial assessment and other related levels of assistance to entrepreneurs.

CONCLUSION

Entrepreneurs play an important role in the development of society. For example, the use of jeans in America has created the demand for it throughout the world. Similarly, Coca-Cola has been accepted as a social drink. The introduction of colour T.V. has provided the society a means of information and entertainment. The society has accepted the innovations of such entrepreneurs as Gillet, Wright Brothers, and Henry Ford. The inventions of these great entrepreneurs has revolutionised the lifestyle of men in the society today.

The role of entrepreneurs in economic development varies from economy to economy, country-to-country, depending upon its material resources, industrial climate and more importantly, the responsiveness of the political system to the growth of entrepreneurs. By and large, entrepreneurs' contribution to development and growth is relatively higher in favourable opportunities, conditions than in less favourable situations. The growth of an entrepreneurial society will bear fruitful results in a short span.

Entrepreneurship is a key driver of economic growth. However, entrepreneurial attributes are under threat in the wake of international competition. These threats provide immense opportunities for innovation, which holds the key to a country's ability to participate and reap the benefits of globalisation. A country that fosters innovation and supports entrepreneurs will emerge the strongest in the future.

Indians need to emulate the early pioneers and move towards opportunity-driven entrepreneurship. In jump-starting any such process, it would help immensely if successful entrepreneurs play the role of mentors and incubators to the late starters. This has succeeded in the IT industry, but the mentors and incubators have primarily been Indian-American entrepreneurs who have made it big in the Silicon Valley. India needs successful entrepreneurs within the country who will spread their knowledge and expertise across industries.

Entrepreneurship, the *de facto* barometer of overall economic, social and industrial growth, has brought revolutionary changes in the society. It is the *sine qua non* of a nation's progress. It has facilitated large-scale production and distribution. It has widened the area and scope of the marketing of goods and services. Perhaps it is for these reasons that the small business sector has been given priority in our national development programmes, for entrepreneurship flourishes when the size of business remains relatively small and viable.

Modern business studies have a distinct entrepreneurial discipline. The approach to the study of entrepreneurship is multidisciplinary. It images on such areas as demography, economic anthropology, business history, politics, sociology, psychology, marketing and finance. That is why entrepreneurship development becomes an integral part of the overall economic, social and industrial development of a country. This is what makes the identification and management of entrepreneurial functions a highly complex exercise.

CHAPTER 6

ENTREPRENEURIAL MOTIVATION AND ACHIEVEMENT

Work as a team

Make sure you're paying attention to people, being sensitive to the culture, and absolutely make sure that the organisation is working together as a team. It's critical for long-term success.

— ***John Thain,*** CEO, Merrill Lynch, in *Business Week*

INTRODUCTION

Behaviour is a manifestation of what a person thinks, feels and acts. An entrepreneur is a creative person. Need for self-actualisation as manifested in the need for achievement forces him to create something new, a new product, a new way of doing things, a new source of raw material, a new market, etc. Behaviour is always caused and is never spontaneous. Human behaviour is goal directed or is directed towards satisfaction of needs. Whenever a person feels any need, he feels uneasy and tension starts building in his mind. This tension provokes him to initiate some action which may lead to the satisfaction of the need. If that need is not satisfied that individual is required to resort to some alternate action for the satisfaction of the need. It is a systematic process which can be explained in the following manner:

RECOGNITION OR REALISATION OF THE NEED → TENSION → ACTION → SATISFACTION OF NEED

Entrepreneurial behaviour is the result of entrepreneurial motivation. Motivation refers to the inner urge that ignites and sustains behaviour to satisfy need. Motivation has been derived from the word 'motive' which implies the inner state of mind that activates, provokes and directs our behaviour towards the goal.

Behaviour is defined as a response of an individual or group to an action, environment, person as stimulus.

The attempts to discover the secret of entrepreneurs' success has pre-occupied writers and analysts from a variety of disciplines. Biographies of successful entrepreneurs and businessmen, for example, frequently reflect the tendencies of the subject of such studies in terms of simple virtues of thrift, hard work and clean living. As an alternative to the biographical models are those studies that turn the entrepreneur into a superman, manipulating the complexities of an uncertain world with a sure and omnipotent touch. Thus emerges the notion of the "genius entrepreneur" whose success is in large measure caused by his unswerving dedication to setting high goals and to reaching for them. He has vision on which he bases his own objectives and sets his own goals. And he does this not simply on the basis of last year's results plus some growth factor, but on the basis of his own perception, of his own capabilities and to satisfy his own needs.

Among other distinguishing attributes of entrepreneurship are a willingness to assume risks; a sense of acquisition or unceasing curiosity; insight into the relationship between concepts, objectives, needs, and needs satisfaction; sound judgement as to what is central and peripheral to attaining his objectives; imitative and creativity; problem-solving ability, ability to marshall resources needed to achieve his objectives and goals; and the administrative ability to organise those resources to accomplish his goals and satisfy his minor needs.

Motivation

Motivation is an indispensable function of management. When man is at work, he cannot be forced to work like a machine. He is a human being who has his dignity, self-respect, values, sentiments and aspirations apart from the economic status. Under such circumstances the efficiency of the enterprise is related not merely to the efficiency of sophisticated machines installed but more importantly upon the satisfaction and the spontaneous desire of man to put his mind and heart into the work. This spontaneous urge to involve in work is not merely related to monetary awards or assignment of position or the direction to perform the duty or even the fear of punishment but to the mechanics and system of motivation.

> "Motivation refers to the way in which urges, drives, desires, aspirations, strivings or needs direct, control or explain the behaviour of human beings."

Motivation encompasses complex aspects of human behaviour to which contribution has been made by sociologists, social anthropologists, psychologists and business executives. This concept has its roots in motives within a person which induce him to behave in a particular manner. Generally speaking, the concept of motivation is by and large psychological which "relates to those forces operating within the individual employee or subordinate which impel him to act or not to act in certain ways" —

This is a deep-seated definition of Motivation. It includes three things:

(*i*) The urges, drives, desires, aspirations, strivings or needs of human beings influence human behaviour.

(*ii*) The factors which influence human behaviour — psychological, sociological, economic or managerial.

(*iii*) The efficiency of such behaviour — this may be tested by the resultant action. Whether this behaviour has directed, controlled or implemented the desired action.

If the entrepreneur feels motivated his behaviour will bring about the desired action.

Here, one reaches the most crucial point in the Regional or District Development Strategy of the underdeveloped regions. The development agency, with all the institutions concerned, will have to formulate a motivation programme and by continuous and ingenious methods, involve people in the process of development so that they acquire new attitudes and confidence to enter into new activities and to show the propensity of enterprise. Appropriate values will have to be inculcated and risk-taking capacity be cultivated. Unless this aspect is given its due weightage in the Development Plan, in spite of all the incentives, most of the projects will hardly make much progress. Development is the consequence of motivated people.

Motivational factors constitute the inner urge present in an individual which continuously demands from him to do something new and unique as also to perform better than others. The motivational factors again are comprised of three basic elements — entrepreneurial motivation, personal efficiency and coping capability. The achievement motivation is also termed *efficiency motivation*. McClelland and Winter have made considerable studies and concluded that what motivates a person to do something new or something to seek better is the inner urge which directs him towards such ends. This urge also force a person to use the resources efficiently than to be negligent of it. Also important is the power of motivation which is really the urge to have control over others and to direct their course of activities towards the end which one seeks to attain. These motivational factors induce the person to undertake entrepreneurial activities which relate to creating a new business where there was none. This also means to excel the performance in carrying out any activity by striving through persistent efforts unlike others who do not have sufficient capacity for hard work.

It's not difficult to understand how and why a motivation to achieve translates into strong leadership. If you set the performance bar high for yourself, you will do the same for the organisation when you are in a position to do so. Likewise, a drive to surpass goals and an interest in keeping score can be contagious. Leaders with these traits can often build a team of managers around them with the same traits. And of course, optimism and organisational commitment are fundamental to leadership just try to imagine running a company without them.

Hierarchy of Needs

Most psychologists who study human behaviour and personality generally are convinced that all behaviour is caused, goal-oriented and motivated.

There is a reason for everything that a sane person does. People constantly are striving to attain something that has meaning to them. Often we may not be aware of why we behave in a certain manner but we all have subconscious motives that govern the way we behave in different situations.

One of the most widely accepted theories of human behaviour is that people are motivated to satisfy certain well-defined and more or less predictable needs.

Abraham H. Maslow formulated the concept of hierarchy of needs. He maintained that these needs range from lower-level needs to higher-level needs in an ascending priority.

These needs actually overlap and are interrelated, and it may be preferable to consider them as existing along a continuum rather than as being separate and distinct from one another.

Maslow's Need Hierarchy Theory

Maslow's theory is based on human needs. He developed a conceptual framework for understanding human motivation. He was of the opinion that every individual has a complex set of exceptionally strong needs and the behaviour of an individual at a particular moment of time is usually determined by his strongest need. He defined a person's effectiveness as a function of matching man's opportunity with the appropriate position of hierarchy of needs. Process of motivation begins with the assumption that the behaviour, at least in part, is directed towards the achievement or the satisfaction of needs. Maslow felt that the needs have a definite sequence of domination. Second need does not dominate till first need is reasonably satisfied and third need does not dominate until first two needs have been reasonably satisfied. Man is never fully satisfied, if one need is satisfied the other will arise and so on. Once a need or certain order of needs is satisfied, it ceases to be a motivating factor. Maslow stated that human beings have five basic levels of needs, which they tend to satisfy in a hierarchical manner. He proposed that human needs can be arranged in a particular order from the lower level needs to the highest level needs. This hierarchy of human needs can be shown in the following figure:

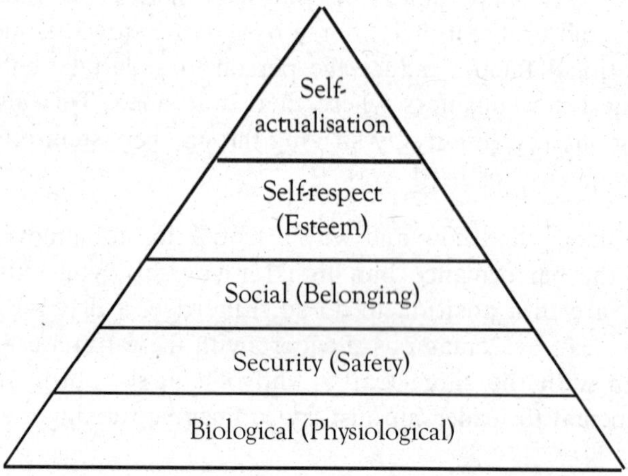

Fig. 6.1: Hierarchial Structure of the Needs

Various researchers are actively engaged in finding answer to one basic question, i.e., what motivates people? Or what makes them work? Various theories have been propounded by different experts to focus attention on this basic issue. Prominent and relatively more relevant to entrepreneurship are as under:

Theories of Motivation

Need is the starting point of motivation. A satisfied need does not motivate an individual. It is only the unsatisfied need which creates tension and stimulate drives within the individuals for the satisfaction of the need and reduction of tension. The efforts or actions initiated by the individual will yield results which will lead to satisfaction of need or removal tension. Classical theorists and scientific management thinkers were of the opinion that people were mainly interested in maximising economic gains as they were primarily concerned with satisfying their basic needs of food, water, air, shelter, etc. Thus, they tried to link up performance and productivity with monetary rewards or incentives. F. W. Taylor, father of Scientific Management proposed

Differential Piece rate system for motivating workers to work at their level best. The traditional thinkers were mainly concerned with the monetary reward and were treating human beings as mere machines, which do not have any inner feelings or emotions. Under Hawthorne experiments it was proved that there was no direct relationship between productivity and economic rewards. Money is an essential condition but not a sufficient one for motivating people to work. Human beings are not machines and they have also social and psychological needs.

Motivational factors constitute the inner urge present in an individual which continuously demands from him to do something new and unique as also to perform better than others. The motivational factors again are compressed of three basic elements — entrepreneurial motivation, personal efficiency and coping capability. The achievement motivation is also termed *efficiency motivation.* McClelland and Winter have made considerable studies and concluded that what motivates a person to do something new or something to seek better is the inner urge which directs him towards such ends. This urge also force a person to use the resources efficiently than to be negligent of it. Also important is the power of motivation which is really the urge to have control over others and to direct their course of activities towards the end which one seeks to attain. These motivational factors induce the person to undertake entrepreneurial activities which relate to creating a new business where there was none. This also means to excel the performance in carrying out any activity by striving through persistent efforts unlike others who do not have sufficient capacity for hard work.

Need of the Basis of Behavioural Change

Need is the basis of behavioural change. The executive before deciding a motivational model should study the need hierarchy of the man working in his factory. Needs are generally stated to be existing in a hierarchical fashion. Needs are generally classified under two heads: (*i*) Primary needs, and (*ii*) Secondary needs. Primary needs are the basic physiological needs which are required to be fulfilled by the man so as to maintain his bodily functions to remain in existence. Secondary needs are both psychological and sociological which are by culture, society, personality and temperament.

Masan Haire gives an elaborate description of need continuum. He describes: (*i*) physical needs similar to primary needs (*ii*) social needs like the need to affiliate and associate with others and to give and receive affection, and (*iii*) egoistic needs relating to one's ego. It includes even the will to dominate.

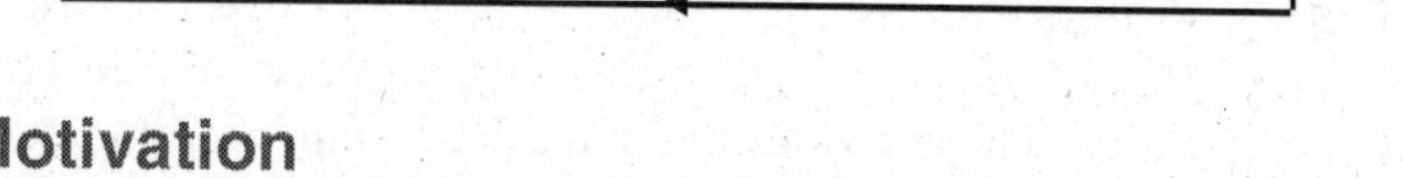

Theories of Motivation

Need is the starting point of motivation. A satisfied need does not motivate an individual. It is only the unsatisfied need which creates tension and stimulate drives within the individuals for the satisfaction of the need and reduction of tension. The efforts or actions initiated by the individual will yield results which will lead to satisfaction of need or removal of tension. Classical theorists and scientific management thinkers were of the opinion that people were mainly interested in maximising economic gains as they were primarily concerned with satisfying their basic needs of food, water, air, shelter, etc. Thus, they tried to link up performance and productivity with monetary rewards or incentives. F. W. Taylor, father of Scientific Management proposed Differential Piece rate system for motivating workers to work at their level best. The traditional thinkers were mainly concerned with the monetary reward and were treating human beings as mere machines, which do not have any inner feelings or emotions. Under Hawthorne Experiments it was proved that there was no direct relationship between productivity and economic rewards. Money is an essential condition but not a sufficient one for motivating people to work. Human beings are not machines and they have also social and psychological needs.

Maslow's theory implies that people attempt to satisfy these needs in the order in which they are arranged. As one level of needs is satisfied to some extent, the individual focuses on the next level, which then becomes the stronger motivator of behaviour. Once a lower level of needs is reasonably satisfied, it no longer motivates behaviour, at least in the short-term.

Table 6.1 describes various types of needs under Maslow's need hierarchy theory.

Table 6.1: Maslow's Need Hierarchy

Nature of Need	*Description*
Physiological needs	Biological needs to pressure human life. These needs include food, clothing, shelter, drink, sleep, etc. These are the basic needs which are recurring in nature. They must be satisfied repeatedly on priority basis.
Safety needs	Human beings search for a protected environment. Safety and security needs kindle the urge for freedom from present and future physical and economic hazards. Though these needs are finite, still they may serve as motivators in case of arbitrary and unpredictable management action. Therefore, people put by money in form of insurance, provident fund, etc.
Social needs	Man is a social animal and his desire to be loved and accepted by his near and dear ones is enormous. Thus, he seeks social affiliation and interaction with the people with whom he works together. In the home front, family members and the neighbours fulfil these needs.
Ego (esteem) needs	These needs arise after physiological, safety and social needs are fulfilled. Self-esteem, self-confidence, self-respect, competence, independence and achievement are vital elements in this process. They determine the entrepreneurial action of the human beings. A person desires to gain reputation, respect, status and appreciation from others.
Self-actualization needs	This desire arises after other needs are fulfilled. These are the needs for realizing one's full potential for continued self-development for being creative. These are aesthetic needs to attain moral maturity, contentment, authority, etc. It is an infinite growth need. This presumes man's inner urge for making the best use of his potentialities.

- At the first level are the biological (or physiological) needs such as food, rest, shelter and recreation. The pay check enables a person to purchase the necessities vital to survive as well some of the comforts of life.

- Security needs include the need to protect ourselves against danger and to guard against the uncertainties of life. Job security, medical, retirement, disability and life insurance plans are benefits designed to satisfy safety needs of employees.
- Social needs are those that people have for attention, for being part of a group, for being accepted by their peers, and for love. Many studies have shown that group motivation can be a powerful influence on employee behaviour at work in either a negative or a positive direction. Some employers provide off-the-job social opportunities for their employees as a means of helping them satisfy their social needs.
- Self-esteem or ego needs are needs that people have for recognition, achievement, status and a sense of accomplishment. They relate to personal feelings of self-worth and importance. Managers should look for ways of satisfying these internal needs by providing variety and challenge in work tasks and recognizing good performance — if possible publicly.
- Self-fulfillment (or self-realization) needs — the desire to use one's capabilities to the fullest. Managers can try to assign tasks that challenge employees to use their abilities more fully or allow them to use their creativity and resourcefulness.

The key for the manager is to recognize where each employee is in the hierarchy, what needs are currently driving the employee and then to design formal and informal rewards to motivate him.

It is formal for employees to expect good wages, generous benefit plans, and job security. For many employees (for example, those who see other employment option as being available in the market), these items may play a secondary role in day-to-day motivation. The key to longer-term, positive motivation of employees lies in better satisfying their higher level needs (social self-respect, self-fulfillment).

For sometime now, employee surveys have been saying that money is not everything. According to a recent survey, one-third of the respondents place a positive work environment at the top of a list of factors for keeping employees satisfied.

Maslow was of the opinion that people put emphasis on lower-level needs and then proceed to higher-level needs in a step-by-step approach. Satisfied need ceases to be a motivator, while unsatisfied needs regulate an individual's behaviour.

Merits of the theory: The merits of Maslow's theory are as follows:

(*a*) This theory is easy to understand.

(*b*) This theory is generally applicable to a wide range of culture.

(*c*) This theory is capable enough to explain how needs influence human behaviour and motivate the human beings to chalking out their work plans.

(*d*) This theory gives an opportunity to the entrepreneurs and the managers to understand the needs of the people at different levels and to motivate them according to their needs.

Criticism: Maslow's Need Priority Model of motivation has gained extensive popularity because of its simplicity and logical explanation. This theory also explains how human behaviour differs in two similar situations. Nevertheless, there is little impartial support for it because its proposition could not be vigorously tested through empirical research. However, the theory is widely criticized for the following reasons:

(*a*) The theory does not give any scientific explanation or tool for measuring needs.

(*b*) The theory gives an oversimplification of human needs and motivation.

(*c*) Not everyone strives for higher-level needs.

(*d*) The hierarchy of needs is not always fixed. It varies from person-to-person, place to place and time-to-time. For example, in case of creative people like singers, artistes, etc., self-actualization need may be a dominant force, even before the lower-order needs are fulfilled. Similarly, the need priorities of the same individual may change over a period of time.

(*e*) Motivation and needs are not directly linked. The same need may lead to different types of behaviour in different individuals.

(*f*) Deprivation of needs may not necessarily motivate, it may cause depression also.

In spite of the criticism, Maslow's theory has a common sense appeal for all managers and entrepreneurs. The theory provides a deep insight into the concept of need and its relation of human behaviour.

What Makes an Entrepreneur?

This is a frequent question. What makes an entrepreneur is the combination of various factors that have enabled the personality formation right from the childhood as also the psychological urge that exists intensively in the person.

These psychological processes which lead men to set up their own successful business enterprises begin in the very early life and have cumulative effect. The influences of early childhood and other social roles are determinant factors for the formation of that personality which motivates an individual towards becoming an independent businessman or entrepreneur.

In the case of persons who take up jobs, it has always been found that they have secured success in the established organisations. These people do not have a rejection towards the established institutions and neither do they attempt to rebel against the traditional path to success. On the other hand, an entrepreneur fails to achieve educational success through the established organisations and this is because of the general rejection of the established organisations at all levels. People who tend to like security and not uncertainty get more satisfied by taking up jobs which are less risk-oriented and hence are not motivated towards building up their own industrial enterprise.

Men who establish new business are men who have right from the childhood faced a different set of environment in their family, school and other social situations. Research studies have indicated that successful entrepreneurs identify a crisis before they venture into new entrepreneurial activities. Even in their childhood most of them had threatening non-supportive and disgusting adult figures who had much say in their social and economic life. Most of these have a childhood of impoverishment and stress. Economic deprivation also works as a motivational factor towards creating something on their own and free oneself from the clutches of oppressing forces which attempt to kill their spirit of individualism. Thus, it has been found that creating a successful new business is not due to an isolated incidence in the life of an individual but it has been as a result of learned response to their total social, emotional and economic environment.

The family plays an important role in developing the personality necessary for turning into an entrepreneur later in life. In family situations where security and non-risk bearing activities are encouraged right from childhood, the individual likes to be more security-oriented rather than attempt on his own in areas where adventures and uncertainty conditions prevail. Also in families where deep attachments and emotional relationship are encouraged, it has been seen that the child growing under such situations tends to take up activities which are more security-oriented than risk-oriented. Since in most of the middle class families attachment and security-oriented activities are encouraged despite seeking academic excellence, it itself does not help the person to develop the urge to be independent and create a framework required for enjoying autonomy.

As a result of this many bright graduates deviate from placing themselves in open positions. On the contrary they choose to stay in the established organisations because they have developed a favourable attitude towards the establishment. On the other hand, the entrepreneurial personality would rather face the impersonal forces of the economy than cope with enter personal relations of the established organisations. Due to this characteristic of an entrepreneur, they tend to shift from job-to-job till they have finally found a field of activity in which they will ultimately have a say and also enjoy the happenings of events by their will, determination and efforts.

While people who take up jobs prefer to see success in the traditional and highly structured roles in the established undertakings, entrepreneurs, prefer to have a different approach towards success and be unique in their own way. They find more satisfaction in their creative faculties getting an opportunity to express themselves fully rather than submitting themselves to structured and rigid forces. The bright graduates may very often lack creativity and be unable to break through the undifferentiated mask of circumstance and make something of their own.

The entrepreneurs, on the other hand, find such situations extraordinarily challenging and attempt with determination and persistence to come out of this web of oppressing factors, which tend to keep him in the rigid framework. Thus, we find entrepreneurial characteristics are formed through a combination of various social, economic and psychological factors to which the person becomes subjected to right from childhood. These factors reinforce in him urge to excel others and seek satisfaction in creating on his own a new enterprise instead of seeking a security-oriented job. In the absence of these reinforcing elements which go into the formation of the entrepreneurial personality, however successful a person may be in his academic life it does not guarantee that he would become a successful entrepreneur. Something more than mere academic excellence is a pre-requisite for becoming an entrepreneur of success and repute. These requisites are embodied in the various qualities that the entrepreneur must have basically within himself in order to establish himself a successful entrepreneur. But many graduates do lack in these qualities.

The Motivating Factors

Several studies have been undertaken to identify the factors that motivate people to start their own enterprises. P.N. Sharma has identified nine motivating factors which are as under:

1. Educational background.
2. Occupational experience.
3. Desire to do work independently.
4. Desire to branch out to manufacturing.

5. Family background.
6. Assistance from government.
7. Assistance from financial institutions.
8. Availability of technology/raw material.
9. Accommodation in industrial estates.
10. Machinery on hire purchase.
11. Financial assistance from venture capital.
12. Encouragement from big business/MNCs
13. Availability of a franchise.
14. Heavy and sustained demand.
15. Profit margin.
16. Sick units available at a cheap price.

Entrepreneurs are tempted to enter industry because of the three main factors:

(*i*) They have strong desire to do something independent in life.

(*ii*) They have technical knowledge or manufacturing experience.

(*iii*) Availability of governmental and non-governmental assistance.

M. Chandra Sekhar and M. Gandhara Rao have classified factors behind entrepreneurial growth into three categories.

Other factors demand of the particular product, utilisation of excess money earned from contractual estate business, started manufacturing to facilitate trading/distribution business since the project was in short supply, unstable policy of the foreign government for non-residents and no chance for further promotion.

The above nine factors were grouped into two major categories — internal and external. First five motivating factors were termed as internal and the last four factors as external. The internal motivating factors like education, occupational experience, family background, the desire to do something independently together make the personality of the entrepreneur. These factors generate an inclination to adopt entrepreneurial activity. The presence of internal factor is a necessary condition for the entrepreneurial activity to take place. But entrepreneurial ideas cannot fructify or take real shape without a proper or conducive environment which provide support in terms of financial assistance, technology and raw material and infrastructural facilities. These facilities form external motivating factors and serve as a spark in igniting the entrepreneurial idea. These factors give a boost to the entrepreneurial activities.

Prof. R.A. Sharma has classified the factors which prompted entrepreneurs to enter industry as follows:

A. Factors Internal to the Entrepreneur

(*a*) Strong desire to do something independent in life.

(*b*) Technical knowledge and/or manufacturing experience.

(*c*) Business experience in the same line.

B. Factors External to the Entrepreneur

(*a*) Financial assistance from institutional sources.

(*b*) Accommodation in industrial estates.

(*c*) Machinery on hire purchase.

(*d*) Attitude of the government to help new units.

(*e*) Financial assistance from non-government sources.

(*f*) Encouragement from big business.

(*g*) Heavy demand.

(*h*) Profit margin.

(*i*) Unsound units available at a cheap price.

It is clear from the above that majority of the new entrepreneurs were tempted to enter industry because of three main factors, viz.,

(*i*) They had strong desire to do something independent in life.

(*ii*) They were having technical knowledge or manufacturing experience.

(*iii*) Availability of governmental and non-governmental assistance.

Another study on entrepreneurial motivation by M. Chandra Sekhar and M. Gandhara Rao have classified the factors behind entrepreneurial growth into three categories as follows:

I. Entreprencurial Ambitions

(*a*) To make money.

(*b*) To continue family business.

(*c*) To secure self-employment/independent living.

(*d*) To fulfil desire of self/wife/parents.

(*e*) To gain social prestige.

(*f*) Other ambitions — making of a decent living, self-employment of children, desire to do something creative, provide employment to others, circumvent Land Ceiling Act, etc.

II. Compelling Reasons

(*a*) Unemployment.

(*b*) Dissatisfaction with the job so far held or occupation pursued.

(*c*) Make use of idle time.

(*d*) Make use of technical/professional skills.

(*e*) Other maintenance of large families, revival of sick unit started by father, etc.

III. Facilitating Factors

(*a*) Success stories of entrepreneurs.

(*b*) Previous association (experience in the same or other line of activity.)

(*c*) Previous employment in the same or other line of activity.

(*d*) Property inherited/self-acquired/wife's.

(*e*) Advice or influence (encouragement of family members/relatives/friends.)

(*f*) Association as apprentices and sleeping partners.

Encouragement and moral support from near and dear inspires the entrepreneurs, reinforces his confidence and prepares him to lace the new challenges with courage.

According to McClelland, executive generally have higher need for achievement than men in other professions. He considers the need for achievement to the most critical to a nation's economic development. McClelland found that achievement motivation was lower amongst people of underdeveloped countries than those of developed countries. Overall better results can definitely be achieved by making people achievement-oriented. According to McClelland achievement motivation can be developed through training and experience. Ambition is the lever of motives and nourishes achievement motivation. McClelland conducted Kakinada Experiment in Kakinada town of Andhra Pradesh. Fifty-two persons from business and industrial community from the Kakinada town were selected. They participated in an orientation programme conducted by Small Industry Extension Training Institute (SIETI), Hyderabad. The experiment was designed to stimulate the imagination and encourage introspection into personal motivation and community goals. The achievement development programme consisted of the following steps:

(*a*) The individuals strived to attain concrete and frequent feedback.

(*b*) The participants sought models of achievement, i.e., watched those who have performed well and tried to emulate them.

(*c*) The participants imagined themseleves in need of success and challenge. They set carefully planned and realistic work goals.

(*d*) The trainees were asked to control day dreaming by thinking and talking to themselves in positive terms.

After two years the trainees were observed. It was observed that they performed better than those who did not attend the programme. McClelland concluded that the participants displayed a more active business behaviour and worked for longer hours. McClelland explains that people with low achievement motivation are prepared to work hard for money or other such incentives but the people with high achievement motivation work for status. He argues that people with the high need for achievement possess the following attributes:

(*a*) Prefer personal responsibility for decision.

(*b*) Are moderate risk takers.

(*c*) Possess interest in concrete knowledge of the results of decisions.

Challenge of Motivation

Since new employees and managers will be of a calibre selected with an eye on the future, they will all be of a high competence level, it will be a challenge to keep motivating them. It is conceivable that organisational structure will have to be looked into order to meet motivational needs of people and "position" them in jobs with the right type of responsibility.

Introduction of high technology and work groups operating without the traditional band of supervisors or inspectors will become more common. Such 'semi-autonomous work groups' will have to be trained so that they are motivated to take care of equipment and meet output targets and tough quality standards.

This will also demand leadership attributes of a high order on the part of people manning such decentralised operations.

V. Lakshmana Rao has aptly summarised the views of various experts on the sources of entrepreneurial supply and motivation as presented in Table 5.1.

Table 6.1 Entrepreneurship: Sources of Supply and Motivation

Author	Entrepreneurial *Phenomenon*	Source of *Entrepreneurial Supply*	Motive Force or *Triggering Factor*
1. Schumpeter	Individual	Extraordinary individuals	Innate urge to achieve success
2. Weber	Status Groups	Extraordinary individuals	Religious beliefs Calninist ethic
3. McClelland	Religious and social groups	Individuals with high n-achievement, creative	Child rearing practices and climate
4. Hagen	Subordinaed Groups	Individuals in the society driven by a duty to achieve	'Status withdrawal' and 'relative social blockage'
5. Cochran	Individual	Society's model, personality determined by its cultural values, role expectations and social sanctions	'Social Acceptance' of entrepreneurial role
6. Young	Homogeneous	Relative subgroups (ethnic communities) occupational groups, or Politically-oriented factions.	Deviant view of the world strengthened by group solidarity
7. Kunkel	Group	Operant conditioning procedures in a society	Reinforcing stimuli and average stimuli
8. Hoselitz	Group	Culturally marginal groups	Gaining social recognition.

Source: V. Lakshmana Rao: *Industrial Entrepreneurship in India,* pp. 85-86.

Ideas to Motivate Self

The gap between knowing and doing is where great men and women are made or lost. Most of us know what we have to do to achieve our dreams but we have a 101 reasons not to act on our knowledge.

Application ideas to motivate yourself:

- Find satisfaction is your daily life, don't wait for your big break to come.
- Make a list of your 20 favourite things to do. Neglecting your personal happiness is a powerful demotivator.
- Ground yourself with solid principles so you don't get distracted from your goal by trends or fads.
- Be able to readily identify the most common de-motivators like fear of failure, change in priorities, uncertainty, anger, jealousy, fear of the unknown and so on.
- Avoid identifying too heavily with what you currently are, it blocks your progress toward something new.
- You can have anything you want in life if you are willing to pay the price to achieve it.
- Never blame other people's action for your lack of action. Anyone can try to make you angry, afraid or depressed but your response to another person's actions will decide whether you are in control or being controlled.
- Rather than viewing life as an endless string of problems to be solved, view it as an unfolding mystery to be revealed.
- When minor failures occur, shift focus to the big goal and assess the impact of the failure on the whole and not only on the area of the failure.
- If you have trouble getting your work day started, choose the task you find most appealing and do it first everyday.
- Do something nice for someone else.
- Avoid comparing yourself to others.
- Don't give too much credit to other people's negative opinions about your goals.
- You have to start somewhere and there is no better time or place than here and now.

Entrepreneurial Behaviour

Achievement motivation and entrepreneurial behaviour are closely associated. Behaviour is a manifestation of what person thinks, feels and acts. Motivation is essentially the process of purposeful or goal-oriented actions. The behavioural pattern of entrepreneurs is summarized below:

(*i*) An entrepreneur is creative. Need for self-actualization as manifested the need for achievement forces him to create something new — a new product, a new way of doing things, a new source of raw material, a new market, etc.

(*ii*) He acts out of desire not necessity. He is proactive not reactive in nature. He influences the environment rather than adopting to it.

(*v*) He is professionally very active but personally lazy. This is reflected in his casual dress and unkept hair. This casualness enables him to work with minimum physical facilities and constraints. His lower order needs are minimum.

(*vi*) He sets his own standards and acts as his own competitor.

(*vii*) He is not satisfied with the present and always looks ahead for more challenging jobs.

(*viii*) He is conscious about time and dislikes time wasters.

(*x*) He learns from his experience.

(*xi*) He is hopeful about future and sees opportunity in a crisis.

(*xii*) He accepts responsibility for his actions.

Entrepreneurship Leadership Style

An entrepreneur is a person who coverts an innovative idea into business. The word entrepreneur is generally associated with small-scale industry. What is an entrepreneurship leadership style? Based on both their personality characteristics, and the circumstances of operating a business, many entrepreneurs use a similar leadership style. The most notable features of this style are:

(*i*) Impatience and brusquences towards employees because the entrepreneur is always busy.

(*ii*) A heavy task orientation combined with a very direct-approach to giving instructions to employees.

(*iii*) A charismatic personality that inspires others to want to do business with him or her despite the impatience.

(*iv*) A much stronger interest in dealing with customers than employees.

(*v*) A strong dislike for bureaucratic rules and regulations.

(*vi*) Anxiety to consolidate business gains as quickly as possible.

Some of the styles described above will be referred to again later in different contexts.

ENTREPRENEURIAL ACHIEVEMENT

Mind field

"For a leader, each hurdle coming his way should be thoroughly understood and methodically eliminated using all the means at his disposal. Howevr, care must be taken to see that these means stand up to scrutiny at a later date."

— P.P. Chhabria, Chairman, Finolex Group

INTRODUCTION

An entrepreneur is a creative person. Need for self-actualisation as manifested in the need for achievement forces him to create something new — a new product, a new way of doing things, a new source of raw material, a new market, etc. Human behaviour is goal directed or is directed towards satisfaction of needs. Whenever a person feels any need, he feels uneasy and tension starts building in his mind. This tension provokes him to initiate some action which may lead to the satisfaction of the need. If that need is not satisfied then that individual is required to report to some alternate action for the satisfaction of the need.

'Creativity'— the very mention of the word fills many of us with awe. It brings our minds, visions of great people — great by virtue of their masterpieces in art and literature, rare inventions and discoveries in science and technology and the like. Recent research indicates that creativity is not such an elusive quality after all. Scientific research is steadily chipping away at the mystery of the creative process — a process many believe is either a divine gift or a black art. And most important, the research is proving that creativity can be taught, in the sense that various techniques have been developed to facilitate creativity. Thus, creativity, innovation are to a greater extent influenced by human behaviour, many entrepreneurial behaviour. In this chapter, we shall examine the entrepreneurial behaviour and motivation.

> Achievement means something accomplished successfully, especially by means of exertion, skill, practice or perseverance.

If there is one trait that virtually all-effective leaders have, it is motivation. They are driven to achieve beyond expectation — their own and everyone else's. The key word here is achieve. Plenty of people are motivated by external factors, such as a big salary or the status that comes from having an impressive title or being part of a prestigious company. By contrast, those with leadership potential are motivated by a deeply embedded desire to achieve for the sake of achievement.

If you are looking for leaders, how can you identify people who are motivated by the drive to achieve rather than by external rewards? The first sign is a passion for the work itself such people seek out creative challenges, love to learn, and take great pride in a job well done. They also display an unflagging energy to do things better. People with such energy often seem restless with the *status quo*. They are persistent with their questions about why things are done the way rather than another; they are eager to explore new approaches to their work.

They say that success comes to those who believe in themselves and never give up; it comes to those who do not stop trying until they achieve their goals. Achievement is thus a benchmark of entrepreneurial activities. Achievement and entrepreneurship reinforce each other. In fact, achievement comes to those who dares and strives to reach their goals.

Achievement and management success is discussed in relation with successful management of enterprises. In this case, the students have to draw their own lessons from the case studies given in this chapter.

Recognition for Accomplishment

Recognition is ingrained in human psychology. If his work and his contribution have not been appreciated properly, he will lose interest in work because it is very difficult to sustain the will to work in the absence of proper recognition. Who recognises the work of the person will be determined by the status or designation of the worker. Herzberg states: "The source could be almost anyone; supervisor, some other individual in management, management as an impersonal force, a client, a peer, a professional colleague or the general public. Recognition may be a word of praise, a letter or a notice, to be published for the accomplishment of the worker. Sometimes, if the verbal recognition may not be there but when an employee gets a wage increase or promotion, they may be perceived as the elements of recognition.

It may, however, be pointed out that increase in wages or monetary awards may be motivating if perceived as award for recognition, otherwise they cease to be motivating. Recognition should be public. Man wants that others should know that he has done good work and, that the relevant agency has recognised his work. If he gets a cheque from the employer closed in the envelope, it may be motivating but not to the extent when even a token medal of one-tenth or of little value is awarded to him in public by the management in recognition of the work done by him.

Recognition should also include "negative recognition" — criticism, blame, reprimand. Even the element of criticism will satisfy his instinct of recognition by his bosses.

Recognition is related to the accomplishment of the challenging task assigned to him. Accomplishment includes "successful completion of a job, solution to problems, vindication and seeing the results of one's work". For instance, and when author finds his paper appearing in a recognised journal of repute or if he finds his book released in the market, he finds biggest satisfaction, though monetarily a writer, who has written a cheap note, may have earned more money.

David McClelland's Theory of Achievement Motivation

In the late 1940s, David McClelland and his associates developed the theory of achievement motivation, which was regarded as one of the best economic theories of entrepreneurial development. They concentrated mainly on the following three aspects:

- Need for achievement
- Need for power
- Need for affiliation.

1. **Need for achievement:** A strong need for achievement 'n Ach' is found within certain individuals, groups and communities. McClelland emphasized that the need for achievement or achievement orientation is the most important factor for explaining economic behaviour. People having this need are more likely to succeed as entrepreneurs. They strive incessantly for success in getting things done in an excellent manner. They try passionately to overcome any odd that comes on their way. They are so much self-confident that they do not believe in mere luck. They look upon money as the index of their achievement but basically they are not money-oriented. Therefore, McClelland wrote: "Need for achievement is a desire to do well, not so much for the sake of social recognition or prestige, but for the sake of an inner feeling of personal accomplishment".

2. **Need for power:** This pertains to the desire by a person to be influential in a group. People with need for power 'n Pow' believe in position of authority. They seek leadership in politics, business, education or arts and feel satisfied having a great number of followers. All successful managers seem to have high need for power. They derive satisfaction to influence and direct authority.

3. **Need for affiliation:** The persons with high need for affiliation are sensitive to social relationship. They are keen on warm and interpersonal relationship. They are associated more with popularity, social support and friendship than with decision making. They love others and wish to be loved by others. This is not predominant among managers but this 'n Aff' greatly helps them in influencing their subordinates.

Thus, the theory of achievement motivation provides a deep introspection to the human behaviour in general and entrepreneurial behaviour in particular. It also glorifies the necessity of the Achievement Motivation Training (AMT) as an important tool for achievement of needs.

Keeping in view the above needs, 'n Ach', 'n Pow' and 'n Aff', David McClelland has pointed out that these factors, especially 'n Ach' are responsible for entrepreneurial development. The following analysis can reveal the impact of need for achievement in accelerating entrepreneurial urge among individuals.

Twin Characteristics of Entrepreneurship: McClelland pointed out the twin important characteristics of entrepreneurship that govern the economic behaviour of a person to become entrepreneurial. They are:

(*i*) Doing things in a novel and excellent manner.

(*ii*) Decision making under uncertainty.

Belief in Personal Accomplishment: According to this theory, 'n Ach' or need for achievement refers to the need for personal accomplishment by the person through excellence. This category of person is fond of shouldering personal responsibility. They are generally moderate risk takers and try to be winners all the time. High achievers aim at personal achievement rather than the reward of success. Persons with high need for achievement behave in the entrepreneurial way.

Psychological Factors for Entrepreneurial Motivation: Need for achievement depends upon entrepreneurial motivation. This need motivates the persons to take risk. The following psychological factors are responsible for the growth of entrepreneurial motivation:

(*a*) Need for achievement through performance evaluation.
(*b*) Goal setting and problem-solving.
(*c*) Strong desire to undertake calculated risk.
(*d*) Willingness for taking personal responsibility.
(*e*) Spirit to achieve success.
(*f*) Anticipating possibilities.
(*g*) Concrete measures of task performance.
(*h*) New instrumental activity.
(*i*) Feeling of personal accomplishment.
(*j*) Organisational as well as decision making skills.

Inner Concerns as the Prime Movers: McClelland opined that inner concerns or motives are the prime movers of entrepreneurship. These forces drive the individuals to take risk, plunge into uncertainty where they find opportunity, discover new ideas, save more and reinvest the savings in the enterprise. According to him: "The internal factors are the human values and motives that lead the human being to exploit opportunities, to take advantage of favourable trade conditions".

'n Ach' Precursor of Economic Growth: McClelland applied his technique of 'n Ach' *to* study the relationship between achievement motivation and economic development. He found that it was the 'n Ach' factor which was a precursor of economic growth both in socialistic and capitalistic system of economy.

Lack of Ambition in Less Developed Countries: Ambition is the basis on which McClelland's 'n Ach' greatly depends. In less developed countries (LDCs), achievement motivation of people is lower than that of developed countries because of low level of ambition. Lack of ambition creates a great barrier for need for achievement and consequently leads to lack of enterprise in LDCs. So in order to bring about economic development, it is necessary that the level of ambition among the people should be high enough to pressurise the need for achievement in them. Then only entrepreneurial spirit can be generated and economic growth can be accelerated.

The 'n Ach' Model

Any behavioural model for entrepreneurial development must, therefore, take care of proportionate development of both Need for power and Need for affiliation in relation to the high priest — Need for achievement.

McClelland applied his technique of 'n Ach' to study the relationship between achievement motivation and economic development. He found that it was the 'n Ach' factor which was a precursor of economic growth both in socialistic and capitalistic system of economy. Entrepreneurship, thus, becomes the pivot around which need for achievement and economic growth to revolve.

EXPERIENCE AT KAKINAD

According to David McClelland, the role of 'n Ach' is the critical factor for entrepreneurial development, which, in turn, leads to accelerate the tempo of economic development. In order to prove this fact, he conducted several experiments with different groups of businessmen in America, Mexico, Mumbai and Kakinada in Andhra Pradesh. Through the experiments, he tried to induce the spirit of achievement motivation in adults and urged them to take up entrepreneurial ventures. Such an inducement was, in fact, essential to increase their level of aspirations and to give rise to confidence-building character in them.

In January 1964, a full-fledged training programme was organized by David McClelland at Kakinada with a total intake of 52 persons. The objectives of such programme were:

(*a*) To instill in them the quality of imagination.

(*b*) To encourage introspection and convert it into personal motivation and community goals.

The training was conducted at small Industries Extension and Training Institute (SIET), Hyderabad. The Achievement Motivation Training (AMT) included the following basics which were supposed to be accomplished by the trainees:

(*a*) Goal setting and goal achievement.

(*b*) Emulating the models of achievement by constant watch and alertness.

(*c*) Attainment of concrete and frequent feedback.

(*d*) Planning carefully the realistic goals through performance appraisal of their own.

(*e*) Converting ideas into opportunities using the positive self-concept and controlling day dreaming.

Thus, the training helped those participants in providing high degree of motivation and subsequently the need for achievement. They displayed a more active business behaviour and took enough stress to accomplish the job. As such, Kakinada experience was considered the most successful experiment so far as the need for Achievement Motivation Training (AMT) is concerned for the benefit of the potential entrepreneurs. This AMT is regarded as a necessary tool for breaking the barrier of limited aspirations among individuals on the one hand and inducing in them high need for achievement on the other. The training also acts as a boost to the risk-taking and decision making behaviour of the potential entrepreneurs.

To conclude with the words of V.L. Rao, a noted economist: "The 'n Ach' factor or 'n' achievement approach suggest promotion of achievement-oriented ways of thinking to foster economic development in the underdeveloped countries".

Motivational factors constitute the inner urge present in an individual which continuously demands from him to do something new and unique, as also to perform better than others. The motivational factors again are composed of three basic elements — entrepreneurial motivation, personal efficiency and coping capability. The achievement motivation is also termed *efficiency motivation.* McClelland and Winter have made considerable studies and concluded that what motivates a person to do something new or something to seek better, is the inner urge which directs him towards such ends. This urge also force a person to use the resources efficiently than to be negligent of it. Also important is the power of motivation which is really the urge to have control over others and to direct their course of activities towards the end which one seeks to attain. These motivational factors induce the person to undertake entrepreneurial activities which relate to creating a new business where there was none. This also means to excel the performance in carrying out any activity by striving through persistent efforts unlike others who do not have sufficient capacity for hard work.

CASE STUDIES

The case studies in management education have the same power to involve our minds, provided the narrative comes alive to us. A case tells the story of an organisation at a point in time. The organisation has a background — a past, an orientation towards the future (goal/s) and a present, which brings us to the moment of the story. The plot involves the key people in the organisation, who are engaged in the action plan in order to achieve the goal/s. The decision maker is the tragic hero: like the winery-owner he ponders the issue — to pick or not to pick. Conflict is at the heart of the organisational narrative: an urgent goal that has to be achieved within a timeframe and a persistent problem.

The case is more fascinating than a ready-made story because it is still evolving. The narrative acquires different shades of reality through case discussions in the classroom and students learn important lessons in creative problem-solving. The analysis of the problem offers alternatives that would otherwise remain unexplored. The transformative power of the narrative holds immense potential to change our view of a problem and generate possible solutions.

The narrative approach provides the opportunity to explore multiple perspectives. Rather than be swayed by the views of one character, the analyst may take an objective approach and distance himself/herself from the scene. What if our Napa Valley farmer were to meet an all-knowing fortune-teller who would tell him whether the welcome storm would hit or not? That would really make life so much easier, wouldn't it? But in its absence our hero would weigh the pros and cons of his choice objectively and plant a decision tree.

Clearly, this exercise in detachment is necessary to solve current problems in organisational and personal life situations. Action should be backed by logic. What if the Napa valley owner waited for the warm storm to hit and it never did? Imagine he has a niece who can give him definite scientific evidence of low pressure and high pressure cycles that can tell him the storm will come to his life, would he be willing to pay for that information? If yes, then the next question is: how much is the rich wine-producer uncle willing to shell out of his thick wallet? That is logical action for you!

Recent research shows that storytelling is one of the most effective tools leaders can use in organisations. Once the placements are over, the much sought-after MBA degree is in the bag, the student is suddenly in the position of the Napa Valley decision maker him/herself. While every problem-situation is like a fingerprint and finding a solution is by no means an easy task, a narrative approach can generate multiple options for the decision maker and suggest unlimited possibilities.

TRANSFORMING DREAMS

Early Beginning

In 1966, a young electrical engineer, R.K. Parasuram, returned to his hometown Madras after working for General Electric Company, U.K., for 10 years, he dreamt of manufacturing world-class electrical transformers and selling them all over the world. Three decades later, his dream is coming true.

The Kappa group of companies (named after his wife Kamala Parasuram) — a bunchy of tiny private limited companies and proprietary firms with a turnover of ₹ 16 crore and an export turnover of ₹ 9 crore — manufacture almost the entire range of transformers. These are low-tech but essential items which require a lot of manual labour.

Having established his products successfully in the domestic market, Parasuram decided to go global. Exports in the early seventies really meant the rupee market. It was not easy to penetrate the European and American markets. So he looked towards South-East Asia which was a relatively easier hard-currency area.

No one had previously attempted to export products like transformers. Right from the outset, Parasuram's emphasis was on quality. The export products were produced to conform to the international standards prescribed by British Standards and International Electro-technical Commission. Due to the availability of cheap skilled labour, the cost of Kappa's transformers was very competitive.

First Order

In 1973, the company got its first export order from Dickson Primer, an engineering firm in Singapore, for 300 pieces of transformers worth ₹ 20,000. Singapore and Malaysia were the major markets then. By late 70s, Kappa decided to expand its activities to the Middle East. The focus was on Beirut. However, when the militarisation of Lebanon became complete in the early 80s exports to Beirut came to a grinding halt.

Parasuram was on the constant lookout for a big deal. Kappa's ability to produce transformers as custom-built original equipment fetched its first order from Siemens, Australia, in 1980. Siemens and Email-Westinghouse became their major buyers in Australia and New Zealand. A bulk of the company's international sales is to Asea Brown Boveri. Worth just ₹ 20,000 in the 80s, business with the Swedish-Swiss giant has grown to ₹ 60 lakh annually, Says Kamala, "With more and more enquiries from abroad, we opened an export office at Singapore in 1983".

In order to broad base exports, it was decided to trade in a wide range of current technology products not necessarily produced by the group. The relays produced by English Electric, semiconductor fuse and voltage transformer fuse links manufactured by S&S Power Switchgear Ltd., are some of the well known products traded by Kappa Exports. Says T.V.G. Menon, general manager, relay division, English Electric, "We cannot export directly because of our agreement with our parent company. So we make our sales to Kappa who are doing a splendid job." Kappa has emerged as the biggest exporter of electrical goods from South India. Today 60 per cent of Kappa's export turnover is from trading.

Kappa's exports reached ₹ 1 crore in 1987. Since then, the annual growth rate has been phenomenal, around 40 per cent now. The main reason for this, according to Kamala, was Kappa's strategic move to become a single-window export house for all electrical engineering equipment. Parasuram is convinced that constant upgradation of technology is the only way for survival. Five per cent of the total turnover is being spent on R&D and another five per cent on technological upgradation. According to Kamala, the neglected but important area in exports is packaging. Says she, "Our special packaging efforts to withstand the wear and tear of the transit costs an additional three per cent".

To ensure quality. Kappa has invested about ₹ 1 crore in various imported testing equipment and this has now proved to be a great advantage as the group is gearing to enter the European market in a big way. Says the founder's daughter Miva Parasuram, an electrical engineer, "We are working with the Indian Statistical Institute to get the ISO 9000 accreditation. Our production systems already seem to conform to international standards. We have to only effect changes in areas like inventory, billing and accounting. We will get our accredition in the middle of 1993." Kappa wants to reach an export figure of ₹ 100 crore by the turn of the century and hence it is seriously studying the Middle East and African markets.

MANTRAS FOR SUPER SUCCESS

Set Goals

Every success becomes a point of departure for new initiatives. Success should be measured in relation to goals. I believe that what has already been achieved, lies in the past. One should always look at the future and set new goals. I have set in my own mind, the goal of contributing, in a modest way, to the building of a resurgent India. I try to explore opportunities that will assist this goal by harnessing technological revolution taking place in a variety of fields — from information, communication, life sciences. India can realise its full potential only by assimilating the latest technological innovations. Given this goal, I have still a lot to do; many many more miles to cover.

Learn from Others

First and foremost, I owe my successes to all that I have learnt and imbibed from my father, Dhirubhai Ambani. He has taught us to think big, think long-term, to pursue excellence unflinchingly, and to trust people.

Secondly, I have also had the fortune of good counsel from a galaxy of well-wishers; eminent persons from various walks of life. In times of trials and triumphs, their advice and guidance have been a tremendous source of strength to me. It helped me look at the real issues and stay focused on the outcomes. Finally, I have been blessed with a large number of the dedicated colleagues, members of the Reliance family. It is on that pair of wings, their unswerving commitment to excellence and hard work — that Reliance has been able to fly to newer heights.

Create Opportunities from Obstacles

The most important lesson that I have learnt from doing business is to convert adversities into opportunities. Lessons drawn from adversities are invaluable. Reliance's history is marked with several encounters with obstacles and road-blocks. From every challenge, we have emerged that much stronger because for us, difficulty and obstacles are great teachers.

Conviction Counts

Proceed with conviction in what you do. Be passionate about achieving your goals. Combine a demanding environment with a humanitarian outlook. Most importantly, place trust in people.

Keep Track of Time

In any business dealing, there must be sincerity of purpose. Meaningful dialogues lead to positive business transactions. It is always helpful to be upfront and candid about the expectations, processes and deliverables because we regard time as a scarce resource. Money lost can be recovered. Time cost can never be regained.

Therefore, it is important to work in a time-bound framework. This facilitates a purposeful and professional approach.

Fair Play Wins

In any business negotiation, it is important to make proposals that are fair to both parties and meet the aspirations of both. Success comes by marrying mutual interest and not by moves to outwit each other. Whenever I come across situations where the principle of fair play is not followed, I tend to take a hard line and attempt to strike a common ground.

Upgrade Standards

Success is a relative phenomenon. More than anything else, it sets a new standard for you to improve upon. So I always look at success as a base for future higher achievements.

Conclusion

Whether in small industry or large, problems always exist. Some face problems as if they are a challenge because that is the road to advancement. If there is no problem or challenge, we lend to feel complacent, which is the beginning of our degeneration. The problems of small industries should, therefore, be treated in this spirit. This, of course, does not mean that the government, the local bodies, financial institutions and banks should create unnecessary obstacles in the path of industrialists; nor that industrialists should function in isolation. Rather, they should be increasingly aware of the fact that they are a part of larger society, each section of which has its own strong and weak points.

In the post-independence period, the Governments as the Centre and the States have established a number of specialised institutions to cater to the varied needs of small-scale units. These promotional institutions assist all and sundry in setting up small units with a view either to fulfilling their objective or over-reach their target: but they do not ensure the provision of adequate working capital, raw materials, power supply; nor do they help them in developing marketing outlets for the sale of their products. This situation has arisen because of the absence of a meaningful co-ordination among the concerned agencies.

The entrepreneur needs to reorient his attitude and develop special leadership qualities necessary for taking decisions based on wider implications rather than the narrow path of urge satisfying action alone. His problem, therefore, is one of growing from professional entrepreneur into a professional manager and finally into an administrator in order to successfully come out of the growth crisis which starts facing once his enterprise grows from a small business into a large enterprise.

The problems of entrepreneurs are multidimensional. These can be solved by the coordinated efforts of entrepreneurs, coordinated functioning of promotional agencies, and governmental assistance without red-tape or bureaucratic delays. The entrepreneur has to be educated: and he should have a proper naming in acquiring the necessary skill in running an enterprise. In fact, the entrepreneur is the kingpin of the industrial spectrum.

INTRAPRENEURIAL ACHIEVEMENT

Anjana Ghosh created a new identity to Bisleri by bringing innovaion to the brand and strategising the re-engineering of Bisleri from blue to green. She also tapped the premium brand in the water segment.

Anjana Ghosh, director of Ramesh Chauhan's Bisleri International Ltd., (BIL) joined the science stream to pursue a career in medicine, but her family could not afford it. In 1986, she had to take a detour and opted for management studies at the S.P. Jain Institute in Mumbai. "I have no regrets", she says.

Today, she looks after new business development and heads sales, marketing and brand strategy at BIL, besides carrying the responsibility for capacity planning and implementation processes. She is driving the packaged water company closer to the consumption centres. Under her stewardship, Bisleri has touched a record sale of one crore cases in 2008-09 in Mumbai, the highest by any bottled water brand in one city. Aquafina has 45 lakh cases and was a second place. Her brand strategy and marketing leadership ensured that Bisleri touched 3.24 crore cases in the last fiscal year.

Ghosh has always stayed away from the rut, doing things differently. From the time she got into management studies, unlike the crowd that looked at majoring in marketing, finance or IT, she chose to go in for project planning. Her first job, via campus recruitment, landed her in a position where she had to plan and prepare feasibility reports on the potential of the market in wildlife resorts and tourism for Indian Adventures Ltd. "I always wanted to do something different. I had the option to join pharma and finance companies, but I did not", recalls Ghosh, whose first job saw her earn a stipend of ₹ 1,000 a month. "It was the magical four-digit figure that lured me, the rest were below that."

In the early 1990s, three years into her wildlife job, not seeing much of a future for tourism, she spent the next three years setting up chemical intermediaries (for pesticides) in Chamundi Chemicals, then moved on to something she could not relate to — steel. "I just do not know how, but I ended up putting in over a decade in this industry; setting up plants and implementing projects across various companies in the steel industry", says Ghosh. In the steel sector she worked with companies like Graham Firth Steel, Rajendra Steels and MAN Industries.

One fine day, in 2006, she felt she had enough of steel. She sat home for two months before being headhunted for the Bisleri job. Recruited at the DGM level.

The Journey from Blue to Green

"I started to question myself. Am I at the right place and should I continue. But in my heart, I wanted a challenge", recalls Ghosh, who joined the company when the sales graph was south-bound (2004 to 2006) and Bisleri's sales was ₹ 150 crore. During this period, there were many new local brands that were being launched; Bisleri was just one amongst them. Kinley, Aquafina, etc., had also come to India. "They were all coming out with blue packaging. There was absolute turmoil in the market", says Ramesh Chauhan. "Ghosh was primarily responsible for bringing innovation to the brand and strategising the re-engineering of Bisleri from blue to green. She played an important role in the peculiar novel green we have today. Getting that shade on plastic, metal and paper is not easy. The change has been historical and fantastic move for Bisleri", recognises Chauhan. However, after the brand re-engineering, the new and young image of a vibrant Bisleri ensured that the company's sales zoomed ahead by almost 60 per cent. In three years, sales had doubled to ₹ 380 crore (March 2009).

The journey from blue to green saw a revolution of change in the perception and demand of the brand. Realising that Bisleri did not have a presence in the natural mineral water segment despite being the first company to launch bottled water, Ghosh decided to tap this premium water segment. Thus, Bisleri Mountain natural mineral water was launched with a bottling plant at Rudrapur.

Now as part of the strategy to grow the brand, Ghosh is working on market penetration through a combination of backward and forward integration. While consolidating the brand presence in the metropolitan and Class-A cities, she ensured that the brand penetrated from metros and satellite cities to B & C class cities, districts, towns and rural markets. "To increase growth we are increasing the number of bottling plants from 35 to 52 and investing ₹ 1,000 crore by 2011-12", adds Chauhan, targeting a 40 per cent growth this fiscal.

"Given the unavailability of clean drinking water, an increase in water contamination and health awareness among consumers has led to the growth of the mineral water segment. In the wake of the rising consumption of mineral water, even in the rural hinterland, there is huge opportunity for growth in India. We will tap it", concludes Ghosh, as Bisleri continues to lead in the ₹ 1,200-crore organised, mineral water market with a 60 per cent market share.

Lancelot Joseph

Source: Business India, September 20, 2009

CONCLUSION

The foregoing discussion highlights two major concepts of motivation. According to the first concept, people react to influences which are known as motivators. They are recognition, achievement, responsibility, development, etc., which have been discussed under the head "Developmental". Apart from motivators, sustaining incentives are also necessary. Whether sustaining or developmental is by and large the leadership factor.

Apart from earning a livelihood and/or making profit, the entrepreneur is also motivated to fulfil his/her innate urge to achieve success in life, improve his/her social standing, gaining social recognition, to provide something to society. The motivational factor vary from place-to-place, time-to-time as well entrepreneur-to-entrepreneur. Yet motivation moulds the different entrepreneurial traits. The traits and motivation are moulded by the socio-economic, political, cultural and psychological environment and varies from country-to-country.

Entrepreneurship is to a great extent the product of motivation. Motivation refers to the inner drive that ignites and sustains behaviour to satisfy needs. Behaviour is always caused and it is not spontaneous. In other words, human behaviour is goal directed or directed towards satisfaction of needs. A person's behaviour is shaped by several socio-psychological factors such as his goals, education level, cultural background, work experience, etc. When a person feels some need, tension arises in his mind until the need is satisfied. This tension motivates him to take action. If the action is successful, need is satisfied, otherwise the person changes the action until the need satisfaction occurs. Motivation implies an inner-state that causes an entrepreneur to act towards the realization of his/her dream and the attainment of the goals.

The study of entrepreneurial behaviour and motivation is useful in developing a profile of a successful entrepreneur. It is indeed a positive approach in developing entrepreneurship and enterprise in the country. Although, the entrepreneurial traits, behaviour and motivation are complex, the goal of entrepreneur is to build enterprises to earn profit and serve the society. Thus, fulfilling his ambition, success, satisfaction, while shouldering social responsibility and earning profit, comfort, status and power. Finally, entrepreneurial behaviour and motivation result in fostering and nurturing entrepreneurship to accelerate the process of socio-economic development.

7 CHAPTER

SETTING UP A SMALL ENTERPRISE

INTRODUCTION

Identifying a Business Opportunity means identifying an unfulfilled need in the market, for which there is a customer willing to pay for in exchange of the service or product.

> Business Opportunity may be defined as a business proposal which an entrepreneur would like to pursue considering risk and the reward involved in the proposal which may be manufacturing or servicing or trading.

WHY START OWN BUSINESS

This is aptly reflected in replies to a typical questionnaire from an enterpreneurship development institute for prospective entrepreneus as follows:

- I want to be on my own
- Demand is very high
- For economic gains
- Status in society
- Opportunity to serve society
- Somebody else is doing it successfully
- I whan to do something new/better
- Somebody has promised to help me all the way
- I am tired of job/service.

HOW TO START BUSINESS

Steps of the Ladder the Entrepreneur (Small) has to Climb
It is a Continuous Process of Industrialisation

10. Identify Target Market
9. Organise Marketing
8. Decide on Pricing Policy
7. Recruit Personnel
6. Plan Finance
5. Decide on location and site
4. Decide whether to purchase a going concern or to start a new one
3. Decide on form of ownership [sole-proprietary, partnership, cooperative company (private/public)]
2. Choose a Line of Business
1. Analyse yourself and your objectives

Entrepreneurial Decision

Entrepreneurial decisions occur despite recession, inflation, high interest rates, lack of infrastructure, economic uncertainty etc. Each of these decisions is a personal human process which, although unique, have some common characteristics. The impulsive motive to change his/her lifestyle and create something new and an inner urge to do something worthy, are the forces behind these decisions. At times, perhaps even more stimulation for change comes from a negative force disruption. At times, the available opportunities force a decision on individuals to take up entrepreneurial work. Like all processes it entails movement from something-to-something new as indicated in Fig. 7.1.

Decision making is the core function of a manager that separates him from any other worker. It needs skills. There are three categories of decision making.

1. Decision on the basis of facts, data and record.
2. Decision on the spot based on a gut call.
3. Decision based on commitment and clarity.

Types of Decisions

- Strategic
- Administrative
- Operational

Strategic: Strategic decisions are the decisions that are concerned with whole environment in which the firm operates, the entire resources and the people who form the company and the interface between the two.

Administrative: Administrative decisions are routine decisions which help or rather facilitate strategic decisions or operational decisions.

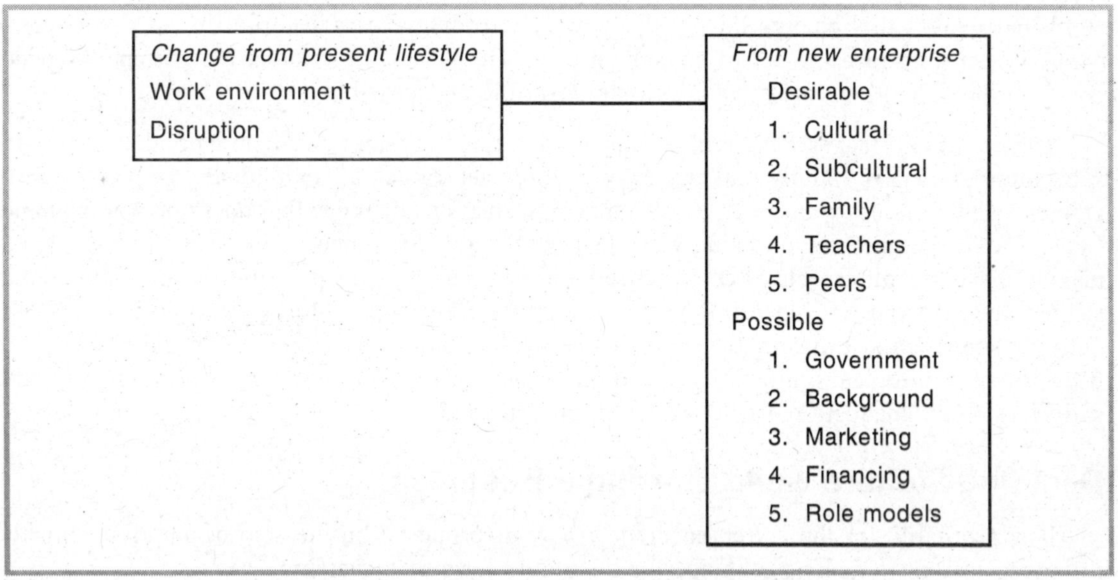

Fig. 7.1: Decision for a Potential Entrepreneur

Operational: Operational decisions are technical decisions which help execution of strategic decisions. Operational decisions are a type of short-term decision by a company in lieu of long-term strategies at the time of acquisition of company assets. These involve the day-to-day operations of the company, and therefore need to be addressed before any grand scheme issues.

To reduce cost is a strategic decision which is achieved through operational decision of reducing the number of employees and how we carry-out these reductions will be administrative decision.

Things to consider before taking a decision

- Inquiring about all possibilities
- Looking at immediate repercussions
- Examining the motivations of people suggesting something
- Priority of decision
- Circumstances under which the decision is taken
- The opinions of others
- Taking the decision at the right time
- Maintaining a balance between optimisation in a particular circumstance
- Looking at the bigger picture — What's good for the department may not be good for the company
- Facts and feelings of people
- Advocating the decision

What causes this change due to the work environment or disruption to result in a new company being formed instead of something else? The decision to start a new company occurs when an individual perceives that it is both desirable and possible.

The perception that starting a new company is desirable results from an individual's culture, sub-culture, teachers, family and peers. A culture that values an individual who successfully creates a new business will spawn more company formations than one that does not. For example, India places a high value on being your own boss, individual opportunity, being a success and making money — all aspects of entrepreneurship. What is more, many different sub-cultures that shape value, systems are operating within a cultural framework. More importantly, these sub-cultures support and even promote entrepreneurship. Thus entrepreneurial decision has more bearing on sociological, cultural, sub-cultural, psychological and political environment, while satisfaction and adequate rewards are the optimistic goals.

Deciding Factors while Starting a Business

It is profitable for the entrepreneur of a new or proposed business to be familiar with the following factors in making a choice for a suitable form of ownership:

1. Type of business — service, trade, manufacturing.
2. Scope of operations — volume of business and the size of the market area served.
3. Degree of direct control and management desire by the owners.
4. Amount of capital funds required.
5. Size of the risk.
6. Continuity of the concern.
7. Costs and procedures and relative freedom from Government regulation.
8. Adaptability of administration.
9. Comparative tax advantage, etc.

Before the above-listed factors stand considered, it must be pointed out that these factors are inter-dependent. In reaching a decision, management is guided by some or all of these factors. The final choice, however, may be a compromise. Thus, the problem in choosing the best form is one of analysing and weighing the relative advantages and disadvantages to find to the onc that will yield the highest net advantage. The obvious flexibility in the form of ownership suggested that most businesses operate under the type most suitable to their needs.

Let us now consider the impact of these factors on the form of business ownership.

1. *Type of business activity:* This is important factor having a direct bearing on the choice of ownership. In small trading businesses, professions and personal service trades, sole proprietorship is predominant. Examples are laundries, beauty parlours, repair shops, consulting agencies, small retail stores, medicine, dentist, accounting concerns, boarding house, restaurants, speciality shops, builders, painters, decorators, bakers, confectioners, tailoring shops, small-scale cobblers and shoe manufacturers, etc. The partnership is suitable in all those cases where a sole proprietorship is suitable, provided the business is to be carried on a slightly bigger scale. Manufacturing contains the highest percentage of companies among all industries. Similarly, large chain stores, multiple shops, superbazaars, engineering companies are in the form of companies.

2. *Scope of operations:* If the scale of operations of business activities is small, sole proprietorship is suitable; if the scale of operations is modest — neither too small nor too large — partnership is preferable; whereas, in the case of large-scale operations, the company form is advantageous. The scale of business operations depends upon the size of the market area served, which in turn, depends upon the size of demand for goods and services. If the market area is small, local partnership is adopted. If the demand originates from a larger area, partnership or company may be adopted.

3. *Direct control and management:* In the sole proprietorship and partnership, the ownership and management and control are completely fused; in the case of a company, there is a divorce between ownership and management. If the entrepreneur is not ready or willing to part with control and management of the business, he will choose the sole proprietorship. If he is just not bothered about it, he will go in for partnership and company.

4. *Attraction of additional capital:* Every business may require additional funds from time-to-time to carry on its business operations. If it cannot obtain adequate capital, it may be headed for failure. In deciding on the legal form of ownership, the top executive must take into account the question of how new money is to be attracted and raised. In a proprietorship, the owner may raise additional capital by borrowing, by purchasing on credit or by investing additional amounts himself. Banks and suppliers, however, will look closely at the proprietor's individual financial resources before sanctioning loans or advances. Partnerships can often raise funds with greater ease, since the resources and credit of all partners are combined in a single enterprise. Companies are better equipped to attract capital from the market.

5. *Size of risk:* Size of risks vary from one organisation to another. The sole proprietor is liable for all the debts of business to the extent of his entire property. Likewise, partners are individually and jointly responsible for the firm's liabilities.

6. *Continuity of the concern:* While continuity of a concern is not guaranteed under proprietary and partnership, companies have the most permanent legal structure. Continuity of the concern is most stable.

7. *Costs, procedure and government regulation:* While proprietary and partnership concerns could be simply initiated, the company form of ownership is more complicated to form. In the formation of a company, a large number of legal formalities have to be gone through which involve a substantial amount of expenditure.

8. *Adaptability of administration:* In the case of a proprietary concern, administration goes with their individual. In a partnership it is shared. In both the cases, adaptability of administration goes with their knowledge and capacity to work. In a company, the administration is centralised in a small group of executives with less involvement.

9. *Comparative tax advantage:* In the case of proprietary concern, the income of the business is taxed as an individual assessee. If the business is higher, partnership form of organisation will be a right choice. As far as companies are concerned, they are taxed at a flat rate.

An entrepreneur has to weigh these major factors, as well as others in deciding the form of organisation while starting a business. Many a time, an enterprise, like a river, may be started as a proprietary concern, converted into a partnership when like-minded people come together, are promoted into a joint-stock company when it grows substantially big. This organisational evolution is an ongoing process through interaction with the socio-political and economic environment.

For example, J.C.Basu put in ₹ 15,000 of his savings and his brother-in-law, Ranjan Banerjee contributed an equal amount and set up the Trinity Forge in 1974. The business rose from ₹ 5.5 lakh in 1974 to ₹ 42 crore in 1996. It has now become a leading company in the forging industry.

The best and the brightest always stand out as the most outstanding. The best invariably prosper which leads to growth. And growth ultimately shows up in increased size. So in a free market economy, the size of the business (enterprise) is a fair indicator of excellence. Managing a larger enterprise is without doubt more difficult than running a small one. And so it is likely that many small enterprises are more profitable than their larger counterparts. But this is in no way detracts from the achievements of the latter. Large enterprises are better, by way of its inherent strength, the capacity to bear shocks and stresses, and simply by the fact that it has grown so big in a world where roughly everyone has had the same opportunities.

TYPES OF OPPORTUNITIES

- An unmet need is met by a new service or product
- A new product or services replaces an existing product or service
- A new product or service may be created because of a new technology, or pure innovation or changing social or economic conditions.
- The new product or service may create additional value to the customer, reduced cost, saves time or increases convenience or saves energy or makes him happy.

A good business opportunity must have:

a. Good Market Scope

b. An attractive Return on Investment

Selecting the right business opportunity: This demands

a. Understanding of one's capabilities, strengths, limitations and preferences.

b. Explore all possible and suitable opportunities available within existing conditions and environment.

c. Taking the final decision about products after comparative analysis of opportunities available.

How to come up with a business idea

In coming up with a business idea, your task should be:

a. To develop new ideas, or

b. To work on variations of an existing idea.

How to Select a Business Opportunity?

In selecting a business opportunity, one has to answer these questions to arrive at an opportunity which is consistent with your likes, skills, market demand, etc.

1) Do I want this?
2) Can I make it?
    a. Is it technically feasible?
    b. What is the capital requirement?
    c. Is the technology/equipment available?
    d. Do I have the skills?
    e. What resources do I require?
3) Is the project compatible with my available resources?
4) Can I access outside help including my resources?
5) Is the project consistent with:
    a. Government priorities?
    b. National goals?
6) Are people ready to pay money for my idea?
    a. Is there a transfer market for my idea?
    b. Do enough people want my idea?
    c. Who are the customers?
    d. Will they have the required purchasing power?
7) Is the venture profitable?
    a. Can I earn from it?
    b. Can I make enough sales?
    c. Can I charge a price above my total costs?

It is important to note that this process enables entrepreneurs to avoid unnecessary wasteful and frustrating efforts in exploiting projects which may later on be found unsuitable.

BUSINESS OPPORTUNITIES IN VARIOUS SECTORS

There is certainly no formula to become a successful entrepreneur. Some may succeed and make good profits, others sink along the way. Which are the most lucrative sectors for entrepreneurs? There are some good buisness opportunities in various sectors for entrepreneurs like:

1. Tourism

Tourism is a booming industry in India. With the number of domestic and international tourists rising every year, this is one lucrative sector on which entrepreneurs must focus on. India with its diverse culture and rich heritage has a lot to offer to foreign tourists. India has everything that tourists are looking for like beaches, hill stations, heritage sites, wildlife and rural life.

2. Automobile

India is now a hot spot for automobiles and auto-components. A cost-effective hub for auto components sourcing for global auto makers, the automotive sector is potential sector for entrepreneurs. The automobile industry recorded a 26 per cent growth in domestic sales in 2009-10. The strong sales have made India the second fastest growing market after China. India being one of the world's largest manufacturers of small cars with a strong engineering base and expertise, there are many segments that entrepreneurs can focus on in India's automobile and auto components sector.

3. Textiles

India is famous for its textiles. Each state has its unique style in terms of apparels. India can grow as a preferred location for manufacturing textiles taking into account the huge demand for garments. Places like Tirupur and Ludhiana are now export hubs for textiles. A better understanding of the markets and customers' needs can boost growth in this sector.

4. Social Ventures

Many entrepreneurs are taking up social entrepreneurship. Helping the less privileged get into employment and make a viable business is quite a challenge. There are many who have succeeded in setting up social ventures. With a growing young population in rural areas who have the drive and enthusiasm to work, entrepreneurs can focus on this segment.

5. Software

India's software and services exports are likely to rise with export revenue growth projected at 13 to 15 per cent to hit about $57 billion by March 2011. With one of the largest pool of software engineers, Indian entrepreneurs can set higher targets in hardware and software development. The information technology enabled services have contributed substantially to the economy. With more companies outsourcing contracts to India, business to business solutions and services would be required. Entrepreneurs can cash in on the rise in demand for these services with innovative and cost-effective solutions.

6. Engineering Goods

India continues to be one of the fastest growing exporters of engineering goods, growing at a rate of 30.1 per cent. The government has set a target of $110 billion by 2014 for total engineering exports. Entrepreneurs must capitalise on the booming demand for products from the engineering industry.

7. Franchising

India is well connected with the world. Hence, franchising with leading brands who wants to spread across the country could also offer ample opportunities for young entrepreneurs. With many small towns developing at a fast pace in India, the franchising model is bound to succeed.

8. Education and Training

There is a good demand for education and online tutorial services. With good facilities at competitive rates, India can attract more students from abroad. Unique teaching methods, educational portals and tools can be used effectively to make the sector useful and interesting.

India's mainstay is agriculture. Entrepreneurs can explore many options in the foodgrain cultivation and marketing segments. Inefficient management, lack of infrastructure, proper storage facilities leads to huge losses of foodgrains and fresh produce in India.

Entrepreneurs can add value with proper management and marketing initiatives. The processed food market opens a great potential for entrepreneurs be it fast food, packaged food or organic food. Fresh fruits and vegetables too have a good demand abroad. A good network of food processing units can help potential exporters build a good business.

9. Corporate Demands

There will be a good demand for formal attire with more companies opening their offices in India. People who can meet this demand in a cost-effective way can make a good business. With corporate gifting getting very popular, this is also a unique business to explore.

10. Ayurveda and Traditional Medicine

India is well known for its herbal and ayurvedic products. With increasing awareness about the ill-effects allopathic medicines, there will be a huge demand for cosmetics, natural medicines and remedies.

11. Organic Farming

Organic farming has been in India since a long time. The importance of organic farming will grow at a fast pace, especially with many foreigners preferring only organic products. Entrepreneurs can focus on business opportunities in this sector. There are many small-time farmers who have adopted organic farming but the demand is still unmet, offering many opportunities for those who can promote organic farming on a large-scale.

12. Floriculture

India's floriculture segment is small and unorganized. There is a lot to be done in this lucrative sector. The floriculture industry in India is poised at about ₹ 3,700 crore, with just 0.61 per cent share in the global floriculture sector, which is likely to reach 0.89 per cent by 2015, said a study titled, 'Indian Floriculture Industry: The Way Ahead' released by Assocham. This is a huge market to be tapped considering the rising demand for fresh flowers. More awareness and better farming and infrastructure can boost exports.

13. Biotechnology

After the software sector, biotechnology opens a huge potential. Entrepreneurs can look at a plethora of options with the application of biotechnology in agriculture, horticulture, sericulture, poultry, dairy and production of fruits and vegetables.

14. Recycling Business

E-waste will rise to alarming proportions in the developing world within a decade, with computer waste in India alone to grow by 500 per cent from 2007 levels by 2020, according to a UN study. This sector opens a viable business opportunity for entrepreneurs in terms of e-waste management and disposal.

SEARCH FOR A BUSINESS IDEA

It's in the attitude: *"I've never run into a guy who could win at the top level in anything today and didn't have the right attitude; didn't give it everything he had, at least while he was doing it; wasn't prepared and didn't have the whole programme worked out".*

— Ted Turner, American Media Mogul

Industrialisation is widely recognised not only as one of the important means to usher in socio-economic transformations and achieving industrial self-sufficiency but also for the accelerated development of agriculture, transport, trade, services and other potential sectors through the forward and backward linkages. It is a process which accelerates economic growth; effects structural changes in the economy, particularly in respect of resource utilisation, production functions, income generation, occupational pattern, population distribution and foreign trade; and induces social change. Jawaharlal Nehru had emphasised that "Real progress must ultimately depend on industrialisation. Throughout the world, industrialisation has indeed become the magic word of the mid-twentieth country."

Persons interested in becoming entrepreneurs must have the ability to generate a large number of ideas so that at least one of the idea has the potential for a business opportunity. These ideas also lead to varied phases of projects. On the other hand, adoption of the ideas is likely to result into a profitable business.

Industralisation is brought about by well-trained entrepreneurs. Entrepreneurship is one of the most important factors of industrialisation in the process of economic growth.

Choosing an Idea

Establishing yourself as a successful entrepreneur depends, in part, upon choosing a good idea. That idea must not only be good for the market, but good for the project and good for the entrepreneurs. It should also be manageable by you without much dependence on others. Importantly, the idea should give satisfacting results to you.

As an entrepreneur, when you are searching for an idea worthy of your commitment, don't pursue one idea at a time. Develop five or ten in parallel until one emerges so appropriate that it begins to dominate your thoughts and fantasies. To adopt one idea at a time has several disadvantages. First, because you are constantly receiving random information from what you read and from people you talk to, having a number of back-burner ideas gives you a greater likelihood of finding uses for information you pick up. Secondly, if you are pursuing a single idea by feigning commitment before you feel it, you may put yourself into a tight corner. It is very hard to be objective when you are down to your last idea.

Box 7.1 **How to Encourage Bright Ideas**

Companies run on ideas, but how do you get people to generate them? Think you're adept at making the most of your employees' brainpower? Try this little quiz (Answer true or false to each statement).

- Big ideas are where the action is.
- Managers are in the best position to come up with ideas on how to do things better.
- Small ideas aren't worth managers' time.
- Without rewards, employees won't offer ideas.
- The best way to encourage innovative thinking is to promise financial rewards based on the monetary value of the ideas.
- An informal approach to gathering ideas works best.
- Suggestion boxes are an effective way to encourage new ideas.
- Creativity is essential to innovation.
- Along with good ideas come a lot of bad ones that waste everyone's time.

If you answered true to any of the above, think again. All those notions, while popular, are also wrong, according to Alan Robinson and Dean Schroeder.

The widespread belief that blockbuster ideas are the only ones that matter is costing companies a wealth of competitive advantage.

If you look at the stats, it's the singles and doubles that win the most games. And don't expect those hits to come only from the "creative" team; any practical-minded, observant player will have his share of RBIs. Okay, but if you're looking to encourage those singles and doubles, why not rely on the old suggestion box? Usually the managers reviewing the stuff in the box aren't close enough to the work to know whether an idea is any good or not.

Smart companies set up a forum where people can discuss ideas, so you get input from everyone who's actually involved. If you value employees' ideas, why not talk with them. Now there's a novel idea.

Choosing an idea is quite difficult and the entrepreneur has to weigh objectively his intrinsic capabilities in finalising an idea.

In the idea stage, suggestions for new products are obtained from all possible sources: customers, competitors, R&D, distributors, and company employees. Frequently, one of the creative problem-solving techniques discussed below are used to develop marketable ideas. The suggested ideas need to be carefully screened to determine which are good enough to qualify for a more detailed investigation. Established objectives and defined growth areas provide a basis for developing these criteria.

Sources for Ideas

Different sources and methods help us to develop a wide range of ideas. Following are some of the sources for ideas:

- Good understanding of economics and the economy.
- Changing needs of the people in a locality/society.
- Emerging trends in the society (e.g., migration of people from rural areas to urban centres, preference for fast food among youth).
- Extensive travelling and a wide range of reading.

The details of these sources for ideas will be discussed at a later stage in this module. Even with such sources of ideas, a creative person is likely to derive more advantages than a person who is less creative and continues to think on traditional lines. Creativity plays a vital role in setting up a small business.

Creativity

Every problem is an opportunity for a creative person. Creativity is a major tool for the survival of an entrepreneur. It not only gives one the edge for recognising needs, generating business and marketing ideas, but it also helps in solving problems. The person who faces a problem and finds a novel solution or is able to quickly convert the problem into an opportunity that has ready solutions, will be a survivor in a field where others, less flexible and less creative, will be left behind.

This is particularly true as small businesses are considered to be more flexible and proactive than large, bureaucratic organisations and thus, can react better and faster to changing circumstances.

Rules for Creativity (and Examples)

Are you good at solving problems? Well, there are ways to expand your mindset. First, let's establish some rules for creativity:

1. Every problem holds an opportunity.
2. Problems are NOT excuses for giving up.
3. Every problem has more than one solution.
4. Think sideways.
5. Creativity is FUN — you get more ideas in an uncritical atmosphere.

We tend to limit our thought processes into traditional and standard ways of doing things which often become security blankets to the point where change scares us and creativity is often stifled by our own mindset of routine experience and also peer pressure. Initially, we have to force ourselves out of our mindset to begin to think sideways (laterally). Let us try a common example:

Thinking Creatively

There are a variety of methods to help you think creatively.

Creativity is an important attribute of a successful entrepreneur. Unfortunately, creativity tends to decline with age, education, and lack of use. Creativity declines in stages, beginning when a person starts school. It continues to deteriorate through the teens and continues to progressively lessen through ages 30, 40, and 50. Also, the latent creative potential of an individual can be stifled by perceptual, cultural, emotional, and organisational factors. Creativity can be unlocked and creative ideas and innovations generated by using any of the creative problem-solving techniques such as those in Table 7.1.

Table 7.1 Creativity and Problem-solving Techniques

- Brainstroming
- Reverse brainstroming
- Synectics
- Gordon method
- Check list method
- Free association
- Forced relationships
- Collective notebook method
- Heuristics
- Scientific method
- Kepner-Tregoe method
- Value analysis
- Attribute listing method
- Morphological analysis
- Matrix charting
- Sequence-attribute/modification matrix
- Inspired (big-dream) approach
- Parameter analysis

Brainstorming

(a) Brainstorming is a process of detaching analysis of ideas from the actual development of ideas. We tend to bog down when we take time to explain or think through an idea and take considerable time to justify or sell the idea to others. Sometimes, non-conventional thinking also gives rise to more ideas and may lead to the best solution.

(b) There are a variety of ways to approach brainstorming, but the principles remain the same:

1. Idea generation is separated from analysis of the idea.
2. You usually get more ideas with a group than by yourself.
3. No criticisms during the idea generating phase.

4. Do not waste time by trying to sell or explain your idea to others during the idea generating stage.
5. The apparently weird and silly ideas often are not so.
6. Weird and silly ideas can lead to more and better ones.
7. Changes in the way you look at something may generate new ideas.
8. Avoid experts in the idea generating group, as they tend to have rigid minds loaded with traditional approaches.
9. At the idea generating stage, you are seeking a large quantity of ideas.
10. Ideas should breed a combination of ideas.

(c) You will find that weird and silly ideas will lead to an *euphoric* or *idea high* which makes the ideas flow. The secret to the idea generating stage is simple: No criticism and no attempt to explain or sell your ideas to others.

Two examples of ideas generated in brainstorming sessions are given in Annexures 2(a) and 2(b).

(d) After a list has been generated, analysis of each idea can take place. In problem-solving, it helps in the analysis stage to have clear objectives of what you want the idea to achieve and a list of the restraints (e.g., cost to be paid out of cost savings) you are working under. You will find the brainstorming method great for both new ideas (e.g., what can we do with this product?) and problem-solving (e.g., how do we handle this?)

Observing Markets for Product Analysis and Market Survey

One major aspect while choosing a project idea should be to ascertain the extent of the marketability of the product proposed to be manufactured, its general use, industries which use it, its end-use and its buyers. One should therefore study the demand and supply of the product over the last few years to estimate its future demand based on the past trend. While doing so it would be necessary to take into consideration the anticipated change in fashions, technology and levels of incomes of the people. If the product proposed to be manufactured has market throughout the country the study takes into account the demand and supply of the product for the whole country. However, if the market for the product would be confined to one/two states/ or a particular region, the study may be confined to the concerned states/region. In this connection, it will be useful to ascertain whether the present demand for the product is elastic (varying with price changes) or inelastic, as also whether it is repeat sole product (like soap or toothpaste) or a comparatively durable article (say, a watch or a refrigerator). Further, attempts should be made to determine the trend of demand and the composition and pattern of the potential users of the product. The extent and the intensity of competition will have to be carefully studied by the entrepreneur before deciding as to whether he should keep the price low to take advantage of larger sales or should fix the price so high that he can get a fair margin even on a smaller volume of sales. An assessment of the market should be supplemented by a survey of the available channels of distribution so that selling campaign can be properly planned well in advance of the production.

The entrepreneur should probe the various consequences of giving a practical shape to his ideas with an analytical mind. He should not only draw upon his past experience but also take advice from his reliable business friends.

There is no difference between a trade fair and an exhibition. The word fair is used to describe a general and large international event which admits a wide range of goods, while the term exhibition connotes a national event or a specialised fair. However, it is the former type that concerns the business community.

Significance of Trade Fairs

Trade fairs and exhibitions offer opportunities for:

1. Meeting a large number of buyers from different countries at one place, and exchanging views on business environment;
2. Assessing the market trend, i.e., market in terms of demand potential and type of products required;
3. Assessing the attitude of the competitors in a particular product or marketing area;
4. Comparing the price and quality of similar products;
5. Establishing personal contacts with the dealers/importers/customers of the products) and organising trade negotiations;
6. Providing education and scope for enhancing the mental horizon of the visitors;
7. Assisting the exhibitors to acquire knowledge of the latest scientific techniques of production and marketing, particularly by their competitors; and
8. Projecting new ideas on commercial publicity for promoting sales in the country and abroad.

BUSINESS PLAN

"Failing to plan is planning to fail"

Planning is a function that ascertains before hand as to what should be done. It is looking ahead and getting ready for future. It is the determination of what is to be done, how and where it is to be done, who is to do it and how results are to be assessed. Setting up and running a business in today's changing world is a great challenge. In fact, if sufficient planning and control measures are not determined early then most of the entrepreneurs will soon find their business getting out of control. A well-thought business plan is a crucial for start-up ventures. Business planning is an essential constituent of starting and growing a successful enterprise.

What is Business Plan?

Various authors and researchers have defined business plan as:

It is formal written expression of the entrepreneurial vision, describing the strategy and operations of the proposed venture.

According to Wikipedia, "business plan is a formal statement of a set of business goals, the reasons why they are believed attainable, and the plan for reaching those goals. It may also contain background information about the organization or team attempting to reach those goals."

A business plan is any plan that works for a business to look ahead, allocate resources, focus on key points, and prepare for problems and opportunities. Businesses need plans to optimize growth and development according to priorities. A business plan is like a map and a compass for a business.

A business plan is a written document prepared by the entrepreneur that describes all the relevant internal and external elements and strategies for starting a new venture.

Benefits of a Business Plan

Writing a business plan helps an entrepreneur to carefully scrutinize all areas of business including marketing, operations and staffing. There are several benefits associated with writing a business plan like:

- It helps to know whether the business idea is viable,
- Helps in setting objectives for a business,
- Reveals threats and opportunities that may not have been considered,
- Helps to know about gaps in planning,
- Increases the chances of business success,
- Provide a basis for evaluating and controlling the company's performance, and
- Communicates company's message to middle managers, outside directors, lenders and potential investors.

The four interdependent factors crucial to every new venture:

- ***People***: parties providing vital services or important resources for setting up and running a venture such as lawyers, accountants, suppliers, etc.
- ***Opportunity***: a report of the business itself — what it will sell and to whom, whether the business can grow and how fast, who and what stand in the way of success, etc.
- ***Environment***: assessing the regulatory environment, interest rates, demographic trends, and inflation (factors that inevitably change but cannot be controlled by the entrepreneur), etc.
- ***Risk and Reward***: an assessment of the possible risks involved in a venture and the gains/profits associated with it.

Elements of Business Plan

- **Introductory Section** – Contains cover sheet, table of content, executive summary and fact sheet. It should tell people about who are you, what you are and what you want.

- **Company Plan** – It includes company description, merchandising plan, operating plan and organizational plan.
- **Marketing Plan** – It covers all the details like market description, competition analysis, selling strategies and marketing approach.
- **Financial Plan** – It should take account of capitalization plan, uses of fund statement, current financial statement, business financial history and risk assessment.
- **Supporting Document** – All records that backup the statements and decisions made in the company plan, marketing plan and financial plan.

Business Plan Outline

Detailed summary of a business plan has been discussed below:

I. Executive Summary

A. Objectives

B. Mission

C. Keys to Success

II. Company Summary

A. Company Ownership

B. Company History (for ongoing companies) or Start-up Plan (for new companies)

C. Company Locations and Facilities

III. Products and Services

A. Product and Service Description

B. Competitive Comparison

C. Sales Literature

D. Sourcing and Fulfillment

E. Technology

F. Future Products and Services

IV. Market Analysis Summary

A. Market Segmentation

B. Target Market Segment Strategy

C. Market Needs

D. Market Trends

E. Market Growth

F. Industry Analysis

G. Industry Participants

H. Distribution Patterns

I. Competition and Buying Patterns

J. Main Competitors

V. Strategy and Implementation Summary

A. Strategy Pyramids

B. Value Proposition

C. Competitive Edge

D. Marketing Strategy

E. Positioning Statements

F. Pricing Strategy

G. Promotion Strategy

H. Distribution Patterns

I. Marketing Programmes

J. Sales Strategy

K. Sales Forecast

L. Sales Programmes

M. Strategic Alliances

N. Milestones

VI. Web Plan Summary

A. Website Marketing Strategy

B. Development Requirements

VII. Management Summary

A. Organizational Structure

B. Management Team

C. Management Team Gaps

D. Personnel Plan

VIII. Financial Plan

A. Important Assumptions

B. Key Financial Indicators

C. Break-even Analysis

D. Projected Profit and Loss

E. Projected Cash Flow

F. Projected Balance Sheet

G. Business Ratios

H. Long-term Plan

Why Some Business Plans Fails?

- Goals set by the entrepreneur are inconsistent.
- Goals are not measurable.
- The entrepreneur could not fully give his/her commitment to the business.
- The entrepreneur could not foresee potential threats or weaknesses of the business.
- Customer need was not fully assessed for the proposed product or service.

TYPES OF BUSINESS PLAN

According to Tim Berry the different kinds of business plans are:

- **Start-up plan** which defines the steps for a new business. It includes the company, product or service, market forecasts, strategy, implementation milestones, management team and financial analysis.
- **Internal plans** are not intended for outsiders like investors, banks or other third parties. They might not include detailed description of company or management team. They may cover only main points rather than detailed texts.
- **Strategic plan** focuses more on high-level options and setting main priorities than on the detailed dates and specific responsibilities.
- **Growth plan or expansion plan or new product plan** focuses on a specific area of business, or a subset of the business. These plans could be internal plans or not, depending on whether or not they are being linked to loan applications or new investment. For example, an expansion plan requiring new investment would include full company descriptions and background on the management team, as much as a start-up plan for investors. Loan applications will require this much detail as well.
- **Feasibility plan** includes summary, mission statement, keys to success, basic market analysis and preliminary analysis of costs, pricing and probable expenses. This kind of plan is good for deciding whether or not to proceed with a plan, to tell if there is a business worth pursuing.

BANKABILITY OF PROJECT

Lenders take high risk while lending money for launching a new project because in case the project fails to generate sufficient returns, their money would be at stake and sometimes they may have to bear huge losses. Therefore, before funding any project, the lender would like to know whether the project is viable and is capable of giving sufficient returns.

Bankable project can be defined as project or proposal that has sufficient collateral, future cash flow and high probability of success to be acceptable to institutional lenders for financing. Bankability is determined by how the project is defined and the constraints that are imposed or the incentives that are provided in respect of the implementation through the Concession Contract or Regulations. This means that many projects could be made bankable if they are well defined and environment provides sufficient incentives.

The process of selecting bankable projects, therefore, comprises of selecting projects that can be given a serious chance of success by providing sufficient incentives through Government support and Regulations whilst keeping these incentives within acceptable limits and in line with risk transfer objectives. Thus, a bankable project is one that generates revenue, has a significant local contribution, sound institutional framework and sufficient guarantee that the loan will be repaid.

FORMAT OF BANKABLE PROJECT FOR FEED PLANTS

It should cover the name of the company, location of plant, activities, products, capacity of plant and project outlay.

Company

It should cover the location of registered office, date of formation, registration and authorised share capital. It should also cover the date of incorporation and commencement of business, the objectives, areas of operation, subscribed share capital.

Promoters and their Background

Name and address of promoters, their background, experience and net worth.

Management of the Company

Persons looking after the day to day management, their background, experience, etc., should be covered.

Project Profile

i) Land and Location

This should cover the area of land, location of the plant, distances from nearby town, availability of approach roads, power and water supply and other communication including schools, banks, hospitals, etc.

ii) Civil Structures

Name of the architect, type of structures proposed, drawings and detailed cost analysis of various civil structures along with the present position of implementation may be indicated. The technical specifications of civil structures are given in Annexure-III.

iii) Plant and Machinery

The major plant and machinery (imported and indigenous separately), sources of supply, specifications and quotations for various items of equipment need to be given. List of major suppliers of feed plant machinery is given in Annexure-IV.

iv) Technical Collaboration

The name of the technical collaborators for monitoring and marketing of the products along with their addresses and the type of collaborations should be indicated. Technical collaboration fee/royalty to be paid should also be indicated.

v) Manufacturing Process

It should cover the manufacturing process of feed (mash/pelleted feed) in the form of flow chart, proportion of various feeds to be manufactured and the composition of the different feeds.

vi) Infrastructural Facilities

a) Raw Material

The feed ingredients (grains, cakes, brans, fish meal, molasses, vitamins, minerals, etc.), source and method of procurement, basis of price fixation, agreements if any for regular supply of raw material may be indicated. BSI standrads for feed ingredients are given in Annexure-V. Average nutritive values of common feed ingredients and the reasonable levels for their inclusion are given in Annexures-VI and VII respectively.

b) Packing Material

The type of packing material required (jute/plastic bags), source of supply, capacity and price of bag, approximate quantity required per month and method of purchase need to be furnished.

c) Utilities

- **Power:** The total power requirement of the unit, source of power supply, position of power supply in the area and standby arrangements made by the company, whether permission is obtained or applied to the State Electricity Board for power connection.
- **Water:** The source of supply, quantity available *vis-a-vis* daily requirement and arrangements made for supply of water.
- **Fuel :** The requirement of coal, diesel and gas, source of supply, adequacy of availability and cost of material may be mentioned.
- **Steam:** Quantity required, source and capacity of boiler.
- **Transportation:** The mode of transportation of raw material as well as feed, whether owned or hired vehicles, availability of vehicles and cost per kilometre.

- **Laboratory :** Whether the company is planning to set up a laboratory for testing the raw material as well as feed, specification of laboratory equipment, quality and cost, the proposed tests to be carried out and the adequacy of manpower for carrying out these tests.

vi) Pollution Control

The type of measures proposed for controlling the air pollution inside the unit and also for the employees of the company.

vii) Manpower

It should cover the technical skill and unskilled labourers required, their availability and source, method of recruiting them and also their salary structures/wage rates should be mentioned.

Marketing and Business Prospects

a) The product mix, capacity of the plant, year-wise capacity utilisation and actual quantity of products produced per year.

b) Areas of marketing of the product and strategies i.e., talukas, district or state-wise quantities proposed for sale, methods of sale, agencies/contractors, method of transportation of products, incentives or commission proposed to be paid, expenditure on publicity and brand name should be indicated. It should also cover the proposed marketing network in terms of staff and material.

c) Market survey for raw materials as well as for the products to be sold covering the demand/supply position, other sources of supply of products, the average price of products for the last 4-5 years and also the potential for selling the products should also be covered.

Socio-economic benefits: The number of villages, farmers and number of animals benefited and also number of persons employed either directly or indirectly in this activity.

Schedule of Implementation

The proposed implementation schedule of the scheme may be indicated starting from purchase of land till commercial production.

SWOT Analysis

The strengths, weaknesses, opportunities and threats should be discussed separately.

Project Cost

i) Land

Area of land, cost of land and conversion charges.

ii) Site and land development

It should cover the land levelling, fencing/compound wall, internal roads, drainage,etc. The specifications, unit cost and the total cost should be furnished.

iii) Civil structures

The civil structures comprises of factory building, raw material and finished products godowns, office, laboratory, quarters, garage, canteen, etc. Detailed plan layouts along with cost estimates certified by the engineer should be given.

iv) Plant and machinery

Imported/indigenous components, major suppliers, quantities, unit cost and the total cost of the plant and machinery including the misc. equipments should be given. The quotations along with the specifications is required to be enclosed.

v) Electrical system

Covering transformer, diesel generators, internal and external electrification and also the deposits to be paid to the State Electricity Boards. The specifications of transformer as well as generators along with the quotations should be furnished. With reference to electrification – the break-up is required to be given.

vi) Water supply and other utilities

Source of water, specifications and expenditure on water supply system, cost of boilers for steam generation, etc.

vii) Vehicles

Number and cost along with justification on requirement of the various vehicles, price quotations from the dealers along with specifications should be furnished.

viii) Pre-operative and preliminary expenses

The item-wise cost and justification should be given.

ix) Contingencies

Percentage of contingencies and its reasonableness

x) Margin money for working capital

The margin money for working capital may be worked out taking into account the requirements of various raw material, packing material, fuel, etc., finished products and sundry debtors for one cycle of operation.

Sources of Finance

The total project cost and source of funds (equity/public issue, subsidy, loan, etc., should be furnished.

Techno Economic Parameters

Should cover the capacity of the plant, year-wise capacity utilisation, quantity of feed manufactured, commission on sale of feed, transportation charges, power and fuel charges, packing material charges, salaries and wages, marketing expenses and other overheads. The procurement prices of various ingredients as well as the sale price of various brands of feed should be indicated.

Economics of the Project and Cash Flow Analysis

Considering the capacity utilisation and also the various techno-economic parameters, the income and expenditure streams have to be worked out to arrive at the gross profit. From the cash flow analysis, the Benefit Cost Ratio (BCR), Net Present Worth (NPW) and Internal Rate of Return (IRR) of the project may be worked out to establish the economic/financial viability of the project.

Documents and Clearances Required

Site Plan, structural drawings,quantities and detailed cost analysis of various civil structures certified by an architect, price quotations and specifications for various items of plant and machinery, approval from State Electricity Board for load connection, NOC from panchayat, approval from Inspector of Factories, Registrar of Copy Rights, approval for brand registration, Registration of Company, Memorandum of Articles of Association, Registration of Unit under SSI (if applicable), permission for procurement of molasses, agreement between the company and the collaborator for technical assistance and market survey report.

STEPS FOR STARTING A SMALL ENTERPRISE

> Small enterprise are those enterprise whose investmentes is above ₹ 25 lakh and up to 5 crore in case of manufacturing sector and ₹ 10 lakh and up to ₹ 2 crore in case of services sector.

The development of small-scale industries has been one of the most significant and characteristic features of industrial development in India. One of the distinctive characteristics of small-scale sector is that, the development of these industries would create broader employment opportunities, assist in entrepreneurship and skills development, and ensure a better use of scarce financial resources and appropriate technology. Furthermore, they can play a main role in the achievement of national economic and socio-political objectives. The gestation period is very short and they need smaller amount of capital to start. It also helps in the dissemination of productive capacity unlike the large-scale industries which tend to concentrate in a few hands. This part, establishment of such industries in rural areas and small towns helps to check the influx of population into bigger towns.

The procedural aspects of the small-scale industry are quite formidable. Each and every entrepreneur is often overwhelmed by the multitude of procedures which help to face at every stage of the development of a small-scale industry. It is therefore, necessary to emphasise here that the student should concentrate more on the purpose and the principles underlying the various procedural formalities than on such routine formalities as filling in various forms, applications, etc.

Basic Objectives

The basic objectives underlying the development of small and medium scale industries are the increase in the supply of manufactured goods, the promotion of capital formation, the development of indigenous entrepreneurial talents and skills and the creation of broader employment opportunities. In addition, they include socio-economic goals such as the decentralisation and dispersal of manufacturing activities from the metropolitan to the non-metropolitan and rural areas, the reduction of regional economic imbalances within a country and the diffusion of entrepreneurial and managerial abilities and skills and technology throughout the country.

In the Indian economy, cottage and small-scale industries have a significant role to play. With increasing pace of industrialisation and sophistication of the large-scale industries, a new orientation is inevitable in the relationship of the SSIs with the large and medium industries. This relationship calls for integration of the production methods, upgradation of the qualities of production, ability to meet stringent delivery schedules and very many other problems that arise in a dynamic and changing environment not only in the country but also in the international field.

The success of a small-scale industry solely depends upon doing the right thing at the right time. In other words, a small-scale industrialist has to be conversant with the varied regulations governing the small-scale industry and the procedures to be followed in order to acquire the necessary assistance and incentives offered by the Government from time-to-time.

The procedural aspects of the small-scale industry are quite formidable. Each and every entrepreneur is often overwhelmed by the multitude of procedures which help to face at every stage of the development of a small-scale industry. It is therefore, necessary to emphasise here that the student should concentrate more on the purpose and the principles underlying the various procedural formalities than on such routine formalities as filling in various forms, applications, etc.

Right Thing at the Right Time

In this chapter, the treatment of procedures — right from conceiving a small-scale industry until the repayment of creditors and ploughing back of profits — is based on the personal and practical experience of a small industrialist. In the latter part of the discussion, a reference has been made to the varied regulations that a small-scale industrialist has to abide by. They are mentioned later.

A discussion of the relevant procedures to be followed when setting up a small-scale industry has been dealt with reference to various phases of its development. These phases are:

(i) Selection of a small industry and preparation of feasibility and project reports;

(ii) Accommodation, power and other infrastructural facilities;

(iii) Machinery;

(iv) Raw materials;

(v) Finance;

(vi) Marketing; and

(vii) Securing various incentives offered for the development of the small-scale industry.

SELECTION OF A SMALL-SCALE INDUSTRY

The process of setting up a small-scale industry has been indicated in Fig. 7.2, which has been drawn on the basis of practical experience gained in its promotion. It indicates all the important stages in the setting up of a small-scale industry.

The objectives of the promotional regulations are to provide an impetus to the growth of a small-scale industry and regulate the supply of machinery, electricity, water, premises, finance,

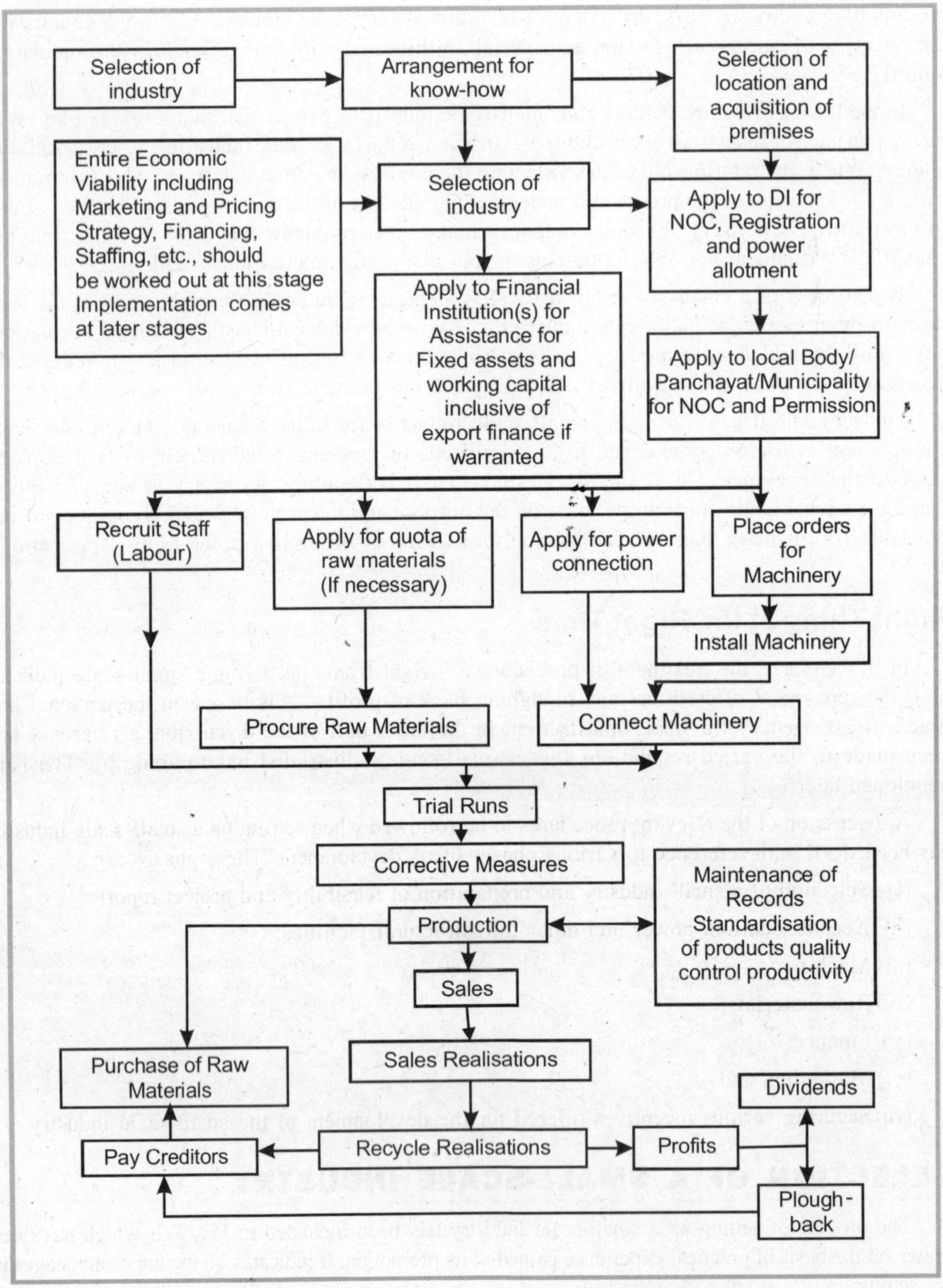

Fig. 7.2: Process of Setting up a Small-scale Industry.

raw materials and markets. The process of production and marketing is governed by a series of rules and regulations. In a way, these regulations are a boon to the small entrepreneur.

A potential entrepreneur has to pass through various stages for setting up his small-scale unit and these are:

(i) Decision to be self-employment

(ii) Identification of opportunities

(a) Idea generation

(b) Screening product/service idea

(c) Concept testing

(iii) Selection of the line of business

Business Analysis

Market Analysis

- Demand estimation, analysis, factors affecting demand
- Derived and autonomous demand
- Forecasting demand
- Marketing methods
- Marketing feasibility
- Market research

Technical Analysis

- Proper location of the unit
- Proper size of the plant
- Suitable process of manufacture
- Factory layout
- Organisational set-up

Financial Analysis

- Fixed assets of units
- Requirement of working capital
- Manufacturing cost of the product
- Sources of finances
- Repayment schedule
- Profitability and production statements
- Cash flow statements
- Break-even point
- ROI in each year

Economic Analysis

- Social cost benefit analysis

- Economic benefits and costs measured in terms of efficiency, impact of project on distribution of income in society, level of savings and investment in society
- Contribution of project towards fulfilment of merit wants, e.g., employment, self-sufficiency, social orders

Market and Demand Analysis

(iv) Selection of product/products

Product Development

(v) Selection of site (location)

Purchase/lease of land/shed in industrial estate

Development of the plot

(vi) Building the factory

(vii) Selection of ownership form

(viii) Preparation of the project report

A comprehensive appraisal of proposed project should cover the following:

(i) Technological Aspect
(ii) Financial Aspect
(iii) Economic Aspect
(iv) Managerial Aspect
(v) Market Aspect
(vi) Break-even Analysis
(vii) Planning Commission's guidelines for feasibility report
(viii) Project Life Cycle
(ix) Project Manager Role Responsibilities
(x) Network Analysis — PERT and CPM
(xi) Financial Appraisal methods
(xii) Registration in case of company or partnership type of organisation
(xiii) Agreement with collaborator, if any
(xiv) Obtaining letter of intent or provisional registration of SSI
(xv) Preparation of detailed project feasibility report
(xvi) Obtaining import licence, customs clearance, etc.
(xvii) Power connection/water connection etc.
(xviii) Completion of civil works
(xix) Delivery of imported and indigenous machinery
(xx) Erection of machinery and equipments
(xxi) Obtaining clearance from pollution control board
(xxii) Obtaining industrial licence or permanent SSI registration
(xxiii) Acquiring manufacturing know-how
(xxiv) Selection of personnel — technical and administrative
(xxv) Procuring unskilled labour

(xxvi) Training the labour
(xxvii) Designing financing schemes
(xxviii) Arranging finance by all means
(xxix) Arrangement of raw materials
(xxx) Apply for getting grants/subsidies from the government
(xxxi) Trial run and commissioning of plant
(xxxii) Start of commercial production
(xxxiii) Arrangement for sale of products
(xxxiv) Registration of designs and trademarks.

A small entrepreneur can obtain the necessary information and guidance from the Government Departments, Organisations and Agencies like Director of Industries and Commerce, Manager of District Industries Centres, Kerala State Industrial Development Corporation, etc.

Starting a Small-scale Industry

A small entrepreneur is the chief executive of his unit, its floor supervisor, accounts clerk, purchase manager, salesman, legal and economic adviser, planner and visionary — all rolled into one.

Every now and then, you will come across advertisements and announcements enticing you to set up small industries under the aegis of the State Small Industries Corporations, which promise a fully developed industrial shed with power and water, assistance in getting you raw materials, machinery on hire-purchase basis, common services facilities, training facilities and facilities in the marketing of your product. Assurance of term loans on attractive terms and working capital in time and at concessional rates. In backward areas, a number of additional subsidies are available.

An entrepreneur may be a qualified engineer. Even so, he should not dream of becoming a small entrepreneur unless he is confident of meeting the following twelve essential requirements:

(i) The entrepreneur should be fully conversant with the product-line. It is not enough that he knows the method of manufacturing; he has to know how to operate the machines, etc.

(ii) He should have adequate shop floor experience to guide the machine operators in fool-setting techniques or the die-maker on the specific needs of his press tools.

(iii) He should be familiar with the raw materials he requires, their specifications, how to ensure their quality and where to get them at reasonable prices.

(iv) He should know how to keep accounts, how to maintain stores, how to prepare the balance sheet, etc.

(v) He should have knowledge of marketing channels, distribution network, agency practices, transport intricacies, and the economic of packaging.

(vi) He should know how to ensure the stipulated quality of his product.

(vii) He should be well-versed in taxation and other laws governing SSIs.

(ix) He should be willing to put up with bureaucratic regulations and insults, and be fractional under any circumstances.

Phases	Objectives
Project Selection Phase	To select those products, processes or systems in an organisation where the value and cost ratio is low and where analysis will lead to increased benefits
Information Phase	(a) To gather, organise and analyse data (b) To define functions (c) To establish a functional monetary value
Creative Phase	To generate alternate methods for providing necessary functions
Evaluation Phase	(a) To develop, refine and evaluate alternate methods generated during the creative phase (b) To determine the cost (c) To select feasible method offering best value
Recommendation Phase	To prepare and present a report containing recommendation along with benefits.
Implementation Phase	(a) To establish a plan to action for implementation of the selected method (b) To obtain approval (c) To perform all other actions necessary to put the proposal into effect
Follow-Up Phase	(a) To follow-up and audit actual results (b) To resolve problems, if any, during proposal implementation.

Fig. 7.3: Project Objectives

(x) He should know how to avail himself of the various benefits available to the SSIs.

(xi) He should possess expertise, shrewdness, resourcefulness and, most important, perseverance in his business dealings. There is no substitute for hard work.

(xii) He should have the guts to withstand the high pressure climate in which he has to build his unit.

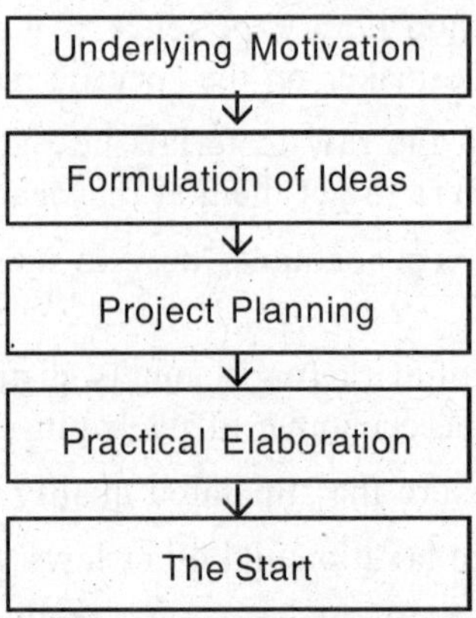

Fig. 7.4: Process of Starting a Small Enterprise

Any entrepreneur desirous of starting a small-scale industry should have a clear picture of the objectives of his project. It is advisable to prepare a comprehensive check list. Such a list, embracing all the important matters, has been given below for the guidance of prospective entrepreneurs. Students will get an insight into the various processes of a small-scale industry.

1. Feasibility Report

Before starting a small-scale industry, one should consult the Director of Industries and the Small Industries Service Institute (SISI) located in one's State. The SISI guides entrepreneurs as to the type of industry to start, where to start and how to start it. The SISI helps them to select the various items of manufacture which have scope for development in different areas. It suggests the lines on which a project report for the proposed units should be prepared for the consideration of various financial institutions with a view to securing financial assistance. Similarly, technical help in the selection of proper raw materials and type of machinery is also provided. Apart from this, the SISI gives valuable information of the various incentives available to the small-scale industries from various organisations.

2. Project Feasibility Analysis

A project feasibility analysis includes market analysis, technical analysis, financial analysis and social profitability analysis. Although each feasibility analysis is different and is tailored to the product, its goal is to identify the strengths and weaknesses of the project.

The starting point of a project analysis is the establishment of the objectives to be attained. The next stage is the pre-selection stage — the advisability of having an indepth study. The analysis stage consists mainly of three factors — market, technical and financial analysis. A market analysis is a method of screening project ideas as well as a means of evaluating a project's feasibility in terms of the market. A market analysis should cover the following areas:

(i) A brief description of the market including the market area, methods of transportation and existing rates of transportation. Channels of distribution and general trade practices are also included.

(ii) An analysis of past and present demands, including the determination of quantity and the value of consumption and identification of the major consumers of the product.

(iii) An analysis of past and present supply, broken down as to source (whether imported or domestic) as well as information which will assist in determining the competitive position of the product such as selling prices, quality and marketing practices of the competitors.

The technical analysis of a project feasibility study establishes whether the project is technically feasible or not, and whether it offers a basis for the estimation of costs. Moreover, it provides an opportunity for a consideration of the effect of various technical alternatives on employment, ecology, infrastructure demands, capital services, support or other industries, balance of payments and other factors. A technical analysis should contain a review of the techniques or processes to be applied and should incorporate:

(i) A description of the product, including specifications relating to its physical, mechanical and chemical properties, as well as uses of the product.

(ii) A description of the selected manufacturing process, showing detailed flow charts and presenting the alternative process which may have been considered and the justification for the adoption of the selected process.

(iii) A determination of the plant size and production schedule, which includes the expected volume for a given time period on the basis of start-up and technical factors.

(iv) Selection of machinery and equipment, including specifications, equipment to be purchased and its origin, quotations from suppliers, delivery dates, terms of payment and a comparative analysis of alternatives in terms of cost, reliability, performance and spare parts availability.

(v) An identification of the plant's location and an assessment of its desirability in terms of its distance from raw material sources and markets. For a new project, this part may include a comparative study of different sites, indicating the advantages and disadvantages of each.

(vi) A design of the plant layout and an estimate of the cost of the erection of the proposed buildings and land improvements.

(vii) A study of the availability of raw materials and liabilities and utilities, including a description of physical and chemical properties, quantities needed, current and prospective costs, terms of payment, locations of sources of supply and continuity of supply.

(viii) An estimate of labour requirements, including a detailed breakdown of direct and indirect labour requirements, and the supervision required for the manufacture of the product.

(ix) A determination of the type and quantity of waste to be disposed of together with a description of the waste disposal method, its costs and the necessary clearance from proper authorities, and

(x) An estimate of the production cost of the product.

In the financial analysis of a project feasibility study, emphasis is on the preparation of financial statements, so that the project may be evaluated in terms of the different measures of commercial profitability and the magnitude of financing required may be determined. The financial analysis requires the assembly of the market and technical costs estimated into various proforma statements. If it is necessary to have more information on which to base an investment decision, a sensitivity analysis or possibly, a risk analysis may be conducted. The financial analysis should concentrate on —

(i) Projects that involve new companies, statements of total project cost, initial capital requirements and cash flows relative to the project time table;

For all projects, financial projections for future time periods including income statements, cash flows and balance sheet are imperative.

(ii) For all projects, supporting schedules for financial projection, stating the assumption made as to the collection period of sales, inventory levels, payment period of purchases and expenses, and the element of production cost, selling, administrative and financial expenses.

(iii) For all projects, prepare a financial analysis showing returns on investments, returns on equity, break-even volume and price analysis.

(iv) For all projects, if necessary, a sensitivity analysis to identify items which have a substantial impact on profitability or possibly a risk analysis.

For the small entrepreneur, the studies conducted during the analysis stage of the project provide the material for an assessment. If positive results are obtained, the entrepreneur, in seeking finance will want to prepare an investment proposal. The planners or government officials, however, having obtained positive conclusion from the economic feasibility study, will want to evaluate the element of social profitability.

The purpose of the investment or loan application is to convince a lender (financial institution) that the project is a desirable investment; that it not only possesses the potential for profit but that the proposed management team has the capability to achieve the potential. The investment proposal normally contains:

(i) General information on the product, company history, the nature of the industry and the reputation and qualifications of the existing or proposed management.

(ii) A description of the period, which usually consists of extracts from economic feasibility studies and includes information on such items as market, production, selected manufacturing methods (with detailed indication of the cost of equipment and operational expenses) and a financial statement, and

(iii) Miscellaneous information, such as the steps taken for the implementation of the project and the qualifications of the technical partners envisaged or selected.

3. Break-even Analysis

Let us first address 'why break-even analysis?' While discussing preparation of a project report of feasibility report, we stated that the level of estimated capacity utilisation, i.e., quantum of production in terms of goods or services as the case may be, needs to be spelled out in advance in the project report. Our business experience tells us that when the enterprise/business is actually started, in other words, the project is actually implemented, the projected or targeted level of capacity is not achieved due to various unforeseen reasons.

Such a situation entails financial implications. Then, the entrepreneur needs to decide to what extent the curtailment in production can be afforded to meet all its liabilities. Steinhoff and Burgess put it as "How much must I sell before I start making profit". The answer to this question is called the 'break-even analysis' where income exactly equals expenses. Let us now understand "What is break-even analysis?" In simple words, it is an analysis of production point at which profit starts. This point is where income and expenses are exactly equal and the point is called 'break-even' point. Thus, break-even analysis is used to find the break-even point.

Having understood the concept of break-even analysis, we now intend to expose you to the mechanics involved in finding out break-even point. In carrying out any enterprise, profit comes from sale of goods or services as the case may be and expenses emerge out from the cost involved. Expenses to be incurred refer to cost. Cost is broadly divided into two types, viz.: (1) Fixed cost, and (2) Variable cost. What are these costs?

Fixed Cost: Fixed costs are defined as those that do not change with increase or decrease in production. No matter what the production is, the fixed cost remains the same. Examples of fixed costs could be the monthly rent paid for the factory, interest on long-term loans, administrative expenses, etc. Even if there is zero production, the fixed cost will remain unchanged. Say, if factory rent, i.e., ₹ 10,000 per month is the only cost, it will remain fixed at ₹ 10,000 if there is a production of 500 units or 200 units or even no production at all.

Variable Cost: In short, what is not fixed cost is variable cost. Variable cost is defined as expenses that change with the volume of production. It varies proportionately with changes in production. Thus, if production is zero, variable cost would be zero. The absolute total variable cost increases or decreases along with increase or decrease in production. But the variable cost per unit is constant at any level of production. The following example clears it.

There are some variable costs that do not vary proportionately with the change in production. In fact, these vary in varying degrees. As a result such costs are called semi-variable. The popular examples of such costs could be telephone, electricity and gas charges if they are billed on a usage basis. In such cases that proportion of expenses which continue even if production falls are considered as fixed and expenses which increase or decrease as production increases or decreases are considered as variable cost.

After knowing sales and total cost in terms of fixed cost and variable cost, now the break-even point can be calculated.

According to the simplest method, Profit is the excess of sales over cost, i.e., sales – cost = profit. The calculation of break-even point involves four steps. These are:

1. Segregation of fixed and variable costs
2. Percentage of variable costs to sales
3. Calculate the contribution or margin, i.e., the difference between 100 and the percentage of variable cost to sales as worked out above.
4. Divide the fixed cost by the percentage of contribution or margin as worked out above.

It will be better, at least for those of you who are coming across to the concept of break-even point for the first time, to calculate break-even point with the help of an example.

4. Licences

An impression seems to have gained ground among some people that there are some restrictions on the getting up of small-scale industrial units and that licences from either the Central or State Governments have to be taken out before an entrepreneur to set up an industrial unit in the small-scale sector; no formal permission from the State or Central Government is necessary for this purpose. Also, industries employing less than 100 workers and having fixed assets of less than ₹ 10 lakh need not obtain any licence under the Industries (Development and Regulation) Act.

Small-scale units have, however, to conform to the rules and regulations prescribed by state or local authorities under the Factories Act, Commercial Establishments Act, Town Planning Rules, and rules made for the issues of quotas of raw materials, etc.

However, powerlooms do not come under the purview of the small-scale industries programme. For installing powerlooms, the prior permission of the Textile Commissioner, Government of India, Mumbai is required.

5. Registration of Small-scale Industries

In their own interest, all existing small-scale units or intending entrepreneurs employing more than 10 workers should get themselves registered with the Director of Industries in their State. A copy of this application for registration should be sent to the Director of Small Industries Service Institute in the concerned State. Such registration with the Director of Industries and the Small Industries Service Institute will be of considerable help to small-scale unit in obtaining financial assistance from the government and for obtaining machinery on hire-purchase basis from the

National Small Industries Corporation. Assistance in the supply of controlled raw materials, specific certificate for imported raw materials and components, and facilities for export promotion, would then be easily made available to small-scale units registered with the State Director of Industries. The registration number is now required to be quoted while submitting import applications.

6. Infrastructure

The Director of Industries and/or the SISI in the State can be approached to provide you with built-up factory space in an industrial estate, or develop the factory site, power, etc. After the initial clearance from the State Director of Industries, the Municipality or the Panchayat issues a "No Objection Certificate".

The mechanics of putting up a new factory in Greater Mumbai are:

(i) Apply to the Industries Commissioner, Industries and Labour Department, Government of Maharashtra, and obtain a "No Objection Certificate". (NOC)

(ii) With a copy of the above NOC, apply in Factory Form "A", to the Word Engineer of B.M.C.

(iii) Clarifications and submission of further details on the information supplied in Form "A" may follow.

(iv) The sub engineer will inspect the premises and submit Form No. '2' to his assistant engineer.

(v) The assistant engineer will scrutinise and confirm if the applicant's activity conforms to the zone and will intimate to the applicant in Form No. '3' if there is no objection or in Form No. '4' if there is any objection.

(vi) Form 'B' will be received by the applicant if Form No. '3' is issued to him. This form should be filled in and submitted.

(vii) Within 21 days after the submission of Forms 'A', 'B' and the factory plans in triplicate, the assistant engineer will issue Form No. '5' and '6' in which he will specify;

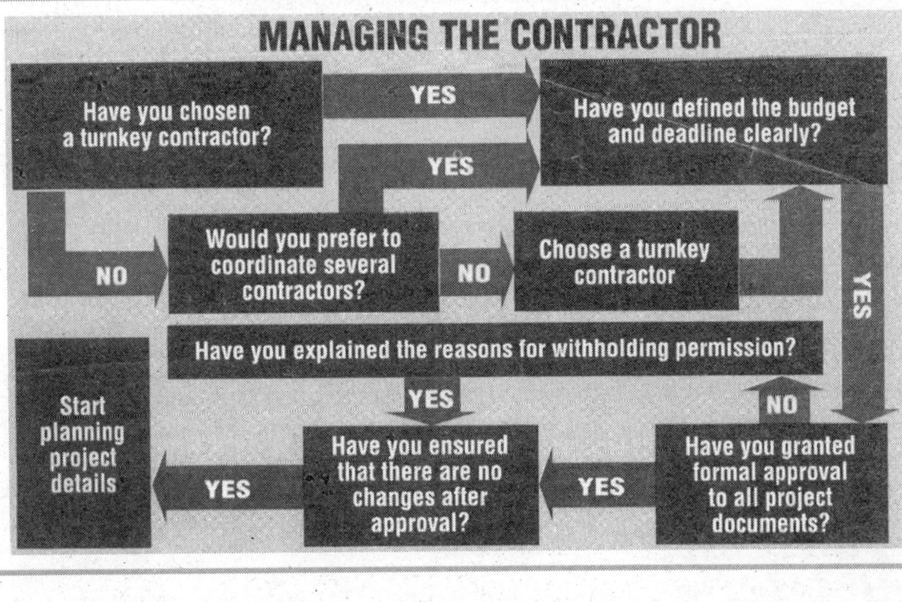

(a) The electric power sanctioned (thereafter, the BEST provides current);

(b) Adequate water facilities provided;

(c) The various requirements, requisitions and conditions for operating the factory, including those required by the chief inspector of factories.

Form 'C' will also be issued along with these forms. (Upon complying with the stipulations in Form 'B', the BMC should be informed thereof in writing.)

Subsequently, permission to commence production will be given.

7. Machinery

The small entrepreneur needs the requisite type of machines for production. He can get the necessary machinery from the National Small Industries Corporation under a hire-purchase scheme.

The scheme for the supply of indigenous and imported machines on hire-purchase basis was launched in March 1956 to enable small entrepreneurs without substantial means to avail themselves of assistance. The scheme is different from the credit operations scheme for entrepreneurs. The NSIC has acquired the necessary experience and expertise in the procurement of machines from the right sources. It also takes care of the problems up to the stage of delivery of machineries to the entrepreneurs. Also, while financial institutions plan to look mainly to the creditworthiness of entrepreneurs, the NSIC would look primarily to the motivation of the individual applicant, his capacity, his technical competence and his managerial ability to run the enterprise.

The small entrepreneur should enlist himself as a member with the NSIC. His application form should be accompanied by the Registration Certificate and report of the Director of Industries. The application for obtaining machines under the hire-purchase scheme of the NSIC is quite comprehensive. The small entrepreneur has to provide full details along with the relevant documents.

The application form for hire-purchase of machinery calls for information regarding the organisational set-up of the unit, its programme of production, and the marketability and profitability of the enterprise. It also calls for additional information regarding the cost of production, the infrastructural facilities available for the unit, the technical capability of the entrepreneur, etc. The details in the application are self-explanatory.

8. Raw Materials

The raw materials required by SSIs may broadly be classified as under:

(i) Raw material components and spares, both indigenous and imported;

(ii) Non-ferrous materials — both indigenous and imported;

(iii) Iron and steel — both indigenous and imported; and

(iv) Chemicals — indigenous and imported.

Under the liberalised scheme, the actual users are provided with adequate foreign exchange to meet their justifiable requirements of imported items of industrial materials. The *"priority"* industries are assured of an adequate supply based on requirements by way of grant of rotational licences.

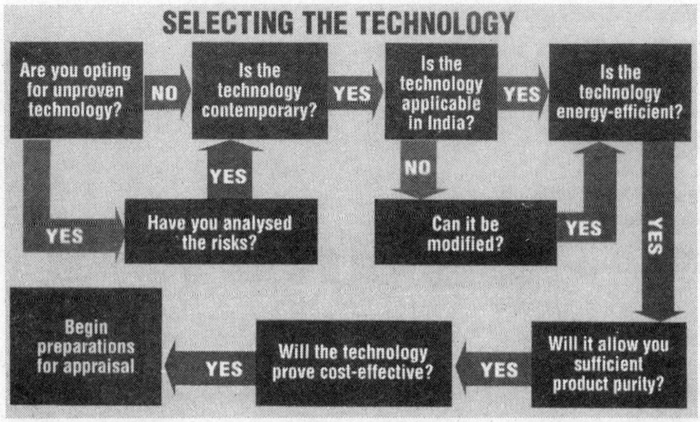

Small-scale units should apply directly to the Regional Licensing Authority, and not through the sponsoring authority, for import licences for raw materials, components and spares after utilising the previous set of licences to the extent of 90 per cent by way of opening their own credit or 60 per cent by way of actual import, covering six months' requirements of the unit. New units should submit their applications through their respective sponsoring authority.

The State Director of Industries allocates indigenous non-ferrous metals. Some of the non-ferrous items are canalised through the State Trading Corporation of India (STC). The raw materials imported by the STC are given to the SSI units in accordance with the recommendations of the Director of Industries concerned.

The same applies to iron and steel raw materials are canalised through the MMTC.

In times of difficulties, the decontrolled chemical raw materials are canalised through the DGTD in accordance with the recommendation of the State Director of Industries. Indigenous controlled chemicals are allocated through the State DIS/SICs. Imported raw materials are canalised through the STC.

In short, controlled and imported raw materials are to be obtained through the State DIS, SICs (SSI).

9. Finance

The financial function in a small-scale industry is similar to the financial function in any other organisation, but with this essential difference — that there are a host of banking and insurance regulations to be strictly adhered to and quite a few precautions to be taken.

The areas where finance would be needed, after the small-scale industrialist fixes the land accommodation, are:

(i) Purchase and installation of machinery;

(ii) Procurement of raw materials and components and the manufacture of products;

(iii) Working funds;

(iv) Availability of funds until the realisation of sales.

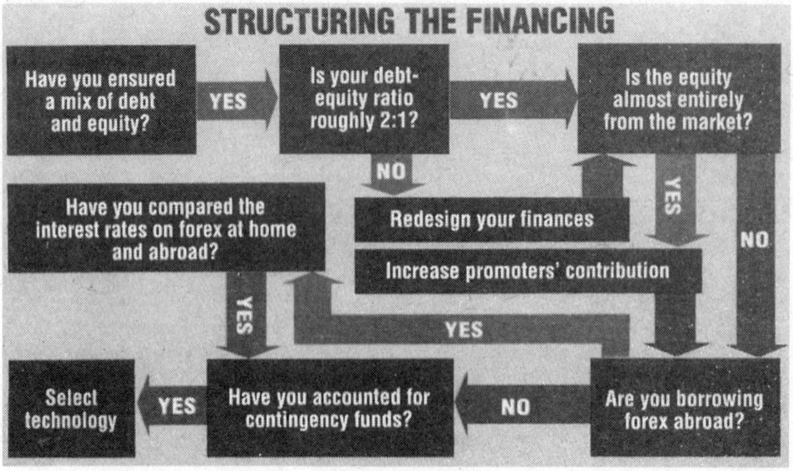

The State Director of Industries provides loans for block capital under the Industries Act. One should apply through the sponsoring authority. State Financial Corporations provide long-term credit for the purchase of fixed assets. The application should be submitted to the SFCs along with the following documents:

(i) Project Report; *(ii)* Copy of Registration; *(iii)* Cash Flow Statement; *(iv)* Stock Statement.

In some states SFCs and the banks agreed to process the common applications for loans. Up to an amount of ₹ 2 lakh, a commercial bank provides medium-term instalment credit. It also provides loans for meeting needs for working capital for the purchase of raw materials as also for day-to-day requirements.

In order to get a loan from a commercial bank, the entrepreneur has to fill in an application form as per the specimen provided by the financial institutions including banks and submit it to the bank along with the following documents:

(i) Authentic copies of Balance Sheets and Profit and Loss Accounts (if the industrial concern is a limited company or an industrial cooperative society).

(ii) A statement of total assets and liabilities in the prescribed form in the case of partnership and proprietary concerns.

(iii) Perform statements in all other cases.

(iv) Copies of the affidavit in regard to the size of the unit.

(v) Technical Feasibility Report from the Small Industries Service Institute, the Director of Industries, if obtained, may also been closed.

10. Recruitment of Personnel

Even single proprietary concerns cannot be run with the sole owner doing all activities. In some enterprises, it is just possible the owner and his family members may be able to manage the affairs. In these days of specialisation and competition, professionals and skilled workers would have to be recruited. Depending on the size and nature of the industry, skilled and unskilled workers would have to be recruited to run small-scale enterprises. After making realistic assessment of the actual manpower requirements of an enterprise, suitable arrangements should be made for recruitment of personnel. It would always be advantageous to decide beforehand and ascertain the norms of production for a year or any shorter period. On the basis of the manpower requirements contemplated in the project report for the smooth and effective functioning of the unit, decisions to recruit the stipulated number of persons may be implemented.

The next step would be to resort to advertisements or request the Employment Exchange to send suitable persons with the requisite skills, training and experience.

If the prospective entrepreneur is merely a matriculate or a graduate and is keenly interested to take up the manufacture of a chemical item, say, calcium carbide, it would always be advantageous to appoint a works manager well-versed in chemical engineering. Besides, the technical personnel in an industrial unit should possess certain basic skills such as —

(i) Technical knowledge relating to the job;

(ii) Experience relevant and adequate;

(iii) Academic knowledge;

(iv) Ability to express ideas.

The time of installation of machinery should always synchronise with the time of recruitment of personnel. If personnel were recruited several weeks before the installation of machinery, most of the workers may idle away their time and it would be a wasteful expenditure. On the other hand, if machinery is installed, and there are no workers to operate the machines, the unit would not be able to start production and the gestation period would prolong. Adequate planning is, therefore, essential to match the various stages of activities and start production at the earliest.

Training is one of the important industrial extension services rendered by the Small Industries Development Organisation (SIDO) through various Small Industries Service Institutes, Branch SISIs, and Extension/Production Centres. The training courses organised by SIDO are aimed at upgrading the skills of workers as well as the managerial capabilities of personnel.

Regular and *ad hoc* training courses in various technical trades are conducted by the Small Industries Service Institutes, Branch SISIs, Extension Centres and Production Centres for artisans, both skilled and semi-skilled, sponsored by the small-scale industries. Broadly, the technical courses are divided into four categories:

(i) Shop practice courses, viz., tool room practices, foundry techniques, blacksmithy and forging, electrical shop practice, etc.

(ii) Trade-oriented courses which provide advanced know-how in the trade of tool-making (press tools) machinist, filter, sheet metal, pattern making, carpentry, etc.

(ill) Process-oriented courses, viz., heat treatment, gas and electric welding, food and vegetable preservation, anodising, leather tanning, etc.

(iv) Product-oriented courses, viz., lens grinding, paints and varnishes, glass beads, footwear, sports goods, thermometer making, scientific glass blowing, etc.

With a new thrust on the development of industries in the backward and rural areas, SIDO diversified its Entrepreneurship Development of industries in the backward and rural areas, SIDO diversified its Entrepreneurship Development Programmes in the year 1978-79 to serve new categories of entrepreneurs like Educated Unemployed, Women, Rural Artisans, Weaker Sections, Handicapped, Defence Personnel and Students. The Entrepreneurial Development Programmes are broadly classified into two categories, namely, (a) motivation campaign for identification and selection of entrepreneurs and (b) Entrepreneurial Development Training Programmes for the target groups. In the year 1985-86, SIDO also introduced Entrepreneurial Development Programmes for the beneficiaries of the Self-Employment Scheme.

11. Marketing

The rationale of the Government Purchase Scheme of the Corporation lies in the fact that the Government of India is the largest single buyer, and by channelising these purchases in favour of small-scale units, it gives a tremendous boost to the marketing of their products.

The salient features of the scheme are:

(a) The small-scale units, desiring to avail themselves of assistance, have to enlist themselves with the NSIC;

(b) Instead of purchasing tender sets from the DGS&D, the small units enlisted with the NSIC automatically get them from it and its branches free of cost;

(c) If their prices are acceptable to the DGS&D they are not required to pay a security deposit on the issue of a competency certificate by the NSIC;

(d) Price preference up to 15 per cent over the quotations of large-scale units is considered by the Purchasing Agency, depending on the merits of each case;

(e) Wherever they feel that injustice has been done to them, the NSIC takes up their cases with the DGS&D and other Government Departments such as Defence, the Railways and the P&T in order to find out the reasons for non-placement of contracts with the units, and tries to redress their grievances.

In the beginning, purchases in respect of only 16 items were reserved exclusively for the small-scale sector; the number of such items has steadily increased to 409 items in 1995-96.

Besides, in respect of 13 items, purchases up to 75 per cent and in respect of 28 items, purchases up to 50 per cent of the requirements are earmarked for the small-scale sector.

The corporation also helps small-scale industries in securing contracts from other Government Departments such as the Railways, Posts and Telegraphs, etc.

Hitherto, the purchase programme has been restricted purely to Central purchase houses like DGS&D, the P&T and the Railways. It is proposed to extend the base further to cover State Government Departments such as the State Electricity Boards, PWDs, etc., and provide liaison offices at each of the principal centres of the State.

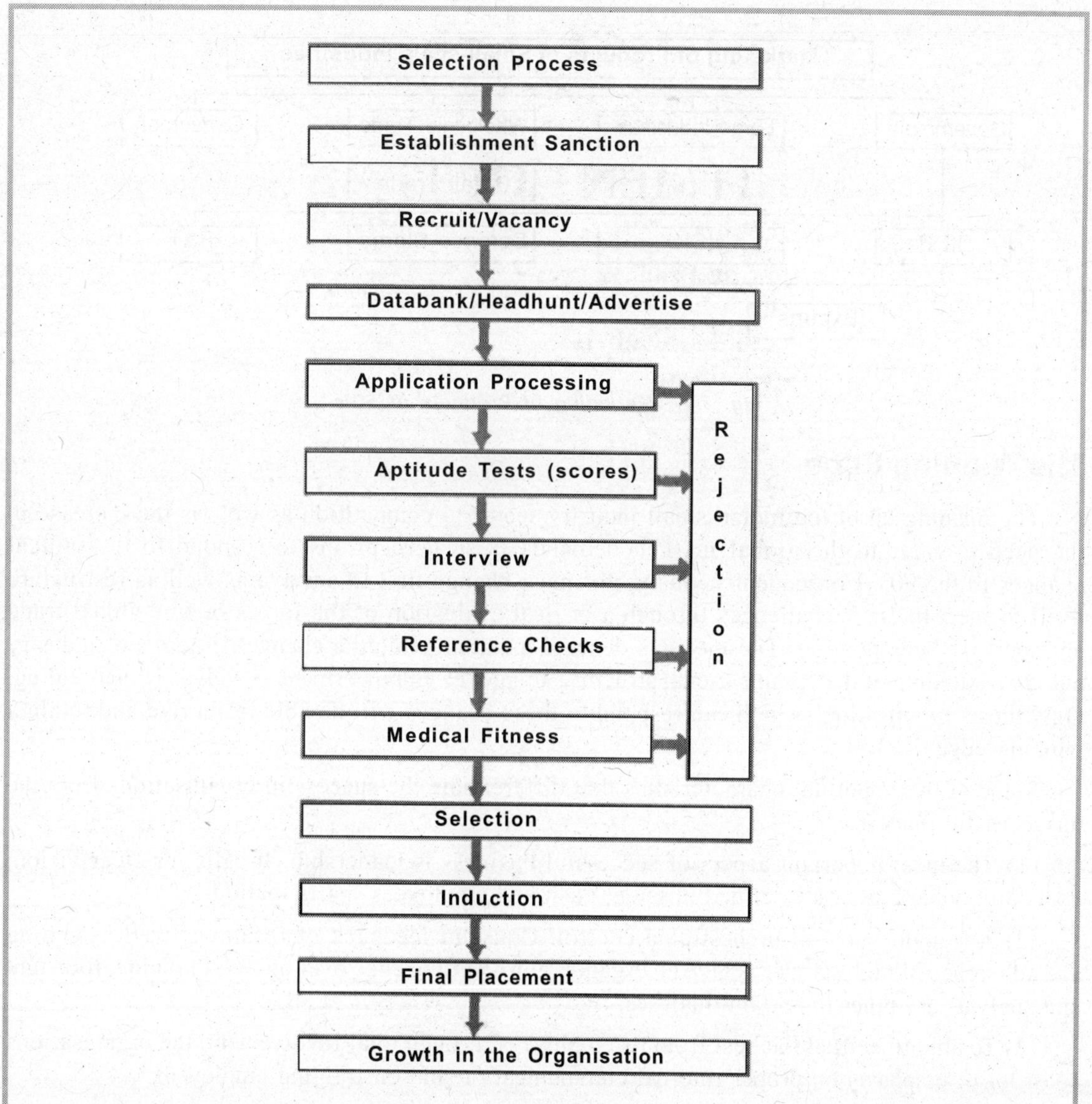
Selection Process
Establishment Sanction
Recruit/Vacancy
Databank/Headhunt/Advertise
Application Processing
Aptitude Tests (scores)
Interview
Reference Checks
Medical Fitness
Rejection
Selection
Induction
Final Placement
Growth in the Organisation

Fig. 7.5

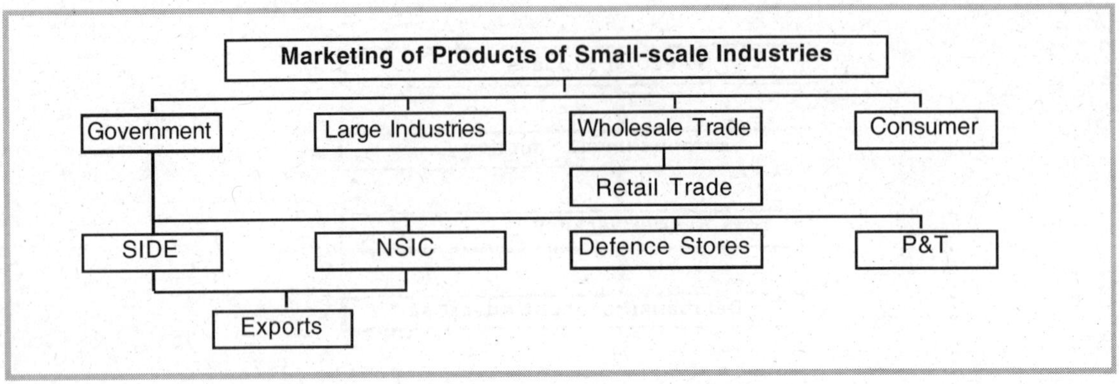

Fig. 7.6: Marketing of Products of SSIs

The Winning Edge

The opening up of the Indian small industry sector to competition as well as the increase in the need to cater to the global market, demands fresh perceptions to respond to the radical changes in the 90s. Consequently, this sector must change first to survive as well as restructure itself to meet the new challenges through a critical evaluation of the forces of free global trade and increased competition. These events demand quantum strategic changes in terms of industry culture, flattening of the organisational structure, employee empowerment as well as team building. Only those organisations which can respond to these changes will be able to survive and retain a winning edge.

Some of the important characteristics that differentiate the successful organisations from the unsuccessful ones are:

(1) The most important aspect of successful business is leadership. It calls for clear vision, goals and objectives, well defined mission, dash and employees' participation.

(2) Adequate but well-orchestrated control. Constant feedback of results as well as setting and adherence of high standards give an organisation a cutting edge over others. Planning, foresight and analysis are other important qualities.

(3) To able to extract the best from its employees through total involvement, the organisations put a lot of emphasis on proper internal communication and on training employees.

(4) The successful organisation is one which is very close to the marketplace. The process of systematic market is used to develop products or process of systematic market research is used to develop products or process and to provide value for money to the customers. This helps to gain the market share.

(5) The next most important characteristic of a winning business organisation is "Zero Basing" or sticking to the last — knowing what business the company is in swiftly recognising and preventing when it has diverted into an unsuitable path and preventing risks.

Instrumental Synergy

Comprehensive coverage of dynamic needs cannot be ensured unless this strategy incorporates the necessary organisational support. In the development of backward areas, two things are of fundamental importance. Firstly, the needs of the entrepreneurs or the target-groups are wider than those immediately related to an enterprise. Unless the complex structure of his private and social needs is understood, our assessment of his requirements which will have to be met to sustain him in a desired enterprise like a small industry or a farm will be unrealistic and lopsided. The amount sent on his enterprise tends to remain unproductive. Unless we support the entrepreneur in all his needs and exigencies till his enterprise yields profit, entrepreneurs are often coerced out of their enterprise during the initial years, because they lack the capacity to withstand inevitable risks, if any. In order to develop small enterprises and small farmers in an integrated manner with an industrial project, the socio-economic conditions of these people have to be understood to appreciate their needs, and devise appropriate loan schemes. The weaker sections of the population are likely to benefit from a programme is designed to meet the varying needs of beneficiary groups *(Development Programme for the Door: Do Strategies Make a Difference?*, Samuel Paul and Ashok Subramaniam). Sometimes, even the consumption needs of the poor artisans have to be provided for in order to sustain in their work.

Secondly, an integrated approach to rural industrialisation which has to deal with a complex structure of differential needs requiring regular monitoring and timely intervention of promotional agencies calls for active coordination among institutions. "The more backward a country's economy, the greater was the part played by the special institutional factors designed to increase the supply of capital to nascent industries and in addition to provide them with less decentralised and better informed entrepreneurial guidance; the more backward the country, the more pronounced was the coerciveness and comprehensiveness of these factors." (A. Gershenkson: *Economic Backwardness in Historical Perspective)*. In a backward place, the role of government institutions is of the highest significance. The institutions should not only cater to a variety of needs but also fulfil their role in the desired sequence so as to make the project work. This is what has been described by some as "synergistic effect or congruence". For example, small industrial units get term-loans from term-lending institutions but the desired working capital is not sanctioned at the right time as a result of which the entire scheme goes wrong. Similarly, if raw materials are not supplied for the essential utilities, the investment may remain idle, unproductive and eventually succumb to heavy accumulated liabilities. Various institutional supports must permit coverage in a synergy to make a success of an enterprise which needs all of them in a given order. In urban or developed areas, institutional synergy can perhaps be overcome by the resilience of the entrepreneurs, but in backward areas, the staying power of the entrepreneurs is so feeble that they quickly wear out with the smallest obstruction. Institutional patronage must, therefore, be comprehensive, continuous and synergistic.

Training

It is only against this background that we can effectively plan out training programmes for the development of entrepreneurship in the backward areas. The basic difference between a backward area and a developed area is that unlike the latter, backward areas do not have a hidden reservoir of potential entrepreneurs who through motivation, training and support can quickly become competent entrepreneurs. Entrepreneurs from the backward areas have to be given comprehensive functional training based on the specific conditions of the entrepreneur and the choice of the enterprise. The entrepreneurship development programme must deal with the following:

(1) On the basis of an elaborate action-plan based on environment analysis, various areas of entrepreneurial activities should be identified and specific projects formulated. These areas should

be suitably assigned to develop the inherent skills of artisan groups and high school dropouts, educated unemployed, farmers and men of other trades.

(2) For each area of activity, institutional linkages should be clearly spelt out. Simultaneous attempts where necessary, should be made to build new institutions which are needed to give financial marketing or other necessary support. For example, if we are promoting a large number of dairy farms, a central refrigeration plant in the area should simultaneously come up.

(3) On the basis of institutional linkages, thus worked out, an inter-agency team should be constituted to take up each identified group of entrepreneurs for training. Since the product an entrepreneur of such a group is to manufacture is known, and his own socio-economic conditions are also known, a series of needs of each entrepreneur in implementing his project should be clearly identified by the agency to look after each need or group of needs in a timebound programme.

(4) The training programme should briefly make the entrepreneurs by a multi disciplinary familiarisation course aware of the nature and problems of entrepreneurship in their context. Further, the training programme should discuss their schemes and proceed with the implementation. No training is more effective than the actual experience in implementation — the agencies must ensure that the entrepreneur gets all assistance and guidance in the implementation of his project. This would eliminate inter-agency disputes and the consequent delay which prove fatal to many entrepreneurs.

(5) There should be a nodal agency, preferably an agency which organises the training programme, to monitor the progress of the implementation of each trainee's project. This calls for coordination of the functions of various promotional agencies in order to make its specific services available to the entrepreneur in right time.

Training programmes for entrepreneurship development which involve all promotional agencies and financial institutions have proved to be the most successful. Involvement in the training programme does create a continuing interest to prove advantageous to the entrepreneurs among these agencies. And since for backward areas, project-oriented training programmes have been considered indispensable, the multiagency involvement in the training programme helps in a better appraisal and quicker implementation. These agencies should work in a manner as if they are escorting an entrepreneur right from the conception of a project-idea to the state when the unit starts production. Even after that stage, specific institutional arrangements have to be made to extend continuing marketing support.

Such a multiagency "escort" approach compensates for many deficiencies which the entrepreneurs of backward areas are beset with by their birth and circumstances, and it helps engender entrepreneurial qualities among them through practical experience.

ANNEXURE 1

Process of Setting up a Small-scale Industry — Guidelines

I. *Selection of Industry*

- **Small Industries Service Institutes** — They guide entrepreneurs in the selection of industries, areas, suitable raw materials and machinery.
- **Indian Investment Centre Parliament Street, New Delhi-1** — It advises on foreign capital participation and technical collaboration. Provides guidance to entrepreneurs regarding government policies, procedures, available incentives and facilities for investment, economic size of unit and the magnitude of investments required, demand forecast, availability of raw materials, etc.
- **Ministry of Industrial Development and Company Affairs, New Delhi.** — It approves the cases of foreign collaboration.

II. *District Industries Centres*

In each district, there would be one agency to deal with all requirements of small and village industries, which would be called the Districts Industries Centre. Under the single roof of the centre, all the services and support required by small and village entrepreneurs would be provided. The Centre would have a separate wing for looking after the special needs of cottage and household industries as distinct from the small industry. The Rural Industries Project and Rural Artisans Programme would be merged with the programme of the District Industries Centre. Each DIC would have a General Manager and seven managers of different disciplines for looking after planning and economic investigation, credit, marketing, etc.

III. *Factory Accommodation*

- **Directors of Industries** — They provide built-up factory space in industrial estates or developed factory sites, power, water, etc. (The building designs have to be approved by Municipalities or Corporations while power and water connections are sanctioned by State Governments/ Undertakings.

IV. *Industrial Estates*

There are more than 600 industrial estates in India which provide constructed accommodation in developed areas. Main facilities include common facility services, workshops, allotment of sheds on hire-purchase, concessional charges on water and power, exemption from octroi duty on building materials, etc.

V. *Registration*

Although it is not mandatory, it is certainly helpful to obtain the SSI Registration Number from the Director of Industries.

VI. *Machinery*

- **Small Industries Service Institutes** — They advise about the kind of machinery and equipment needed for the manufacture of different products.
- **National Small Industries Corporation, New Delhi** — It supplies indigenous as well as imported machinery on hire-purchase basis.
- **State Small Industries Corporations** — They provide indigenous machinery on deferred credit basis.
- **Chief Controller of Imports and Exports, New Delhi** — He issues import licences for machinery of foreign origin on the recommendation of the Directors of Industries.
- **Consultants** — Install machinery as per the layout drawn by them.

VII. *Raw Materials*

- **Development Commissioner, Small-scale Industries, New Delhi** — He procures raw materials for the small industry and distributes them among State Governments. He also arranges imports of raw materials through the Minerals and Metals Trading Corporation and the State Trading Corporation of India.
- **Directors of Industries** — They allot quotas of scarce raw materials.
- **State Small Industries Corporations** — They supply raw materials.
- **Chief Controller of Imports and Exports and His Port Offices** — They issue licences for the import of raw materials.

VIII. *Finance*

- **Small Industries Development Bank of India, Lucknow, 1989** — Small Industries Development Bank of India (SIDBI) has started operations through its 25 offices located in different states of the country. The SIDBI has been set up under an Act of Parliament as the principal financial institution for promotion, financing and development of industry in the tiny and the small-scale sector. The SIDBI is also expected to coordinate the functions of the institutions engaged in similar activities. The SIDBI is a wholly-owned subsidiary of the Industrial Development Bank of India (IDBI). It has taken over IDBI's financing activities relating to the small-scale sector.
- **State Financial Corporations** — They provide long-term credit for the purchase of fixed assets.
- **State Directors of Industries** — They provide loans under State Aid to Industries Act/Rules for block capital.

Agency	Assistance
State Bank of India and its Subsidiaries	They sanction medium-term and instalment credit loans for the purchase of machinery and the construction of factory buildings. They also provide working capital for the purchase of raw materials and meeting other day-to-day requirements.
Commercial Banks	They sanction loans for working capital needs
Small Industrial Service Institutes	They furnish technical reports to Institutes, the State Bank of India on the applicant units.
IX. Technical know-how	
Small Industries Service Institutes	They prepare improved designs and Institute's drawings for products. They assist in making tools, dies, jigs and fixtures. They help in the optimum utilisation of men, materials and machinery. They prepare management control charts for the maximisation of profits. They train managers and supervisors in industrial management. They train workers to upgrade their skill They demonstrate modern technical processes.
National Small Industries Corporation, New Delhi	They give advanced training in their prototype Production-cum-Training Centres in the operation of modern machines.
Council of Scientific and Industrial Research, New Delhi	It develops new technological processes and disseminates the same to the industry.
Productivity Councils	Train factory-owners to increase productivity.
Small Industry Extension Training Institute, Hyderabad	It gives full-time management training to managers/proprietors in the small industry sector.
Central Institute of Tools Designs (CITD) Hyderabad	Specialises in provision of technical consultancy and tool facilities, training in design and manufacture of tools.
Institute for Design of Electrical Measuring Instruments (IDEMI) Mumbai	Provides technical know-how and testing, calibration laboratory, workshop and training facilities to electrical measuring instrument manufacturers.
X. Standardisation	
Small Industries Service Institutes	They provide technical guidance in the production of goods according to prescribed standards.
Indian Standards Institution	It prescribes specifications for the products and issues ISI certification.
Directors of Industries	They prescribe standards and give 'Q' Mark to the small industry's products.
Quality Control	Those in charge provide technical guidance in maintaining the quality of products.
XI. Marketing	
Small Industries Service Institutes	They conduct distribution and surveys for the benefit of small industrialists. They enlist the units for participation in the Central Government Stores/Purchase Programme. They issue competency certificates to the units receiving government orders. They promote ancillary relationships with large and medium-scale units in public and private sectors.
National Small Industries Corporation, New Delhi	It secures contracts from the Director General of Supplies and Disposals, Railways, and Defence Departments for supply of manufactured goods by small-scale units.
State Small Industries Corporations	They secure orders from the State Government and other semi-government organisations for the supply of stores.
XII. Export	
Small Industries Service Institutes	They enlist small units for participation under the Export Aid to Small Industry Scheme of the State Trading Corporation of India. They render technical counselling services for a satisfactory execution of export orders. They disseminate information about the items having export markets. They maintain a close liaison with specialised agencies like the Export Promotion Councils to have up to date knowledge about the products having export markets.
Chief Controller of Imports and Exports, New Delhi	He issues licences for the export of products to foreign countries.
Directorate of Export Promotion, Udyog Bhavan, New Delhi	It collects and supplies information on foreign markets. It carries out market studies for particular products. It publishes Trade Directories, Brochures and Bulletins.
Export Promotion Councils	They organise exhibitions and showrooms. They maintain a close liaison between Indian exporters and foreign buyers. They settle commercial disputes. They frame special export promotion schemes.
State Trading Corporation of India, New Delhi	It registers units for participation under Export Aid to Small Industry Scheme. It helps the small-scale units in the preparation of sales leaflets, price lists, etc. It secures export orders for small industries.
Trade Fair Authority of India, New Delhi	Organises National Small-scale Industries Fairs. Conducts publicity work. Project image of the industry and assists in finding potential markets.
XIII. Inventions	
The Inventions Promotion Board, 39 Ring Road, Lajpat Nagar IV, New Delhi-110 014	It promotes workable inventions of practical utility through financial assistance and other incentives. It produces tools, jigs, fixtures, dyes and moulds.

The Central Institute of Tools Design, Hyderabad.	It trains practicing personnel in the design and manufacture of tools, etc.
XIV. Training	
Small-scale Industries Development Organisation	It trains practicing managers and technologists.
Small Industries Service Institutes	They conduct management courses for senior managerial personnel.
Extension Centres	They conduct regular and *ad hoc* training courses in various technological trades for skilled and semi-skilled workers.
Indian Investment Centre	Conducts regular entrepreneurial development programme courses. Assistance is given to the trainees in the identification of project reports. They are also helped in obtaining the necessary financial assistance from the financial institutions and guidance is also provided up to the stage of trial production.
Small Industry Extension Training Institute (SIET)	Offers training in industrial management and other aspects of small industries development; undertakes feasibility and research studies and collects and disseminates technical information through its Documentation Centre. Under assistance to Young Engineers programme, training is provided through specified agencies and interest subsidy, i.e., difference between interest rate of 7 per cent per annum and the normal rate charged by the financial institutions is provided subject to a maximum of ₹ 20,000 per annum for a period of five years in backward areas and three years in other areas.
National Institute for Entrepreneurship and Small Business Development (NIESBUD)	NIESBUD is an apex body established in 1983 for coordinating and overseeing the activities of various institutes/agencies engaged in entrepreneurship development in the small industry and related business.
XV. Problems	
The Federation of Associations of Small Industries of India, Rohtak Road, New Delhi,	They represent the problems faced by the small industries to the government.
Chambers of Commerce and Industry	They discuss the problems and represent them to the appropriate authorities.
XVI. Monitoring	
The National Alliance of Young Entrepreneurs (NAYE)	It is a national level apex organisation of entrepreneues. It assists in promoting new enterprises through first-generation entrepreneurs. It also monitors the programmes of entrepreneurial development in India.
XVII. Other Voluntary Organisations	Association of Women Entrepreneurs of Karnataks (AWAKE) Women Entrepreneurs Association of Maharashtra (WIMA) Self-employed Women's Association (SEWA) World Association of Small and Medium Enterprises (WASME) National Alliance of Young Entrepreneurs (NAYE) National Association of Software and Service Companies (NASSCO) Consortium of Women Enterprises of India (CWEI), etc.

ANNEXURE

Formalities in Setting up of an Enterprise

1. Identification of project which should be a viable one, i.e., depending on demand and supply of raw materials
2. Preparation of project report
3. If project report is less than ₹ 10 lakh, promoter has to submit three copies of EM – Part-1 form along with scheme, photo and status report. If it is more than ₹10 lakh then the promoter has to file three copies EM – Part-1 along with CAF (combined application form). If project report is less than ₹ 10 lakh but requires shed or government land from IDCO then it has to go through the single window scheme to get all clearances. If project report is more than ₹ 3 crore, then an amount of ₹ 20,000 has to paid towards fees but if it is less than ₹ 3 crore then a sum a ₹ 1,000 is to be paid towards fee charges.
4. All the clearances can be obtained through the single window schemes. A single window scheme has been launched by the government in order to enable the entrepreneurs to get all clearances (nearly 23 clearances) under single window where the Collector is the Chairman.
5. Within three days EM – Part-1 is issued.

8 CHAPTER

ENTREPRENEURSHIP ENVIRONMENT

> *"Entrepreneurship plays a key role in the economic development of a country."*

INTRODUCTION

There have been many attempts to shed light on what makes somebody want to become an entrepreneur, and there is still a widespread idea that entrepreneurs are, by and large, people who drop out of school when they are in their teens, go and invent something in the shed at the bottom of the garden, start a company, and go on to fame and fortune. Clearly, entrepreneurs with this profile do exist, but despite popular entrepreneur folklore, they are very much in the minority.

In fact, the only recipe that stands up to critical examination is that you are more likely to become an entrepreneur if someone in your environment is or has been one, your father for instance, or some other family member.

However, your environment includes more than just your family and so it can also be said that if there is a strong entrepreneurial community where you are brought up — your hometown, or even a cluster of towns in your area — then this can also encourage you to think of becoming an entrepreneur yourself. It's not just a question of icons, or role models; it's more than a matter of entrepreneurship appearing to you in those you see around you as a perfectly normal and widely practiced way of pursuing a career.

In this chapter we discuss the environmental influence on entrepreneur and entrepreneurship.

ENTREPRENEURSHIP ENVIRONMENT

Entrepreneurship environment refers to the various facets within which enterprises — big, medium, small and others have to operate. The enterprise is, therefore, influenced by the environment. By and large, entrepreneurship is influenced by an environment created by political, social, economic, national, legal forces, etc.

> Entrepreneurship environment means total surrounding, which have a direct/indirect bearing on the functioning of business.
>
> Environment means setting of conditions in which a particular activity is carried on.

Entrepreneurial environment is broadly classified into six important segments, namely, (1) Political environment, (2) Economic environment, (3) Social environment, (4) Technological environment, (5) Legal environment, and (6) Cultural environment. (See Fig. 8.1).

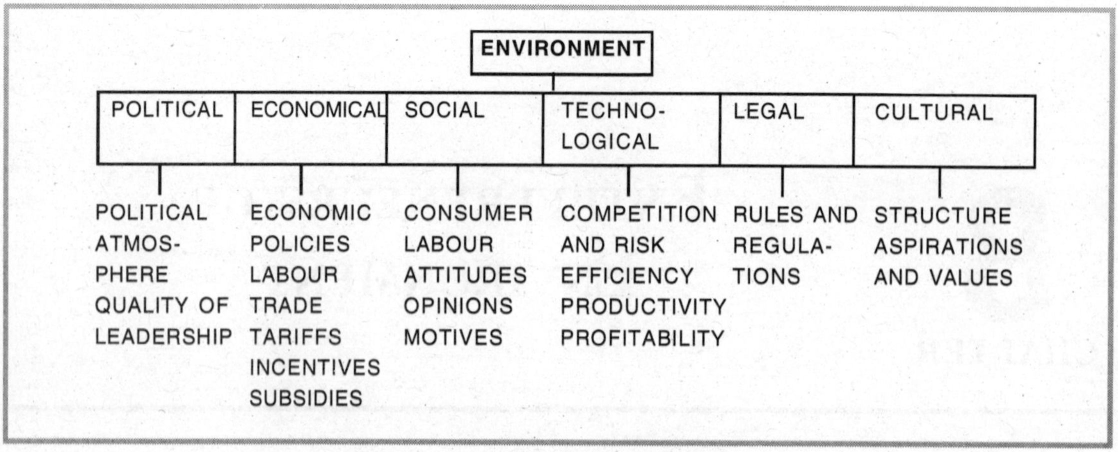

Fig. 8.1: Entrepreneurial Environment

Significance of Entrepreneurial Environment

A study of socio-political and economic environment has a great social and economic significance to the growth of entrepreneurship. Modern business is treated as a social and economic institution and is affected by the political, social and economic forces. The political environment, industrial policy, licensing policy, foreign exchange regulations, banking policy, technological development and social change form the framework within which an enterprise has to work. It is for these reasons that all business plans must be based on the immediate environment. An entrepreneurial plan cannot be framed and finalised for its implementation without its relevance to the political, social, economical and technological requirements. In fact, it is environment which regulates entrepreneurial activities. Business environment has a positive relationship with the development of entrepreneurship.

POLITICAL ENVIRONMENT

Political environment affects the entrepreneurial growth and accelerate the process of economic activity. Law and order is of high priority, followed by Government policies in regard to the promotion of entrepreneurship, followed by incentives, encouragement and right institutional structure will go a long way in fostering entrepreneurship.

Economical Environment

(a) Economic Conditions: The economic conditions of a nation refer to a set of economic factors that have influence on business organisations and their operations. These include gross domestic product, per capita income, markets for goods and services, availablility of capital, foreign exchange reserve, growth of foreign trade, strength of capital market, etc. All these facotrs help in increasing the pace of economic growth.

(b) Economic Policies: All business activities and operations are directly influenced by the economic policies framed by the governmnet from time-to-time. Some of the important economic policies are:

(i) Industrial Policy

(ii) Fiscal Policy

(iii) Monetary Policy

(iv) Foreign Investment Policy

(v) Export Import Policy (EXIM Policy)

The government keeps on changing these policies from time-to-time in view of the development taking place in the economic scenario, political expediency and the changing requirement. Every business firm has to function strictly within the policy framework and respond to the changes therein.

Important Economic Policies

(i) ***Industrial Policy:*** The industrial policy of the government covers all those principles, policies, rules, regulations and procedures, which direct and control the industrial enterprises of the country and shape the pattern of industrial development.

(ii) ***Fiscal Policy:*** It includes govenment policy in respect of public expenditure, taxation and public debt.

(iii) ***Monetary Policy:*** It includes all those activities and interventions that aim at smooth supply of credit to the business and a boost to trade and industry.

(iv) ***Foreign Investment Policy:*** This policy aims at regulating the inflow of foreign investment in varous sector for speeding up industrial development and take advantage of the modern technology.

(v) ***Export-Import Policy (EXIM Policy):*** It aims at increasing exports and bridge the gap between export and import. Through this policy, the government announces various duties/levies. The focus nowadays lies on removing barriers and controls and lowering the custom duties.

(c) Economic System: The world economy is primarily govened by three types of economic systems, viz., (i) Capitalist economy; (ii) Socialist economy; and (iii) Mixed economy. India has adopted the mixed economy system which imples co-existence of public sector and private sector.

SOCIAL ENVIRONMENT

Social environment strongly affect the entrepreneurial behaviour which contribute to entrepreneurial growth. The social factors can be: (i) family background, (ii) kith and kins (relatives, friends and teachers), (iii) religion, (iv) social status, (v) social mobility, and (vi) social marginality.

Family background greatly affects the entrepreneurial environment and maintenance of social system. Joint family or nuclear families have their own benefits and disadvantages. There is more sentimental attachment of family members of joint family as compared to nuclear family. But even in nuclear families, sentimental association or emotional bonds are stronger in India as compared to those in the Western countries where "out of sight out of mind" is the type of attitude of people. In the words of Desai, "the joint family is perhaps the most faithful in which he lays stress on generation depth and sentimental belongingness among the members of the family". The joint family according to him is a three and more generational groups of lineal descendants.

The environment of the family also influences the entrepreneurship. If the father is a professional or a businessman or the like, the son is more likely to adopt the same occupation because of certain inherent advantages by virtue of his father being in the similar line.

The reference also affects the environment. A person is likely to adopt the guidelines or rules of the reference group to which he belongs. The reference group can be church groups, armed services and otherwise, informal circle of friends and relatives. The prospective entrepreneur would discuss his ideas with them and seek their advice while starting a new business.

Similarly, social status has its own role to play. Every human being aspires for a high social status and once he achieves a reasonable level, his aspirations and desires for it start getting multiplied. People, therefore, become quite responsible in the wake of protecting and developing their status. Chester Barnard said that the desire for improvement of status and especially the desire to protect status appears to be the basis of a sense of general responsibilities. People work hard to maintain their status as it also contributes to their entrepreneurial growth.

Caste and religion of entrepreneur are the contributory factors of entrepreneurial growth. History reveals that the entrepreneurial traits do not belong to a specific caste rather the entrepreneurs emerge from varied communities. James Berna conducted a study of 52 medium-scale manufacturing entrepreneurs and found that his firms had mostly grown from small beginnings and his entrepreneurs had come from a wide range of social and economic backgrounds. Many of his entrepreneurs had to face formidable obstacles but their enterprises did grow. But sociologists still claim that caste and religions do have an impact on the environment. For example, Parsis of Maharashtra, Jains of Rajasthan and Gujarat have been the mainsprings of entrepreneurial activity.

Social mobility involves the degree of social and geographical mobility and the nature of mobility channels within a system. There are varied opinions about the influence of social mobility on the entrepreneurial environment. Hoselitz and McClelland's need for openness of a system and flexibility in role relations respectively reveal an imperative role of mobility within a system for entrepreneurship development. Their viewpoint is that high degree of social mobility would help in the emergence of entrepreneurship. But Hagen's belief is that the lack of mobility possibilities promote entrepreneurship. Brozen's emphasis is that the system should neither be too flexible nor too rigid because the former would pull the entrepreneur away from his role and the latter would restrict the entrepreneur. However, social mobility does not work in the system in isolation but there are many other factors which influence the entrepreneurial environment.

Social marginality also positively influences entrepreneurship. Stauworth and Curran stress that a person belonging to a social group traditionally constrained to enter economic activity and barred from many other activities by the society is expected to choose the owner-manager role in a small industry.

TECHNOLOGICAL ENVIRONMENT

Technology represents the application of scientific knowledge for practical purposes. While the 20th century and certainly the 1st half up to 1950 gave us a massive industrial base, shift from agriculture and rural life to urban life, utilisation of energy and power for our benefit, the ongoing progress of technology through R&D efforts have led to more comfortable lifestyles. The last three decades of the 20th century brought in what we call an Information Revolution.

Technological advancement has become a catalytic agent in the promotion of entrepreneurship growth of industrial and allied services. Thomas DeGregori sets forth thirty operational principles demonstrating that technology creates resources and that with intelligent policies in science our society can be sustainable and will continue to invent new resource creating technologies. Conversely, he argues, "living within limits: is a course that, if followed, would lead to certain decline and destruction. The technological impact on agriculture, industry are immence. Further, technology bring in cultural changes as well as the quality of life. Technological development continues to give fillip to entrepreneurship in multi-facet manner, affecting the life of the entrepreneurs as well as the common man. The entrepreneur's endeavour is to stay ahead technologically in products and services with a penchant for quality. This will not only enhance profits, but also maintain balance in the ecosystem.

Next two decades will see a Knowledge Revolution, leading to large-scale adoption of new technologies in India. Most of them will be based on information technology using tools such as computer and mobile phones for processing, storage and transfer of data, internet communication and e-commerce. Many new industries, arising out of application of new technologies, will flourish in countries of Asia, depending on their stage of economic and technological development.

The Knowledge Revolution has made it possible to routinise processes — a shift from the traditional manual control of conventional machinery for using the computer brain to operate the machinery. Computer software is an alternate way to reorganise traditional work processes, through application of overseeing knowledge aided by systematic, logical analysis.

LEGAL ENVIRONMENT

There are various rules and regulations applicable to different groups of industries, for various purposes. Some of them relate to:

Registration, licensing, pollution, location, acquisition, payment of wages and labour related laws, pollution and environmental rules, laws relating to organisation, product, patent, resource and taxes. According to a recent study, there are over 150 legal requirements an entrepreneur has to take care of.

Some legal entity — may be a business, a government agency, or a large non-profit organisation — may well contain in its fold a network of diverse autonomous organisations. The old model of corporations is fast becoming obsolete and is being replaced by new ones. We are witnessing the operation of Schumpeter's doctrine of "creative destruction" in practice. Traditional geocentric way of industrial operations are being replaced by innovative, multi-location industrial operations tapping the synergies of "outsiders" from different countries. This is happening in China and India now; and in countries like Korea, Singapore, Thailand and Malaysia this process began almost a decade or two ago. Indeed Australia, being closely aligned to the Western countries, had the advantage of a headstart.

CULTURAL ENVIRONMENT

Every organisation has an invisible quality — a certain style, a character, a way of doing things — that may be more powerful than the dictates of any one person of a formal system. This invisible quality 'the corporate culture' decides how effective the organisation is in the marketplace. Achieving cultural change to maintain a prime market position is the key preoccupation of every chief executive these days.

Max Weber emphasises that cultural factors have a crippling effect on entrepreneurial growth. Culture consists of: (i) tangible man-made objects like furniture, buildings, etc. (ii) intangible concepts like laws, morals, knowledge, etc. (iii) values and behaviour acceptable within the society. America is a capitalist country, Russia followed a socialist pattern, democracy has no touch in China, but Indian culture encourages democracy and accepts mixed economy. At the time of independence, India was in such a state that the economy could not be left in the hands of people. The government had to intervene and chalk out plans to take the country towards development. Culture of Hindus is to worship 'Ganesha' before undertaking any financial affair. Whether it is a superstition or not is a debatable point. While going on some long journey or on some special days or while tying up a nuptial knot, it is in our culture to seek the recommendations of priests, pandits or sufis.

Catalysing change in corporate cultures by managing people and talent better seems to be the new mantra on the Indian corporate landscape. Better people management is being recognised as the key to sustained success — from managing internal relationships to building corporate cultures that nurture talent. It is no longer enough to be a blue chip IIT-IIM manager, it is equally necessary to update one's EQ to become emotionally engaged with employee and customer need.

Gone are the days when the dictat ran down from the top and the boss's words were carved out in stone. In place of fear and distruct of management policies, is creeping in, slowly but surely, a culture of inclusiveness and openness which starts at the very bottom of the ladder. There is a growing understanding that it is people-driven strategies that sow the seeds of consistent growth.

Hence, there is a growing demand for change managers and culture interventionists who are putting in place a wide range systems and templates which handle issues from employee attrition rates to the business perceptions within the company, to nurturing talent by matching people with the right jobs and bringing in new talent.

And most often these are people who have been associated with that company either as employees and consultants but have since become specialists in one or more areas of change management. Take Ashoke Maitra, former head of Tata Share Registry whose focus is on organisational development and institutional building.

Although he quit the Tata group years ago, today he is mentor to three top MDs and CEOs of the group and is actively coaching them on a one-to-one basis on a wide spectrum from intra-organisation relationships to developing organisational structures. "It is often lonely at the top. There is no one to look up to or discuss things with. Having a mentor helps because he or she is also a sounding board. And it is always better if it is someone who knows the company and its culture."

Besides demographic advantages, other factors that will contribute to the shifts in economic power are cultural traits, lifestyles, new technologies, and globalisation. Demographically young nations capable of efficient absorption and application of new technologies enabling sharper competition in business, will not only thrive, but will emerge as key drivers of globalisation.

The pace of India's ascendancy will be accelerated, when India move up the value chain, supplying high-value products and services in the global market. The emergence of the internet will provide added thrust to the process.

It will be interesting to watch how the Western countries will respond to these changes. How will societies living with their old attitudes adapt to the new environment of changing equations? Will it mean increased tensions between nations on either side of the Digital Divide? Or will it give rise to occasional outbursts of frenzy, like the one we witnessed during two World Wars and later during the Cold War?

Infrastructural Network

It has been argued that the development of industries be preceded by development of agriculture which introduces certain economic changes that culminate in industrial activities. "A developed mass agriculture is normally needed before you can have widespread successful development in other sectors" (Michael Lipton: *Why Poor People Stay Poor?*). But we cannot, perhaps, wait that long till a "developed agriculture sector provides wage goods and savings capacity" needed to support rapid industralisation. If agricultural development does not create savings for industralisation, an industrial development process can be induced by substantial investments on certain selected nucleus industries, leading to a number of ancillary and other related industrial units. This method has gained wide acceptance. But before such nucleus industries are set up in backward areas, necessary infrastructural facilities have to be provided. Even then, the location of these industries may not necessarily lead to a development process in which the poor people of backward areas whose development is the real development area successfully participate — unless the choice of nucleus industries is such that it can utilise the available skills and capacities of a large number of small artisans or farmers. Otherwise, the entrepreneurial opportunities thrown up by such nucleus industries will be exploited by affluent entrepreneurs from outside who have the capacity to invest. It has been seen that entrepreneurs from developed areas have normally gravitated towards these backward areas which are *contiguous* to developed business centers with a view to availing themselves of the incentives and concessions. But such enterprises have not created any economic impact on the people of the backward areas except, perhaps, creating some negligible employment avenues.

It is, therefore, very important to ensure that the infrastructural facilities created to pave the way for nucleus industries are extended to cover a vast multitude of small artisans or farmers whose products can be processed in the nucleus industries. "An integrated infrastructural programme geared to the needs of small-holder farms and small-scale enterprises is the best means of promoting both types of productive activity." (J. Muller: *Promotion of the Manufacture of Rural Implements in the United Republic of Tanzania*). For example, if there are a number of small dairy farmers, a central refrigeration plant can serve all the farmers in the area by an active network of communication. As a result, each farmer can get the benefit of an assured market and an enhanced income. If a large number of farmers are producing soyabean, a central soyabean processing unit would serve as ideal nucleus plant. Such a step would not only integrate agricultural development with industrial development, it would also bring about a pervasive growth of both. On the other hand, if a unit manufacturing some sophisticated machinery is the nucleus plant, its ancillaries would also need the precision or sophistication which will not be possible to achieve within the capabilities of the target-beneficiary group whom we want to develop through the development of backward areas. As Paul Streeten has said, "Industry should produce consumer goods required by the people, the majority of whom live in the countryside, hoes and simple power-tillers and bicycles, not airconditioners or expensive cars and equipments. Much of the recent criticism of inefficient, high cost industrialisation behind high walls of protection and quantitative restrictions should be directed at the types of product and technique which cater for a highly unequal income distribution and reflect entrenched vested interests" (Paul Streeten: "Industrialisation in a United Development Strategy", *World Development,* January, 1975). Actually the production of simple goods depends on the character and potential of a particular backward area; and the essential infrastructure so developed that it would be capable of sustaining active linkages between the subsidiary units in the villages and the central unit.

Environmental Analysis

This integrated approach which is the key to the development of backward areas implies a very careful environment analysis or research study of the target groups of beneficiaries, their activities and differential needs; and the practical modes of operation by which their activities can be linked with the covering enterprise. Unless these studies are made meticulously, the entire planning will only give unproductive results. Most of the development schemes fail to benefit the target clientele because elaborate linkages are not identified and built up. An imaginative study should —

1. Identify the beneficiaries or target groups;
2. Analyse the environment for immediate feasible enterprises in an integrated manner;
3. Delineate the linkages and institutional arrangements;
4. Recommend appropriate organisational structures to provide necessary promotional support.

Unfortunately, in most of the studies on backward areas, there is a tendency to make generalisations and ignore the specific details of really feasible projects. As a result, immediate perception of concrete opportunities by interested entrepreneurs is left in confusion. Sometimes "Area Studies" make a general statement of demand and resources and recommend certain enterprises which are not immediately feasible due to important reasons unaccounted for in such studies. It is also not seriously contemplated whether the recommended enterprises are feasible within the capabilities and investment capacity of the target-group. In short, most of the studies fail to discern the real issues of growth in the target area and fail to identify the concrete and specific needs of these endowments like resource, skill, etc., to flourish. Enunciation of general objectives and generic beneficiaries tend to blur the distinct contours of one homogeneous group from the other. Also, the extension of certain standard facilities or services does not serve their actual needs. All this possibly happens because in such basic studies, we fail to identify clearly the target-groups and their specific problems, and make theoretical studies on resources and demand in an impersonal manner, as a result of which even the schemes devised on the basis of such studies tend to become too impersonal and rigid. Sometimes, the schemes become so inflexible on account of a standardised petrified approach that in some most genuine cases demanding a certain departure from the fixed framework, the scheme is incapable of giving requisite help. It is, therefore, absolutely necessary that any action plan for a backward area must first identify the target-group, identify the specific services they need for monitoring their enterprises and devise an appropriate structural support for comprehensive coverage of their needs.

CONCLUSION

Entrepreneurship, therefore, will flourish only under the right atmosphere said to be conducive to the social, political and economic issues. Even though the urge to excel others and to create something new is inborn and psychologically oriented in the larger analysis, this urge to excel others will fail to obtain the full freedom of expression unless the right environment is available. Entrepreneurial environment, therefore, a high awareness of incorporates existing potentials and enough source of capital is available, and also where there are sufficient number of individuals and institutions which provide adequate help and advice for the establishment and growth of industrial enterprises.

Thus, since entrepreneurship involves a complex of economic and social behaviour, it can only survive where conditions are ideal in terms of political, economic, social and ethical concerns, and when economic changes are free from restraints — for the benefit of all concerned.

An integrated approach to backward area development requires a unified administrative machinery itself animated by a passion for distributive justice. And in no small measure, the proselytising entrepreneurial zeal of the deprived and the down-trodden is a reflection of that passion.

9

CHAPTER

ENVIRONMENTAL POLLUTION ACTS

INTRODUCTION TO ENVIRONMENTAL PROBLEMS

The differences in economic activities may be partly explained by the interaction between man and his environment. Although physical environment does not, absolutely determine the character of economic life, it does exercise a control over it which is more apparent in integrated development. Environment offers certain opportunities which man may or may not utilise. His abilities in exploiting the resources of the environment depend upon their knowledge, intelligence and culture as well as on the social structure of the country they live in. The environment and human ability together determine the economic growth of the country.

The environment is considered an integral part of planning, policy framing and development. It plays a crucial role in economic planning, improving productivity, growth and above all, in maintaining the ecological balance as it affects each segment of our economic and social life. In recent years, the planners and economists have focussed their attention on the environment, moreso on the acute environmental problems and this becomes clear only if the concern for environmental protection is understood in its proper context.

Corporate concern for the environment is not merely a social obligation, or a fashionable 'flavour-of-the-month' recipe to which lip service needs to be paid, but a hard core business proposition. What is required, therefore, is a change in the mindset of corporate managers today, and an understanding of business and environment on the part of graduate students undergoing business education. After all, on them rests the responsibility to manage growth and development in a sustainable world – one in which future generations are not left to pay the price for the follies committed by their forebears. Whilst environmentalists the world over are concerned about the gross inequities being perpetrated and are quite radical in their approach to the problem, corporations need to imbibe a more rational approach which balances the need for environmental preservation on the one hand, with concern for economic development and business viability on the other.

National Environmental Policy

Life owes its existence and obtains its sustenance, growth and fulfilment from the environment which is the product of complex and dynamic interactions of physical, chemical, biological and social systems. The quality of life is linked with the quality of environment. Man is continuously altering the environment to satisfy his needs and aspirations. Nature has, however, finite capacity to accommodate such changes without degradation. Pressures of the growing population and technological capacities often inflict undesirable and irreversible changes, outstripping nature's regenerative capacity. In many cases, these have adversely support systems. Conservation and improvement of the environment are vital for the survival and well-being of man. National resources of land, air and water have to be used wisely as a trust to ensure a healthy environment for the present and future generations.

Environmental pollution in many cities and larger towns has been increasing rapidly. Pollution affects river water and land, besides polluting air and posing health risks to the inhabitants. Industrial units contribute to pollution through solid wastes, liquid effluents and gases. The inappropriate handling of industrial wastes creates problems for the human and the natural environment. Increasing industrialization without proper treatment of effluents has been considered a major cause of pollution. Further, poor working conditions in the SSIs are often the cause of occupational health hazards. Small industries tend to cause more pollution due to inefficient production methods, inferior equipment, poor housekeeping and the inability to adopt proper treatment technologies. In order to encourage cleaner production, the Government of India extends incentives like custom duty waiver, soft loans, etc., and provides other concessions for installation of pollution control equipment in industrial units.

The National Environment Policy (NEP) must ensure effective and judicious use of resources-natural, man-made and human – to meet the needs of the population without undermining the carrying capacity of the environment or pre-empting future choices. The Government of India, therefore, had resolved that the objectives of the National Environmental Policy shall be to:

(i) Conserve and develop a safe, healthy, productive and aesthetically satisfying environment.

(ii) Upgrade, develop and manage rural and urban settlements to enhance the quality of life.

(iii) Plan development on sound ecological principles with environmental impact assessments and incorporating appropriate environmental safeguards.

(iv) Promote environmental safety technologies, recycling of resources and utilization of wastes.

(v) Conserve the biotic diversity in the country by creating nature reserves and sanctuaries for specific habitats such as mountains, rain, forests, pastures, deserts, wetlands, lakes, beaches, mangroves, estuaries, lagoons and islands.

(vi) Safeguard the environment within the national maritime Exclusive Economic Zone.

(vii) Evolve environmental norms and establish effective mechanisms for monitoring surveillance and collection and dissemination of information.

(viii) Preserve scenic landscapes and cultural monuments and their environs.

(ix) Promote environmental education at all levels and create public awareness.

(x) Encourage research of environmental sciences and technological and social investigations to conserve and improve the environment.

(xi) Develop adequate manpower within the country of ecologists, environmental scientists, planners and managers of the highest quality and recognise their work as an important component of national development.

Environmental problems in India can be classified into two broad categories:

(a) Those arising from conditions of proverty and underdevelopment, and

(b) Those arising as negative effects of the very process of development.

The first category has to do with the impact on the health and integrity of our natural resources (land, soil, water, forests, wild-life, etc.) as a result of poverty and inadequate availability, for a large section of our population to fulfil basic human needs (food, fuel, shelter, employment, etc.). The second category has to do with the unintended side effects of efforts to achieve rapid economic growth and development. In this, the latter category would fall on the distortions imposed on national resources from poorly planned development projects and programmes as well as from lack of attention to long-term concerns by commercial and vested interests. Thus, it is clear that a concern for environment is essentially a desire to see that national development proceeds along rational sustainable lines.

India's focus on industrial progress has apparently consumed unlimited resources of air and water, which play a vital role in industrial processing. They bring about the necessary chemical and physical transformations required for converting the raw materials into products and for product separation, isolation and purification in downstream processing.

The residuals of the manufacturing activities together with the undesired products of side reactions and chemical intermediate constitute the three principle categories of industrial wastes – process waste water, atmospheric emission, sludges and solid residues. These contribute to the problems of water pollution, air pollution and solid waste management problems of the industries.

While it is generally acknowledged that the generation of some wastes or residuals is inevitable in any industry, it is necessary to utilise the available resources in an effective integrated manner for multi-product activities. This will minimise the total quantum of process residuals.

Industries are now engaged in implementing waste minimisation strategies through better plant operation, process modification and by-product development through recovery and reuse schemes. In addition to these, recent world wide developments targeted towards a cleaner process technology to reduce the pollution potentials have also been adopted. Environmental management and pollution control pose a major concern to all.

State of the Environment

At present, pollution of air, water, land, noise, radiation and odour affect the quality of life in India. Most of the environmental and ecological problems are mainly due to the pressure on land and adoption of technology which releases effluents in a larger quantity than nature can neutralise by physical, chemical and biological processes without losing the ecosphere's equilibrium. For example, the petrochemical technology has become a menace to environmental stability since their effluents are invulnerable to enzyme attack and are thus inherently bio-non-degradable. Similarly, chemical fertilisers and other modern industries have been adding various oxides affecting the health of the living species.

Environmental Protection Laws

Environmental pollution as a subject matter of legislation did not find a place in the Indian law books until as late as 1974. Prior to 1974, the only recourse available to citizens against pollution of any nature was under the provisions of the Indian Penal Code. Suits claiming damages for tortuous liability were also possible. However, there was nothing in the nature of regulatory or preventive enactments as far as environmental pollution was concerned. All that the law provided for was to proceed under civil or criminal law after the damage to environment took place.

The procedural requirements of a regular civil court made relief very difficult. Very often cases were lost on account of mere procedural and technical irregularities. It was only in the year 1974 that the Water (Prevention and Control of Pollution) Act, 1974 was enacted. Then came the Water (Prevention and Control of Pollution) Act, 1977, the Air (Prevention and Control of Pollution) Act, 1981.

Until 1981, the legislation with regard to environmental pollution were drawn up piecemeal. Moreover, even these legislations were only punitive in nature and not preventive. Whatever little regulatory measures were provided for in the laws were never implemented. There was no clear demarcation of powers of the various authorities under the Acts and this often led to further confusion.

The Environmental (Protection) Act, 1986, was the first comprehensive legislation with regard to environmental pollution. It evoked encouraging response and support from all environmental groups. It was widely acclaimed as the first legislation to tackle the problem of pollution. But the Act itself was a major disappointment as it was not very comprehensive in its scope and was not provided with sufficient powers to effectively bring to book offenders and control environmental pollution.

There are two major statutes that govern water and air pollution control. The majority of SSI units in the country do not fall within the ambit of these pollution control laws. However, certain highly polluting industries are required to obtain a No Objection Certificate (NOC) prior to establishing a unit, even in the SSI sector.

The Water (Prevention and Control of Water Pollution) Act, 1974:

The Act applies to all establishments discharging effluents into water or on land. A unit while making the project report is required to meet pollution control requirements and obtain an NOC (from the State Pollution Control Board) before setting up the unit. The effluents so discharged have to be managed at all times or else there are penalty provisions under the Act for violations. Further, the unit is not permitted to install any new or altered outlet for discharge of effluents/ sewage into a stream or well, without prior consent of the Board. In a major initiative to reduce industrial waste pollution, the Government of India in partnership with the World Bank (WB), Washington, has launched an Industrial Pollution Control Project for assisting clusters in setting up common effluent treatment plants.

The Air (Prevention and Control of Pollution) Act, 1981:

The Act applies to all industries, which have to declare air pollution control points and install necessary equipment. At the time of making the project report, provision has to be made for pollution control requirements and an NOC is to be obtained before establishing the unit. During operation of the unit, discharges into the air are to be managed within prescribed standards at all time, failing which penalty provisions will be applicable.

Environmental Measures in SSIs

Specific attempts have been made to liberalize environmental laws wherever possible as applicable to small-scale industries. In fact, except for 17 categories of polluting industries in other areas, small-scale industries have only to file a memorandum of information which will serve the purpose of consent.

Specific areas where measures for pollution control are urgently required to be taken in the small-scale sector were identified. These are dye-stuffs, pesticides formulation, storage batteries, lead oxides, reclamation of used lubricating oils, manufacture of chromic acid, sodium dichromates, chrome pigments, basic chrome, chrome sulphates acid-slurry and blown bitumen. A paper of pollution control on safely aspects of synthetic detergent industry was prepared for circulation. Similarly, the areas have been identified for energy conservation that include design improvements in the boilers attached to different chemical groups of industries, improved design for evaporation/distillation process and improved design for ball mill/grinding equipment for paint industry.

There is environmental awareness among thc small-scale industries and are acting thereupon within the available resource at their disposal.

Environmental Action

Liberalisation of Industrial Licensing Policy has necessitated greater attention being paid to environmental related issues of industrial development both because of resultant increase in industrial activity and freedom being given to entrepreneurs for location of industrial enterprises. Suitable measures are required to be taken to abate industrial pollution and for conservation of natural resources though promoting suitable technologies.

Following actions have been/are being taken with respect to environment:

1. Monitoring of pollution control measures being undertaken by different industries.
2. Ensuring adherence to environmental guidelines issued by the Ministry of Environment for location of industries wherever applicable.
3. Efforts are being made to introduce the concept of Common Effluent Treatment Plant in industrial estates developed by the State Government. One such cluster approach has been successfully executed in Ambur, Tamil Nadu. More such clusters are being taken up in Vaniyambadi, Ambur, etc.
4. An Inter-departmental Fuel Efficiency Committee has already worked out fuel efficiency standards for the various industrial sectors including the automobile industries.
5. Based on the recommendations of the Inter-departmental Task Force headed by Department of Industrial Development, the National Strategy on Phasing out of Ozone Depleting Substance has been formulated by the Ministry of Environment.

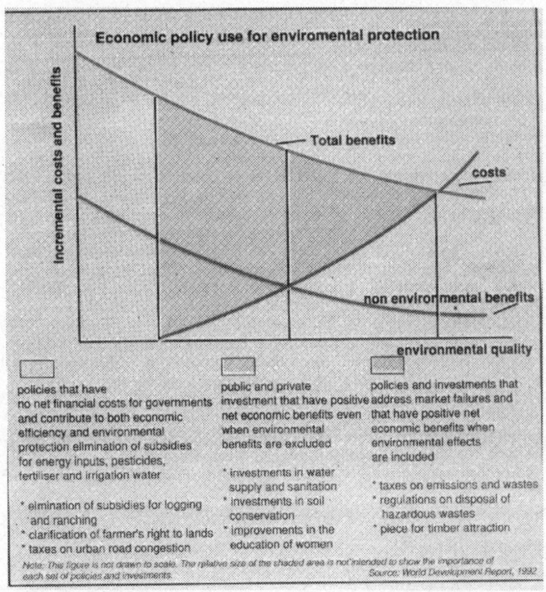

6. National Productivity Council (NPC), an autonomous organisation under this department, has pioneered significant steps in the field of pollution, prevention and control especially in the small and medium scale industries. NPC provides pollution control and prevention services to the small-scale industries.

Approach to Pollution Control

Measures needed for prevention of pollution include: (i) policy approach, emphasising regulations for use of less polluting materials, introducing clean technologies and recycling of waste streams either on site or as a useful by-product, (ii) technical assistance approach, emphasising training, technology transfer and development, and (iii) financial assistance approach, support for fulfilling environmental conditions and technical incentives for research and development facilities.

For controlling the level of pollution in the SSI sector, support is needed both from the Government as well as from the NGOs in the matter of: (i) raising awareness of risks, occupational health and pollution, and providing training at enterprise level, (ii) providing representation to Industries Association in the policy formulation committees to fill the gap between policy level and enterprise level co-operation, and (iii) co-ordination of environmental policy incentives and programmes for a sustained development.

POLLUTING UNITS

Over 9,000 industrial units in Delhi have been notified by the Central Pollution Control Board (CPCB) to be shifted out of Delhi, in compliance with the Supreme Court order of March 24, 1995. Most of these are small-scale units, employing locals.

Pollution is undoubtedly a major problem, which concerns all. But while dealing with a problem which involves the livelihood of lakh of people, the human angle should always be kept in mind. Logically, first of all, these small units should not have been allowed to come up. Again, the units which were set up before the master plan for Delhi came into force should have been asked to shift their activities to safer places, but these were not done.

The Green Arm of the Law

Three important Indian legislations presently enjoin the industry to remain within the pollution control standards set by the Government:

1. Water (Prevention and Control of Pollution) Act, 1974, with amendments made in 1988:

- Following the 1988 amendments, permission is necessary to set up any industry which is 'polluting' – one that uses or discharges any poisonous, noxious or polluting matter. Standards must be those set by state pollution boards. Industries set up prior to the amendment need to obtain clearance within three months of its coming into force.
- State pollution control boards (PCBs) have the power to obtain information regarding the construction, installation or operation of any process of the industry.
- After the 1988 amendments, the PCBs can issue directions or order for closure or stoppage of electricity or water supply, if standards are not being met by the polluting industry.
- Penalties for not-compliance have been increased to ₹ 10,000 for defaulting and ₹ 5,000 per day for continued default.

Environmental Statement

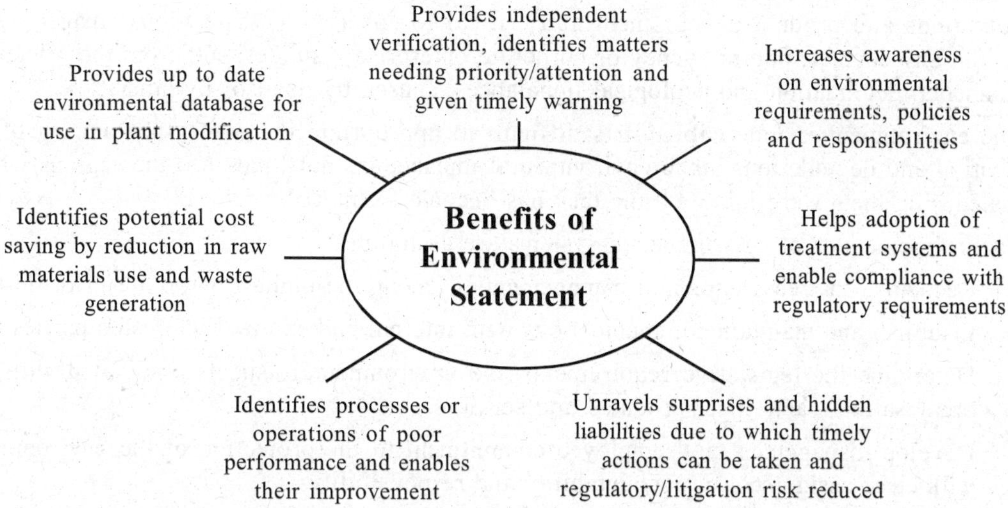

2. Air (Prevention and Control of Pollution) Act, 1981, with 1987 amendments:

- The definition of air pollutant was extended from harmful solid, liquid or gaseous substances present in the atmosphere to include noise pollution.
- Unlike the practice earlier, now all air polluting industries must have the sanction of their respective PCBs.
- After amendments, powers have been given to PCBs to issue directions which include the closure, prohibition, stoppage of electricity, etc., for violation of standards set.
- Penalties are as those in the Water Act.

3. Environment (Protection) Act (EPA), 1986:

- The Central Government has the power to take all such measures as it deems necessary or expedient for protecting the environment.
- Section 3 of EPA empowers the Central Government to: (a) restrict areas in which any industry, operations, process or class of industries can be carried out under certain safeguards; (b) lay down procedures and safeguards for the prevention of accidents which may cause environmental pollution and remedial measures for them; (c) lay down procedures for handling hazardous substances; (d) examining manufacturing process and materials, and (e) widespread inspection powers.
- As in the other two Acts, the EPA gives the Centre wide powers to direct closure, prohibition and regulation of any industry if it contravenes the provisions of the Act.
- In addition, the Marpol Convention, pertaining to marine pollution control, was drawn up by the International Maritime Organisation, a United Nations agency, and ratified by India in 1978.
- The five annexures of this convention deal with: prevention of oil pollution; prevention of pollution by noxious liquid substances in bulk; prevention of pollution by noxious packaged substance; pollution from sewage and from garbage.
- The Indian Government has ratified only the first two annexures. Thus, a vessel can be penalised for oil or chemical pollution. But the remaining forms of pollution go unchecked.

The ecological environment of business is slowly but surely emerging as an important factor in the decision making process of corporate enterprises. It will become central to cost considerations and product development and critical to ensure access to global markets. No longer can any country, public agency or corporate enterprise insulate itself from the effects of environmental degradation and ecological imbalances, caused by itself or by others.

The environment is indivisible. It is difficult to appropriate the ownership or cost of its exploitation and degradation. Since environmental impacts are not limited to the regions where actions causing them were initiated, the task has become formidable.

The key principles of environmental systems are as follows:

- Recognise that environmental management is among the highest corporate priorities.
- Establish and maintain communications with internal and external interested parties.
- Determine the legislative requirements and environmental aspects associated with the organisation's activities, products and services.
- Develop management and employee commitment to the protection of the environment, with clear assignment of accountability and responsibility.
- Encourage 'cradle-to-grave' environment strategic planning, i.e., throughout the product or process life cycle.
- Establish disciplined management process for achieving targeted performance levels.
- Provide appropriate and sufficient resources, including training to achieve targeted performance levels on an ongoing basis.
- Evaluate environmental performance against appropriate policies, objectives and targets, and seek improvement where appropriate.
- Establish a management process to review and audit the EMS and to identify opportunities for improvement of the system and resulting environmental performance, and
- Encourage contractors and suppliers to establish an EMS (Environment Management System).

Environmental Clearance Procedures

Under the Environment (Protection) Act, 1986, 24 categories of projects and industries require environmewntal clearance from the Central Government. In addition, any project proposed to be located within 10 kms of the boundary of a reserved forest or a designated ecologically sensitive area or within 25 kms of the boundary of a national park or sanctuary require environmental clearance from the Central Government. For all other projects, environmental clearance need to be obtained from the State Government. Clearance is required from the environmental (for site clearance) and pollution control angle, which has to be obtained by all units other than certain specified non-polluting units in the small-scale sector. No Objection Certificate for the site clearance usually involves clearance from the concerned State Pollution Control Board. NOC is also required for adequacy of pollution control measures. In general, the State Pollution Control Board is the authority concerned which usually specifies certain pollution control measures to be taken by the unit.

The Environment Rules

1. Apply to the Union Ministry of Environment and Forests for obtaining a pollution clearance certificate.
2. Obtain a No Objection Certificate from the office of the State Pollution Control Board.
3. Provide a copy of the Project Report to the State Pollution Control Board.
4. Provide a copy of the Risk Analysis Report to the Union Ministry of Environment and Forests.
5. Submit a comprehensive rehailitation programme to the Ministry if more than 1,000 people will be displaced.
6. Provide evidence of water-supply connection to the Ministry.
7. Provide evidence of electricity connection to the Ministry.
8. Submit Form XIII for the consent of the Ministry to establish an industrial unit under the Water (Prevention and Control of Pollution) Act, 1974.
9. Submit Forms I and XII for the consent of the Ministry to establish and operate an industrial unit under the Air (Preventíon and Control of Pollution) Act, 1981.
10. Provide evidence of installing an Effluent Treatment Plant (ETP) on the factory premises to the Ministry.
11. Provide a chart of the manufacturing process to the Ministry.
12. In case the industrialist is an importer of environment-sensitive items, apply to the DGFT for an import-licence.

Environment Management

The small-scale sector which accounts for a significant portion of the total industrial production in the country is yet to adopt pollution control measures on a significant scale. Environment management has, therefore, been identified by the Bank as a thrust area for assisting the SSI units in complying with pollution control norms. Taking cognisance of the limitations in ensuring unit-level pollution abatement measures by the small scale units, the route common to treatment facilities is being encouraged especially in case of homogeneous group of units located in clusters.

ISO 14000: Environmental Management Systems

ISO 9000, the corporate *mantra* that has swept India over the last five years has made corporations aware of the quality of products and processes required to attain world-class standards. But not any more... by March 1996, when the ISO 14000 draft for Environmental Management Systems (EMS) superseding the ISO 9000 is expected to be finalised, the mad rush for accreditation under this system will begin. An audit of the corporation's EMS will be essential for exporting to the European Community, NAFTA, APEC, and other trade blocs.

An EMS provides order and consistency to organisational efforts that address environmental concerns through allocation of resources, assignment of responsibilities, and ongoing evaluation of practices, procedures and processes. As enviro management is part of an organisation's overall responsibility, its structure, process, policies and objectives need to be integrated with current efforts in other areas such as operations, finance, quality, marketing, etc.

Image / *Damage*	*Low*	*High*
High	Reactive threat driven	Reactive legislation driven
Low	Discretionary management driven	Reactive communications driven

As in the case of ISO 9000, the ISO 14000 framework has the following components: Commitment and Policy, Planning, implementation, Measurement and Evaluation, Review and Improvement. The key principles for managers, as enumerated in the draft include:

The quality paradigm has helped managers refocus their mindsets from one that viewed defects as an inevitable by-product of the manufacturing process to one that viewed defects as a result of inefficiencies in product and process design. Similarly, the environment paradigm will hopefully refocus managerial mindsets from one that is focussed on pollution control for one that focusses on environment management, by changing over from the view that effort on pollution reduction and prevention adds to costs, slows down progress and makes companies uncompetitive to one that regards pollution as a result of incomplete, inefficient or ineffective use of resources, and enables companies to increase competitiveness by improving their resource utilisation.

CONCLUSION

The entrepreneur's concern for the environment is not merely a social obligation, but a hardcore business proposition. Indian entrepreneurs need to awaken themselves urgently to the environmental imperatives facing them, and integrate environmental perspectives within their business strategies for organisational development. Environment is a key issue of sustained industrial growth.

10 CHAPTER

FINANCIAL MANAGEMENT

> *"Ratios are measurements of business operation results studied over the years. They indicate the trends of an enterprise's financial soundness, growth and intrinsic problems. They also reveal the inter-relationship between various aspects of enterprise operation. In this chapter, we discuss the use of financial analysis as a key to project appraisal as well as its implementation."*

MEANING

Financial Management is that specialised function of general management which is related to the procurement of finance and its effective utilisation for the achievement of common goal of the organisation.

"Financial Management is an area of financial decision making harmonizing individual motives and enterprise goals." **– *Weston and Brigam.***

"Financial Management is the application of the planning and control functions to the finance function." **– *Howard and Upton.***

"Financial Management is the operational activity of a business that is responsible for obtaining and effectively, utilizing the funds necessary for efficient operations." **– *Joseph and Massie.***

From the above definitions, it is clear that financial management is that specialised activity which is responsible for obtaining and effectively utilizing the funds for the efficient functioning of the business and, therefore, it includes financial planning, financial administration and financial control.

Functions

(i) Financial Forecasting. The first and foremost function of financial management is to forecast the financial needs of the concern. In the initial stage, it is done by promoters but later on it is performed by the executive chief or by the officers of the finance department. In estimating the financial requirements of the concern, help of various budgets, i.e., salès budget, production budget, etc., profit and loss account and Balance Sheet is sought.

(ii) Establishing Asset Management Policies. In order to estimate and arrange cash requirements of an enterprise, it is very necessary to decide how much cash will be invested in fixed assets, and also the kind and coverage of insurance that a company will carry. Establishing a sound asset management policy is a pre requisite to successful financial management. The financial manager, in deciding about the asset management policies seeks cooperation of marketing executive in making decisions involving the carrying of inventories of finished goods and credit policy, etc., and that of the production manager in making decision concerned with the carrying of inventories of raw materials and factory supplies, purchases, etc.

(iii) Allocation of Net Profit. How to allocate the net profits of the concern is another problem before the financial manager. After paying all taxes, the available net profits of the concern can be allocated for three purposes: (a) for paying dividends to the shareholders of the company as a return upon their investment. (b) for distributing bonus to the employees; and (c) retention of profits for the expansion of business. As far as the second alternative is concerned, the amount to be paid to employees is generally fixed by statutes or on contractual basis and therefore, there is no problem in allocating profits for that purpose. But a considerable attention is to be paid in so far as first and third alternatives are concerned namely the dividends to be distributed to the shareholders and the amount to be retained for future expansion plans.

(iv) Cash Flow. It is the prime responsibility of the financial manager to see that an adequate supply of cash is available at proper time for the smooth running of the business. A good financial executive should ensure that cash inflow and outflow must be continuous and uninterrupted. Inflow of cash originates in sales and cash outflows or cash requirements are closely related to volume of sales. Here the financial manager is to decided how much cash must retain to meet the current obligations so that there would be no idle cash balance earning nothing for the company. But there is a dilemma because inflow of cash is not precisely predictable and seldom offset one another. Therefore, the financial manager must maintain a balance between inflow and outflow of cash.

(v) Deciding upon Borrowing Policy. Every organisation plans for the expansion of the business for which he requires additional resources. Personal resources being limited, the cash can be arranged by borrowing money either from commercial bank, and other financial institutions or by floating new debentures or by issuing new shares. The financial manager, at this juncture, will take a decision about the time when the funds from outside sources are needed, the source from which they are to be received, how long they will be needed and from what sources they will be repaid.

(vi) Negotiation. Finance function does not stop with the decision to undertake outside financing; it extends towards carrying on negotiations with the outside financing agencies. Finances are needed by an establishment to meet its short-term and long-term requirements. The financial manager must assess short and long term financial requirements of the organisation and start negotiations for raising these funds.

(vii) Checking upon Financial Performance. The financial manager is required to check the financial performance of the funds invested in the business. It requires analysis of the operating period to evaluate the efficiency of financial planning. An unbiased assessment of financial performance shall be great value to the business in improving their standards, techniques and procedures of financial control.

Objectives

(1) Profit maximisation. Maximisation of profits is generally the main objective of a business enterprise. Each company collects its finance by way of issue of shares to the public. Investors in shares purchase these shares in the hope of getting medium profits from the company as dividend. It is possible only when the company's goal is to earn maximum profits out of its available resources. If the company fails to distribute higher dividend, the people will not be keen to invest their money in such firm and persons who have already invested will like to sell their stocks. On the other hand, higher profits are the barometer of its efficiency on all fronts, i.e., production, sales an management.

(2) Return Maximisation. The second goal of financial management is to safeguard the economic interest of the persons who are directly or indirectly connected with the company, i.e., shareholders, creditors and employees. All such interested parties must get the maximum return for their contributions but this is possible only when the company earns higher profits or sufficient profits to discharge its obligations to them.

Financial Planning

Planning is very necessary for the smooth running of the business. Planning means deciding in advance what is to be done. It is a continuous and never ending process. Planning is a preparatory step for action to be followed. According to Kontz O'Donnel planning is "an intellectual process, the conscious determination of courses of action, the basis of decisions on purpose, facts and considered estimates. Planning is done for each functional area of management. Each functional manager plans for his area of management and acts accordingly. The planning of each area should be linked to the objectives of the organisation.

Financial management, being one of the branches of the management also needs planning. Financial planning is necessary for the control of inflow and outflow of cash so that necessary funds may be made available as and when they are required. The highest earnings can be assured only through sound financial plans. A faulty financial plan may ruin the business completely. So, sound financial planning is necessary to achieve the long-term and the short-term objectives of the firm and to protect the interest of all parties concerned, i.e., firm, creditors, shareholders and public.

Financial planning means deciding in advance, the financial activities to be carried on to achieve the basic objective of the firm. The basic objective of the firm is to get maximum profits out of minimum efforts. So, the basic purpose of the financial planning is to make sure that adequate funds are raised at the minimum cost (optimal financing) and that they are used wisely. Thus, planners of financial policies must see that adequate finance is available with the concern, because an inadequate supply of funds will hamper the smooth functioning of an enterprise. A proper planning is therefore necessary.

Capitalisation

The term capitalisation is used only in relation to companies and not in respect of firms or sole-proprietorships. Capitalisation refers to the par value (i.e., face value indicated on the security itself) of the long-term securities (shares and debentures) plus by any reserves which are meant to be used for meeting long-term and permanent needs of a company. 'Capital' includes all the loans and reserves of the concern but 'Capitalization' includes only long-term loans and retained profits besides the capital.

Overcapitalisation

If a company raises more capital (by the issue of shares and debentures and through long-term loans) than is warranted by the figure of capitalisation of its earning power, the company will be said to be overcapitalised. In other words, a company is overcapitalised when its actual profits are not sufficient to pay interest and dividends at proper rates. It means that an overcapitalised company is unable to pay a fair return on its capital investment.

Undercapitalisation

Undercapitalisation is just the reverse of overcapitalisation. It means the condition when a company doesn't have enough cash to carry on its business and pay its creditors capital.

Budgeting

Capital expenditure budget or capital budgeting is a process of making decisions regarding investments in fixed assets which are not meant for sale such as land, building, machinery or furniture.

(a) Capital expenditure plans involve a huge investment in fixed assets.

(b) Capital expenditure once approved represents long-term investment that cannot be reserved or withdrawn.

(c) Preparation of capital budget plans involve forecasting of several years profits in advance in order to judge the profitability of the projects.

It may be asserted here that decision regarding capital investment should be taken very carefully so that the future plans of the company are not affected adversely.

FINANCIAL ANALYSIS

Financial analysis assumed an increasingly important role as a scientific tool for appraising the real worth of an enterprise, its performance during a period of time and its pitfalls. This strategy helps in drawing out the complications of what is contained in the financial statements.

Concept of Financial Analysis

> Finance is the study of funds management. Financial analysis is defined *as the process of discovering economic facts about an enterprise and/or a project on the basis of an interpretation of financial data.*

Financial analysis also seeks to look at the capital cost, operations cost and operating revenue. The analysis decisively establishes a relationship between the various factors of a project and helps in manoeuvring the project's activities. It also serves as a common measure of value for obtaining a clear-cut understanding about the project from the financial point of view.

An analysis of several financial tools provide an important basis for valuing securities and appraising managerial programmes. Financial analysis is vital in the interpretation of financial statements. It can provide an insight into two important areas of management — return on investment and soundness of the company's financial position. David Hawkins observes that the analyst evaluates results against the particular characteristics of the company and its industry. He seldom expects answers from this process; but he hopes that it would provide him with clues as to where he should focus his subsequent analysis.

Internal management accounts provide information which is valuable for the purpose of control. The information is made available in the form of accounting data, which may be manifested as financial and accounting statements. A financial analysis reveals where the company stands with respect to profitability, liquidity, leverage and an efficient use of its assets. Financial reports provide the framework within which business planning takes place. They are the key through which an effective control of a business enterprise is exercised. It is the process of determining the significant financial characteristics of a firm. It may be external or internal. The external analysis is performed by creditors, stockholders and investment analysis. The internal analysis is performed by various departments of a firm.

Financial analysis is the process of obtaining relevant economic information relating to a project for finding out its financial viability.

Key Areas

- Capital and operating costs
- Funds flow
- Cash flow
- Ratio analysis
- Break-even analysis
- Profitability analysis
- Social co-benefit analysis
- Investment process

Scope of Financial Analysis

Financial analysis primarily deals with the interpretation of the financial data incorporated in the proforma financial statements and the presentation of the economic facts in such a form as to make a comparative evaluation/appraisal of projects. In other words, it is mainly concerned with the development of financial profile operational aspects. Its main purpose is to establish whether the project would enable to achieve the objectives for which it is undertaken. For easy and better comparison and explanation, ratio analysis is used. Through the ratios, the relationship between various financial factors of a project is explained and their trend forecasts are developed.

In order to complete the financial profile of a project it is also necessary to evaluate the operational strategy and the investment strategy of the project. The break-even analysis is used to explain the operational characteristics of a project. Financial strategy is evaluated in terms of financial leverage, i.e., debt-equity mix and its effect on financial returns from the project. Theoretically different types of capital structure are available and the ultimate objective is to choose an ideal capital structure, i.e., investment criteria such as IRR, NPV, etc. These project selection criteria depict the net contribution of the project towards the improvement of the economic position of the project implementing body.

Significance of Financial Analysis

Financial analysis primarily deals with the interpretation of the data incorporated in the proforma financial statements of a project and the presentation of the data in a form in which it can be utilised for a comparative appraisal of the projects. It is, in effect, concerned with the development of the financial profile of the project. Its purpose is to find out whether the project is attractive enough to secure funds needed for its various constituent activities and once having secured the funds, whether the project will be able to generate enough economic values to achieve the objectives for which it is sought to be implemented. It deals not only with the financial aspects of a project but also with its operational aspects. As such, it is necessary to undertake such an analysis not only in the case of industrial projects but also in the case of non-industrial projects.

Analysis of financial statements has become very significant due to the widespread interest of various parties in the financial results of a company. In recent years, the ownership of capital of most public companies has become broad-based. A number of parties and bodies, including creditors, potential suppliers, debentureholders, credit institutions like banks, industrial finance corporations, potential investors, employees, trade unions, important customers, economists, investment analysts, taxation authorities and Government have a stake in the financial results of a company. Various people look at the financial statements from various angles. A number of techniques have been developed to undertake analysis of financial statements in order to reach conclusions about the financial health, profitability and efficiency of an enterprise and also to compare an enterprise with other similar undertakings. The technique of ratio analysis is the most important tool of financial analysis. It helps in comparing the performance of various companies and judge their financial soundness.

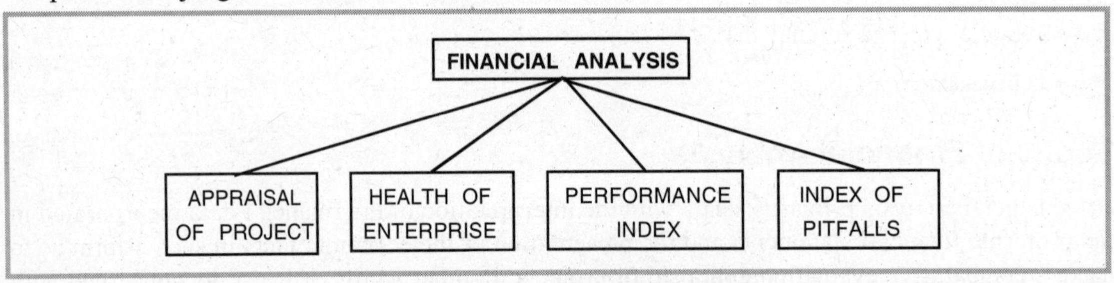

Fig. 10.1: Utility of Financial Analysis

Utility of Financial and Accounting Statements

Financial statements play a vital role in the internal financial control of an enterprise. These should, therefore, be properly constructed, analysed and interpreted by executives, bankers, creditors and investors. The following factors enhance the utility of financial statements:

1. *Large-scale Production:* The ability to analyse financial reports is essential bridging the gap in personal relationships created by the size of business units.

2. *Regulatory Provisions:* Financial statements are often required by Government regulations. Accounting procedures are standardised to obtain correct and adequate data for the construction of financial statements.

3. *Income Tax Accounting:* The income-tax authorities insist on the maintenance of proper and suitable accounting records.

4. *Executives:* Executives need information so that they may be in a position to plan for profits and ensure a sound financial condition for the firm. Financial statements serve the business executive as gauges and charts serve the engineer.

5. *Bankers:* The banker seeks liquidity, but looks upon his debtors not merely as clients but also as ordinary customers. His analysis has, therefore, to be thorough.

6. *Investors:* Whether buying an interest in a firm or purchasing the securities of a corporation, the investor's interest in the enterprise is continued for a number of years.

7. *Mercantile Credit:* Mercantile credit refers to the grant of credit by one merchant to another. The usual object of granting credit is to enable the customer to have sometime in which he many realise his dues on the merchandise he has sold.

The entire future of a company hinges on the manager's ability to decide relevant financial data with a view to planning profit ability moves. Learning to read financial statements is the first essential element in any businessman's attempt to acquire financial management skills. The change in the elitism of stock ownership to broad public ownership has necessitated a concomitant change in the entire process of reporting corporate financial results. The role of management in the matter of preparation of financial statements is to add understanding to these statements, the fairness of which is to be viewed through the eye of the user, while that of the accountant is to close the communication gap and of the auditor to add credibility to them. For evolving a good economic information system, accounting innovations are of great economic information system, accounting innovations are of great importance. Without these, communication with the financial community would be difficult, the interest of present and future potential investors would not be served, the ability of the company to raise additional capital would be impaired and the government's regulatory measures and policies would not serve the best interests of society. Though a financial statement reveals less than it conceals, it provides the indicators of the enterprise's performance during the year.

Financial analysis seeks to spotlight the significant facts and relationships concerning managerial performance, viz., corporate efficiency, financial strengths and weaknesses and creditworthiness of the enterprise.

Financial Tools

Financial tools are of immense use to entrepreneurs in carrying out his planning and controlling functions. The financial tools are helpful to top management, creditors, investors, and labourers. The principal financial tools are:

(i) Trend analysis

(ii) Variable analysis

(iii) Ratio analysis

(iv) Funds flow analysis

(v) Break-even analysis

(vi) Common size statements

(vii) Cash budgetary and

(viii) Proforma statement

Techniques of Financial Analysis

Having estimated the projected capital costs, projected operating costs and operating revenue of a project and presented them in projected financial statements, the next step is to discover the economic facts about the project on the basis of an interpretation of such projected financial data. The objective of the financial analysis is to find out whether the project is attractive enough to secure funds needed for its various constituent activities and once having secured the funds whether the project will generate the benefits to realise the final objective for which it is undertaken. A large number of analystical tools have been developed to assist the process of financial analysis. Some of the tools are described below.

Financial analysis is a continuous process which may be employed to analyse the past and/or future financial position of a firm. In other words, it may be used to interpret the past and/or projected financial data. For the purpose of such analysis the most commonly employed techniques are the funds flow analysis, the cash flow analysis and the ratio analysis. Similarly, the operational strategy can be evaluated by employing the cost-volume-profit analysis.

INTRODUCTION TO RATIO ANALYSIS

> *"Ratio analysis is an invaluable aid to management in the discharge of its basic functions of planning, forecasting, control. It is useful to assess important chracteristics of business like liquidity, solvency, profitability, etc."*

Ratio analysis is a key dimension of financial management, suggesting a relationship between profit and loss as mentioned in the balance sheet of an organisation. Its appropriate use will go towards giving a true picture of the financial health of the unit. Its benefits can be seen in areas of management, production, marketing, personnel management, etc.

An enterprise keeps fit by ensuring that *inter alia*, its various financial proportions are feasible. The absolute accounting figures reported in the financial statements do not provide a meaningful understanding of the performance and the financial position of a firm. These figures convey effective meaning when it is related to some other relevant information.

In assessing the financial stability of a firm, a management should, apart from profitability, be interested in relative figures rather than in absolute figures. In fact, an analysis of financial statements is possible only when figures are expressed as percentages or ratios.

What is Ratio Analysis?

The latin word *'ratio'* stands for reason. In English 'ratio' stands for the relationship.

A ratio shows the arithmetical relationship between two figures. Thus, we can say that the ratio of gross profit to sale is 1:4 or 25 per cent (stated as percentage) or 25. It is obvious that absolute figures do not convey much. Thus, if we say that Co. A made a profit of ₹ 50,000 and Co. B a profit of ₹ 60,000 we cannot automatically conclude that Co. B is more profitable. If we say that Co. A has made a profit of ₹ 50,000 against ₹ 5,00,000 employed as capital, it can be concluded that Co. A is more profitable since its net profit to capital employed ratio is 10 per cent as against 5 per cent of B. Ratios show the relationship between the relevant figures. With their help, we can reach useful conclusions about the performance and financial health of a company.

> Ratio analysis is defined to mean "the establishment of a reasoned relationship" of a fixed variable character between measurements of certain phenomenon having some kind of linkage.

It goes without saying that ratios should be worked out on the basis of figures which are significantly related to each other. For example, the relationship of total debtors to authorised capital will be meaningless but that of total debtors to credit sales definitely is. It will be no use establishing ratios between figures which do not influence one another. It has been suggested by some accounts that in the arrangement of ratios properly, the "more desirable" item should be divided by the one that is "less desirable" so that any favourable change reflects itself by an increase in the ratio. For example, it is more desirable to have more current assets than current liabilities; hence current assets should be divided by current liabilities. This suggestion, however, is not universally accepted. Consequently, there is lack of uniformity in the expression of results; while discussing the ratios, along with name of each ratio, the formula for the ratios also need to be stated.

The ratios are conveniently classified as follows:

(*i*) Balance sheet ratios which deal with the relationships between two items or groups of items which are both in the balance sheet, e.g., the ratio of current assets to current liabilities (Current Ratio).

(*ii*) Revenue Statement Ratios which deal with the relationships between two items or groups of items which are both in the revenue statement, e.g., ratio or gross profit to sales, or gross profit margin.

(*iii*) Balance Sheet and Revenue Statement Ratios which deal with relationships between items from the revenue statement and items from the balance sheet, e.g., ratio of net profit to own funds (Composite Ratios).

(*a*) Revenue Statement Ratios:

- (*i*) Gross Profit Ratio.
- (*ii*) Operating Ratio.
- (*iii*) Expense Ratio.
- (*iv*) Net Profit Ratio.
- (*v*) Stock Turnover or Turnover of Inventory.

(*b*) Balance Sheet Ratios:

- (*i*) Current Ratio or Working Capital Ratio.
- (*ii*) Liquidity Ratio or Quick Asset Ratio or Acid Test.
- (*iii*) Debt to Equity Ratio.
- (*iv*) Asset to Equity Ratio.

(*c*) Composite Ratios:

- (*i*) Return on Total Resources.

(*ii*) Return on Own Funds.

(*iii*) Turnover of Fixed Assets.

(*iv*) Turnover of Debtors.

Advantages of Ratio Analysis

1. The process of producing financial ratios as observed by Lee, is concerned with the identification of the significant accounting data relationships which give the decision makers insights into the company being assessed.
2. A ratio analysis involves a study of the total financial picture. By basing conclusions upon a thorough understanding of the importance of each ratio, the analyst can recommend and indicate positive action with confidence.
3. One of the most fruitful areas for the use of traditional financial ratios seems to be that of predicting company failures.
4. Ratios enable the company's management to analyse business situations and to monitor their performance as well as that of their competitors.
5. Ratio analysis helps the management to diagnose the situations, monitor the performance and chalk out future plans of the company.
6. There are certain priority ratios for the chief executives into key areas which are common to nearly all business and with which the top management is seriously concerned with. These priority ratios enable the chief executives to understand the relationship between his organisation, at one end, and the market, investors, suppliers and employees, at the other. He is also in a position to watch how well is the organisation using its assets and how well it is providing for the future.
7. There are ratios which help the marketing manager, the purchase manager, the financial manager and others representing the middle management to know what the positions are like and how to find a way out in typical situations from time to time.

Limitations

1. Erich Helfert has pointed out that it is essential for a person analysing business performance to have a clear awareness of the tests he should apply and the specific reasons for which he should apply them. Temptation arises in financial ratio analysis to run all numbers, yet select only a few relationships which would provide clues for judgement.

2. Industry ratios pose a more difficult problem to the financial analyst because of the following reasons:

(*a*) It is difficult to determine the industry to which a company belongs.

(*b*) The whole emphasis of the system of accounting is on consistency rather than profitability among different companies at a single point in time.

3. There is clearly some latitude for window-dressing. Within limits, a company may be able to arrange its current assets and liabilities so as to have the desired ratios at the time the balance sheet is presented to stockholders.

4. Financial standard data are not exact, and have, therefore, to be treated with great caution.

5. The valuation contained in the final statements does not represent the actual position because it is based on the assumption that the financial statement presents a reasonable picture of what is happening in the business. The information relates only to a particular period and cannot be relied upon excessively. The ratios refer to past events and may not represent the present or future events.

6. Financial statements are generally based on historical or original cost. The current economic conditions are ignored.

7. V.V. Desai points out that the advancing artistry of the technique of ratio analysis has miserably failed to accomplish the expected impeccability or immaculacy. Moreover, it has made the technique more complicated and complex far beyond the understanding of ordinary businessmen.

8. Not all ratios and percentages are significant and useful. One should beware of the temptation to calculate them for their own sake.

9. R.H. Parkar is of the opinion that the limitations of conventional accounting should always be kept in mind and that accounting figures should not be treated as more precise than they really are.

10. A ratio is of little value in isolation. It is necessary to have some standard with which to compare it. The standard may be a budgeted one. It may be set by a company. It may be a historical one. It may be based on the past performance of the company. It may be based on industry comparison.

11. In using ratios computed by others, one should realise that the computation of a particular ratio has not necessarily been standardised.

12. A frequent comparison of ratios between companies is questionable, particularly when there are important differences between companies, such as industry, nature of operations, etc.

13. Most ratios represent averages and, therefore, may tend to obscure large variations in the underlying causative factors above and below the average.

14. Ratios are based on financial statements and suffer from the limitations inherent in these statements.

15. Changes in many ratios are closely associated or connected with one another.

16. While comparing the size of a ratio during the current period with the corresponding ratio during a previous period, it is possible that the conditions, during the two periods may have changed; for example, product lines, markets, economic conditions, prices, etc.

17. While comparing the ratios of a particular firm with those of similar firms, the differences between the firms should be recognised; for example, methods of accounting operations and financing.

18. Not many results of financial statement analysis can be used by themselves as direct indications of good or poor management. Such analysis merely indicates probabilities or matters which might be investigated further. Davidson, Schindler, Stickney and Weil have pointed out that ratios derived from financial statements should be combined with an investigation of facts before valid conclusions can be drawn.

19. Ratios are likely to be misused. There are some situations in which they may appear to be misleading.

20. Westwick observes that ratios need the upper and lower warning lines because in most cases they have an optimum level.

21. Ratios are mathematical but this does not ensure that they are useful because the mathematical process does not attest to the fundamental relationship between the two factors in the computation. Unfortunately, everyone does not understand this fundamental fact and some financial ratios which have been advocated may have little or no value.

22. A ratio analysis is a guide rather than a solution to the present problems and future plans. It is not possible to suggest absolute ratios for a firm, which makes it imperative to consider issues as competition, financial resources and objectives of a company.

Quantitative Approach

Ratio analysis may be defined as "the establishment of a reasoned relationship" of a fixed or variable character between measurements of certain phenomena having some kind of linkage. It is not confined to the four walls of financial management. There are vast and fruitful opportunities for its application to production (operations), marketing, personnel and general management.

The quantitative approach to management has manifested itself mainly in three forms:

(i) the theory of probability and other branches of statistics;

(ii) operations research; and

(iii) applications of mathematics to economics, psychology, sociology and other behavioural studies having their bearing on decision-making, commercial viability or managerial efficacy of various types of entities.

Various factors have added to the significance of quantitative approach in management:

(i) tremendous increase in the quantum of activity;

(ii) technological change;

(iii) needed fineness in the process of comparison;

(iv) need for a computerised capsule approach;

(v) emphasis on objectivity in decision-making; and

(vi) call for greater conviction through the language of numbers.

Among the limitations of quantitative approach are:

(i) unreal assumptions;

(ii) an excuse for not existing common sense;

(iii) vast scope for window-dressing in accounting/manipulation of financial ratios; and

(iv) phoney relationships not based on any significant linkage.

Classification and Significance of Financial Ratios

Financial Ratio Analysis (FRA) is a quantitative technique for assessing the financial health of a unit from the accounting data. FRA helps to describe the significant relationship between two comparable figures in the financial statements.

Ratios need to be interpreted:

(i) to decide the perspective from the point of view of the shareholder, management, creditor, labour and the government.

(ii) to compare with norms/budget, previous year's figures, industry average, inter-firm comparison.

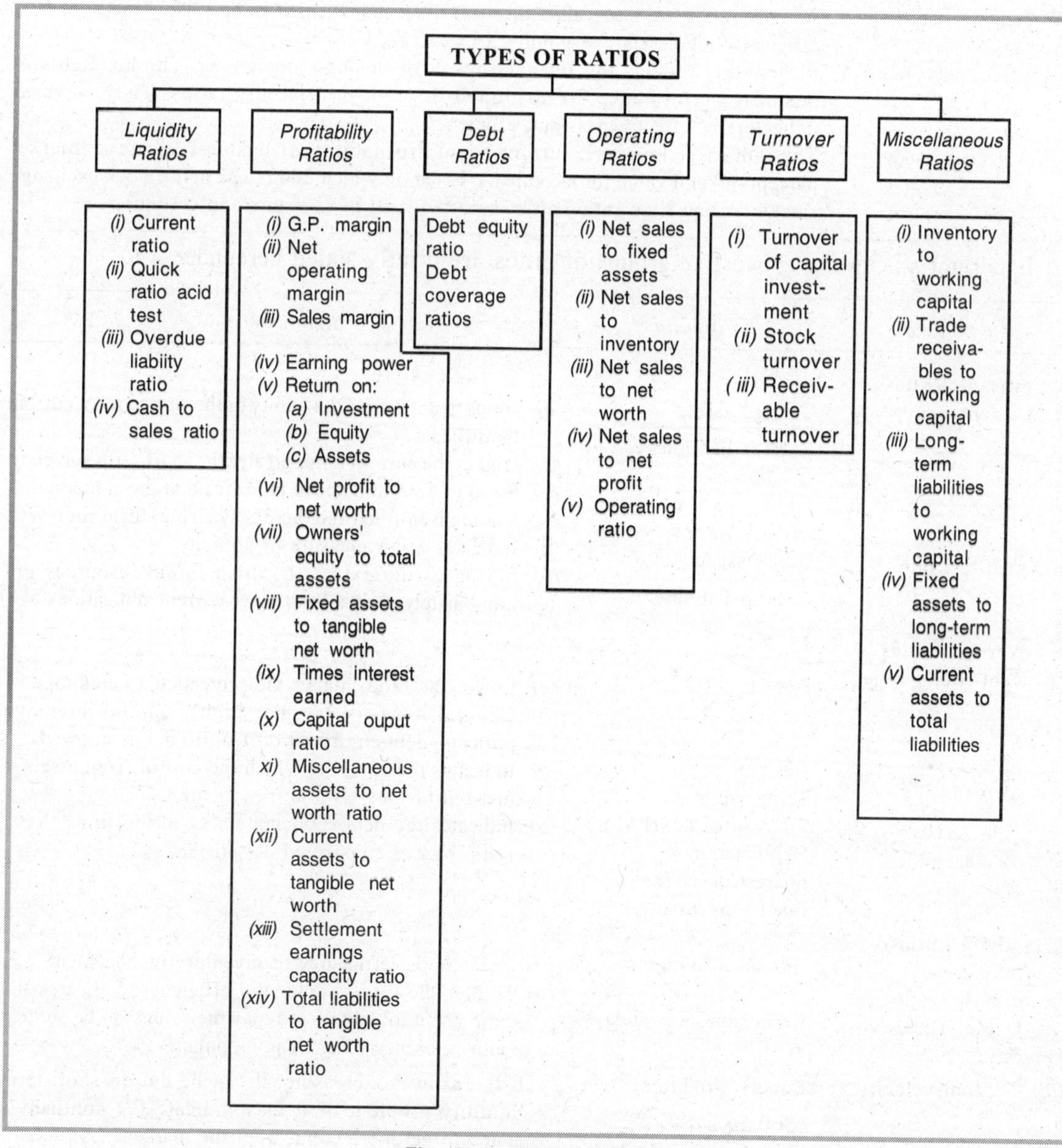

Fig. 10.2: Types of Ratios

The ratios can be conveniently classified under five categories:

Important among the above five groups of ratios are briefly stated hereunder:

The ratios can be conveniently classified under five categories:

Classification of Ratios	Significance
(i) Liquidity ratios	Liquidity refers to the ability of the firm to meet its obligations in the short run, usually one year. These ratios help determine the solvency of the firm.
(ii) Leverage ratios	Financial leverage refers to the use of debt finance, which is cheaper but a riskier source. Leverage ratios help in assessing the risk arising from the use of debt capital.
(iii) Activity ratios	Activity ratios are also called turnover/asset management ratios. They measure how efficiently the assets are employed by the firm.
(iv) Profitability ratios	Profitability reflects the financial result of business operations. The highlights of business performance are exhibited through profitability ratios. They serve as indicators of effectiveness and efficiency.
(v) Valuation ratios	The solvency, leverage, turnover and profitability of business create a 'market perception' and value for a company, based on which quotations in the stock exchange fluctuate. Valuation ratios offer important tips to investors and creditors.

Important among the above five groups of ratios are briefly stated hereunder:

Ratio	Formula	Significance
A. Leverage Ratios		
(i) Current ratio	$\frac{\text{Current assets}}{\text{Current liabilities}}$	(a) Helps to determine the ability of the firm to meet current liabilities. (b) Higher the current ratio, greater the short-term solvency. (c) Ratio of 1.33 and above indicates that the II method of lending is fulfilled and there is available sufficient NWC.
(ii) Acid test ratio	$\frac{\text{Quick assets}}{\text{Current liabilities}}$	(a) Indicates a fair measure of liquidity. (b) Measures the extent to which liquid resources are immediately available to meet current obligations.
B. Leverage Ratios		
(i) Debt-equity ratio	Debt Equity	(a) Lower the ratio, higher the protection to creditors. (b) General norm is 2:1. For highly capital-intensive projects, debt-equity ratio of up to 4:1 is allowed.
(ii) Asset coverage ratio	Net block Term liabilities	(a) Indicates the extent to which the cost of fixed assets is met out of long-term borrowed funds.
(iii) Debt service coverage ratio	Profit after tax (PAT) + Depreciation + Interest on LTL + Loan repayments	(a) Indicates the debt servicing ability of the firm. (b) Ratio of 2 is considered as satisfactory.
C. Activity Ratios		
(i) Inventory turnover ratio	Net sales Inventory	(a) Reflects the efficiency of inventory management. (b) Higher the ratio, higher the efficiency.
(ii) Debtor-velocity ratio	Receivables x 360 days	Indicates the time given to debtors to repay their dues; to be studied with reference to company's policies.
(iii) Creditor-velocity ratio	$\frac{\text{Sundry Creditors} \times \text{360 days}}{\text{Purchases}}$	If the ratio is increasing, it can be due to short-term liquidity problem or it may indicate the company's ability to get more credit from the market.
(iv) Fixed assets-turnover ratio	$\frac{\text{Net sales}}{\text{Fixed Assets}}$	Measures the efficiency of all assets.
D. Profitability Ratios		
(i) Gross profit ratio percent	$\frac{\text{Gross profit} \times 100}{\text{Gross sales}}$	(a) Ratio shows the margin left after meeting the manufacturing costs.

INTRODUCTION TO INVESTMENT PROCESS

> *"An investment decision depends on alternative selection. A good investment decision can be reached by choosing between two alternative opportunities. A company makes an investment only after studying the conditions of market; demand, consumers, competition, Government policies, etc., before taking a decision."*

> Investment is putting money into something with the expectation of gain, that upon thorough analysis has a high degree of security for the principal amount, as well as security of return, within an expected period of time.

Indian economy is vibrant and growing. Opening up of the economy, globalisation and the new technology have contributed to push up the economic growth rate to over 9 per cent. In the process, there is a continuous growth of entrepreneurial activities. The past few years of the Indian economy have truly been a phase of transformation. The transformation has affected various parts of Indian society and one of the important and positive developments in this period has been the unleashing of the entrepreneurial talent of Indian promoters. In fact, many of the top businesses that we see today in the IT, pharma or the telecom industry have really been built by entrepreneurs who were not even well known in their own cities a few decades ago.

Since India looking more and more towards free market capitalism for future growth, this change had huge positive spin-offs for the society at large and individual entrepreneurs in particular. India has always been a land gifted with entrepreneurial talent. As soon as controls on vision and nurturing of new businesses were lifted, we saw the advent of several high quality professionals in the area of setting up and development of new businesses.

K.P.Singh and Mittal: The spirit is soaring high

And so, emerging sectors like energy, information technology, pharmaceuticals, real estate, media and telecom presented themselves as ideal areas where intellectual property, quality capital and entrepreneurial drive could all be harnessed together to create great businesses.

With new age business idols like Sunil Mittal, Kishore Biyani and Jeh Wadia stepping up on to take the mantle of entrepreneurship and change the face of the Indian entrepreneurial segment, a new wave entrepreneurship spirit is setting in. Not only have they broken grounds and set trends but also made entrepreneurship aspirational.

This apart, a lot of other factors like the ready availability of capital have also given a great impetus to Indian entrepreneurship. Many international venture capital firms are looking at emerging economy to invest in. This has given a fillip to investments in manufacturing, pharma, retail, IT, finance and other sectors.

Prospects for rapid industrial growth both in manufacturing, infrastructure and service sectors in India in the coming years are exceedingly well. The investment climate is quite bright.

India has been investing in infrastructure and entrepreneurs are investing heavily in start-ups, modernisation and technological upgradation. Growth opportunities are plenty for innovative entrepreneurs. And, in this context, investment process is a key factor.

Information on the utility and importance of ratio analysis has been aptly presented earlier. In this chapter, the investment process will be dealt in all its aspects.

The investment process helps the entrepreneur to make a clear assessment of the rate of return on his investments in a short and long-term basis.

Characteristics of Investment

The entrepreneur has to weigh the alternative investment process in accordance with his preferences to achieve his business goal.

The principal charactristics of investment are:

(i) Risk
(ii) Return
(iii) Safety
(iv) Utility
(v) Liquidity
(vi) Benefits

Investment Profile of an Entrapreneur

The investment process of an entrepreneur are multi-dimensonal. He invests in land and building, machinery and tools, procuring raw-material, marketing etc. The entrepreneur has to evaluae each process in an indepth manner to gain from the investment decision.

Classification

Investment proposals are broadly classfied as follows:

1. Replacement Investments
2. Modernisation Investments
3. Rationalisation Investments
4. Expansion Investments
5. New Product Investments
6. Research and Develoment Investments
7. Marketing and sales investments
8. Human resource development investments
9. Welfare investments
10. Obligatory investments

Investments are also broadly classified into short-term and long-term.

Investment Outlay

The invest outlay of a project may be classified as follows:

Tangible Fixed Investment

Land and site development

Buildings and civil works

Plant and machinery

Miscellaneous fixed assets

Intangible Fixed Investment

Intangible assets

Preliminary expenses

Pre-operative expenses

Working Capital

Inventories

Receivables

Cash and bank balance

Entrepreneur has to plan these investment and budget for it carefully.

Utility of Investment

Investment plays a vital role in the overall economic development. In fact, the quantum of investment decides the process and direction of growth. In case of manufacturing enterprises investment determines its performance.

Broadly, the utility of investment is directed towards development, profit, power, wealth, capital generation and social good.

Investment Decision

For an entrepreneur, investment decision is tough, complex as well as crucial. An entrepreneur has to weigh all possible variables and then take the investment decision.

Analytical tools like foreseeing, scenario planning, derivatives, etc., provide better insights to entrepreneurs. At thc same time, a vastly competition-driven business, aided by the very advancements in information technology, has reduced the time available to managers for making decisions. But speed in decision making, much like in the case of an automobile, increases the chances of a crash in the event of even a small miscalculation.

Notwithstanding the above, there is every need for managers to analyze their decision making process to improve the quality of their decisions. Although there are many approaches to decision making, a simplified approach involves the following steps:

1. Clearly define the issue.
2. Develop maximum alternative solutions.
3. Collect relevant information.

4. Evaluate the alternatives to arrive at the best choice on the basis of available information.
5. Take the decision and get the same implemented.

A right investment decision will go a long way in the progress of the dream entreprise of an entrepreneur.

The Investment Process

The investment process is generally described in four stages. These stages are investment policy, investment analysis, valuation of securities, and portfolio construction.

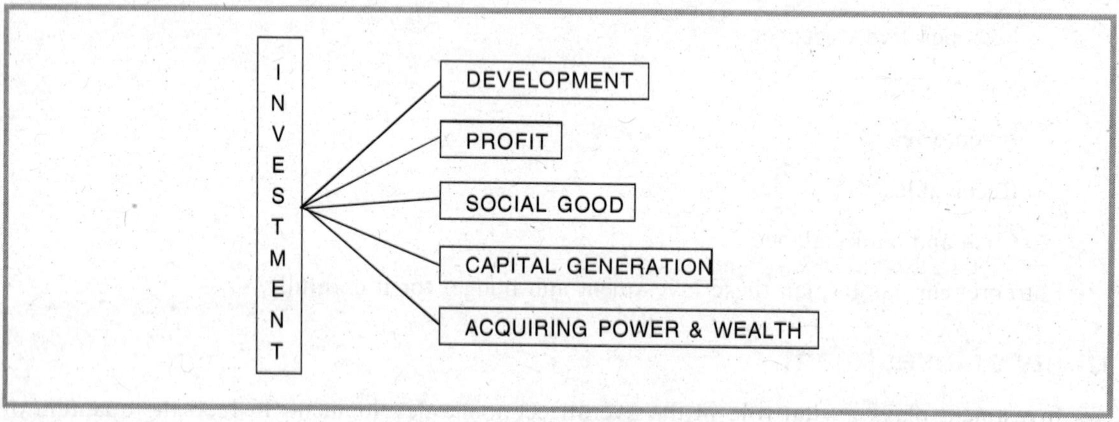

Fig. 10.3: Utility of Investment

Portfolio construction requires a knowledge of the different aspects of securities. These are briefly recapitulated here, consisting of safety and growth of principal, liquidity of assets after taking into account the stage involving investment timing, selection of investment, allocation of savings to different investments and feedback of portfolio as given in the table below:

The Process of Investing

I. Investment Policy

Determination of investible wealth
Determination of portfolio objectives
Identification of potential investment assets
Consideration of attributes of investment assets
Allocation of wealth to asset categories.

II. Investment Valuation

Valuation of stocks	Valuation of Debentures and bonds	Valuation of other assets

III. Investment Analysis

Analysis of the Economy

Equity Stock Analysis	*Debentures and Bond Analysis*	*Other Assets Analysis*
Screenings of industries	Analysis of yield structure	Qualitative analysis
Analysis of industries	Consideration of debentures	Qualitative analysis
Quantitative analysis of stocks	Quantitative analysis of debentures	

IV. Portfolio Construction

Determination of diversification level
Consideration of investment timing
Selection of investment assets
Allocation of investible wealth to investment assets
Evaluation of portfolio for feedback.

Return on Investment (ROI) — A Key Profitability Ratio

A Key Profitability Ratio is the return on investment ratio (RoI), which is a measure of efficiency and provides a starting point for analysing the influences and trends in a company's performance.

It is defined as

$$\text{Return on Investment} = \frac{\text{Profit}}{\text{Capital employed}} \times \frac{\text{Profit}}{\text{Sales}} \times \frac{\text{Sales}}{\text{Capital employed}}$$

In determining the capital employed, any of the following three definitions can be used:

(a) Gross Capital Employed = Fixed Assets + Current Assets

(b) Net Capital Employed = Fixed Assets + (Current Assets – Current Liabilities)

(c) Proprietors' Net Capital Employed = (Fixed Assets + Current Assets) – (Current Liabilities + Long-term borrowings)

The proprietors' capital employed can also be defined as Proprietors' net capital employed = Equity Capital + Preference Capital + Accumulated Reserves and Profits.

The definition of profit, used in calculating ROI, will change according to the meaning of capital employed.

Briefly:

(1) If some asset has been excluded from the calculation of amount of capital employed, its income must also be deducted from the profits. Usually, fictitious and intangible assets are not included in the capital employed.

(2) If "capital employed" is the gross capital, then interest paid on debentures/long-term liabilities/preference shares dividends should also be included in profits, i.e., added back to profits.

(3) If capital employed is calculated in the sense of "net equity capital employed" then both debenture interest and preference dividends should be deducted from profits.

Generally, profits calculated for any type of capital employed must not include abnormal and non-recurring gains or losses, e.g., gains or loss on sale of fixed assets, gains on foreign exchange fluctutations, gains on insurance claims, etc.

A low ROI could be due to either low gross profit margins, a low rate of assets turnover or a combination of both. Therefore, if profit margins on sales cannot be improved due to strong domestic/international competition, then the only way to improve the return on investment is by increasing the rate of assets turnover, i.e., by increasing productivity. This could be further broken down, by working out the ratio of Sales: Fixed Assets and Sales: Working Capital, in order to find out whether these are satisfactory and whether there is room for improving the productivity of the fixed assets or of the working capital component of the capital employed. In other words, the Fixed Assets Turn-Over (Sales/Fixed Assets) or the Working Capital Turn-Over (Sales/Working Capital) must be separately assessed in order to find out which offers scope for improving productivity.

An important aspect of measuring the operating efficiency of management is to assess the Operating Ratio which is defined as:

Operating Ratio = Operating Costs/Sales

The higher the operating ratio, the lesser is the margin available for net profit to owners (and shareholders or proprietors) and for ploughing back into the company. A high operating ratio is indicative of inefficient management and must immediately be investigated.

Investment Ratio

Ratio analysis is defined to mean "*the establishment of a reasoned relationship*" of a fixed or variable character, between measurements of certain phenomena having some kind of linkage. They are the key tools of management. In this sense, investment variable ratios have acquired greater significance in financial management.

Incentives to Investment

Fiscal measures play a major role in the process of economic development. In fact, state intervention is used to sustain the level of effective demand for investment through various incentives. And, incentives stem from different instruments of fiscal policy, monetary policy and commercial policy (Chart 10.1).

Develop Capabilities

Advanced economies have grown through the centuries with the development and diversification of the industry and the resultant commerce. Every country slowly, and many times unknowingly, develops a sense of economic proportion. This sense ultimately determines,

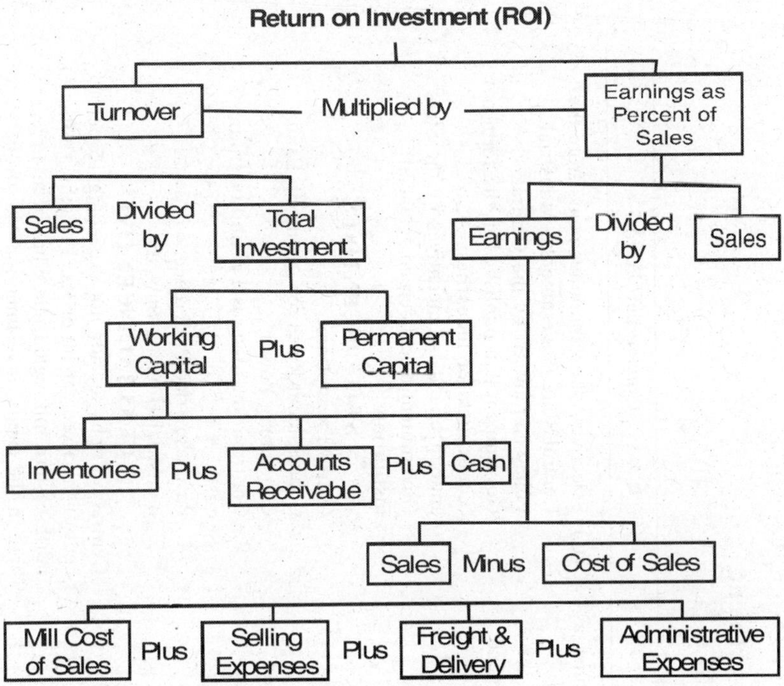

N.B.: Alternatively total investment can be analysed as shareholders' equity plus long-term borrowed fund plus current liabilities.

Fig. 10.4: Du Pont Chart

along with the scale of economies. This sense of economic proportion brings with it the consciousness of capabilities — technological, managerial, financial and organisational. The advanced economies in the developed countries are due to their developed capabilities. So long as such capabilities have not been developed, large projects and larger conglomerates would prove to be sterile, difficult to establish, and much more rigorous to manage. Any national industrial economy must develop, as far as possible, naturally. On its inception, it must be properly protected and nourished. Then, with the passage of time, it will grow into healthy proportions. It will outgrow the gestation stage and eventually become selfreliant, self-sustained and self-accelerating, with stout muscles and stronger nerves. The national enterprise, which is equivalent to the sum-total of the entrepreneurial, managerial, financial, and technological capabilities, is the growth of time. Therefore, small industries in underdeveloped countries when they are emerging out of the traditional agricultural economy provide a cradle for modern medium and larger industries.

The sense of economic proportion at any point of time determines the direction of economic development. There are several constraints which influence the process of industrialisation. The underdevelopment of a country is really the reflection of inadequate development of entrepreneurship in that country. When entrepreneurial growth is accelerated, modern industrial development automatically gains momentum. Narrow or non-existent entrepreneurial in various countries. How to broaden and strengthen the entrepreneurial base in the society is the real challenge facing the developing countries today.

Chart 10.1

Incentives for Investment
STEM FROM

Fiscal Policy	*Monetary Policy*	*Commercial Policy*
(A) Budget Proposals eventually enacted as an Act of the Parliament, viz., The Income Tax Act (and periodic amendements thereof).	(B) Interest Rate & Lending Policy as announced by the Financial Institutions in consultation & collaboration with the Financial Institutions	(C) Selective Adhoc announcements from the Central/State Governments. Industrial Policy announced by the Central Government/and published in the form of 'Guidelines for Industries'. Also announcements of incentives by the State Government or concerned financial institution.
1. S 32 Normal Depreciation 2. S 32 *(i) (ii)* — Extra Depreciaton @ 50% of Normal Depreciation. 3. S 35A Amortisation of Patents and copy rights. 4. S 80J/80I Tax Holiday 5. S 32A Investment Allowance 6. S 35B Export market development allowance 7. S 35C Agricultural develoment allowance 8. S 35D Amortisation of Preliminary Expenses.	1. Concessional Interest Rates 2. Repayment Moratorium 3. Extended Amortizaion Period 4. Participation in Risk Capital 5. Concessions in Undertaking/ Underwriting Commissions 6. Commitment Charges 7. Consultancy Services 8. Reduced Security Margins 9. Refinancing Facilities 10. Concession with respect to promoters' Contribution.	**STATE INCENTIVES** 1. Octroi Exemptions. 2. Concessional Rates for Acquiring Land/ Consuming Power. 3. Contribution towards Feasibility studies costs. 4. Purchase Price Preference. 5. Industrial Housing Subsidy. **CENTRAL INCENTIVES** Central outright subsidy not exceeding 15 per cent of the fixed capital or Rs. 15 lakhs. (In the north-eastern hill region, there has been a recent hike in the capital investment subsidy from 15 to 20 per cent from March 1983. Transport subsidy under the Transport subsidy Scheme of 1971).

INTRODUCTION TO BREAK-EVEN ANALYSIS

> *"The break-even analysis is the most widely known form of cost volume profit (CVP) analysis. A narrow interpretation of break-even analysis refers to that system determining that level of activity where total cost is equal to total sales, i.e., the point of zero profit and zero loss. In a broad sense it refers to a system of analysis that can be used to determine the probable profit at any level of activity."*

The determination of the break-even point of a firm is an important factor in assessing its profitability. It is a valuable control technique and a planning device in any business enterprise. It depicts the relation between total cost and total revenue at the level of a particular output. Ordinarily, the profit of an industrial unit depends upon the selling price of product (revenue), volume of business (it depends on price) and cost price of the product.

If an entrepreneur is aware of the product cost and its selling price, he can plan the volume of his sale in order to achieve a certain level of profit. The break-even point is determined as that point of sales volume at which the total cost and total revenue are identical.

Break-even Point

Break-even point is an important measure being used by the proponents and banks in deciding the viability of a new project, especially in respect of manufacturing activities. This technique is useful dealing with a new project or a new activity of the existing unit.

The break-even point (BEP) establishes the level of output/production which evenly breaks the costs and revenues. It is the level of production at which the turnover just covers the fixed overheads and the unit starts making profits.

From the banker's point of view, the project should achieve a break-even position within a reasonable time from the start of production. The project which reaches a break-even point earlier is considered as a viable project by bankers. They cannot only expect earlier repayment of their advances in the case of such projects but can also be assured that the project can fairly adapt itself to the day-to-day developing technology. The projects which are unlikely to reach the break-even point in the third or fourth year of its commencement of production will not be a viable proposal for the bankers.

The break-even analysis also determines the margin of safety, i.e., excess of budgeted or actual sales over the break-even sales so that the bankers would know how sensitive a project is to recession. This is an important factor in determining the feasibility of the project and its ability to absorb the ups and downs in the economy. The bankers, as lenders of funds, insist upon a reasonable margin of safety so that fixed costs are met at a fairly earlier stage.

Algebraic Formulate of Break-even Analysis

(A) Break-even point (BEP) in terms of sales:

$$\text{BEP} = \frac{\text{Fixed cost}}{\text{Total contribution}} \times \text{Total amount of sales}$$

(Total Sales – Total variable costs – Total contribution)

Example:

Sales	1,000 units
Selling price per unit	₹ 60
Variable cost per unit	₹ 40
Fixed cost	₹ 1,500

$$\text{BEP (Unit volume)} = \frac{1{,}500}{60 - 40} = \frac{1{,}500}{20} = 75 \text{ units BEP in terms of units}$$

BEP in terms of sales = ₹ 75 × ₹ 60 = ₹ 4,500

(B) BEP (in terms of capacity utilisation)

$$\frac{\text{Total fixed costs}}{\text{Total contribution}} \times \text{Production in terms of per cent to installed capacity}$$

In this method, BEP in terms of capacity utilisation is calculated with reference to capacity utilisation in the normal year of production. For instance, if the unit is expected to achieve a capacity utilisation of 40%, 45%, 60%, 80% and of the installed capacity in the first five years, the BEP computation will be with reference to 80%.

Calculation of BEP

The break-even point can be calculated in terms of physical units and in terms of sales turnover.

(i) In terms of physical units: The number of units required to be sold to achieve the break-even point can be calculated using the following formula:

$$\text{BEP} = \frac{FC}{SP - VC} \text{ or } \frac{FC}{C}$$

where

FC = fixed cost
VC = variable cost
SP = selling price
C = contribution per unit (C = SP – VC)

Example, if:

FC = ₹ 1,00,000
VC = ₹ 2 per unit
SP = ₹ 4 per unit, and

Maximum productive capacity = 1,00,000 units per year.

$$\text{BEP} = \frac{1{,}00{,}000}{4 - 2} = 50{,}000 \text{ units (i.e., 50 per cent of the capacity)}$$

(ii) In terms of sales volume: BEP in terms of sales volume can be calculated using the following formula:

$$\text{BEP} = \text{SP}\,\frac{\text{FC}}{\text{SP} - \text{VC}}$$

where

FC = fixed cost
SP = selling price per unit
VC = variable cost per unit

A different way of calculating BEP is

$$\text{BEP} = \frac{\text{Fixed Expenses} \times \text{Sales}}{\text{Total Contribution}}$$

where total contribution is the total sales minus the total variable expenses.

In this case, the EBP will be in Rupees. Graphically, BEP is represented as below:

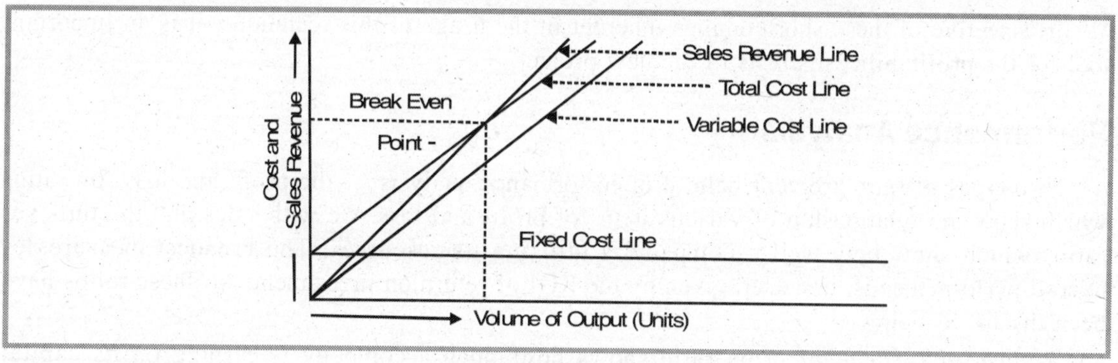

Fig. 10.5: Break-Even Analysis

Utility of the Break-even Analysis

The utility of Break-Even Analysis is as follows:

- It serves as the most useful and important managerial tool to study Cost-Output-Profit relationship at varying level of output.
- It is useful in reviewing pricing policies.
- It aids in planning capitalisation of the enterprise.
- It provides the entrepreneur to decide whether to acquire or not assets involving additional fixed costs.

Shortcomings of the Break-even Analysis

The BEP analysis is based on some assumptions, such as sales price, costs, production, sales, etc. The technique will be only of financial value unless all these assumptions are well-calculated. Besides, the technique is a preliminary and supplementary tool in the whole exercise of ratio analysis.

Another important factor in using the technique is to provide cost-escalation as a built-in safeguard against increase in prices.

The most important factor while using the technique, however is the proper analysis of various costs into fixed costs and variable cost as there are some types of costs which do not fall into either of the categories. These are the expenses which are partly fixed and partly variable. In a break-even analysis, these semi-fixed costs cannot be treated independently but have to be isolated into the usual categories of fixed and variable elements.

Break-Even analysis may not prove useful to rapidly growing enterprises and to enterprises which frequently change their product mix.

It has limited utility in the case of multiproducts.

It does not take due cognisance of factors like uncertainty and risk involved in estimates for costs, volume and profits.

It is not a potent tool for long range planning.

Irrespective of these shortcomings inherent in the usage of this technique, it is an important tool for the profitability analysis of the new project.

Performance Analysis

Two types of ratio are very helpful in performance analysis — the profit and loss A/c ratios which show the relationship of various items of profit and loss A/c with sales and the turnover ratios which show how well a company is utilising its resources. The broadest measures of overall performance is, however, given by the ROI of return on investment. All these ratios have been discussed below:

Return on Investment: This ratio shows how much a company is earning on its capital employed. Thus, if a company has ₹ 5 lakh as equity capital and ₹ 3 lakh as loan, its total capital employed would be ₹ 8 lakh. Suppose it earns ₹ 80,000 in a year before interest and taxation, and RoI will be 10 per cent. It is calculated thus:

$$\frac{\text{Net Profit before Interest and Income Tax}}{\text{Capital Employed}} \times 100$$

Net capital employed is the amount of funds invested in business. It can be calculated from the balance sheet in one of the following two ways:

(a) Equity Share Capital + Preference Share Capital + Reserves and surplus + short-term and long-term liabilities minus non-operating assets (e.g., investments) and miscellaneous expenditure if any such item appears on the assets side of the balance sheet).

Or

(b) Fixed Assets + Current Assets – Current Liabilities

It is obvious that the amount of net capital employed would be the same whichever way it is calculated. The following points may be noted in this regard:

(c) It is not generally proper to include outside investments when calculating the net capital employed. The profit is also the profit before interest on such investments. The idea is that the return on investment for funds employed within the business should be calculated separately from the return on investment for funds employed outside a business. However, if the RoI for the total business is to be calculated, investments should be included in the figure of net capital employed, and the income from such investments should also be taken into credit when calculating net profit before interest and tax.

Intangible assets (assets which have no physical existence like goodwill, patent and trade-marks) should be included in the figure of capital employed, specially if they have been paid for. Only if these are totally fictitious and represent no rights or benefits to the business, should they be excluded from the figure of 'net capital employed'.

ROI is a very significant measure for inter-firm comparison and for evaluating performances of various units within a firm. Actually, ROI combines in itself the net effect of all types of performance ratios. Ratios of the profit and loss account and turnover ratios indicate the performance of a company. All these ratios are ultimately reflected in ROI. A slight fall in turnover efficiency or a rise in costs would immediately affect the ROI. It is because of this that ROI is called the broadest measure of performance.

The impact of Net Profit ratio and Turnover ratio on ROI can be seen as given below:

$$\text{Net Profit Ratio} = \frac{\text{Net Profit before interest and tax}}{\text{Sales}} \times 100$$

$$\text{Capital Turnover Ratio} = \frac{\text{Sales}}{\text{Net capital employed}} \times 100$$

If we multiply the two, i.e.,

$$\frac{\text{Net Profit before interest tax}}{\text{Sales}} \times \frac{\text{Sales}}{\text{Net capital employed}} \times 100$$

We get ROI.

Example:

	₹	*Rate of Return*
Sales	5,00,000	
Capital	20,00,000	$\frac{5,00,000}{50,00,000} \times \frac{50,00,000}{20,00,000} \times 100$
Profit	5,00,000	
		or 10% × 2.5 = 25%

Thus once ROI is worked out, a further analysis is undertaken by working out the Net Profit Ratio (and Profit and Loss A/c ratios which affect it) and the Turnover Ratios (with other ratios affecting it). The table given on the next page shows these relationships. The exact cause of a low ROI can be treated only after a complete analysis through Profit and Loss Account ratios and turnover ratio, mentioned in Fig. 10.6.

Sensitivity Analysis

Under the sensitivity analysis, instead of using one estimate of each variable, several estimates used under varying conditions.

The element of uncertainty can be reduced by applying sensitivity analysis at the project planning stage by finding the optimistic and pessimistic alternatives. For example, considering the pessimistic solutions, the project's viability in the worst of all possible situations can be determined. If the sensitivity analysis shows that the project will be commercially viable under pessimistic conditions, the project can be considered non-risky.

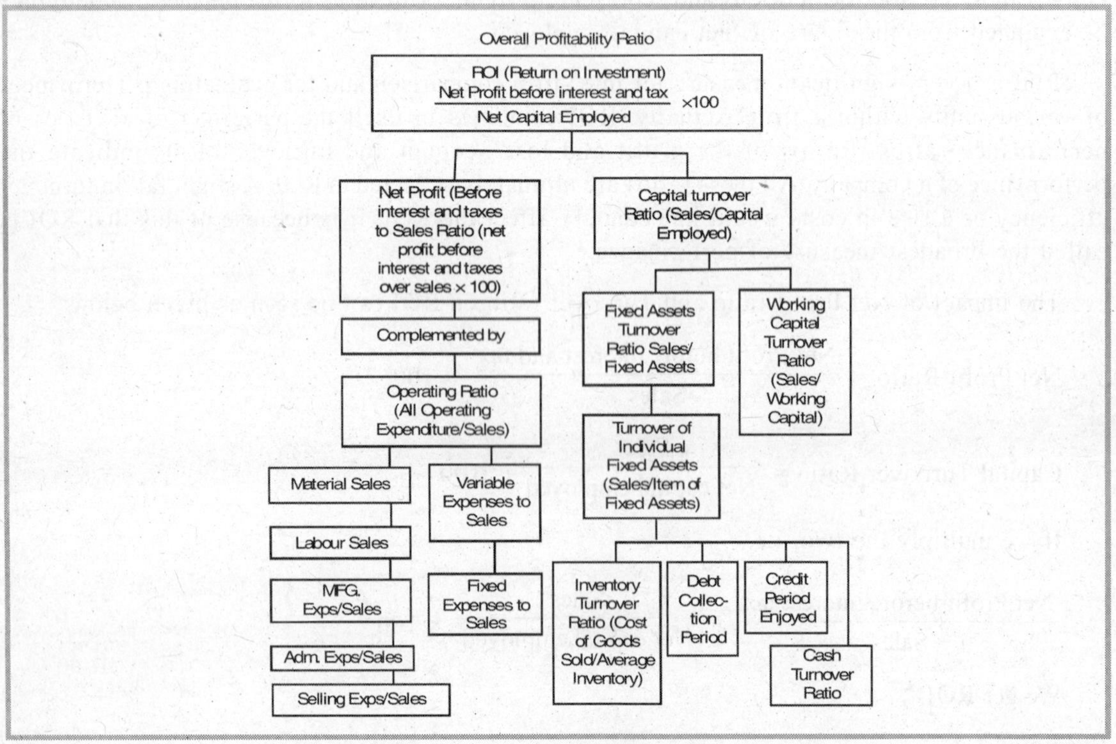

Fig. 10.6: Profitability Ratios

With the help of sensitivity analysis, it is easy to identify the most important factors in a project, such as raw materials, labour and energy and to determine any possibilities of input substitution.

The break-even analysis can be made more realistic by applying the sensitivity analysis. For example, alternative break-even calculations can be done with optimistic and pessimistic estimates of costs and selling prices. Similarly, alternative estimates of the business prospects can be made on the basis of optimistic and pessimistic estimates of demand or capacity utilisation.

Sensitivity analysis, thus, helps to understand the extent to which a project can face adverse conditions.

Probability Analysis

Probability as used here refers to the frequency of occurrence of an event, measured as a ratio of the number of different ways that the specific event can happen to the total number of possible outcomes.

The purpose of probability analysis is to eliminate the need for restricting to a single optimistic, pessimistic or realistic estimation by identifying the possible range of each variable and attaching a probability of occurrence to each possible value of the variables within this range. These judgements take the form of probability distribution of each possible value and each variable is associated with a number between 0 and 1, so that for each variable the sum of all these numbers (probabilities) is equal to one. This numerical description of the likelihood of an event's occurrence makes possible on objective measure of many situations that could otherwise be gauged only intuitively. Therefore, from a mathematical point of view, probability analysis consists of aggregating probabilities.

This analysis is carried out in the context of project preparation with the objective of improving the accuracy of cost estimates and, in turn, of probability forecasts.

The term investment is to be understood in its economic sense. Economical investment means to lay money for profit. In its broader sense, investment means utilising money for development.

PROFITABILITY ANALYSIS

> *"Profit is a dominant goal of a business. It is the prime motive force for all enterpreneurs to venture on their dream projects. In fact, profit is the reward for entrepreneurship. Hence, profit analysis is a key input to entrepreneurial activities."*

Profitability analysis technique employed in several industrial countries are vitally important to assess the operational efficiency of a project and its profitability. It also seeks to correct the structural deficiencies and improve productivity and profits.

Profit is the primary objective of an enterprise. In view of the heavy investment which is necessary for the success of most enterprises, profit in the accounting sense tends to become a long-term objetive, which measures not only the success of a product but also of the development of the market for it. The word "profit" implies a comparison of the operations of business between two specific dates, which are usually separated by an interval of one year. In order to optimise these corporate resources of wealth on which national prosperity depends, the basic financial objective of companies is to maximise, within socially acceptable limits, profits from the use of the funds employed by them. The maximisation of profit within a socially acceptable limit implies that a proper regard for public interest has been shown. No company can survive long without profit, for profit is the ultimate measure of its effectiveness. Also, and in a capitalist society, there is no future for a private enterprise showing repeat losses. The crucial measure of the effective performance of a business is profit, which really is a measure of how well a business performs economically.

Profit is a signal for the allocation of resources and a yardstick for judging managerial efficiency. It is wrong to believe that the importance given to profit planning in the literature on business finance does not reflect its genuine importance in the financial activities of a modern business firm. In fact, it is the growth of profit which enables a firm to pay higher dividends to its ordinary shareholders.

Profit results from transactions which should satisfy both the parties to it. The vendor should be satisfied that the price is acceptable, and that it gives him an appropriate return for the work he has done and the risks he has taken. The purchaser should be satisfied that he has had a full value for his money. Irrespective of the way in which a company's profitability is expressed, its profit potential depends on its ability to price its products so that they provide value not only to the customer, but also to the company itself. Good pricing results in good profits.

Profit is a dominant goal of a business, and profit-making should be the main objective in terms of which the general effectiveness of an organisation is measured. Economists have long been concerned with profits and have framed theories to explain both their meaning and distribution. According to them, *profit is the reward for entrepreneurship.* A source of funds which is completely within the internal system is that of profit-making. The exact contribution which profits make to funds is a disputable matter. But the fact that funds are augmented by profits and reduced by losses should be beyond controversy.

Goals or objectives are the ends which a business enterprise seeks to achieve through its existence and operations. A typical business establishment seeks to achieve more than one goal and there are always restraints to the attainment of some goals. Objectives vary with the passage of time. Goals common to most contemporary business establishments are explained in figures 10.7.

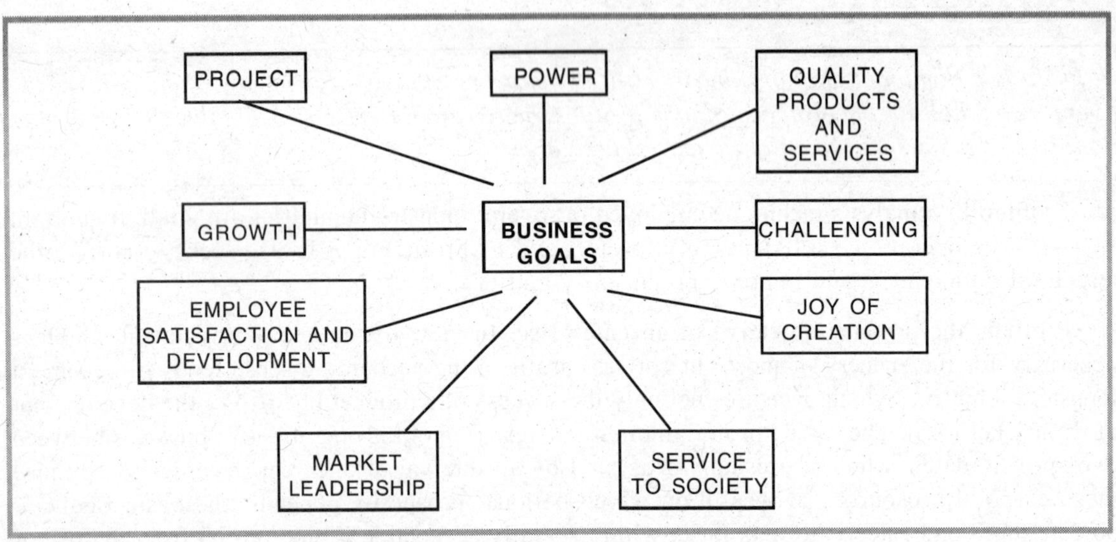

Fig. 10.7: Business Goals

Factors Affecting Profit

A number of factors influence profit variations. These are:

1. *Mix of product changes:* The effect of the mix of product changes upon profits is fairly easy to interpret and record, if a good system is in use.

2. *Volume of fluctuations:* The volume of sales plays a tremendous part in profit-making. So long as a sustained maximum volume continues at the top of capacity curve, break-even point would be far away. The profit path is wide and deep at the point.

3. *Performance changes on any volume:* To attain real sophisticiation in profit calculation, the true profits at any given volume which should exist at a planned break-even point are separated from the profits created by the performance at one attained volume.

4. A change in fixed costs changes the break-even point, but not the marginal profit. The marginal point is the profit picked up above the break-even point.

5. A change in variable costs and selling prices changes both the break-even point and the marginal profit.

6. The rate of marginal profit is affected by a change in variable costs, selling price and operating performance as against planned performance.

7. When both the fixed and variable costs change and when they move in tandem, the effect of the break-even point is pronounced and definite. When they move in opposition to each other, the effect is very weak.

8. The marginal break-even point is that point of output at which out-of-pocket costs are recovered. Depreciation and amortisation costs are excluded from them.

If the fact that the central purpose of a business is to earn a profit is accepted, the first problem is to determine the factors which determine the level of profitability. Profitability should first measure the relationship between profits and the funds committed in the business to earn that profit.

The first step in devising the strategy is to measure the task. For private industry, the measure of a task is the gap between the level of profit achieved by a business without the introduction of any major changes and the level of profit which the target profitability measurement indicates should be earned. Value is what people think it is. Any analysis is in the final test, subject to the values that the world at large is prepared to place upon it. The final word is, of course, said by the people who are prepared to buy it. The value of the decision-maker to the sensitivity analysis is that he can choose that which, he thinks, is the most likely value for any variable and read off the resulting rate of return or NPV. He does not have to accept a single-valued estimate based on somebody else's appraisal of the outcomes. The measurement and control of profitability in a company or any other business organisation should form one of the principal objectives of the finance function of a management.

A return on investment has come to be regarded as perhaps the most important measure of industrial and commercial efficiency. This is, as it should be, whether in the different activities of a capitalist economy or in the field of public investment. Even the communist regime of the USSR which eschewed the profit motive, had recognised return on investment as a proper measure of efficiency.

Indicators for Measuring Income

T. A. Lee has suggested following indicators for measuring income. He is of the opinion that income is:

1. A guide to dividend and retention policy.
2. A measure of management effectiveness.

Mapping a Profit Pool

Step 1 *Define the pool*	*Step 2* *Determine the size of the pool*	*Step 3* *Determine the distribution of profits*	*Step 4* *Reconcile the estimates*
Task Determine which value-chain activities influence your ability to generate profits now and in the future	Develop a baseline estimate of the cumulative generated by all profit-pool activities	Develop estimates of profit generated by each activity	Compare the outputs of steps 2 and 3 and, if necessary, reconcile the number
Guidelines Take a brand view of the value-chain; look beyond traditional industry definitions	Seek a rough, but accurate, estimate	Shift between aggregation and disaggregation in your analysis	If the numbers don't add up, check all assumptions and calculations
Examine your industry from 3 perspectives: your own company's, other players; and the customer's	Take the easiest analytical routes available; go where the data are	Look at your own company's economics first, then look at large pure players, then look at large mixed players, then at a sample of smaller players	Collect additional data if necessary
Talk to industry players and analysts to uncover new or emerging business models	Try to take at least 2 differnt views of poolsize — for example, company-level and product-level	If relevant company data are unavailable, use proxies, such as product-level or channel-level sales	Resolve all inconsistencies; don't ignore them
Don't disaggregate activities more than is necessary	Focus on the largest components — for example, large companies, high-volume products; extrapolate smaller components from a sample	Think creatively	
Output List of all value-chain activities in your profit pool, in sequential order	Estimate of total pool profits, usually expressed as a range	Point estimates of profit for each value-chain activity	Final estimates of activity and total pool profits

Source: How to Map Your Industry's Profit Pool

3. A measure of a management's stewardship of the entity's resources.
4. A means of evaluating the result of past decisions and of working on future decisions.
5. A managerial aid in a variety of decision areas within and outside the business entity.

Profit Pool

A new theory argues that the value chain must actually be used to identify the deepest sources of profits. And that identification must be the starting point for formulating corporate strategy. Although the concept of profit zones generates maximum profits, Gadiesh and Gilbert have come up with another profit perspective that provides a starting point for devising a strategy: profit pools.

A profit pool is the total quantum of profits that can be earned at all points along an industry's value-chain. Expectedly, the depth of the pool varies between differnt points on the chain. And the extent of this variation is a function of the products a company makes, the markets in which it decides to sell them, the customer group it targets, and the distribution channel it uses. The shape of the profit pool is actually a manifestation of the industry structure, and it reflects the competitive dynamics of a particular business. Profit pools are deepest in areas where potential competitors face entry-barriers, or in those overlooked by competitors.

Profit pools are not stagnant. Any change in the external environment — competitive activity, change in customer preferences, and supplier initiatives — will alter its shape and size. As a strategic tool, it can help companies answer one basic question: where and how are profits being made in the industry? The versatility of the concept, though, lies in its use as a diagnostic tool.

A Starting Point for Strategy: The shape of a profit pool is a function of the market and competitive forces that influence a particular industry. Companies can use their understanding of profit pools to decide on the right strategies which will help:

- Identify new sources of profit in industries faced with shrinking margins.
- Regulate M & A decisions.
- Identify profitable customer segments to target them.
- Influence decisions related to the 4 Ps: Product, Price, Promotion and Place.
- Identify new business models that improve profitability.

Mapping Profit Pools: Gadiesh and Gilbert suggest a 4-step process to map a profit pool: definition of its boundaries; calculation of its size; estimation of the importance of each value-generating activity in the pool; and review of the calculations.

Profit Planning

It has already been pointed out that profits do not just happen. They must be produced. When a management plans its profit performance, projects its plans to possible multiples of volume, and then realises its profit plans, it may be said to have achieved profit control. Profit planning is a part of an overall planning process in which finance plays a major role.

This activity is now an important responsibility of the finance manager. While activities of this sort require an accounting background, they also rest heavily upon the knowledge of the business principles, economics, statistics and mathematics. Hence, from a company's viewpoint, any effort to confine profit planning activities within the framework of accounting procedures would be detrimental to the long-range interests of the firm.

Profit planning represents an overall plan of operations, covers a definite period of time, and formulates the planning decisions of management. It consists of the operating budget, the financial budget and the appropriation budget. The operating budget covers revenues and expenses. Its crucial elements are the sales budget and the various expense budgets. The financial budget contains the budgets, the balancesheet and supporting schedules. The appropriation budgets cover expenditure on advertising and research. The preparation of a profit plan begins several months before the end of the current year. The chief executive has the ultimate responsibility of profit planning and control programmes.

Effective profit planning cannot be carried out in a casual manner. It should emerge from a rigorously disciplined examination of all aspects of business aspects and alternative strategies which may become indispensable.

Long-term profit-planning implies a sacrifice of today's profit for tomorrow's. The sacrifice made in the immediate profit is taken by the management as an investment in the future on the basis of the philosophy that a management makes the future of a business today. In certain industries in India, competition has already become very keen. The doctrine of the *survival of the fittest* implies that managerial dynamism must be developed to cope with problems not only today but also in the foreseeable future. Take the situation in Great Britain, where the switchover from insulated conditions to keen competition in the early fifties was so sudden that a large number of enterprises were in the red before they could realise what was happening. It is very likely that such a situation may eventually develop in India in the near future. Long-term profitability ensures sustenance and dynamic growth of enterprise. A myopic view of the question is a good riddance before it is too late. In this respect, Indian enterprises still have a long way to go.

Long-range profit planning is a systematic and formalised process for purposefully directing and controlling future operations with a view to achieving the desired objectives for periods extending beyond one year. Forward planning is vital in a competitive profit-and-loss economic system. The success of each enterprise in realising its optimum profit is determined by the extent to which it attains its objectives, develops co-ordinated plans to realise them and exercises control of all its activity so as to reach and even exceed expected results. The entire process constitutes a budgetary planning-and-control programme. It includes income, costs, profits, working capital, fixed capital, fixed assets, financing, and dividend distribution. It extends throughout the entire organisation, from the chief executive to the front-line supervisory staff.

Advantages of Profit Maximisation

Profit maximisation has been considered to be the most important business objective for the following reasons:

1. It is rational to accept profit for a business enterprise.
2. It is difficult to survive without profit maximisation.
3. Even for the attainment of social and economic welfare, profit maximisation has to be achieved.

4. A business with a high level of profitability will generate a high level of funds, out of which it can provide for expansion, in addition to a substantial and increasing return to its shareholders.
5. In the absence of profit, business activity would remain static. A firm cannot afford to do this because:
   (a) Price levels are not stable. Profits, therefore, have to be made to create additional resources.
   (b) Investors in business would expect a positive return on their investment. Profits are essential for ensuring this return.
   (c) It would not be possible to maintain the same level of activity because of the pressures for the expansion of business. The resources required for this purpose have to be provided through profits.

Limitations of Profit Maximisation

1. Profit is essential, but it would be wrong to assume that every action initiated by the Board of Directors is aimed at maximising profits, irrespective of its social consequences.
2. One of the difficulties in looking at the comparative profitability of a number of companies lies in their different standards of valuing business assets.

Profitability Index

Profitability Index is worked out by dividing the present value of the cash inflows with the initial investment cost. The value must be more than one for a project to be viable.

Example

• Initial capital cost of the project	..	₹ 50 lakh
• Present value of the cash inflows from the project	..	₹ 250 lakh
• Profitability Index	..	250 ÷ 50 i.e., 5

Profitability Indices

After the details of net sales, net savings, cost of production etc., have been worked out, various profitability indices shall be calculated. These indices are:

- Return on Investment (ROI)
- Internal Rate of Return by DCF (IRR)
- Net Present Value Method (NPV)

The above indices are now discussed in more detail.

Pay Back Period Method

This method indicates the time required to recover the initial project cost through its benefits/ savings. The projects with the minimum pay back period are only accepted.

This method is most suitable for the projects where chances of obsolescence losses are very high. However, it ignores the time value of money to be received in later years and also the income which will be earned in the later years after the payback period. Still this method is very popularly used because of its simplicity.

Payback period is calculated in the following way. After determining the total net cash inflow, then the total initial cost should be divided by the annual net cash inflow and the resultant (factor) quotient is known as payback period.

$$\text{Payback period} = \frac{\text{Total cost of Investment}}{\text{Annual net cash inflows or savings}}$$

In order to identify the viability of the project, the promoter has to compare the payback period with some predetermined period known as cut off period, in which the investment should pay for itself. If the project pays for itself in less time than the pre-determined period, then the project is considered viable and profitable. On the contrary, if the project takes a longer period to payback, then the project is not viable and unprofitable.

Return on Investment (RoI)

Return on investment is worked out by dividing the net benefit/net savings after depreciation but before interest by the capital employed. This method is simple like payback period method. However, this method also lacks in not considering the time value of money to be received in the future years of the project.

Merits of Return on Investment Method

1. This method takes into account the total earnings from the project during its entire economic life. This method gives importance to the viability or profitability of the project.

2. Since the total earnings are calculated after deducting depreciation and taxes, the fiture gives clear and correct picture about the project.

Demerits

1. This method ignores the time value of money.

2. It does not take into account the fluctuations in the profits.

Internal Rate of Return (IRR)

It is the rate of discount that equals the present value of the expected future cash inflows to the present value of the cash outflows. This method is very popular and is very widely used. This is mostly used as an important profitability index in major investment proposals. In this method cash flows for income as well as expenditure are discounted to bring the same to the present value. It is done on the logic that money received today shall not be the same amount, if received after one year or after two years or so on. Thus ₹ 100/- @ 10 per cent interest shall become ₹ 110/- on simple interest in a bank if deposited. This gives to understand that present value i.e., value today of ₹ 110/- is ₹ 100/-. In this method income as well as expenditure are considered for the entire life of the project. Decision is based on the cost and benefits in terms of present value.

Internal rate of return is worked out by discounting the cash outflows and cash inflows from the project. The rate of discount is the result of various trials of calculations. Thus, the internal rate of return is worked out by trial and error method. However, to avoid many calculations an indicative rate may be known on the basis of pay back period.

Symbolically, the IRR may be expressed as follows:

For a conventional investment,

$$\text{NPV} = \sum_{t=1}^{n} \frac{B_t}{(1+1)^t} - C_0 = 0$$

(Aggregate discounted cash inflows) minus (aggregate initial investment)

$$\sum_{t=1}^{n} \frac{B_t}{(1+1)^t} = C_0$$

Where the discount rate '1' is the IRR.

For a non-conventional investment,

NPV = [Aggregate discounted cash inflow] – [Aggregate discounted cash outflow] = 0

OR

$$\sum_{t=1}^{n} \frac{B_t}{(1+1)^t} \sum_{t=1}^{n} \frac{C_t}{(1+1)^t}$$

Where B_t represents cash inflows during the years 1,2,3,...n; C_t represents cash outflows during the years 0,1,2,3,...n; and '1' represents the IRR.

IRR indicates the maximum rate of return that a project can contribute and is mainly based on the internal cash inflows generated by it. In other words, its most straightforward interpretation is as a 'break-even' rate of interest, showing the highest rate of interest consistent with the project not making a loss. However, in order to judge the profitability of the project, IRR should be compared with a cut-off rate of return which might be the company's cost of capital.

Net Present Value Method (NPV)

This method also like IRR method considers the income of the entire life of the project and time value of money. The present value of the expected cash flows by the project is determined by discounting these cash flows by the company's cost of capital or a specified rate. The rate of discount is generally considered as the prevailing borrowing rate or current bank rates of interest. When the present value equals or exceeds the investment, the proposal is considered favourable. In case of alternatives, the alternative is selected with comparatively higher NPV.

Merits of Net Present Value Method

1. This method recognises the time value of money and can be applied where there is uniform cash outflows and uneven cash inflows or cash flows at different periods of time.
2. This method evalautes the true and maximum profitability of the investment proposal.
3. Considering the earning over the entire life of the project the true profitability of the investment proposal can be evaluated.
4. This method summarises the merit of an investment proposal, i.e., it determines the profitability of the investment proposal in objective terms.

Demerits

1. Comparing to other methods, this method is not easy to understand and operate.
2. This method does not give good results as the projects are compared with unequal investment of funds.
3. It is not easy to determine an appropriate discount rate.
4. Under this method, profitability is not related to the capital required to produce it. The project may have a high NPV but it can still be unattractive, for it requires very high capital outlay.

CONCLUSION

Ratio analysis is a powerful tool of financial analysis. Financial analysis is the process of identifying the financial strength and weaknesses of the firm by properly establishing relationships between the items of the balance sheet and the profit and loss account.

Financial analysis can be undertaken by management of the firm or by parties outside the firm, viz., owners, creditors, investors and others. The nature of analysis will differ depending on the purpose of the analyst. For example, trade creditors are interested in the fact that the firm should be able to meet their claims over a very short period of time. Their analysis will, therefore, confine to the evaluation of the firm's liquidity-position. The suppliers of long-term debt, on the other hand, are interested in the firm's long-term solvency and survival. They analyse the firm's profitability over time; its ability to generate cash to be able to pay interest and return their claims and, the relationship between various sources of funds (capital structure relationships). Long-term creditors not only analyse the historical financial statements, but also require the firm to supply them with the projected or proforma financial statements to make analysis about the firm's future solvency and profitability. Similarly, investors, who have invested their money in the firm's shares, are more anxious about the firm's earnings. They repose much confidence in those firms that show steady growth in earnings. As such, they concentrate on the analysis of the firm's present and future profitability. They are also interested in the firm's financial position to the extent that it influences the firm's earning ability. Finally, management of the firm would be interested in every aspect of the financial analysis as it is their overall responsibility to see that the resources of the firm are used most effectively and efficiently; and that, the firm's financial condition is sound.

The financial analysis is a unique technique useful in the sphere of financial control, planning and review of financial condition of the business organisation. With the help of financial tools the entrepreneur can nationalise his decisions and reach the business goal easily.

The objective of financial analysis is to develop the project from the financial angle and to identify financial characteristics.

It is a tool in judging the performance of a project/enterprise. It helps the entrepreneur, banker and other concerned people to know about the health of an enterprise. It also indicates the direction in which it is progressing. It also gives the warning signals, if any, in its own way. Financial analysis gives a clearer picture of a project as far as its financial factors are concerned. Financial statements, particularly the ratios, require a detailed, critical examination to test their validity. This examination is possible by looking into the internal management of the concern. Briefly, financial analysis is a right step in financial management.

It should be particularly emphasised that one particular ratio used without reference to other ratios may be very misleading. In other words, the combined effect of the various ratios must be considered in arriving at a correct diagnosis which will be of assistance in interpreting the financial condition and earning performance of the business. Each ratio plays its part in this interpretation.

Finally it should be realised that ratios are only preliminary step in interpretation and must be supplemented by rigorous investigation into all aspects of operations of the company before safe conclusions can be drawn from them. Trend analysis should supplement the ratio analysis to assess the good and bad aspects of working of a company.

A ratio is a mathematical relationship between two parameters. Ratio analysis is of major importance for financial analysis. Ratio is both a quantitative as well as qualitative index of measurement. Though it is primarily related to financial managment, there are vast and fruitful opportunities for its application to production, marketing, personnel and general management. Thus ratio analysis equips the entrepreneur with timely and correct status of varied activities of his/her enterprise, its utility enhances with the deepening knowledge and involvement of the enterpreneur in his project work.

Ratios enable the mass of accounting data to be summarised and simplified. Besides, they provide the means of showing the interrelationship which exist between various segments of business, as revealed through accounting statements and thereby prevent any distortions that may result from the study of absolute figures.

The trend ratios may be useful for predicting likely events in the future. The plans made can be "sign posted" by accounting ratios and thereby become an integral part of the standard costing and budgetary control system.

Ideal ratios can be established and the relationship between primary ratios and the ideal ratios may be used to establish the desirable coordination. Ratios may also be used for control of performances as well as control of costs. Ratios are an effective means of communication and play a vital role in informing the position of and progress made by the business concern to the owners or other parties.

Ratio analysis is an effective instrument which, when properly used is useful to assess important characteristics of business, like liquidity, profitability, solvency, etc. A study on these aspects may enable conclusions to be drawn relating to financial requirements and capabilities of business. The ratios may also be used as an effective measure of efficiency.

Rapid industrial development would involve mobilisation of productive resources, investments and entrepreneurial energies. Investment is a continuous process of economic development. In particular, an enterprise's needs for investment is an ongoing business. The entrepreneur invests in enterprises and services after ascertaining adequate returns (Profit), Power and Wealth. Thus, investment is one of the basic foundation of development.

It is an effective management tool as it provides an insight into the effects of and inter-relationships or factors which influence profits of the project. The relationship between cost, volume and profits make up the profit structure of a project. Hence it is very much useful for budgeting and profit planning. As an ultimate objective it helps project analysis to find the most profitable combination of cost and volume. Hence, it is used to predict and evaluate the implications of its short run decisions about fixed costs, variable cost, sales volume and selling price for its profit plans on a continuous basis.

The break-even analysis is an analytical technique for studying the cost-volume-profit relationship and operational leverage in an enterprise. A narrow interpretation of break-even analysis refers to a system determining the level of activity where total cost is equal to total sales, i.e., the point of zero profit and zero loss. It is a unique technique often used by the new enterprises and bankers in determining the viability of a new project. Its utility enhances with careful interpretations.

Profit motive is the prime mover of business activity. In fact, profitability is the most useful overall measure to the health of an enterprise. In other words, the profitability of an enterprise in any one year is the relationship between the profit made and the funds employed to earn the profit. Profitability analysis is a useful tool/technique to entrepreneurs to take right decisions in maximising profits and to bankers and financial institutions to arrive at the viability of the enterprise and its financial needs.

In the emerging free market and entrepreneurial driven economy, for a healthy and sustainable growth of businesses in the future, the entrepreneur has to weigh the profitability in the new sectors. In this context profitability analysis is one of the key inputs to all entrepreneurs. The entrepreneurial drive and vision will identify the potential transformation opportunities and harness them ahead of time.

11
CHAPTER

ACCOUNTING AND BOOK KEEPING

INTRODUCTION

For a constant check on the working of a small-scale industry at all the stages of the manufacture of a product, an entrepreneur has to keep up to date records of all the business activities of a unit. These records help him to evaluate its working and introduce corrective steps at crucial time.

A small-scale industry has to maintain two types of records:

(i) Records which would enable the taxation authorities to determine the sales, purchase, income, expenses, profit and/or loss of a unit; and

(ii) Main cost records to keep a check on the costof a product. These records are known as *(a)* Financial records, and *(b)* Cost records. Both are inter-related and inter-dependent.

According to a survey of small industries, about 80 per cent of the total complied and kept up to date account which reflected their true financial position. A cross-check was provided in the questionnaire in the form of an annexure requiring the responding units to furnish an account of their assets and liabilities. About 13 per cent stated they did not maintain such up to date records, while 3 per cent of the respondents did not state their specific positon on the subject.

It may be assumed that of the units which received loans, about 95 per cent compiled and maintained up to date accounts, while only 3 per cent did not. Of the units which had applied to banks/co-operatives for credit facilities and did not receive them, about 8 per cent had maintained up to date accounts. Of the 3,267 units which maintained accounts, a large proportion (about 47 per cent) received credit facilities. A good proportion (about 41 per cent) of the units which maintained accounts did not approach any bank/co-operative for credit, while 12 per cent were not granted loan facilities. It is of importance to note that as many as 75 per cent of the units which did not maintain up to date accounts did not approach any bank/co-operative, while about 15 per cent were not granted loans when they sought credit from banks/co-operatives. It is clear from these facts that the maintenance of up to date accounts was a factor in institutional lending.

Table 11.1

	Number of Units Which			
	Did not Approach any bank or Co-operative	*Approached and Granted Credit*	*Approached but were not given Credit*	*Total*
Maintained up to date accounts	1,331 (40-7) (74.8)	1,442(47.2) (95.3)	394 (12.1) (81.9)	3,267 (100) (84.2)
Did not maintain up-to-date accounts	372 (75.0) (20.9)	51 (10.3) (3.2)	73 (14.7) (15.2)	496 (100) (12.8)
No response	76 (66.1) (4.3)	25 (21.7) (1.5)	14 (12.2) (2.9)	115 (100) (3.0)
	1,779 (45.9) (100)	1,618 (41.7) (100)	482 (12.4) (100)	3,878 (100) (100)

Although a large number of small-scale entrepreneurs, artisans and cottage industrialists maintain accounts in a very crude manner in a small notebook, no accounts or records are maintained by many. However, a model small-scale industrialist has to maintain the following registers and records:

A. Financial Records

(i) Cash Book

(ii) Ledger

(iii) Record of Bills Receivable

(iv) Record of Bills Payable

B. Cost Records

(i) Register for Raw Materials

(ii) Production Schedule

(iii) Stock Register

A. Financial Records

(i) *Cash Book:* The cash book is a book, wherein cash transactions are recorded by a small-scale unit. it is a subsidiary book of the ledger. The cash book folio is divided into two parts — credit and debit.

The largest number of transactions in any concern, particularly in small-scale industries, necessarily relate to the receipt and payment of cash or its equivalent. Cash has been aptly termed as the lifeblood of every business activity. For a small-scale industry, cash is a tool of development. The cash book is a combination of the cash journal and cash account in a ledger. It is a book of original entry for cash transactions; an entry therein constitutes a part of the double entry system. In actual practice, the cash book is ruled to provide information and facilitate an easy entry of transactions. Usually, the following types of rulings are used:

(a) Cash book with a cash column only; and

(b) Cash book with cash and bank columns.

(c) Cash book with cash, discount and bank columns.

The cash book is divided into two parts; the left hand side is known as the credit side, recording all the receipts in cash, and the right side is known as the debit side, recording all the payments. Each half page consists of the following particulars:

Date of receipt/Payment
Particulars of the transaction
Ledger Folio

Amount received/paid (in cash or through a bank).

All the receipt and payment vouchers are arranged and kept in a file, and classified under different heads. Generally, a small-scale industrialist maintains cash transactions in a serial order. This is the easiest way of maintaining accounts.

Illustration

(a) Cash Balance in hand ₹ 100 and Bank Balance ₹ 1,500.

(b) Paid to Mr. X, ₹ 250 by cheque in full settlement of dues of ₹ 265.

(c) Received cash from Mr. Y, ₹ 750.

(d) Deposited ₹ 500 in bank and paid coolie charges, ₹ 5.

(e) Goods sold for cash, ₹ 250 and against cheque for ₹ 1,100.

(f) Remitted to Mr. Z ₹ 980 by cheque.

(g) Received a cheque from Mr. A, ₹ 750, in full settlement of our dues of ₹ 760; deposited the above cheque in the bank.

Ledger: Ledger is a principal book used for posting transactions to various accounts. It provides in a summarised and classified form a permanent record of all transactions. For example, all purchase transactions are posted to purchase account. The small-scale entrepreneur can know the total purchases or sales from the ledger. Ledger is the most important book of account as it provides necessary information regarding various accounts. Personal accounts in the ledger show how much money the firm owes to its creditors and the amount debtors owe to it. The real accounts show various assets of the firm.

Nominal accounts indicate various sources of income and expenditure. The financial position of the business can be ascertainned easily at anytime with the help of a ledger.

Each ledger account has two sides. The left-hand side is the debit side and the right hand side is the credit side. On each side there are columns for data, particulars, folio and amount. The format of ledger is given below:

Dr. **NAME OF THE ACCOUNT** Cr.

Date	*Particulars*	*Folio*	*Amount (₹)*	*Date*	*Particulars*	*Folio*	*Amount (₹)*

Posting. It is the process of transferring entries from journal to ledger. It can be explained with the help of an example. Suppose, Mohan purchased on June 1 furniture for ₹ 10,000 on credit from Modern Furnitures. Its journal entry will be as follows:

Furniture Account	Dr.	₹ 10,000	
To Modern Furnitures			₹ 10,000
(Being the credit purchase of furniture)			

This entry will be posted to ledger as follows:

Dr. **FURNITURE ACCOUNT** Cr.

Date	*Particulars*	*Folio*	*Amount (₹)*	*Date*	*Particulars*	*Foilo*	*Amount(₹)*
1995 June 1	To Modern Furnitures A/c		10,000				

Dr. **MODERN FURNITURES** Cr.

Date	*Particulars*	*Folio*	*Amount (₹)*	*Date*	*Particulars*	*Folio*	*Amount (₹)*
				1995 June 1,	By Furniture A/c		10,000

The differnce between total of debits and total of credits in an account is called balance. If debit total is greater, then it is called 'debit balance' and is put on the credit side to close the account. When the credit total is greater it is called 'credit balance and is put on the debit side to make both sides equal.

FORM 1

LAXMI ELECTROPLATING — GOREGAON (EAST), MUMBAI - 400 063

CASH BOOK

CREDIT						DEBIT					
Date and Month	***Receipts***	***L/F No.***	***Dis-count***	***in Bank***	***Cash***	***Date and Month***	***Receipts***	***L/F No.***	***Dis-count***	***in Bank***	***Cash***
1.	To Opening Balanace b/F			1,500.00	100.0	2.	By. Mr. X (paid in full Settlement of ₹ 265)			1,500.00	250.0
3.	To Mr. Y (being cash received)			500.00	750.00						
4.	To Cash (being cash deposited Contra entry)					4.	By bank (being cash deposited Contra entry)				500.00
5.	To cash sales (being cash sales ₹ 250 and By cheque ₹ 1,100.00)			1,100.00	250.00	4.	by Coolie charges				10.00
						6.	By MR. Z (payment by cheque)		980.00		
7.	To Mr. A (being cheque received in full settlement of ₹ 760)			10.00	750.00		By bal. c/d				

FORM II

LAXMI ELECTROPLATING — GOREGAON (EAST), MUMBAI - 400 063

LEDGER BOOK

Month	*Date*	*Particulars*	*L/F No.*	*Amount (₹)*	*Month*	*Date*	*Particulars*	*L/F No.*	*Amount (₹)*
		(Mr. A's Account)							
Aug.	1	To goods		900.00	Sept.	2	By Cash		900.00
		(GOODS ACCOUNT)							
		(CASH ACCOUNT)							
Sept.	2	To Mr. A's A/c		900.00	Aug.	1	By. Mr. A's A/c		900.00

Illustration

	Journal Entry	Debit	Credit
Aug. 1.	Sold goods to Mr. X on credit X's Account. Dr.	900	
	To Goods Accounts (being goods sold on credit.		900
Sep.2.	Received cash from Mr. X in settlement of account.		
	Cash Account	900	
	To X's account (being cash received)		900

(iii) *Bills of Exchange,* Bills of exchange are bills receivable and bills payable. They are governed by the Negotiable Instruments Act. If A draws an instrument on B for goods received by B and the same is accepted by B in good faith, then for A it is a bill receivable and for B it is a bill payable.

Illustration

(a) A draws a bill on B for ₹ 1,000 for goods sold to him and B accepts it.

(b) A accepts a bill of ₹ 400 drawn by B for goods received by A.

In the book of A, the journal entry would be as follows:

	Debit	Credit
Bills Receviable A/c Dr.	1,000	
To B's Dr.		1,000
B's A/c Dr.	600	
To Bills Payable		600

In the book of B, the journal entry would be as follows:

	Debit	Credit
A's A/c Dr.	1,000	
To Bills Payable		1,000
Bills receivable A/c Dr.	600	
To A's A/c		600

Ledger Account with A

	Debit	Credit
Bills Receviable (B/R) Account		
To B's A/c		1,000
Bills Payable A/c (B/P) Account		
To Bills Payable	600	

Ledger Account with B

	Debit	Credit
B/R Account		
To A's Account	600	
B/P Account:		
By A's Account		1,000

B/R or B/P Ledger Account

Debit | **Credit**

Date	Particular	Amount (₹)	Date	Particular	Amount(₹)
	To			By	

B. Cost Records

(i) Register for Raw Materials: This is maintained by the stores department. By means of this register, it is easy to identify the materials received against the materials ordered. It enables the small entrepreneur to check prices against invoices. In this register, details of the raw material, *e.g.,* quality, quantity and prices, are recorded.

(ii) Production Register : To record the progress of a manufacturing order through all the main stages until the delivery of goods, a production register is maintained, in which the following information is entered:

(a) Particulars of production items;

(b) Quantity of production, quantity scrapped;

(c) Weight and measurement of the units;

(d) Date of issue.

In addition to this information, columns are provided for estimated material costs and comparing them with the actual costs. On the cost and accounts copy of the manufacturing order, the estimated total cost, including overheads, packaging, etc., is compared with the actual cost. The columns in the register are arranged in such a manner that they can be operated as simply as possible. At the same time, provision has been made for duplication.

(iii) Stock Register: A stock register is maintained to show the quantity of raw materials required, the quantitiy on order and the balance in stock, so that, as orders are received, decisions may be taken whether the purchase of additional materials is necessary.

The main items of information entered in the register are :

(a) Date;

(b) Serial number;

(c) Company's name;

(d) Quantity and price;

(e) Date of delivery ;

(f) Balance;

(g) Remarks.

If the small-scale unit utilises more than one type of raw material, separate folios are allotted for each item purchased and held in stock. The stock register enables an entrepreneur to record the location of the materials or components in stock. It is worthnoting that, in a store for a small-scale industry, it will not be a difficult matter for a storekeeper to keep a constant check on a number of stock items per week. In this way, physical stocks will be kept in line with the balance shown in the stock register. Every half-year, a physical check of the stock is undertaken. A specimen of a folio of a stock register is reproduced in Form 3.

FORM III
STOCK REGISTER

Date	*S. No.*	*Company's Name and Details*	*Quanity and Price*	*Date of Delivery*	*Balance*	*Remarks*

TRIAL BALANCE

After posting the accounts in the ledger, a statement is prepared to show separately the debit and credit balances. Such a statement is called 'trial balance'. The totals of debit and credit sides must he equal. If the two sides do not agree, there is definitely some error. Trial balance is prepared on a particular date which should be mentioned at the top.

The specimen form of a trial balance is given below:

TRIAL BALANCE OF MOHAN

as at March 31, 2007

Name of account	*Dr. (₹)*	*Cr. (₹)*
Capital Account		20,000
Drawings	6,000	
Sales		50,000
Purchases	30,000	
Shop rent and lighting	4,000	
Wages	6,000	
Shop fixtures and fittings	15,000	
Amounts due to suppliers		5,000
Amounts due from customers	6,500	
Cash in hand	1,500	
Cash at bank	6,000	
Total	**75,000**	**75,000**

Objectives and Functions of Trial Balance

Trial balance is prepared for the following reasons:

(i) ***To judge arithmetical accuracy of ledger.*** Trial balance helps to ascertain whether the posting and other accounting processes have been carried out accurately.

(ii) ***To get summary of accounts.*** Trial balance provides a summarised version of each account in the ledger. It enables the owner to know his assets, the amounts due from others and the amounts owed to others.

(iii) ***To locate errors.*** Trial balance helps in locating errors in books. However, it does not disclose all the errors.

(iv) ***To help in preparation of final accounts.*** Trial balance serves as the starting point for preparing profit and loss account and the balance sheet. The various adjustments that are to be made can be made only after the trial balance is ready.

Limitations of trial balance: The agreement of trial balance is not a conclusive proof of the accuracy of books and accounts. In spite of the trial balance agreeing, the following types of errors might remain:

(i) A transaction has not been entered at all in the journal.

(ii) A wrong amount has been written in both columns of the journal.

(iii) A wrong amount has been mentioned in the journal.

(iv) An entry has not at all been posted in the ledger.

(v) An entry is posted twice in the ledger.

Methods of Preparing the Trial Balance

(i) **Total method.** In this method the total of each side of an account is entered respectively in the debit and credit columns of the trial balance. Such a trial balance is called 'gross trial balance'.

(ii) **Balances method.** In this method, only the debit or credit balances are entered separately. This is known as the 'net trial balance'.

(iii) **Totals and balances method.** In this method, the total as well as balances are entered in the trial balance. Such a trial balance has four columns. The first one for the totals of the debt side of the various accounts, the second for the totals of the credit side of the various accounts, the third for debit balances and the fourth for credit balances.

(iv) **Totals method for excluding closed accounts.** This is similar to the first method. But those accounts which do not show any balance are omitted altogether.

Preparation of Final Accounts

Final accounts consist of profit and loss account and balance sheet.

Profit and Loss Account. It is prepared to calculate the net profit or loss of the business for a given accounting period. All incomes (gains) and expenses (losses) are included in it, except capital gains and capital expenditure. If the credit (income) side exceeds the debit (expenditure) side, there is net profit and *vice versa.* Net profit or net loss is transferred to the capital account of the owner. Profit and loss account not only helps to ascertain profit or loss, its analysis is useful in exercising control over expenses. Profit for a particular year can be compared with those of previous year to find out trends in efficiency of business.

From the trial balance given above, Profit and loss account would be as follows:

TRADING AND PROFIT AND LOSS ACCOUNT

for the year ended March 31, 2007

To purchase	₹ 30,000	By sales	₹ 50,000
To Gross Profits c/d	20,000		
	50,000		50,000
To Shop Rent and Lightings	4,000	By Gross Profit b/d	20,000
To Wages	6,000		
To Net Profit	10,000		
	20,000		20,000

Notes:

(i) *c/d* means carried down and b/d means brought down.

(ii) Opening stock, if any, would appear on the debit side and closing stock on the credit side of the Trading A/c.

(iii) Carriage inwards and other manufacturing expenses would appear on the debit side of Trading A/c.

Balance Sheet. It is a statement containing the assets and liabilities of a firm. It is prepared to show the financial position of the business on a particular date. Assets are shown on the right side and capitals and liabilities on the left side. The total of the two sides must always be equal.

On the basis of the trial balance and the profit and loss account given above, the balance sheet of Mohan would be as follows:

BALANCE SHEET

as at March 31, 2007

Liabilities		₹	*Assets.*	₹
Amount due to Suppliers		5,000	Shop fitting and fixture	15,000
Capital Account balance	20,000		Amount due from customers	6,500
Add: Net profit	10,000		Cash at bank	6,000
Drawings	30,0000		Cash in hand	1,500
Less:	6000	24,000		
Total		**29,000**		**29,000**

CONCLUSION

Maintenance of accurate and up to date accounts and records is quite essential for small business. The records come handy to the entrepreneur to know the way the enterprise is moving as well as exercise effective control of funds, overall performance of the enterprise. They also help to know the financial position of the business. Modern technology has made this much easier for the entrepreneur.

ANNEXURE

Books of Original Entry

In a business, most of the transactions are first recorded in subsidiary books like cash books, purchase-book, sales book, etc. A separate book is maintained for each class of transactions. An entry is recorded as and when the transaction takes place. These books are called books of original entry, because transactions are entered first of all in these books. From these books, the entries are posted in ledger and thereafter a trial balance is prepared. Generally, the following books of original entry are used in a business:

(i) **Cash Book.** It is used to record receipts and payments of cash, including receipts into and payments out of the bank. Cash receipts are recorded on the debit side and cash payments are recorded on the credit side. The cash book also serves as the cash account and bank account. Its balances are carried directly to the ledger. Therefore, cash book is also treated as a principal book. Several types of cash book are maintained, e.g., one column, two-column, three column cash books and petty cash book.

(ii) **Purchase Book.** It is used to record credit purchases of goods dealt in or of the material and stores required in the factory.

(iii) **Purchases Return Book.** It is maintained to record the returns and materials previously purchased.

(iv) **Sales Book.** It is to record sales of goods on credit.

(v) **Sales Return Book.** It is kept to record the returns made by customers.

(vi) **Bills Receivable Book.** It is used to record the receipts of promissory notes or hundis from various concerns.

(vii) **Bills Payable Book.** It is maintained to record the issue of promissory notes or hundis to other parties.

(viii) **Journal (Proper).** It is used to record the transactions which cannot be recorded in any of the books mentioned above. In the journal, transactions are originally recorded in a chronological (day-to-day) order. The format of a journal is as follows:

Date	*Particulars*	*L.f.*	*Dr.* (₹)	*Cr.* (₹)

Here date is the date of the transaction. Particulars contain the details of the account to be debited and credited along with a brief narration of the transaction. Ledger Folio (L.F.) refers to the page of the ledger where the particular account appears.

Thus, the books in which transactions are first of all recorded to enable further processing (preparation of ledger accounts) are called books of original entry or subsidiary books. These books by themselves are not complete. Only when ledger accounts are prepared, the information becomes meaningful.

The main advantages of journal are:

(a) It provides a chronological record of all transactions.

(b) It reduces the possibility of error because amounts to be debited and credited are written side-by-side. The two can be compared to see that they are equal.

(c) It provides an explanation of every transaction due to narration.

Advantages of Books of Original Entry

The use of subsidiary books offers the following advantages:

(i) *Division of Work.* The accounting work can be divided amongst different clerks, e.g., cash clerk for cash book, sales clerk for sales book, etc.

(ii) *Efficiency.* When a person performs the same accounting work over a period of time, he acquires its full knowledge and becomes an expert in handling it. As a result efficiency of accounting work increases.

(iii) *Time Saving.* Various accounting processes can be performed simultancously. Therefore, work gets completed quickly.

(iv) *Facility in Checking.* When the trial balance does not agree, the error can be located easily with the help of subsidiary books. Check can also be kept on errors and frauds.

(v) *Availability of Information.* Information relating to a particular class of transactions becomes available at one place because a separate book is maintained for each class of transactions.

12 CHAPTER MARKETING MANAGEMENT

"Marketing is a dynamic, exciting and challenging activity. It affords ample employment opportunities in the modern business world. The success of business enterprises depends upon the efficiency of marketing management."

"Marketing management is the anatysis, planning, implementation and control of programmes designed to create, build, and maintain beneficial exchanges with target buyers for the purpose of achieving organisational objectives. Marketing management seeks to influence the level, timing, and character of demand in a way that will help the organisation achieve its objectives. Simply put, marketing management is demand management."

— ***Philip Kotler***

Marketing is a system of integrated business activities designed to develop strategies and plans including marketing mixes to the satisfaction of customer wants of selected market segments or targets. It is an ongoing process involving a set of multidirectional as well as multidimensional activities. Marketing is a matching process by which a producer provides a marketing mix (product, price, promotion and physical distribution) that meets consumer demand of a target market within the limits of society.

The term market has come from a Latin word "Mercatus" meaning "to trade"

Promotion is the process of marketing communication involving information, persuasion and influence. Promotion is a systematic attempt to move forward from a stage of awareness to purchase action.

Of late, marketing management has been given much importance, especially by the SSI sector. This could be attributed to the vastly different market situations existing now. The demand for most products then exceeded the supply and anybody having the resources could normally do well. In a competitive environment small-scale industries face marketing problems from stage-to-stage.

Some of the factors which contribute to marketing problems of the small-scale industry could be identified as under:

(i) increasing competition from within the small-scale sector as well as from large industries with established brand names and marketing set up;

(ii) consumer awareness, even in rural and semi-urban areas, for quality goods;

(iii) the need to set up distribution networks for reaching out widely dispersed markets;

(iv) Inability of the SSI units to exploit the export markets.

(v) Use of inferior quality of technology

(vi) Lack of marketing knowledge

(vii) Poor as inadequate market research

(viii) Weak bargaining power

(ix) Inadequate sale promotion

Considerable difficulty is being experienced by small-scale industrial units in marketing their products due to their size, limited scale of operations and inability to set up an adequate network of retail outlets. With a view of facilitating the marketing efforts of small-scale units, it is considered desirable to encourage the operations of marketing organisations specially engaged in promotion of sales of products of cottage, tiny and small-scale industrial units. Any requests from such marketing organisations for financial assistance to meet their working capital needs should, therefore, be favourably considered by banks with due regard to the performance of such organisations in respect of recycling of bank credit.

The requirement, therefore, of systematic marketing efforts for survival and growth of small-scale industries, cannot be overemphasised. Basically, marketing involves:

— finding out what consumers want;

— planning and developing a product or a service to satisfy these wants;

— determining the best way to price, and distribute that product or service.

The various activities required to be looked into in detail for arriving at a sound marketing strategy comprise product planning, market segmentation, market research, sales promotion, advertising, pricing and distribution. However, depending upon the product, the market and the environmental conditions, the intensity of usage of these activities will differ.

The resources required for taking care of the various marketing aspects are obviously lacking with the small-scale sector with which they are not in a position to compete with large well-established business houses and have to face unfair competition. A small detergent manufacturer, for example, cannot compete with Hindustan Lever or Tatas for a market share due to his inability to conduct surveys, create a brand image, establish marketing channels etc. He has therefore to remain content with whatever residual market is left over after the major share is covered by these corporations. The Government has banned the large sector from producing certain items but such preventive measures have not solved the basic marketing problem of making available quality goods at a reasonable price to the consumer, *the ultimate aim of all manufacturing activities.* The consumer's interests must therefore be safeguarded. As a buyer he would certainly like to get quality goods at a reasonable cost without bothering to know whether the goods are produced by a small entrepreneur or by a big industrial house.

The strategy for marketing goods produced by entrepreneur must therefore be ultimately beneficial to the consumer. No consumer is going to purchase goods unless he is satisfied with their quality and wherever necessary by an efficient after-sales service.

The Marketing Concept

It is necessary to distinguish between marketing as a concept and marketing as a group of activitics that executives carry-out, between marketing as a *'thought-process'* and marketing as a *'doing-process'*. Marketing must start as a concept which defines the purpose of marketing operations rather than as a description of the operations themselves. For when a company has cmbraced the marketing concept there are many different ways in which the marketing functions can be organised according to the particular circumstances and environment in which the individual company finds itself. There is no universal formula for mobilising and organising the marketing effort and no single mould for casting a firm's marketing structure. There is, indeed, no universally accepted definition of *'marketing'*.

The American Marketing Association (AMA) defines marketing as *'the performance of business activities that direct the flow of goods and services from producer to consumer or user'*. As it stands, this definition is purely factual and descriptive. It emphasises activity rather than effective accomplishment. It does not provide an adequate explanation of which goods or services in what quantities and with what characteristics ought to be produced or of the importance of planning and integrating these and related activities concerned with the movement of goods and services from the producer to the consumer. Marketing does not merely take over where production leaves off but is concerned with determining the nature and scale of production and with profitability, exploiting a firm's capacities and technological know-how in relation to marketing opportunities. In other words, marketing decision precedes production decisions and investment decisions. The economies of large-scale production and return from long-range investments cannot be realised unless the output can be sold and the added capacity resulting from investment fully utilised, at least for most of the time. There is nothing so wasteful as doing with great efficiency that which should not have been done at all. Finally, the above definition places the consumer or user at the tail-end of the production-marketing sequence.

J.H. Buck, a Unilever food marketing specialist, gave his organisation's definition of marketing as *'the planning and execution of all aspects and activities of product so as to extent optimum influence on the consumer to result in maximum long-term profit'*.[1] The key element in this definition is 'maximum consumption at optimum price resulting in maximum long-term profit.' A company must first establish the benefits of its products to the prospective purchaser and these benefits must be saleable at a price at least sufficient to cover the cost of initial product development and of getting them across to the purchaser or user. Further, the bundle of benefits represented by the product must be recognised by the potential purchaser as value for the money he is asked to pay. At this stage, marketing aims to ensure that the quality and performance of the product, its penetration and the advertising, all combine to give the most effective share in the market. It is right and proper that this should be so since one of the major criteria by which a company's performance is judged is the profit earned in relation to capital employed in the business.

Allowing for varying degrees of generalisation and emphasis, most of the foregoing definitions are broadly in accord. The danger to be avoided, of course, is ending up with a definition which sacrifices precision for the sake of the generalisation. What is required is a precise and concise definition which is both meaningful to the individual firm, and at the same time, is applicable to all types of business in the consumer and industrial goods and service fields. Therefore, marketing can be defined as the primary management function which organises and directs the aggregate of business activities involved in converting customer purchasing power into effective demand for a specific product or service and in moving the product or service to the final customer or user so as to achieve company-set profit or other objectives.*

The term *'customers'* in the foregoing definition of marketing, means not only the ultimate consumer or user of product but the manufacturer's own customers, importers, retailers and wholesalers who must be induced to stock, distribute and give active selling support to the product if the final user is to be able to buy it. Effective demand means demand at price the customer is both able and willing to pay and at a profit that makes it worthwhile for a company to make and supply the product. By *'specific product or service'* is meant a product or service which by virtue of its differentiation, real or imaginary, can be readily distinguished from competitive substitute products or services. The differentiation, whether of a characteristic of the product itself, of its packaging or pricing, of its advertising and promotion, must be significant enough to form the basis of preference by the potential customer.

The Institute of Marketing codified a new definition in September 1986, with acknowledgement, and incorporating the following slight word changes: marketing is the management function which organises and directs all those business activities evolved in assessing and converting customer purchasing power into effective demand for a specific product or services to the final consumer or user so as to achieve the profit target or other objectives set by a company.

A very large part of the marketing effort of most companies and an ever-increasing share of marketing expenditures, is taken up with keeping the company's products on the move between the factory's warehouse and the final customer. The whole of the company's sales, effort, through personal selling and advertising, as well as the location of supply — warehousing, depot location, stock control and shipment, represent a major component in marketing costs. Whenever products stop moving for any reason on their journey towards the ultimate user, they accumulate cost — for warehousing and storage, insurance, stock-handling, order processing and packing, stock-obsolescence and deterioration.

Ideally, marketing aims to secure the optimum rate of movements of products from factory to final user, that is to say, that rate which combines the most profitable rates of sale and stock turn and the minimum level of investment in stocks consistent with providing adequate service to customers. This last point can be critically important in the case of certain goods subject to cyclical or seasonal supply and demand. Where it is necessary to hold strategic reserves of a particular commodity or product then the accumulation of cost by holding heavy stocks may be less than the accumulated cost of frequent or irregular short run production.

Finally, in our definition no assumption is made as regards the profits maximising or cost-minimising goals of the company. In any given set of circumstances, the profit objective is not the sole measure for judging a company's performance over a given period of time. Factors such as building up the company's prestige or status in the industry, the fear of attracting new entrants to the market, the fear of government intervention and regulations, the desire to an 'average-rate of profit' between the highest attainable short run profits and the greatest risk of maximum losses are other legitimate objectives or considerations. However, it is fair to say that every company goal, regardless of the language in which it may be couched, has an economic dimension.

---

1. Institute of Marketing and Sales Management, published paper No. 128, April 1962.

* The Institute of Marketing codified a new definition in September 1986, with acknowledgement, and incorporating the following slight word changes: marketing is the management function which organises and directs all those business activities evolved in assessing and converting customer purchasing power into effective demand for a specific product or services to the final consumer or user so as to achieve the profit target or other objectives set by a company.

Traditional Marketing vs. Modern Marketing

Traditional Marketing	*Modern Marketing*
1. Meaning It deals with production and products to be sold out at any cost to consumers.	It deals with production and distribution, satisfying the needs of consumers.
2. Satisfaction of consumers It deals with circulation of products, irrespective of satisfaction of consumers.	It considers consumer satisfaction as an important aspect.
3. Profit generation Profit-earning has weightage.	Profit motive is secondary to the satisfaction of the consumers.
4. Approach It is product-oriented.	It is consumer-oriented.
5. Mutual relations It does not find any relationship among the various marketing functions.	It takes into account relationship, coordination and integration among all the marketing functions.
6. Social responsibility It has such an approach.	It deals with satisfaction of consumers as a social responsibility. Therefore, it provides quality products, in time at reasonable prices. Moreover to pay taxes in time to govt. and participate in govt. welfare programmes.
7. Research and development It is absent in this regard.	However, it has a basis of research and development of products, marketing research for products, consumers and publicity.

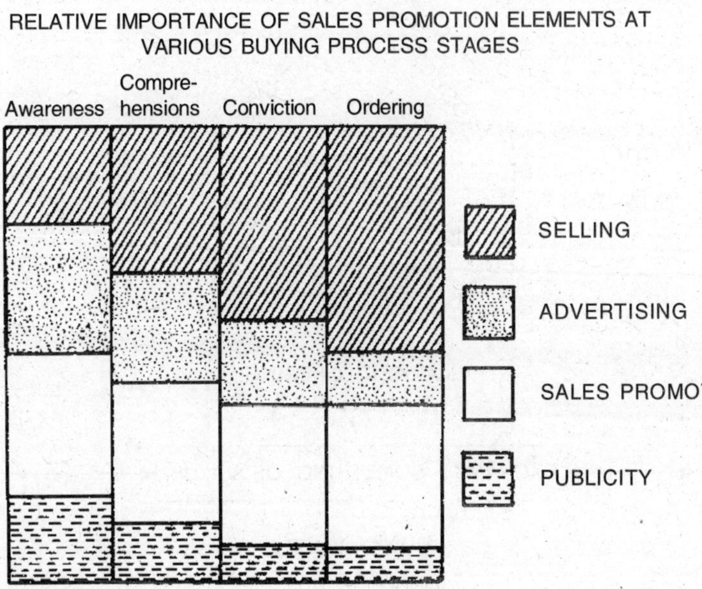

Fig. 12.1:

Source: Puzzullo, M.A. (1982), "Marketing for Bankers", American Bankers Association, Washington, p. 298.

The British Institute of Marketing has defined marketing as *'the creative management function which promotes trade and employment by assessing consumer needs and initiating research and development to meet them; it coordinates the resources of production and distribution of goods and services; determines and directs the nature and scale of the total effort required to sell profitably the maximum production to the ultimate user'*.

This definition is more explicit than that used by the AMA since it makes specific reference to the research and development responsibilities of marketing; to the key coordinating role it plays between the linked process of production, selling and distribution. According to the definition, marketing is nothing more or less than the total business function of producing a saleable product.

Salient Features of Marketing

The salient features of marketing are:

(i) It is a creative function;

(ii) It promotes business and employment;

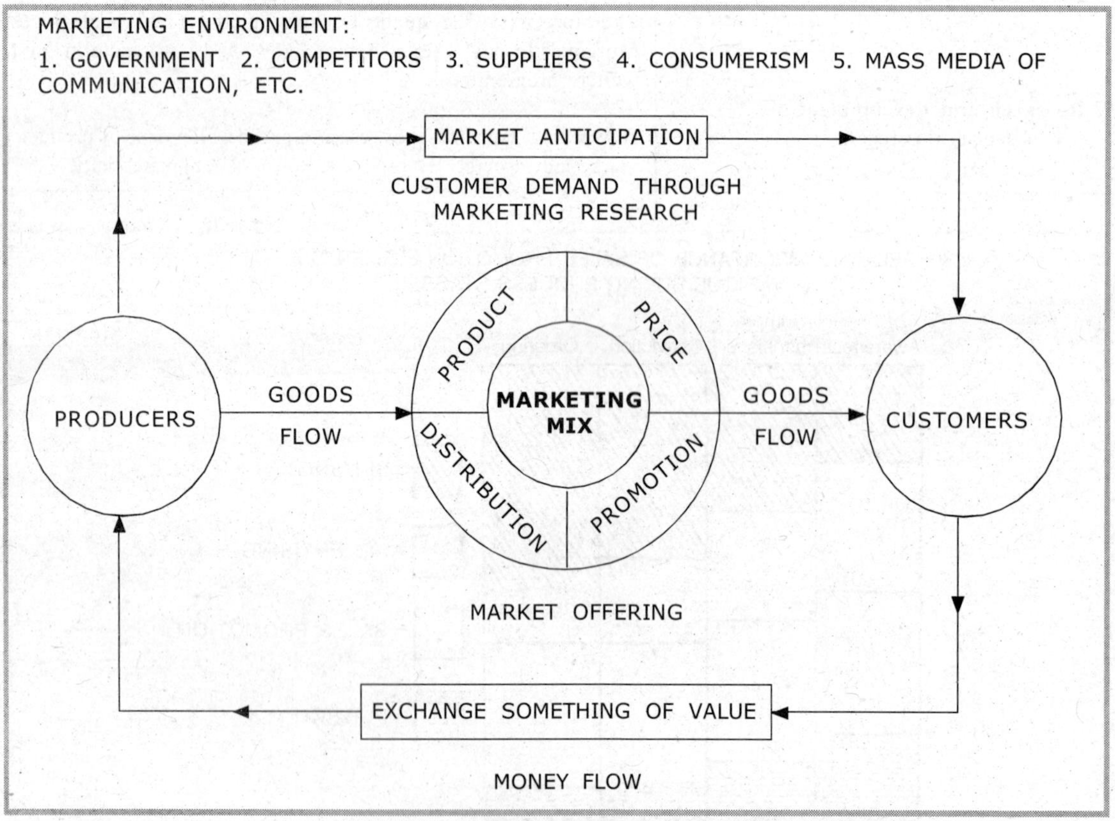

Fig. 12.2: Modern Marketing Process

(iii) It co-ordinates finance, production and distribution, and determines and directs the scale and value of the total efforts;

(iv) There is an emphasis on what the customer/borrower wants;

(v) There is an emphasis on the social good, on increasing employment, by giving the customer/consumer the chance to decide; and

(vi) It is a process of exchange between seller and buyer. It may be a commodity or a service.

Business firms in competitive markets must abandon the historical approach of manufacturing what they want to sell and instead manufacture what their customers want to buy. However, this does not mean that through market research, customers can provide the manufacturer with a fairly detailed specification of the product they want. In practice, consumers cannot demand product not already in existence; they are not very articulate when it comes to specifying their particular requirements; they have difficulty in visualising what the product should look like and what they expect it to do for them. The basic idea for a product comes from the manufacturer, arising out of his detailed knowledge and understanding of consumer needs, and his ability and ingenuity in translating, in technological terms, a specific need into a workable product at a price which the consumer is prepared to pay and which gives the manufacturer sufficient profit to make it worth his while to market it.

Thus, management decisions and the policies based on them are taken in the fullest possible knowledge of market factors and awareness of the effects of those decisions and policies on the market. This should not be taken to imply that all management decisions are reached in this way but simply that, in the final analysis, management has the responsibility for making a profit through supplying a marketable output, out of a company's technological facilities and know-how that creates saleable products. Production and investment plans, raw materials procurement and employment programmes can only be based on confidence in what can be sold.

Chart 12.1 Four Basic Business Strategies

	Products	
Markets	*Present Products*	*New Products*
Present Markets	Market Penetration	Products Development
New Markets	Market Development	Diversification

Source: Adapted from, Ansoff, H. (1965), *Corporate Strategy,* McGraw-Hill, New York.

Marketing Characteristics

Packaging	Product Price
Promotion	Distribution
Adaptability	Simplicity of operations
Building bonds with customers	Product Demonstration
Client education	Cost-based analysis
Competitive depositioning	Psychological repositioning
Product differentiation	Demographic International Education

The Principal Marketing Functions

A marketing function may be defined as a major specialised activity or group of activities performed in the marketing of goods and services. Although the performance of a specific function may be inescapable, it is frequently transferable; in other words it has to be performed by someone regardless of his official title and responsibilities. Another characteristic of a function is that, whereas its purpose may be unchanging, its content, in terms of the number and kinds of activities involved, may be subject to constant change. Newer and better ways of doing things and carrying out traditional functions are continually being developed.

Traditionally, some seven or eight so-called marketing functions have been listed and normally include: *(a)* the exchange functions of buying and selling, *(b)* the physical distribution functions of transporting, warehousing and handling goods between producer and customer, *(c)* what are usually described as the *'facilitating'* functions which take in product standardisation and simplification, commercial and market information, financing and risk-bearing. (It is questionable whether risk-bearing, in the true entrepreneurial sense of committing one's own resources to a speculative venture, really belongs in any list of marketing functions, risk-bearing is a responsibility jointly undertaken by the managers of a business or solely by the chief executive).

This kind of analysis is inadequate as a description of modern marketing activities since it fails to distinguish clearly between major functions and the specialised activities which comprise the different functions. Under the modern marketing concept, there are four principal functions — marketing research and information, product planning, selling and distribution, and advertising and promotion. Chart sets out those major functions and the specialised activities involved in each.

Marketing Mix

A successful marketing strategy depends upon a marketing mix of all the marketing elements and resources.

The basic marketing mix is the blending of four inputs or sub-mixes which form the core of the marketing system: (1) Product mix, (2) Place mix, (3) Promotion mix, and (4) Price mix. The outputs are optimum productivity and satisfaction.

Marketing Process

Marketing involves three basic inputs: the product, the promotional methods and the distribution system. These three are the core of the marketing programme and must be integrated to achieve maximum consumer satisfaction and optimum profits. The marketing process brings together producers and customers — the two important segments in any exchange. An exchange or a transaction takes place when a market offering is acceptable to the customer who is prepared to give something in return for the product he purchases.

The marketing process starts with knowledge of the customer, his needs and ends with a customer purchase and the satisfaction of those needs. Through technical product research and customer research, generalised needs are translated into specific product sales opportunities. Product planning identifies and specifies the particular product-price-package combinations to exploit these opportunities. Products are engineered or formulated (a number of variations of a single prototype may be made up), screened and tested with customers for overall acceptance

Chart 12.2 The Principal Marketing Functions

Specific function	*Activities involved*
Marketing Information and Research	Economic, business, trade, industry, consumer, user, product, sales and advertising research and analysis. Information handling and data processing. Marketing operations research. Competitive intelligence.
Product Planning	Determining and developing the company's product mix. Matching the products' specifications, packaging, pricing, performance and servicing to customer needs through product and service improvements and new product development.
Sales and Distribution	Field selling Selection of distribution channels Warehousing Transport Sales analysis Sales reporting Sales forecasting Sales budgets and quotas Merchandising Sales communications
Advertising and Promotion	Advertising to the customer or user in all media (press, television, cinema, radio, outdoor posters, etc.) Consumer promotion directed at the customer or user, e.g., reduced price offers, banded pack offers, premiums, competitions, couponing, etc. Point-of-purchase display material. Trade promotion, e.g., incentive schemes, display competitions, sales contests.

Extracted from *Marketing in a Competitive Economy* by Lesile Rodger.

and performance. Final decisions have to be taken on packaging design, pricing and trade terms. Assuming that one product stands out as eminently suitable in all major respects the next step is to prepare a marketing plan, in writing, setting down all the relevant facts about the product, the market, and the competition, the company's marketing objectives and sales goals and the means by which they are to be achieved.

Market Segmentation

No organisation can effectively serve all sections of the market. This is so, because customers are numerous, widely spread over and differ in their buying practices/requirements and perceptions. This is more relevant to SSI units, in view of their resource constraints. It is, therefore, essential to first decide which segments of the market the organisation would be in the best position to serve. This can be facilitated through market segmentation.

This country has many diversities with regard to consumption patterns. Thus, in reality, it is a conglomeration of several markets in which people tend to differ. People can be regrouped demographically, economically, and socially, but even within these groups, each set of consumers can be differentiated further. For instance, individuals sharing a common demographic profile may show variations in terms of a cultural and demographic mosaic. The marketer has to recognise all these differences since each individual represents a unique opportunity.

Segmentation is dynamic and extends beyond the traditional two-dimensional classification. We need to treat it as three- four- or five-dimensional segmenting. Many intelligent companies

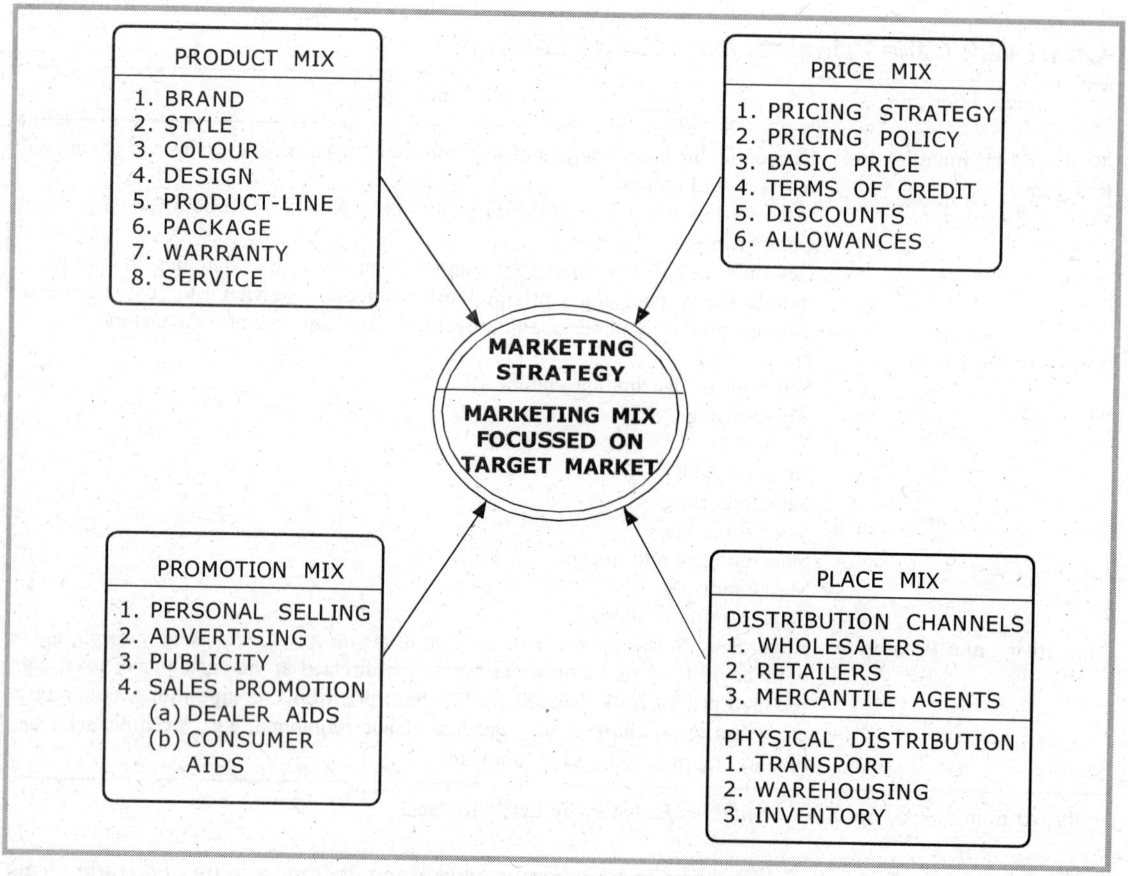

Fig. 12.3: Elements of Marketing Mix

have been able to do beyond two-dimensions. However, it is only the gut feeling of the marketer that will help him venture into the fourth and fifth dimensions of segmentating. Thus, segmentation itself becomes a multi-dimensional issue, and a marketer has to face a complex matrix in terms of positioning products.

Segmentation or subdivision of the market is based upon the modern marketing concept, i.e., market-oriented strategy and philosophy. Segmentation places special emphasis on the demand side of the market. It is a more rational and more precise adjustment of the product and marketing effort is tuned to consumer of user needs and requirements. Segmentation implies bending of supply to the will of demand as far as feasible and desirable. It recognises that there are several demand schedules and not necessarily a single demand schedule or curve. For each demand schedule representing a group of buyers with similar needs and characteristics, we can prepare a separate and precise market offering or marketing mix.

Market segmentation is a method for achieving maximum market response from limited marketing resources by recognising *differences* in the response characteristics of the various parts of the market. In a sense, market segmentation is the strategy of *divide and conquer, i.e.,* dividing markets in order to conquer them. Its philosophy is something for everybody, within practicable limits. Marketing strategy is adjusted to inherent differences in buyer behaviour. For different groups of customers, *i.e.,* market segments, we have different sets of marketing strategies. Segmentation strategy is an answer to the question, "*To whom* should we sell our products, and *what* should we sell them?" It is a strategic choice concerned with "doing the right things" as opposed to the tactical choice, "doing things right".

Market segmentation enables the marketers to give better attention to the selection of customers and offer an appropriate marketing mix for each chosen segment, or a group of buyers having homogeneous demand. Each subdivision or segment can be selected as a market target to be reached with a distinct marketing mix.

Marketers must go beyond the age-old classifications based on consumer locations, age-profiles, gender, and economic strata, among others, and take into account several other factors that differentiate the market.

Cultural Factors: Societal and cultural factors play a significant role in defining markets for particular products. Unfortunately, although marketers often talk about this, they rarely address it properly. This is particularly true when the product is of a personal nature. Another example of cultural inhibitors is our psyche to avoid wastage. This holds in the consumer durables replacement market. Try and convince a consumer to junk his existing, but outdated, television set for a state-of-the-art set — and even if he fits into the profile of your ideal customer, the chances are that he will refuse to do so. The solution, then, is to offer him some kind of an exchange scheme. As long as he feels that he is getting some value for his old set — in terms of a reduced price — he can be initiated into making a purchase decision. Of course, cultural factors are also dynamic and changing constantly.

Market segmentation consists of the following steps:

(i) identification of segments of a market;

(ii) evaluation of the target group of consumers; and

(iii) product positioning.

Market consists of buyers, who differ in one or more respects. They may differ in their wants, resources, geographical locations, buying attitudes/practices. One may use one or more of these variables to identify suitable segments or target groups of consumers.

(a) Geographic Variables

These comprise district, region, state, nation, climate, etc. The unit will have to decide on one or a few geographical areas to operate in. It depends primarily on the nature of its product.

(b) Demographic Variables

These include sex, age, family, size, income, occupation, religion, etc. They form an important base for distinguishing consumer groups. For example, a textile unit may use as a demographic variable for market segmentation and may decide to produce sarees, shirting and suiting.

(c) Psychographic Variables

These variables comprise social status, lifestyle and personality traits. Producers of cosmetics, alcoholic beverages and furniture use lifestyle as a base for market segmentation.

(d) Behavioural Variables

Consumers differ in knowledge, tastes, attitudes and response. It is, therefore, necessary for a producer to take into account these factors.

Once the broad segments of the market are identified, the producer has to evaluate those segments and select one or a few segment which he can reach and serve.

Box 12.1 Elements of the Marketing Mix

1. *General Planning:*
   (–) Establishing an acceptable and possible rate of growth.
   (–) Determining the size and extent of market where business may function profitably.
   (–) Determining the costs and expenses needed for the business operations.
   (–) Estimating the finance needed.
2. *Product Planning:*
   (–) Determining the product or service offered.
   (–) The possible improvement and innovation in the product.
   (–) The brand and packaging policies.
   (–) The importance of servicing and after-sales service.
3. *Pricing:*
   (–) The level and psychological aspects of prices.
   (–) The appropriate margin.
   (–) Research price maintenance.
   (–) Government control, if any.
4. *Channels of Distribution:*
   (–) Selling through wholesalers.
   (–) Appointing sole selling agencies.
   (–) Selling direct through own sales force.
5. *Sales Force:*
   (–) The extent of personal selling.
   (–) Extent of approach to wholesalers and retailers.
   (–) Extent of approach to consumers direct.
6. *Advertising and Sales Promotion:*
   (–) The advertising programme.
   (–) Importance given to display and point-of-sale material.
   (–) Extent of sales promotion aimed at consumers.
   (–) Extent of sales promotion to dealers.
7. *Physical Handling:*
   (–) Transportation.
   (–) Warehousing.
   (–) Inventory policies.
   (–) Possible reduction in costs.
8. *Marketing Research:*
   (–) Sales analysis.
   (–) Field surveys.
   (–) Use of outside agencies.

Building the image of a product is an essential pre-requisite for successful marketing. This is referred to as product positioning and can be effected through one or more of the following ways:

(a) Highlighting specific/special features of the product: Some toothpaste manufacturers attribute ayurvedic characteristics to their product.

(b) Indicating specific benefits: A two-wheeler manufacturer advertises the high mileage yielded by his product, in order to highlight fuel economy.

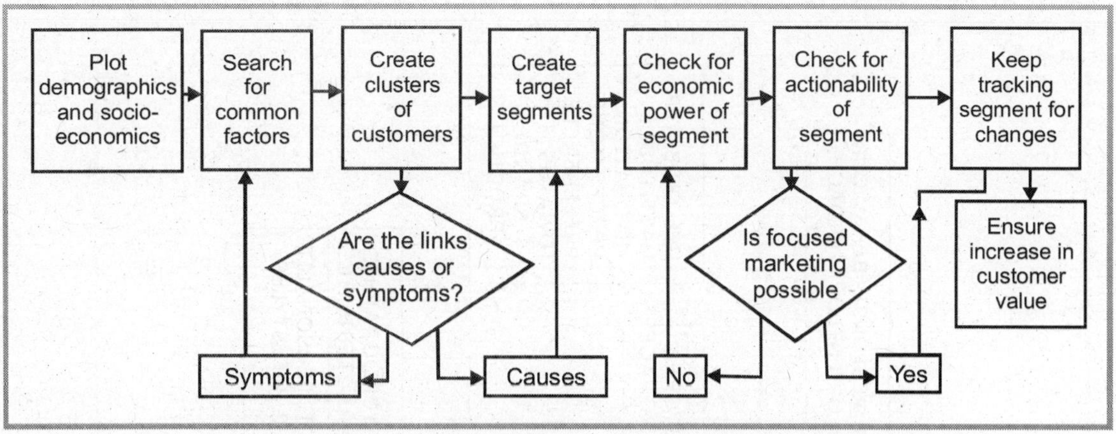

Fig. 12.4: How to Add Value Through Segmentation

(c) *Utility for special occasions:* Identifying usage of product with special occasions, e.g., special occasion sarees or wedding sarees.

(d) *Indicating user category:* The producer highlights the specific category of consumers for whom the product is meant. For example, calculators are being designed and produced for various groups of consumers, e.g., students, engineers, accountants and scientists.

(e) *Comparing against similar product:* In this case, a producer tries to show his customers how his product is superior to other products. For example, a TV manufacturer may highlight the quality of picture tubes which are being used in his TV sets.

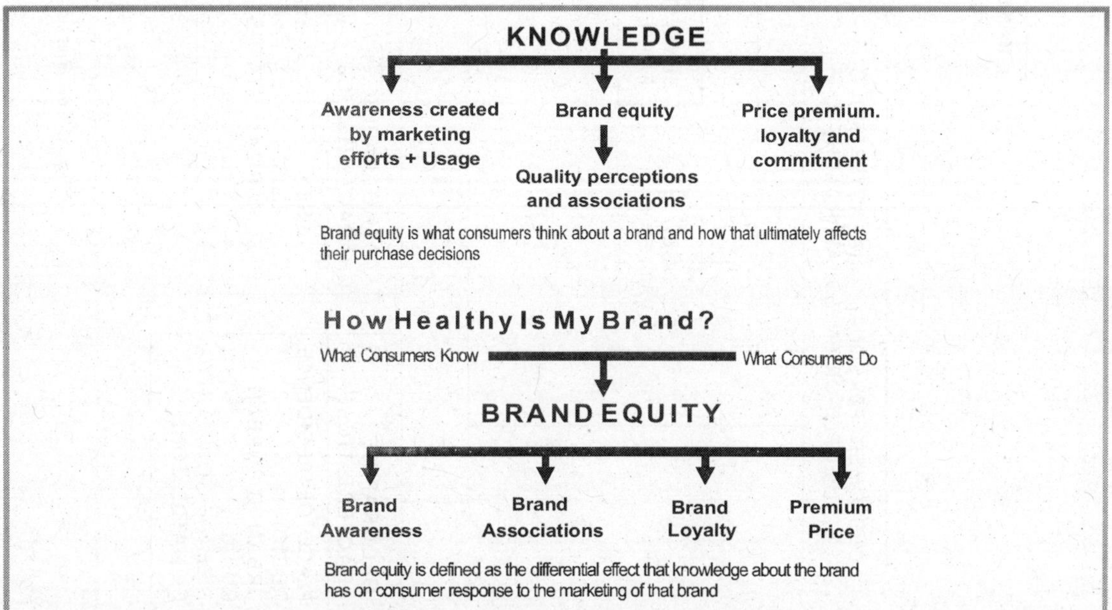

Fig. 12.5: Winning Brands Approach

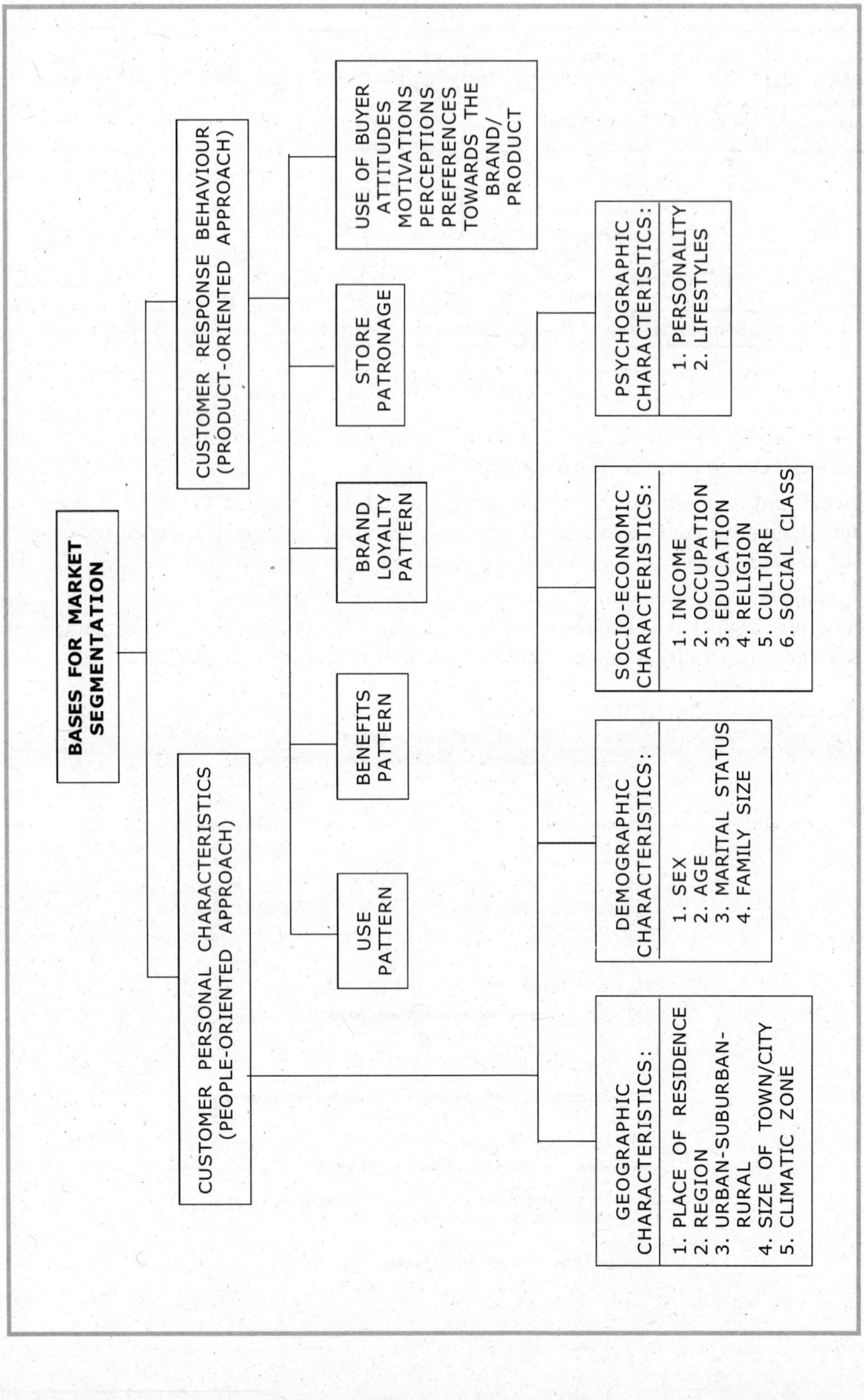

Fig. 12.6: Bases for Market Segmentation

Market Positioning

The market positioning is the process of distinguishing an enterprise or a product from competitors along real dimensions — products or corporate values that are meaningful to customers — to become the preferred enterprise or product in a market. Essentially, the process involves knowing what the market wants and needs, identifying enterprise and competitors' strengths and weaknesses, and assessing abilities to meet market requirements better than enterprise competitors do. There are three logical steps to translate market positioning into reality. They are:

Step-1: Analyse market opportunities for your company: Identify areas in which your company feels it is likely to enjoy a differential advantage over the competition. For example, if a large manufacturer of vinyl products used in the construction industry wants to evaluate opportunities in ₹ 25 cm. floor-covering market, the marketer will have to select a particularly opportune area and develop a positioning strategy for his company's market entry. He studies sales potential of the new market, its growth rate, buyers and buying influences, suppliers, and their influences, cost to make and sell, prices, profit margins, intensity of competition, market dynamics and channels of distribution. The success factors like market size, market growth, barriers to entry, the negotiating power of buyers and suppliers, price sensitivity and environment may be charted, both quantitatively and qualitatively.

Step-2: Select a market and target a specific subgroup: To fine-tune a positioning strategy, segment the market into subgroups, for example, by product (ceramic tile, brick, sheet vinyl) and by purchaser (residential, institutional or commercial). Any segment can be subgrouped, for example, residential sheet vinyl segments into: (1) new and replacement floor covering by contractors, and (2) Do it yourself kit (DIY) – If DIY is selected, research indicates that installation and upkeep are two vital attributes the purchaser looking for in sheet vinyl floor covering. A product space map can be drawn along with the positions of competitors.

Step-3: Devise a competitive strategy: To achieve this, a company must focus primarily on identifying its competitors' weaknesses and capitalizing on its own strengths to differentiate an offer.

A matrix should be drawn, ranking its own and competitors business strengths on a scale of 1 to 5 incorporating, for example, market share, profitability, product range, coverage, corporate profile, financial strength, cost position, product differentiation, quality of management, distribution, technology and company reputation. After such analysis, find gaps to differentiate an offer. Make it look like a benefit bundle, or value package involving products, price, distribution and service mix. If product distinction is not possible, the range of other possibilities is endless: everything from timely response to enquiries, to help in design and application, delivery, warranties, return policies, price and payment conditions, service and maintenance, salesperson skills, process or a strong distribution network.

Marketing Research

In a dynamic economy, marketing research acts as the investigative arm of the marketing manager — a management tool in the planning-control cycle. Marketing research covers: (1) market research; (2) sales research; (3) product research; (4) advertising and promotion research; (5) research on sales methods and policies; (6) distribution research, including dealer research.

Marketing research is an invaluable tool to *plan, measure* and *evaluate* marketing effort so that the marketing management can offer: (1) the right product; (2) the right package, and brand;

Box 12.2 The Right Time Approach

Product Launch

Before time: the product is not relevant to the concerned target audience within the specified geographical area as a function of time; the necessary infrastructure is not available to support the product; the need for the benefits of the product category is more a figment of the marketer's imagination, than based on market realities.

On time: the need-benefit for the product category is just about surfacing; the necessary infrastructure to support the product is in shape or is taking shape; the product is an early mover in its category.

After time: the product's technology is outdated/obsolete or second-grade; the product is the fifth, sixth... entrant in its category.

Promotions

Tie up with the tide (seasonality) if the resources are limited; for a player of size and financial muscle, unconventional timing in promotions can deliver it a strategic marketing edge.

Between Elements of the Marketing Mix/Packaging

Synchronise the timing between promotions and distribution to avoid an advertising and product availability trap; packaging can certainly be a means for differentiation, but futuristic packaging reflects more often than not on high product price.

Exit

Exit first with a replacement to maintain/acquire the position of a technology leader; if existing altogether from the producer category, make a lot of noise, let the competition be confused, and get out.

(3) the right price; (4) the right promotion; (5) the right channels; (6) the right means of physical distribution; (7) the right trade policies, and (8) the right marketing strategies and plans.

The marketing concept also emphasises the role of information as the key resource to accomplish the twin objectives of customer satisfaction and profitability. Thus, marketing research has grown along with the expanded role of marketing as the focus for business decision marketing:

(1) To identify and define the problem, including the causes.
(2) To suggest reasonable and profitable alternative courses of action.
(3) To determine the most desirable alternative courses of action.
(4) To test the feasibility of particular alternative course of action decided upon by management.

Marketing research process is conducted through several steps. The research process steps are as follows:

(i) Defining the problem and objective of the project.
(ii) Conducting a situation analysis.
(iii) Conducting an informal investigation to know whether a detailed investigation is necessary.
(iv) Planning and conducting a formal investigation:
    (A) Selecting the sources of information.
    (B) Selecting the methods for collecting data.
    (C) Preparing forms.
    (D) Pre-testing the forms.

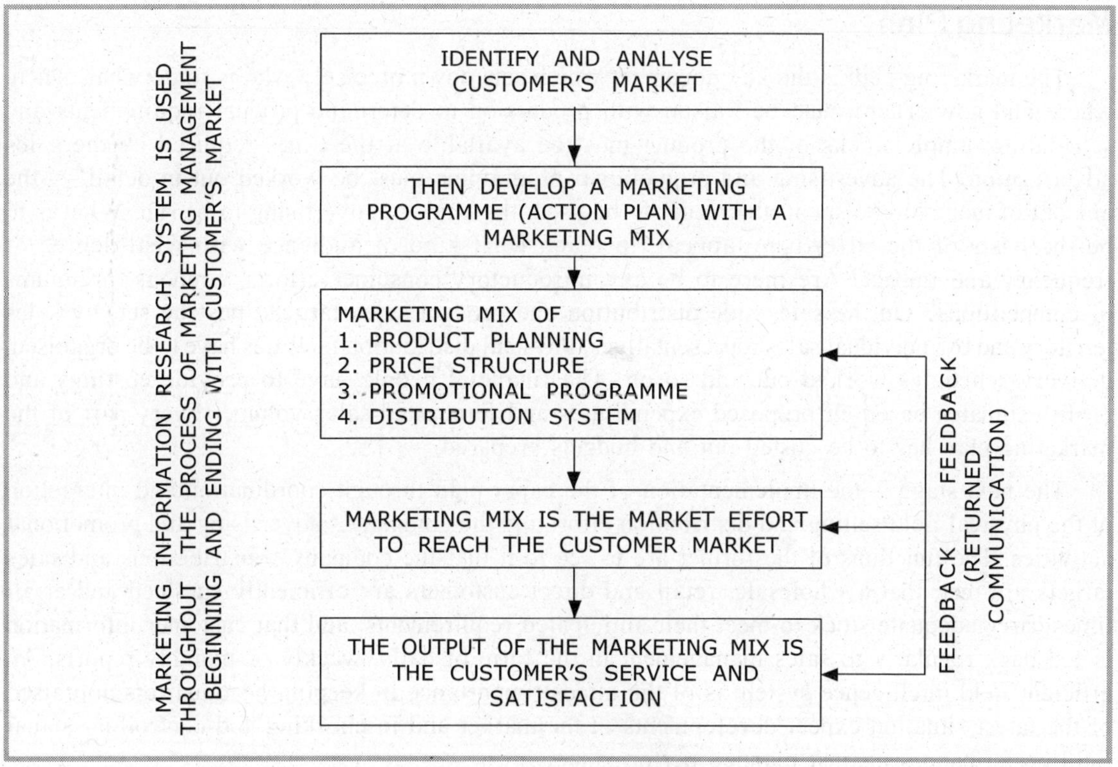

Fig. 12.7: Marketing Research Begins and Ends with Customers

Notes:
1. Company's marketing efforts start and end with customers.
2. Marketing research is a valuable tool to optimise the marketing effort so that we have a minimum of waste and maximum of advantage.
3. Marketing research enables identification and analysis of customer's market.
4. Marketing research is used for devising an appropriate marketing programme.
5. Each component of the marketing mix is formulated on the basis of marketing information and research on product, price, promotion and distribution.
6. Marketing research is also used to evaluate the results of marketing effort when marketing programme is implemented. It provides feedback information on customer's satisfaction and on the achievement of marketing goals.
7. At present, marketing research is also used to evolve the solution of consumers' problems as well as ecological and environmental problems under the societal concept of marketing.

(E) Planning the samples.

(F) Collecting the data.

(v) Analysing and interpreting data.

(vi) Preparing a written report for management.

Marketing research is interested in five vital areas of marketing: (1) Market; (2) Product; (3) Price; (4) Promotion; and (5) Distribution. Market survey indicates information on consumer demand. Marketing mix consisting of the 4 Ps indicates the market offering and effort to serve the demand. Fig. 12.7 provides the details of the aforesaid five vital areas of marketing.

Marketing Plan

The marketing plan is the key document which sets down precisely who is to do what, when, where and how. There must be liaison with production to determine product requirements and scheduling; ample stocks of the product must be available at the times required by the sales advertisation. The advertising and promotional programme must be worked out in detail — the amount of money to be spent, the media to be used, the kind of advertising to be run. What is to be the basis of the advertising appeal, to reach what kind of audience with what degree of frequency and impact? Are there to be any introductory consumer efforts, coupons, premiums of competitions? On the sales side distribution and product sales targets must be set, by sales territory and by individual sales representatives. Physical distribution facilities have to be organised, delivery schedules worked out and so on. The financial people have to provide costings and profit estimates based on proposed expenditures and forecasted sales volume. Every part of the marketing plan has to be costed out and budgets prepared.

The next stage is the implementation of the paper plan through coordination and interaction of the physical field selling and distribution effort and the company's advertising and promotional activities. The functions of the former are to see to it that the company's distributions and sales targets are met, that a wholesale, retail and direct customers are efficiently surviced and at all times carry adequate stock to meet their anticipated requirements, and that customer information is fed back regularly to sales management in the form of daily, weekly or monthly reports. An efficient field intelligence system is of the utmost importance in keeping headquarters appraised of the latest situation expect developments in the market and in checking and controlling actual field performances against planned performance.

Advertising and sales promotion activities run parallel with the physical selling and distribution operations, and include advertising and display material aimed directly at the consumer user; trade and technical press advertising to distributors, trade buyers, professional groups, etc., direct main, trade receptions, and planned sales presentations to trade buyers, committees or associations; consumer and trade incentive schemes, such as special offers, bonuses, competitions, premiums, etc.

India, like many developing countries, is expanding in the number of efficient marketing organisations. Marketing enterprises engaged in meaningful market research on a continuing basis are very few. There are distributing organisations which have undertaken promotional functions. There is just a beginning of designing the products after a study of customer requirements. Very few so-called marketing organisations possess adequate resources to spend on advertising and so stimulate interest of prospective customers. In a developing country, its economy can be greatly expanded, improved and diversified by efficient marketing organisations, manned by expert personnel. Small industries need them more. If their share in domestic, Government and foreign markets is to be secured and expanded, the small entrepreneur should develop a new attitude and assist in the process of building up powerful and prosperous marketing organisations.

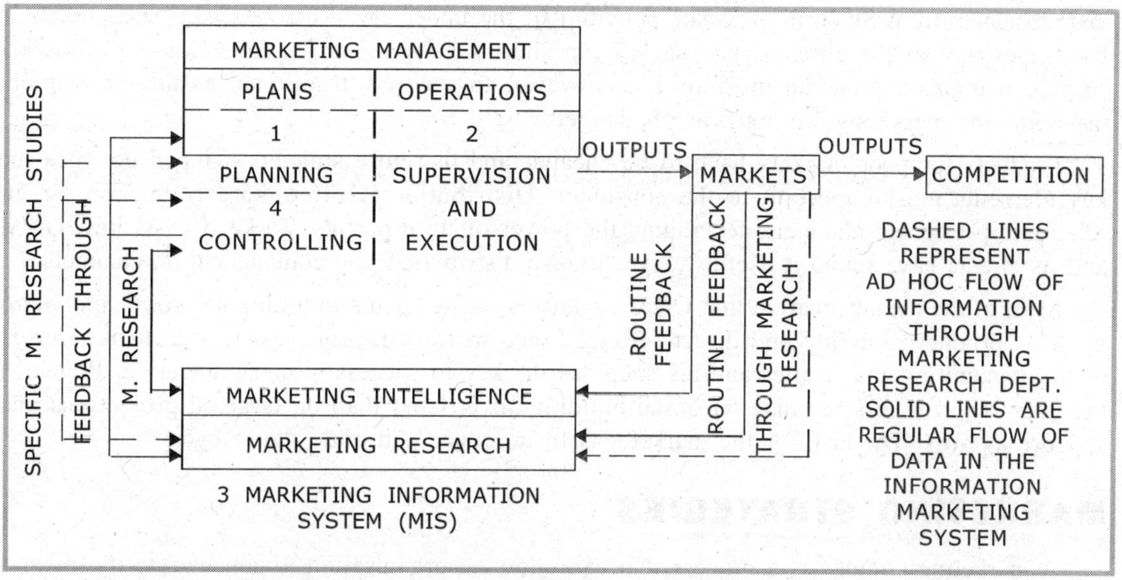

Fig. 12.8: Marketing Research as a Component of Marketing Information System (MIS)

Notes:
1. Planning subsystem decides objectives, policies and strategies and then plans marketing programmes for action.
2. Operations subsystem executes the marketing programme.
3. Marketing information is a subsystem of marketing management. It connects outside environment with the firm. It feeds data on markets, competitors and other external factors. These data are inputs to the control function and to the planning function. The planning function seeks new marketing opportunities and new marketing programmes.
4. Controlling is the fourth subsystem of marketing management. It monitors the marketing operations and their result. If feedback points out deviations from plans, operations are adapted to the changing conditions or objectives (standards) are modified to reflect the changes in the marketing environment.
5. Information is the life-blood of planning, directing and controlling any enterprise. Data circulate, like blood, through the channels or functional areas of a business — production, finance, personnel and marketing. Customers, competitors and external environment interact with marketing.

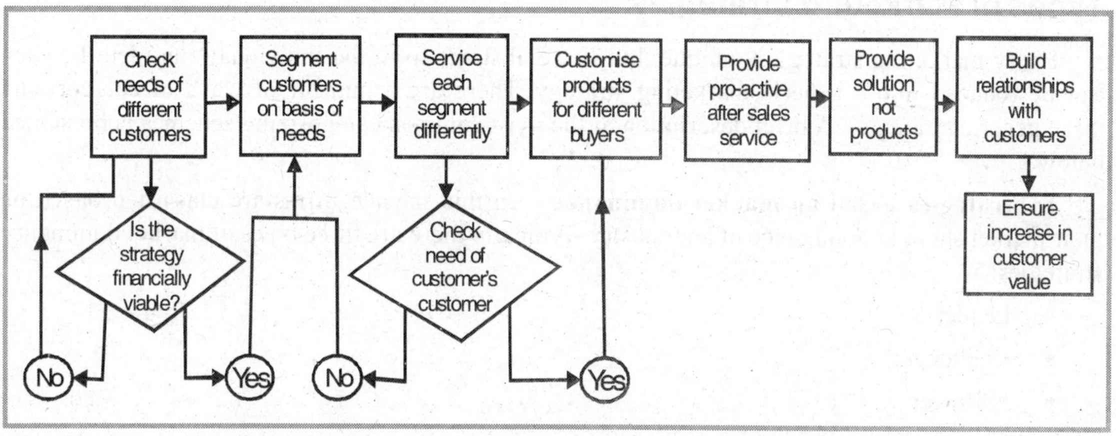

Fig. 12.9: How to Add Value in Industrial Marketing

Target Marketing

Business models targeting low-income consumers require managers to change their mindset from one focused on revenue and margin maximisation to one concerned with sales volume and market penetration. Since the revenue potential of the underserved markets can be as much as five times that of the elite market, sacrificing short-term unit margin for volume and market share can improve long-run profitability. However, to succeed, traditional assumptions about managing the marketing mix must be challenged.

Products for poor markets have to be cheaper and therefore simpler, stripped down to the key elements most important to the consumer. Distribution is often more reliant on direct, relationship-oriented channels, leveraging the power of third parties. To keep costs low, O&M and its clients have found it useful to synchronise distribution and communication channels.

Most of the communication that O&M organises for its clients in traditional *haats* and *melas* includes product sampling and direct selling. Since word-of-mouth plays a significant role in poor communities, the retailer and his shop are the key to successful communication. Reaching the poor requires less reliance on brand-building advertising than on targeted promotions and support services. The task for the marketer is to introduce and build the category.

MARKETING STRATEGIES

A marketing strategy is a process that can allow an organisation to concentrate its (always limited) resources on the greatest opportunities to increase sales and achieve a sustainable competitive advantage.

A good marketing strategy should integrate an organization's marketing, goals, policies, and action sequences (tactics) into a cohesive whole. Many companies cascade a strategy throughout an organization, by creating strategy tactics that then become strategy goals for the next level or group. Each group is expected to take that strategy goal and develop a set of tactics to achieve that goal. This is why it is important to make each strategy goal measurable. Marketing strategies are dynamic and interactive.

Types of Marketing Strategies

Every marketing strategy is unique, but if we abstract from the individualizing details, each can be reduced into a generic marketing strategy. There are a number of ways of categorizing these generic strategies. A brief description of the most common categorizing schemes is presented below:

1. Strategies based on market dominance – In this scheme, firms are classified based on their market share or dominance of an industry. Typically there are three types of market dominance strategies:

- Leader
- Challenger
- Follower

2. Porter generic strategies – strategy on the dimensions of strategic scope and strategic strength. Strategic scope refers to the market penetration while strategic strength refers to the firm's sustainable competitive advantage.

- Cost leadership
- Product differentiation
- Market segmentation

3. Innovation strategies – This deals with the firm's rate of the new product development and business model innovation. It asks whether the company is on the cutting edge of technology and business innovation. There are three types:

- Pioneers
- Close followers
- Late followers

4. Growth strategies – This strategy deals with "How should the firm grow?". There are different ways of growth, but the most common are:

- Horizontal integration
- Vertical integration
- Diversification
- Intensification

5. Marketing warfare strategies/Warfare based strategies – This scheme draws parallels between marketing strategies and military strategies.

MARKETING INSTITUTIONS AND ASSISTANCE

> *"Marketing institutions aim at giving fillip to marketing of products of enterprises by total integration and co-ordination of all the factors that will influence the final sale."*

Over the years, India has worked on beneficial strategies and incorporated technology resulting in the emergence of efficient marketing organisations and distribution centres, thus seeing a shift from the inadequacy of these firms. However, this is just a beginning of designing the products after a study of customer requirements. Very few, so-called marketing organisations possessed adequate resources to spend on advertising and so stimulate interest of prospective customers. In a developing country, its economy can be greatly expanded, improved and diversified by efficient marketing organisation, manned by expert personnel. Small industries need them more. If their share in domestic, government and foreign markets is to be secured and expanded, the small entrepreneur should develop a new attitude and assist in the process of building up powerful and prosperous marketing organisations.

Institutional Support

The success of marketing depends solely on well established institutional set-ups and timely assistance without any hassels. Although the institutional set up for marketing has been broad-based, it is biased towards international marketing in preference to internal markets. Another feature is that a majority of these institutions are in the public sector.

With a view to assisting small-scale industries, the government and other agencies have reserved certain items to be purchased from them. The National Small Industries Corporation and State Small Industries Corporations assist small-scale industries in selling their products to the Government.

The Khadi and Village Industries Commission and the Handicrafts and Handlooms have their own distribution agents and their own marketing arrangements.

Moreover, the Government has established trade centres to cater to the marketing needs of the small-scale industries sector. The NSIC and the STC help this sector to export its products.

Let us discuss in detail the methods of the marketing of the products of the small-scale industries sector:

Central Government Stores Purchase Programme

The Central Government Stores Purchase Programme provides an outlet for the products of industrial units in the country. This programme was then operated by the Director-General of Supplies and Disposals, Government of India. Under the programme, the DGS&D is responsible for arranging the purchase and delivery of all the stores required by the Central Government, certain specified items from the scope of this department. It also purchases the stores needed by State Government, public sector organisations and other government and semi-government bodies.

The two major recommendations of the Stores Purchase Committee set up under the chairmanship of the Deputy Minister of Works, Housing and Supply, and accepted by the Government of India relating to the small-scale sector were:

(i) Price preference to products of cottage and small-scale industries, including reservation of certain items of stores for purchase only from this sector; and

(ii) Greater facilities for the registration of cottage and small industries.

The objective was to encourage the production and utilisation of industrial products manufactured by the small-scale sector by State purchases. To achieve this objective, the items of Government purchases have been divided into the following four groups by the DGS&D:

Group I: Items which are of no interest to small-scale units and can be procured only from the large-scale sector.

Group II: Items which, by their very nature, require large-scale firms as prime contractors but permit substantial scope to purchase components and parts from small-scale units.

Group III: Residuary items which both small-scale as well as large-scale firms can supply. Tenders for items falling under the groups are invited from all parties, including small-scale industries.

Group IV: Items which are reserved for exclusive procurement from small-scale units. The present list consists of 379 items.

Special Facility for Small-scale Sector

The present policy offers the following special facilities to small-scale units:

(i) Application forms for initial registration and renewal are issued free of charge;

(ii) No registration fee is charged;

(iii) Free tender forms are supplied;

(iv) Tenders are accepted without a security deposit from those small-scale units which are registered with the NSIC and whose competency is certified by the Council;

(v) In certain cases, purchase of items in group III is also confined to small-scale industries;

(vi) Where basic considerations like quality and delivery conditions are comparable, or where small-scale industries have an advantage over large-scale industries, or where the former

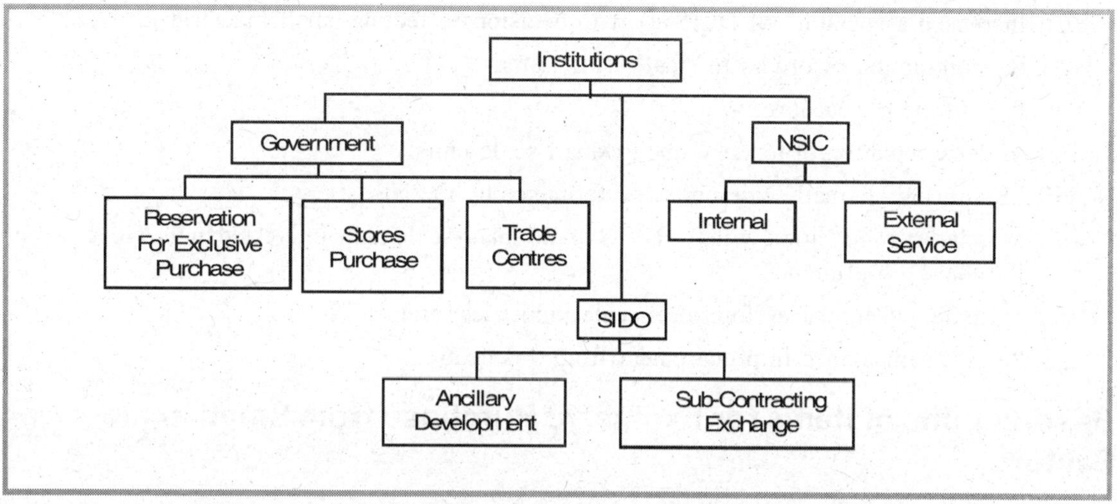

Fig. 12.10: Institutional Market Support to Small-scale Sector

have established themselves as suppliers to the Government on competitive terms, the products of small-scale industries are given preference over products of other manufacturers; and

(vii) In the case of Group III items, which are purchased from both large-scale and small-scale units, the small-scale units are accorded suitable and reasonable price preference up to a maximum of 15 per cent. The actual quantum of price preference is decided in each case on merit.

This price preference is not, however, granted automatically and is subject to certain conditions. The basic consideration is conformity to specification, quality, delivery, capacity, etc.

Price preference is not granted in the following cases:

(a) Where the items are reserved for exclusive purchase from small-scale units;

(b) Where competition against tender enquiries exists amongst the small-scale units alone; and

(c) Where tenders are received from both small-scale units and large-scale units and the lowest offers are from small-scale units and their capacity is more than sufficient to meet the demand.

The offers received from middlemen for the products of small-scale industries are treated as offers from small-scale units for the purpose of price preference. All small-scale units, whether registered with the DGS&D, the NSIC or the Directors of Industries are eligible for price preference.

The subcommittee appointed in 1975 under the chairmanship of the DC (SSI) by the High Power Committee had made recommendations concerning the following aspects:

(i) Categorisation and review of items under groups (referred to above);

(ii) Uniform purchase and price preference to be adopted by all Central and State Government Departments for small-scale units;

(iii) Increased association of DC(SSI) with decisions affecting small industries;

(iv) Subcontracting of orders to small-scale units;

(v) Registration procedure;

(vi) Wider circulation of tenders among small-scale units;

(vii) Monitoring of small-scale units' performance by the NSIC;

(viii) Mandatory registration with the NSIC of the small-scale units interested in the Government Purchase Programme;

(ix) Statistics of purchases for small-scale industries; and

(x) Regional imbalance in procurement from this centre.

Reservations of items for Exclusive Purchase from Small-scale Sector

The reservation of items for exclusive purchase from the small-scale sector has been effective from 1956-57. To begin with, 16 products were reserved. Later 40 per cent products were listed. This apart, 22 items, which were, till now, reserved for civil requirements were to be treated as reserved for purchase from the small-scale sector for defence requirements also. 11 items were notified under the list Group V for graded purchase reservation to the extent of 75 per cent and 15 items to the extent of 50 per cent under the List Group VI.

There was an appreciable increase in the total number of firms registered under the Central Government Purchase Programme during the last five years. But small-scale units have shown a slightly higher rate of increase than the large-scale units. However, the number of large-scale units is much greater than that of small-scale units registered under the programme.

All the firms in India and abroad, dealing in stores purchases by the DGS&D, are eligible for registration under the categories of manufacturers; stockists of imported and certain indigenous stores; sole selling agents of Indian manufactures; and agents of overseas principals.

Registration with the DGS&D has to be renewed every five years.

Until recently, the procedure was that a small-scale unit could participate in the Government Purchase Programme by getting itself registered either directly with the DGS&D, or with the NSIC. For registration with the NSIC the unit could approach any of its regional offices or go through the SISI, the Directorate of Industries and District Industries Officers with an application containing information on the plant and machinery, installed capacity and production, and the specific products for which the unit requests registration. On receipt of the application by the SISI, its officers visit the factory, assess the unit's technical competence to manufacture the products in question and recommend registration with the NSIC.

Subsequently, NSIC would enlist the units and issue competency certificates in their favour. Such units are then supplied with tender forms as and when the DGS&D issues them for specific products. The NSIC and the SSIs help the units to fill up the tender forms wherever required; but they are submitted directly to the DGS&D.

Revised Procedure: A policy decision was recently taken by the Department of Supplies that small-scale units registered with the NSIC would be treated on par with those units registered with the DGS&D. The application form for registration has been suitably revised, all new applications by small-scale units have now to be submitted only on the revised forms to the concerned SISIs.

This has been applicable only in the case of those units enlisted by the NSIC under the revised procedures and which have applied on the new application forms, subject to the condition that the NSIC has followed the registration procedure and observed the conditions laid down by the DGS&D. The revised procedure eliminates the formalities related to the production of various documents, etc., at the time of submission of tenders to the DGS&D, which were necessary earlier. After having satisfied itself of the units' competence, the SISIs will make suitable recommendations to the NSIC, which will register these units, initially for a period of two years, and issue the necessary certificate.

Only manufacturers and sole selling agents will be registered by the NSIC. However, suppliers of safety/difficult items, as specified, will not be registered by the NSIC but by the DGS&D directly, even though they belong to the small-scale sector.

Gradually, all the small-scale units already registered with the DGS/SIC, will be covered under the new procedure. The NSIC, has taken up the registration of firms under the new single-point scheme with effect from 1st May, 1976.

Marketing Services Offered by SIDO

The organisation provided marketing assistance to small-scale units by providing promoting ancillarisation, marketing intelligence and information, establishing trade centres, encouraging small entrepreneurs to participate in the purchase programmes of the Central and State Governments, setting up subcontracting exchanges, organising exhibitions, seminars and training programmes in marketing and publishing information booklets, etc.

Ancillary Development

One of the important activities undertaken by the SIDO is the promotion of ancillary industries in order to help in the marketing of the products of the small-scale sector in collaboration with Bureau of Public Enterprises (BPE) and other Central Government agencies.

The Small Industries Services Institutes are actively engaged in identifying and promoting new items for ancillarisation, besides rendering technical and managerial assistance to the existing ancillaries. Region-wise seminars, exhibitions and buyer-seller meetings are arranged to promote mutually beneficial relationship between small and large industries through ancillarisation.

Sub-contracting Exchange

With a view to providing effective support to small-scale units in securing subcontracting jobs from large and medium undertakings in the country, the SIDO established 16 subcontracting exchanges at the SISIs. The main functions of these subcontracting exchanges are:

— To invite small-scale units to register with the exchange their spare capacity on specific machines;

— To approach large industries with a view to listing out items which may be manufactured in small-scale units;

— To render technical assistance to small-scale units in creating new capacity for specific processes or for the manufacture of items/stores which are required by large-scale undertakings; and

— To furnish information on firms from whom enquiries can either secure orders to meet their requirements or on subcontract their requirements.

The 16 subcontracting exchange (SCEs) established in the SISIs provide a suitable linkage between large industries and small-scale feeder units to maintain up to date information on spare capacities available within the small-scale units and the requirements of large industries.

The Standing Committee on Ancillary Development appointed by the Small-Scale Industries Advisory Board held sittings in all the regions and gathered information from such agencies as the Association of Industries, private institutions (private/public are undertakings), etc., and their recommendations on ancillary development are under preparation. The committee was also furnished with a full techno-economic analysis of all the industries. Suitable recommendations on regular programmes, licensing and direct incentive systems have been made.

Government Purchase Schemes: NSIC

In 1956, the small-scale industry had not grown sufficiently in the technology of manufacturing processes and skills to be able to produce goods according to the rigid specifications of the Government Purchasing Agency. A scheme was, therefore, evolved, according to which the National Small Industries Corporation would take prime contracts from the Purchasing Agencies and get such contracts executed by farming them out to a number of small-scale units scattered all over the country.

This arrangement for the pre-emption of the orders of the corporation was soon stalled by a basic problem. Some small units would quote through the Corporation and others directly; as a result, the Corporation inadvertently became the sponsor of one set of the small units against another when, constitutionally, it was to serve them all equally well. Besides, there were the operational problems of coordinating the production of units located in different parts of a vast country. A fresh thinking was, therefore, called for on the issues involved. The scheme was re-oriented. The Corporation now acts as a liaison agency to enable small-scale units to secure a larger share of Government business. The salient features of the scheme are:

(a) Instead of purchasing tender sets from the DGS&D, the small units enlisted with the Corporation automatically get them, free of cost, from it and its branches;

(b) After verifying the technical competence of the small units, the corporation issues certificates of competency. The units, subsequently do not have to pay any security deposits to Government Purchasing Agencies;

(c) Provided that the specifications and quality are acceptable, the small units get a price preference up to 15 per cent over the quotations of large-scale units, depending on the merits of each case;

(d) Whenever the small units feel that injustice has been done to them, the NSIC takes up their cases with the DGS&D in order to find out the reason for the non-placement of contracts with these units and tries to redress their grievances wherever feasible or possible;

(e) As a result of the efforts of the NSIC, another big purchase department, the Ministry of Defence, has come in line with the DGS&D, and has now started exempting small units from the payment of security deposits.

In addition, the following facilities are available to the small-scale units registered with NSIC under the Single Point Registration Scheme under the Government Store Purchase Programme.

1. Issuc of tender sets free of cost;
2. Exemption from payment of earnest money;
3. Waiver of security deposit into the monetary limit for which the unit is registered;
4. Price preference upto 15 per cent over the large-scale unit.

Internal Marketing

In this field, the NSIC had undertaken the marketing of some products — tapioca starch, hand-made paper and hosiery items. By organising and co-ordinating the productive efforts of a consortium of hosiery manufacturers, the sale of ISI-marked hosiery products has been encouraged. Under its future programme, the NSIC intends:

(a) To cover domestic appliances, hand tools, malleable castings, light engineering products, soap;

(b) To provide marketing intelligence within the country and abroad for the benefit of the small-scale sector;

(c) To assist small-scale units in their survey of the markets and marketing research;

(d) To provide the necessary technological inputs in developing and standardising products in the small-scale sector;

(e) To establish raw material banks to meet the requirements of the small-scale sector in ferrous and non-ferrous raw materials.

Trade Centres

The Government of India has established trade centres to cater to the marketing needs of units in the small-scale sector.

These trade centres provide an integrated marketing system for small industries; they collect and disseminate information relating to all types of small-scale industries in the region, giving full details of products, capacities and prices. They provide a focal point for buyers and sellers who have the required supplementary service for trade centres and transactions, between small-scale industries and the buyers of their products, including large-scale manufacturers, importers and merchant exporters, export houses, purchasing organisations and consumers in general. A library function as an agency for contracts between small-scale units and prospective buyers in the country and abroad. Moreover, they assist the small units in the maintenance of quality control and the introduction of standardisation. About 50 per cent of the total recurring and non-recurring expenditure on equipment, stores, library and documentation, etc., on these centres was met by the Central Government (excluding the cost of land and buildings), subject to a maximum limit of ₹ 200,000 per year for a period of five years.

The need for setting up trade centers for small-scale industries was keenly felt of their phenomenal growth and because of the fact that they manufactured a wide range of products — from simple consumer goods to capital goods and other sophisticated items, such as machine tools, television sets, scientific equipment, automobile ancillaries, drugs and pharmaceuticals, etc. But if the small-scale sector is very important, it is also very vulnerable, so far as its marketing capacity is concerned. It is essential, therefore, that the products of small units should become competitive and should be able to contribute in a large measure to the national industrial output.

Small-scale industrialists cannot organise sales and market promotion activities on their own; they cannot display their products; they cannot spend much on advertising and publicity market research, etc., because their resources are limited and they are handicapped in their exports know-how and trade contacts. Buyers in India and abroad, on the other hand, are not aware of the quality, specifications and range of the products manufactured by the small-scale industry. The setting-up of trade centres in different parts of the country has therefore considerably filled up the information and communication gap between small manufacturers, consumers and buyers.

Exports

Responding to the widespread belief that the small industrial sector has not been marking a proportional contribution to the overall export earning of the country, the NSIC has set up an Export Department to encourage the export of small industry products. Because of their small size and lack of resources and effort the small industrialists do not have an easy access to world markets. Very often, they are unable to infuse confidence in foreign buyers. The NSIC aims at filling this need by functioning as an export house. Following the latest in marketing concepts, the corporation identifies the demand abroad for labour-intensive products. It collects intelligence about specifications, prices, etc. It locates small industries in the countries with the required production facilities and helps such units to make dyes and tools, counter samples, small-units, and takes the entire responsibility for the execution of the contract. It helps small industry products such as hand tools, fasteners, casting, etc., from some of the most sophisticated markets in the world — from the US, West Germany and Canada.

Export Incentives

The Government has offered special incentives to encourage export of the products of the small-scale sector. The minimum export performance limits for the grant of export house certificates have been lowered for small-scale manufacturers and their consortiums. The Government has also made arrangements to educate the small-scale units in the export prospects of different products abroad, by collecting information from various sources and disseminating it among them. Some of the important sources of information are the reports prepared by the Trade Development Authority, the Indian Institute of Foreign Trade, the Export Promotion Councils and the Directorate General of Commercial Intelligence Statistics. Periodical reports from Indian missions abroad are consulted for the purpose of identifying export opportunities for small-scale industries or taking note of the developments affecting such opportunities in foreign countries.

Export Promotion Councils (EPCs)

There are at present eleven Export Promotion Councils in India. The EPCs perform both advisory and executive functions.

Indian Institute of Foreign Trade (IIFT)

The Indian Institute of Foreign Trade (IIFT) was established in 1964 by the Government of India with the objective of strengthening the country's external trade sector through development of human resources; generating, analysing and disseminating data and conducting research and providing consultancy services.

The IIFT is engaged in the following activities:

(i) Training of personnel in modern techniques of international trade;

(ii) Organisation of research, area surveys, commodity surveys, market surveys; and

(iii) Dissemination of information arising from its activities relating to research and market studies.

Commodity Boards

The five statutory Commodity Boards for Rubber, Coffee, Tea, Tobacco and Spices are responsible for production, development and export.

Export Inspection Council (EIC)

The EIC, a statutory body, is responsible for the enforcement of quality control and pre-shipment inspection of various exportable commodities.

Indian Institute of Packaging (IIP)

The main aims of the Institute (IIP) are to undertake research into raw materials for the packaging industry, to develop new types of packaging for export products, to organise programmes on packaging technology and to stimulate consciousness of the need for good packaging.

India Trade Promotion Organisation (ITPO): The ITPO has come into effect from January 1, 1992 with the main objective of promoting exports and imports and upgradation of technology, through the medium of fairs to be held in India and abroad, to undertake publicity through the print and electronic media, to assist Indian companies in product development, to organise export development programmes, buyer-seller meets, contact promotion programmes and integrated marketing programmes.

Export Credit Guarantee Corporation of India Ltd. (ECGC)

The prime objective of ECGC is to support the country's export by providing a range of insurance covers to the Indian exporters against the risk of non-realisation of export proceeds due to political or commercial reasons and guarantees to financial institutions to facilitate grant of credit facilities to exporters on a liberal basis.

It provides: (a) a range of insurance covers to Indian exporters against the risk of non-realisation of export proceeds due to commercial or political causes, and (b) different types of guarantees to banks and other financial institutions to enable them to extend credit facilities to exporters on liberal basis.

Export Processing Zones

The Export Processing Zones set up as enclaves, separated from the Domestic Tariff area by fiscal barriers, are intended to provide an internationally competitive duty free environment for export production, at low cost. This enables the products of EPZs to be competitive, both quality-wise and price-wise, in the international market. India has seven Export Processing Zones at Kandla (Gujarat), Santacruz (Mumbai), Falta (West Bengal), Noida (UP), Cochin (Kerala), Chennai (Tamil Nadu) and Visakhapatnam (Andhra Pradesh). The one at Visakhapatnam (Andhra Pradesh) has become operational only recently.

The Santacruz Electronics Export Processing Zone (SEEPZ) is meant exclusively for export of electronics and gem and jewellery items, whereas the other zones are multiproduct zones.

Export Oriented Units

The EOU Scheme introduced in early 1981, is complementary to the EPZ scheme. It adopts the same production regime but offers a wide option in locations with reference to factors like source of raw materials, ports of export, hinterland facilities, availability of technological skills, existence of an industrial base and the need for a larger area of land for the project. As on 31.12.2006, 2,168 units were in operation under the EOU Scheme.

Box 12.3 Recent Policy Changes in the EOUs Scheme (w.e.f. 7th April, 2006)

- Procurement and export of spares/components up to one-and-a-half per cent of the FOB value of exports will be allowed to the same consignee/buyer of the export article within the warranty period. The exports of such spares/components could be effected separately from the capital goods.
- In order to facilitate the smooth functioning of the EOU units, the Development Commissioners will fix time limits for finalising the disposal of matters relating to EOUs.
- New units engaged in export of Agriculture/Horticulture/Aqua-Culture products have been now allowed to remove capital goods inputs to the DTA farm on producing bank guarantee equivalent to the duty foregone on the capital goods/input proposed to be taken out.
- The EOU units in Textile Sector are allowed to dispose of the left over material/fabrics up to 2 per cent of Cost Insurance Freight (CIF) value of imports, on consignment basis. Recognising that settling the accounts for every consignment is complex and time-consuming it has been decided to allow disposal of left over material on the basis of previous year's imports.

Export Promotion Industrial Park Scheme (EPIP)

A centrally sponsored "Export Promotion Industrial Park" (EPIP) Scheme has been introduced in August 1994 with a view to involving the State Governments in the creation of infrastructural facilities for export-oriented production. The scheme provides that 75 per cent of the capital expenditure incurred towards creation of such facilities, ordinarily limited to ₹ 10 crores in each case, will be met from a central grant to the State Governments. In addition a maintenance grant equivalent to 2 per cent of export turnover of each unit established therein will also be made available to State Governments for a period of 5 years from the date of commercial production of that unit.

The Central Govt. have so far approved 18 proposals for establishments of EPIPs in the states of Punjab, Haryana, Himachal Pradesh, Rajasthan, Karnataka, Kerala, Maharashtra, Tamil Nadu, Andhra Pradesh, Uttar Pradesh, Gujarat, Bihar, Jammu & Kashmir, Assam, Madhya Pradesh, West Bengal, Odisha and Meghalaya.

Export Houses, Trading Houses and Star Trading Houses

The objective of the Scheme of Export Houses, Trading Houses and Star Trading Houses is to give recognition to the established exporters and large Export Houses to build up the marketing infrastructure and expertise required for export promotion. The registered exporters having a record of export performance over a number of years are granted the status of Export/Trading Houses/Star Trading Houses/Super Star Trading Houses subject to the fulfilment of minimum annual average export performance in terms of FOB value or net foreign exchange earnings on physical exports prescribed in the EXIM Policy.

The Export Houses, Trading Houses, Star Trading Houses and Super Star Trading Houses Scheme allows the Registered Exporters certain additional benefits available to them under the policy.

Jute Corporation of India

The Jute Corporation was established on 2nd April, 1971 as a wholly-owned limited company of the Government of India. The main functions of the corporation are:

(i) Export and import of raw jute;

(ii) Internal marketing of jute; and

(iii) Undertaking measures for the export promotion of jute goods.

The objectives of the JCI are to ensure the minimum prices of raw jute; to conduct commercial operations in a judicious manner; to import and export jute fibre as authorised by the Government; to process raw jute and export jute goods; and to undertake export promotion measures for jute goods. It also aims at maintaining stability of jute production and prices.

State Trading Corporation of India (STC)

The State Trading Corporation of India was set up in May 1956 as an autonomous corporation to implement the Government's policies in regard to the promotion and diversification of foreign trade. The principle objectives of the STC are:

(i) To explore new markets for existing as well as new products;

(ii) To diversify and consequently increase India's export trade; and

(iii) To promote long-term export operations and the sale of "difficult-to-sell items".

The Corporation's major export items are semi-processed leather, castor oil, art silk fabrics, rice, jute goods, etc. With the pace of canalisation of India's foreign trade gathering momentum, the share of the STC in India's trade has increased substantially in recent years.

The STC provides a package of services to this sector with a view to encouraging it to produce more and market its products in foreign countries. These services include the supply of raw materials service, and warehousing, exporting, marketing and shipping facilities.

The Corporation deals in agricultural products, chemicals and fats, leather goods, textiles, imported cars and marketing. It has set-up an Industrial Raw Materials Assistance Division to make off-the-shelf deliveries of imported raw materials to manufacturers against import licences.

The business activities, turnover and profitability of STC have grown manifold in the recent years as a result of focussed thrust on diversification and innovation.

In addition, the STC has set-up four subsidiaries, namely: *(a)* The Projects and Equipment Corporation; *(b)* Handicrafts and Handlooms Exports Corporation of India; *(c)* The Cashew Corporations of India Ltd.; and *(d)* The State Chemicals and Pharmaceuticals Corporation Ltd. The subsidiaries assist the parent Corporation in furthering the main objectives of export promotion.

(a) The Projects and Equipment Corporations of India (PEC): The PEC was formed on 21st April, 1971, and has taken over the Railway Equipment and Engineering Divisions from the STC.

This corporation was formed to promote more intensively the export of non-traditional sophisticated engineering and railway equipment. In addition to this, it specialises in large-scale joint ventures and turnkey projects in the railways, public utilities and in complete industrial plants and projects. In view of the promising turnkey project opportunities in most developing countries, the corporation is expected to play a very important role in developing the exports of Indian engineering goods and technical now-know on a continuing basis.

The PEC plans to concentrate on undertaking turnkey projects and large-scale ventures. These vary from the construction of new railway lines of the putting up of complete industrial plants on an integrated basis, from the initial project report stage to that of final commissioning.

(b) Handicrafts and Handloom Exports Corporation of India: The HHEC came into existence in October 1962 as a subsidiary of the State Trading Corporation, with the merger of the Indian Handicrafts Development Corporation (set up in 1958) and the Handloom Export Organisation, a department of the STC. The main objective of the corporation is to develop new markets and expand traditional ones, thus supplementing and aiding the existing private sector trade in handicrafts and handlooms.

With a view to projecting the image of Indian handicrafts and handlooms in international markets, the corporation has opened showrooms known as "Sona of India" in New York, Tokyo, Paris and Nairobi, and also at the Akbar Hotel in New Delhi. A carpet warehousing depot was set up in Hamburg in July 1965.

The HHEC undertakes the export of handicrafts, handlooms, ready-to-wear garments and canalised export of woollen knitwear. Product development is one of the main activities of the HHEC. In its attempts to increase overseas sales of its products, it has secured the help of many popular designers in different countries — France, Japan, Italy and the U.K.

The HHEC also conducts consumer preference surveys abroad and introduces new products which project the excellent craftsmanship of India, helps the trade by means of advice and market exposure: participates in trade fairs and exhibitions abroad; and encourages delegates from abroad to visit India, study the products and offer valuable suggestions for improvement.

(c) Cashew Corporation of India: The Government of India set up the Cashew Corporation of India (CCI) on 19th August, 1970 as a wholly-owned subsidiary of the STC to stabilise the import trade in raw cashew. The import of raw cashew, handled under the Open General Licence (OGL), was canalised through the Cashew Corporation with effect from 1st September, 1970. The CCI has floated a joint stock company to raise cashew plantations.

The Minerals and Metals Trading Corporations of India (MMTC)

The Minerals and Metals Trading Corporation of India was established by the Government of India on 1st October, 1963. The central aim of the corporation is to broaden and enlarge the scope of exports of Indian minerals and ores and to arrange for the import of essential raw materials for distribution to industrial units in the country. Iron ore, fifth largest foreign exchange earner of the country, is the principal item of the export handled by the MMTC. The other items of export handled by it are manganese ore, ferro-manganese, coal, silimanite, ferro-silicon and ferro-chrome.

Besides Japan, which still accounts for more than 65 per cent of MMTC's exports, several other markets have been cultivated. Notable among these are South Korea, Taiwan, Romania, Czechoslovakia, Poland, Hungary, Yugoslavia, West Germany and the Netherlands. It has sought to secure continuous export outlets by entering into long-term contracts with importing countries.

Tea Trading Corporation of India Ltd. (TTCI)

Tea Trading Corporation of India was established in 1971 to create a stable export market for Indian tea particularly in the value added forms, which include packet tea, tea bag, instant tea, etc. Other activities of this Corporation include marketing of tea for domestic consumption, management of tea establishment of other facilities beneficial to the tea industry. TTCI has been a subsidiary company of the State Trading Corporation of India since January 1986, TTCC owns five gardens, namely, Pathini Tea Estate in Assam and Pashok, Looksan, Vah-Tukvar and Potong in West Bengal.

The Spices Trading Corporation Limited (STCL)

Spices Trading Corporation Limited (formerly known as Cardamom Trading Corporation Limited) was established in October 1982 and commenced its trading activities in September 1983. The Corporation was set up to carry on domestic and international trade in spices and their products. The Memorandum of Association permits the Corporation to also carry on business as a dealer/exporter of other agricultural commodities and related products. The Corporation diversified its trading to include agricultural inputs such as fertilisers, pesticides and sprayers.

The authorised share capital of the Corporation is ₹ 5 crores while the paid up share capital is ₹ 1.50 crores. For its commercial activities, the Corporation mainly depends on borrowings from banks.

Small-scale industries have made a significant contribution not only by increasing industrial production but also to non-traditional exports from the country. Programmes for promoting the export capabilities of small-scale units have been further intensified. Export market training courses and seminars have been held in different parts of the country to create the necessary awareness and motivation among the small-scale units engaged in export business.

Promotional Activities

The Small Industries Development Organisation (SIDO), through its network of Small Industries Service Institutes and Extension Centres, provides techno-managerial assistance and extension services for promotion of the exports of the products of these industries. The SIDO intensified its activities relating to the dissemination of information on foreign markets to export-worthy small-scale units; provided on consultancy services in all matters of export procedure to facilitate the disposal of replenishment, claims, drawbacks and other incentives; on export prices; on the identification of small-scale units already possessing the necessary equipment and skills to undertake the production of items having an export potential; on the organisation of training programmes on export marketing; and on the maintenance of liaison with the concerned agencies. A large number of meetings, seminars and open-house discussions on export promotion were organised in collaboration with the concerned promotional agencies and associations of industries. Training programmes on export packaging, too, were organised by some of the Small Industries Service Institutes in collaboration with the Indian Institute of Packaging.

A quarterly 'Small Industry Export Bulletin', which covers the important areas of interest to exporters, continued to be brought out by the SIDO. It contains useful information on export marketing, Government policy announcements and the procedures relevant to small industry exports, abstracts of market/commodity reports prepared by such professional agencies as the Indian Institute of Foreign Trade and Trade Development Authority, special features on export-oriented industries, markets and facilities, etc. The Export Promotion Division has started another feature in the form of Trade Enquiry Service Bulletin, in which the names and addresses of overseas buyers, importers and importing organisations are provided. As a result of these efforts, the communications are provided. As a result of these efforts, the communication and information gap between the small-scale manufacturers/exporters and overseas markets will be partially bridged.

SIDO also dealt with the special problems of small-scale exporting units, especially in regard to import entitlement, cash assistance, duty drawback, etc., and took them up with the authorities concerned.

In order to encourage the formation of export consortia of small-scale units, a scheme for financial assistance to them in the initial years of their formation was formulated and submitted to the Ministry of Industry. Under the scheme, the export consortia of small-scale units would be provided financial assistance during 3 or 4 years till they are able to develop themselves into full-fledged export houses.

Co-operation with Other Organisations

The SIDO actively collaborated with other Central and State institutions in their export promotion efforts, especially for small-scale industries. The SISIs prepared techno-managerial reports on export-worthy small-scale units, and collaborated with State Small Industries Corporations, Export Promotion Councils, the National Productivity Council and associations of small industries in organising seminars, training programmes, exhibitions, etc.

Under the scheme of Export Awards of the Ministry of Commerce, the Development Commissioner (Small-scale Industries) has been designated as a sponsoring authority for small-scale units. The Small Industries Development Organisation, through its network of SISIs, therefore, invited applications from various small-scale units and recommended suitable exporting units for the Award.

One classic instance was when SIDO encouraged small units to participate in buyer-seller meets and exhibitions organised by the Trade Development Authority at Rotterdam and Birmingham. Interested units were given detailed information and advice in this regard.

State Small Industries Corporations

Some of the State Small Industries Corporations have, in recent years, shown interest in export promotion activities. These corporations were actively associated with the various programme of export promotion organised by the SISIs.

Export House and Turnkey Projects: The NSIC, a recognised export house, has been pushing up the export of such small industry products as hardwares, industrial fasteners, sanitary fittings, locks and machine tools, etc. Goods worth more than ₹ 2 crore have been exported to such countries as the UK, the USA and countries in the Middle East. The NSIC has supplied complete plant and machinery for 32 turn-key projects for 62 small-scale units in Tanzania against the IDBI credit line of ₹ 20 million. This has evoked interest for similar projects from other countries, *viz.,* Nigeria, Mauritius, Uganda and Yemen. The corporation also considered proposals to assist Tanzania and Indonesia in setting up industrial estates for small-scale units.

Some small industries have good prospects of selling their products in international markets. If they cannot develop a consortium for the export of their products, they should at least associate with and support an export house. If marketing is a war, it is the most fierce in the international field. Well-equipped and highly professionalised export houses are indeed necessary, if the products of small industries are to be established in overseas markets. India has not made any serious inroads in these markets, not because the products do not conform to specification or are not competitively priced, but because exportability — the organised power to export — is somewhat low. There is a distinct need of large, strong, high-voltage and high resources export houses, which have specialised in the promotion of the export of the products of small industries. Individual small units may succeed when entrepreneurs have a high degree of marketing competence. But this is not true of most small units. They should not, therefore, enter the foreign markets on their own.

Exports have their own attractions; but unfortunately, very few entrepreneurs care to equip themselves adequately to export successfully and satisfactorily. The complaints one hears from foreign buyers of Indian goods, particularly, against manufacturers in the small-scale sector, bear testimony to this fact, though it may be conceded that some Indian small entrepreneurs do enjoy a high reputation abroad; but their number is woefully small. In these circumstances, the small entrepreneur should, as far as possible, utilise the services of an export house. In fact he should help build up the right type of export houses which have specialised in the promotion of the production of small industries in foreign markets. All export houses can neither do justice to the products of the smal sector, nor all their operations likely to be of real benefit to small exporting units. Hence the need for specialised export houses capable of producing and pushing the products of small industries in overseas markets.

Responsibilities of Management

The major responsibilities of the general management are to establish marketing objectives, to make policy decisions and communicate these decisions to the managers of the operating (or implementing) divisions of the company; to establish standards for measuring and guiding the overall performance of the company. The responsibilities of operational or line management are to plan programmes, methods and procedures and implement the decision necessary to achieve the stated objective; to organise and coordinate the activities and resources necessary to carry-out the programmes and to see that operating results conform as nearly as possible to agreed plans and standards of performance.

The Basic Differences Between Production-oriented and Marketing-oriented Organisation

Business function or Activity	*Company Perspective*	
	Production	*Marketing*
Top Management	Technological considerations predominate. Production and engineering personnel in highest level executive positions.	Customer considerations paramount. Marketing personnel in highest level executive positions.
Objectives	Internal influences predominate. Business objective is to match total company resources against production on technical efficiency and method. Want to be known for technical or production know-how.	External market influences predominate. Business objective is to match total company resources against market requirements and opportunities. More emphasis on market strategy and planning. Want to be regarded as style and market leader.
Manufacturing	Production less flexible. The company sells what can be made.	Flexibility in production so as to match product to sales opportunities. The company manufactures what can be profitably sold.
Marketing	Aims to fulfil existing needs and develop workable products to meet these needs. Company's future bound up with markets already supplied, and products already in existence. Marketing function not considered to be as valuable as manufacturing engineering as finance.	Seeks to create markets and develop saleable products. Company's future bound up with markets yet to be identified and developed, and with products not yet in existence. Marketing is considered to coordinate with manufacturing, finance and other major business functions.
Research	Leads in technical and scientific research. Marketing intelligence system relatively undeveloped.	Leads in analytical and marketing research. Market intelligence system well developed.
Product Planning	Based on technical research, suggestions for new or improved products stem from functional performance and applications are prime considerations. Engineering consideration tends to predominate. Laboratory testing more prominent than sales or market. Packaging viewed as a shipping and protective device. Chief concern is engineering, materials handling and packaging machinery.	Based on market research. Suggestions for new or improved products stem from research into customer needs. Performance and applications are prime considerations regarded to be almost as important. Sales and market testing an integral part of planning. Packaging viewed as a sales tool in terms of its user convenience and advertising and promotional effectiveness.

Business function or Activity	*Production*	*Marketing*
Sales Organisation	Salesman regarded as a person who fetches orders for the factory.	Salesman regarded as an order-maker who keeps the factory running and provides employment to production workers. Salesman accorded high status in the company and more likely to be promoted to top management position.
	Salesman lacks the professional status of the engineer, chemist, lawyer or accountant. Less likely to be promoted to top management. Salesman lacks formal training. Tends to get left to his own devices as the man 'out there'. Motivation of the salesman is minimal.	Salesman is given formal and continuous internal and on-the-job training. Motivation of sales organisation given high priority. Chief sales executive regarded as part of the management team.
Advertising and Promotion	Emphasis on cost rather than on the value of its contribution to the total selling effort. Advertising and promotion regarded as an extra cost, not a basic cost like machines, raw materials, research laboratories, etc. Not regarded as one of the skills required to run a modern business successfully.	Advertising and promotion is an integral part of the company's marketing effort and a basic cost. Outstanding advertising and promotion considered to be as equally important to the successful running of a business as outstanding manufacturing technique, technical research ability or financial and legal skills.
	Advertising and promotion not looked upon as an important source of competitive differential advantage.	Advertising and promotion regarded as a potential source of competitive differential advantage, particularly when the differences in own and competitive products become less and less distinguishable.

GLOBAL AND REGIONAL TRADE ARRANGEMENTS

World Trade Organisation (WTO)

The WTO, established in January 1, 1995, as the successor to the General Agreement on Tariffs and Trade (GATT), serves as the legal and institutional foundation of the multilateral trading system.

The Uruguay Round Trade Agreement that created the WTO also eliminated tariffs for some manufactured goods and reduced other tariffs; reduced barriers to trade in agriculture; expanded protection for copyrights, patents, and other intellectual property; and provided some reduction in barriers to services and foreign investment. It also reformed the multilateral trade process itself, including the introduction of a stronger dispute-settlement mechanism.

The WTO has 123 members, and the following 31 governments have applied to join: Albania, Algeria, Armenia, Belarus, Bulgaria, Cambodia, China, Croatia, Estonia, Georgia, Jordan, Kazakhstan, Kirgyz Republic, Latvia, Lithuania, former Yugoslav Republic of Macedonia, Moldova,

Mongolia, Nepal, Oman, Panama, Russia, Saudia Arabia, Seychelles, Sudan, Taiwan, Tonga, Ukraine, Uzbekistan, Vanuatu, and Vietnam.

Extended beyond their original deadlines, WTO negotiations continue now on reducing barriers to trade in basic telecommunications and financial services; a decision on whether to resume failed negotiations on maritime services has been deferred until 2000.

North American Free Trade Agreement (NAFTA)

NAFTA, which built on the 1989 U.S. – Canada Free Trade Agreement, went into force January 1, 1994, phasing out tariffs on trade between the United States, Canada, and Mexico over 15 years. Side agreements require each country to enforce its own labour and environmental laws.

U.S. trade with Canada and Mexico increased 29 per cent in the first two years of NAFTA. Nevertheless, trade disputes between the partners persist, mitigated somewhat by dispute-settlement mechanisms.

Failing for three years to get abroad fast-track authority from Congress to negotiate any trade agreements, the Clinton Administration is grappling with a strategic decision: whether to request fast-track authority solely for negotiating accession to NAFTA by Chile.

Asia-Pacific Economic Cooperation (APEC)

Formed in 1989 as an informal dialogue group with limited participation, APEC has become a forum for negotiations to achieve the goal of freer trade and investment in the Asia-Pacific region – by 2010 for industrialised economies and by 2020 for developing economies.

APEC has 18 members: Australia, Brunei, Canada, Chile, China, Hong Kong, Indonesia, Japan, South Korea, Malaysia, Mexico, New Zealand, Papua New Guinea, Philippines, Singapore, Taiwan, Thailand and the United States.

New Transatlantic Agenda

Part of the New Transatlantic Agenda agreed to at the U.S. European Union (EU) summit in December 1995 in Madrid was an initiative to expand trade between the two sides called the New Transatlantic Market place, assisted by meetings of businessmen called colectively the Transatlantic Business Dialogue.

Among a number of agreed goals were tariff cuts, including elimination of tariffs on information technology products (an information technology agreement), and negotiation of mutual recognition agreements to harmonize product standards and testing. Progress has been slow.

Meanwhile, U.S.-EU relations have been disturbed in 1996 by a number of irritants, especially U.S. imposition of sanctions against third-country investments in Cuba, Iran, and Libya.

CONCLUSION

Industrial liberalisation, globalisation, marketing economy and heightened competition is changing all this permanently. While labour laws have become antiquated and virtually ineffective, Government policies which encourage dispersal of industries into backward area locations have helped improve matters. Market forces are now compelling modernisation, productivity improvement and value of additional efficiency like never before. Some parts of the country where industry had been severally affected by obscurantist trade unionism, are today showing heightened pragmatism to generate and endowed states do not seem to appreciate that in order to stay ahead in the game of economic and industrial development, only one thing counts — efficiency of value addition and an enabling climate along with a degree of reassurance about the future. Marketing, a strategic tool for business development is critical to the growth and survival of enterprises in today's competitive economy.

Marketing management is responsible for creating customers by persuading them through advertising and personal salesmanship that the company's products or services match their indicated needs and preferences more closely than competitors' offerings, by developing products and services through technical and market research which appear to offer profitable sales opportunities and at a price, time and place the customers want.

As with sciences, so with markets, segments change with the passage of time. Only those companies that can adapt to these changes, and innovate to serve the evolving needs of customer can hope to survive. To do this, marketers will have to continuously go back to the basics. Niches or segments are not made by product managers, the changing needs and perceptions of consumers create them. A smart product manager only identifies them and provides products to fill them up. The future, therefore, belongs to the proactive challenger.

Marketing is a system of integrated business activities designed to develop strategies and plans including marketing mixes to the satisfaction of customer wants of selected market segments or targets. It is a process involving a set of multidirectional as well as multidimensional activities. Marketing is a matching process by which a producer provides a marketing mix (product, price, promotion and physical distribution) that meets consumer demand of a target market within the limits of society.

Of late, marketing management has been given much importance, especially by the SSI sector and will continue to get this importance with different market situations existing now.

13 CHAPTER HUMAN RESOURCE MANAGEMENT AND LABOUR LAWS

"On the one hand, factories Acts tries to regulate and promote industrial culture in the country. On the other hand, a number of legislative and executive initiatives have been taken to promote, protect and preserve health, safety and social security for workers through observance of the ethos and culture of tripartism."

"The achievements of an organisation are the results of the combined effort of each individual."

– Vince Lombardi

INTRODUCTION

Management is often included as a factor of production along with machines, materials, and money. Management is the art of getting done things through others. Management is the only activating element of any enterprise for getting things done through its personnel. Wherever and whenever objectives are to be achieved through organized and co-operative endeavour, management becomes essential for directing and unifying the group efforts towards a common purpose. As an activity process, management plans the future course of action, organises people and their work, directs the operation and controls the performance ensuring the accomplishment of enterprise objectives.

Human resource is one of the important elements and has an important role to play in the success or failure of any organization. Right person, in the right place, at the right time is one of the secrets behind the success of an organisation.

Human Resource Management (HRM) includes all activities used to attract and retain employees and to ensure they perform at a high level in meeting organisational goals. Edwin Flippo defines HRM as "planning, organising, directing, controlling of procurement, development, compensation, integration, maintenance and separation of human resources to the end that individual organisational and social objectives are achieved".

Features of HRM

1. HRM involves management functions like planning, organizing, directing and controlling.
2. It involves procurement, development, maintenance of human resource.

3. It helps to achieve individual, organisational and social objectives.

4. It involves team spirit and teamwork.

Scope of HRM

The scope of HRM refers to all the activities that come under the banner of HRM. These activities are as follows:

1. **Human resources planning :** Human resource planning or HRP refers to a process by which the company to identify the number of jobs vacant, whether the company has excess staff or shortage of staff and to deal with this excess or shortage.

2. **Job analysis design :** Another important area of HRM is job analysis. Job analysis gives a detailed explanation about each and every job in the company. Based on this job analysis the company prepares advertisements.

3. **Recruitment and selection :** Based on information collected from job analysis the company prepares advertisements and publishes them in the newspapers. This is recruitment. A number of applications are received after the advertisement is published, interviews are conducted and the right employee is selected thus recruitment and selection are yet another important area of HRM.

4. **Orientation and industion :** Once the employees have been selected an induction or orientation programme is conducted. This is another important area of HRM. The employees are informed about the background of the company, explain about the organisational culture and values and work ethics and introduce to the other employees.

5. **Training and development :** Every employee goes under training programme which helps him to put up a better performance on the job. Training programme is also conducted for existing staff that have a lot of experience. This is called refresher training. Training and development is one area were the company spends a huge amount.

6. **Performance appraisal :** Once the employee has put in around year of service, performance appraisal is conducted that is the HR department checks the performance of the employee. Based on these appraisal future promotions, incentives, increments in salary are decided.

7. **Compensation planning and remuneration :** There are various rules regarding compensation and other benefits. It is the job of the HR department to look into remuneration and compensation planning.

8. **Motivation, welfare, health and safety :** Motivation becomes important to sustain the number of employees in the company. It is the job of the HR department to look into the different methods of motivation. Apart from this certain health and safety regulations have to be followed for the benefits of the employees. This is also handled by the HR department.

9. **Industrial relations :** Another important area of HRM is maintaining co-ordinal relations with the union members. This will help the organisation to prevent strikes, lockouts and ensure smooth working in the company.

Significance of HRM

HRM becomes significant for business organisation due to the following reasons.

1. **Objective :** HRM helps a company to achieve its objective from time-to-time by creating a positive attitude among workers. Reducing wastage and making maximum use of resources, etc.

2. **Facilitates professional growth :** Due to proper HR policies employees are trained well and this makes them ready for future promotions. Their talent can be utilised not only in the company in which they are currently working but also in other companies which the employees may join in the future.

3. **Better relations between union and management :** Healthy HRM practices can help the organisation to maintain co-ordinal relationship with the unions. Union members start realising that the company is also interested in the workers and will not go against them therefore chances of going on strike are greatly reduced.

4. **Helps an individual to work in a team/group :** Effective HR practices teach individuals teamwork and adjustment. The individuals are now very comfortable while working in team thus teamwork improves.

5. **Identifies person for the future :** Since employees are constantly trained, they are ready to meet the job requirements. The company is also able to identify potential employees who can be promoted in the future for the top level jobs. Thus, one of the advantages of HRM is preparing people for the future.

6. **Allocating the jobs to the right person :** If proper recruitment and selection methods are followed, the company will be able to select the right people for the right job. When this happens the number of people leaving the job will reduce as the will be satisfied with their job leading to decrease in labour turnover.

7. **Improves the economy :** Effective HR practices lead to higher profits and better performance by companies due to this the company achieves a chance to enter into new business and start new ventured thus industrial development increases and the economy improves.

HRM activities are made up of:

1. Recruitment and selection.

2. Training and development.

3. Performance appraisal and feedback.

4. Employee benefits.

5. Labuor relations.

A. Recruitment

It refers to the process of attracting, screening, and selecting qualified people for a job. Recruitment is the positive process as it attracts suitable applicants to apply for available jobs.

Recruitment can be of two types:

1. External recruiting: It can be done with the help of advertisements in newspapers, campus recruitment, employment exchanges and through private placement agencies. The organisation can get talented personnel. But it is a costly and lengthy process.

2. Internal Recruiting: In this method positions are filled within the firm.

Internal recruiting has several benefits:

a) Workers know the firm's culture

b) Managers are likely to know the candidates

c) Internal advancement can motivate employees

Selection

After a pool of applicants are identified, qualifications related to the job requirements are determined. It is negative process as it eliminates the unqualified applicants. Selection can be made with help of the following tools.

- **Preliminary Interviews:** It is used to eliminate those candidates who do not meet the minimum eligiblity criteria laid down by the organisation. The skills, academic and family background, competencies and interests of the candidate are examined during preliminary interview. Preliminary interviews are less formalized and planned than the final interviews. The candidates are given a brief up about the company and the job profile; and it is also examined how much the candidate knows about the company. Preliminary interviews are also called screening interviews.

- **Application blanks:** The candidates who clear the preliminary interview are required to fill application blank. It contains data record of the candidates such as details about age, qualifications, reason for leaving previous job, experience, etc.

- **Written Tests:** Various written tests conducted during selection procedure are aptitude test, intelligence test, reasoning test, personality test, etc. These tests are used to objectively assess the potential candidate. They should not be biased.

- **Employment Interviews:** It is a one-to-one interaction between the interviewer and the potential candidate. It is used to find whether the candidate is best suited for the required job or not. But such interviews consume time and money both. Moreover the competencies of the candidate cannot be judged. Such interviews may be biased at times. Such interviews should be conducted properly. No distractions should be there in the room. There should be an honest communication between candidate and interviewer.

- **Medical examination:** Medical tests are conducted to ensure physical fitness of the potential employee. It will decrease chances of employee absenteeism.

- **Appointment Letter:** A reference check is made about the candidate selected and then finally he is appointed by giving a formal appointment letter.

B. Training and Development

"Tell me and I forget, teach me and I remember, involve me and I learn"

– Benjamin Franklin

It is an ongoing process to develop worker's abilities and skills. Training is often given at lower levels of firm, whereas development is more common with managers. Assessment should be made to determine who needs which programme and what areas should be focused upon.

Types of Training

1. **On-the-job Training:** Learning occurs in the work setting as worker does the job.

2. **Vestibule Training:** This method involves the creation of a separate training centre within the plant itself for the purpose of providing training to the new employees.

3. **Case Study:** It is a written description of an actual situation in business which provokes, in the reader, the need to decide what is going on, what the situation really is or what the problems are, and what can and should be done.

4. **Role Playing:** It generally focuses on emotional (mainly human relations) issues rather than actual ones. The essence of role playing is to create a realistic situation, as in case study, and then have the trainee assume the parts of specific personalities in the situation.

5. **Apprenticeships:** A formal occupational training program me which combines on-the-job training and related instruction and in which workers learn the practical and conceptual skills required for a skilled occupation, craft, or trade.

6. **Sensitivity Training:** Training in small groups in which people develop a sensitive awareness and understanding of themselves and of their relationships with others.

C. Performance Appraisal and Feedback: It rates the employees in terms of their performance. Through appraisal it provides information about how to train, motivate and reward workers.

Managers can evaluate and then give feedback to enhance worker performance.

1. **Trait appraisals:** evaluate on traits (skills, abilities) related to the job.
2. **Behavior appraisals:** how a worker does the job. Focuses on what a worker does and provides good feedback options.
3. **Results appraisals:** what a worker accomplishes. Example, sales representatives are usually evaluated on what they sell.
4. **Objective appraisals:** based on facts and figures (sales figures)
5. **Subjective appraisals:** based on a manager's perceptions of traits, behaviour or results.

Who Appraises?

i. **Self:** self-appraisals can supplement manager view.

ii. **Peer appraisal:** co-worker provides appraisal.

iii. **360 Degree:** provides appraisal from a variety of people like peers, customers, superiors, self which helps in evaluation.

iv. **Effective feedback:** appraisals must provide feedback.

v. **Formal appraisals:** conducted at set time period of the year.

vi. **Informal appraisals:** manager provides frequent feedback informally.

Effective Feedback

1. Be specific and focus on correctable behaviour. Provide a suggested improvement.
2. Focus on problem-solving and improvement, not criticism.
3. Express confidence in worker's ability to improve.
4. Use formal and informal feedback.
5. Treat subordinates with respect and praise achievements.
6. Set a timetable for agreed changes.

D. Employee Benefits: Pay structure clusters jobs into categories based on importance, skills, and other issues. High performing employees should be rewarded with raises, bonuses, etc. It is the additional benefit that an employee receives from the organisation besides his remuneration.

Benefits are usually paid in order to enhance productivity, satisfy employee needs, reduce labour turnover, etc. It may be in-form of sick leave, vacation, holidays, travel allowances, child care facilities, medical expenses, health insurance, etc.

E. Labour Relations: Refers to relationship between management and the workers. Managers need to maintain effective relationship with labour unions that represent workers.

Problems in HRM

Labour absenteeism and turnover

High labour absenteeism and turnover can create problem for the management. It can lead to disruption in the flow of production, can affect even good employees, risk of losing competitive advantage due to loss of capable employees in critical sectors or positions and in turn decrease in profits.

Resistance to change

In this ever-changing dynamic world, change is one of the ways to survive and sustain. But sometimes the employees become resistant to change may be due to fear of loosing their present job, depromotion, less salary, etc.

Lack of qualified employees

With the growth and, expansion of an organisation and rising demands, the owners should strengthen human resources management and human resources operations so that they can keep enterprises running. HRM can increase competitive advantage and makes enterprise success but it may also be the biggest problem faced by the enterprise.

Difficult to find and retain talent

As skilled human resources supply in the labour market is limited, training and professional development of enterprises for staff has become a major challenge. Another problem is that of retaining them as because after acquiring necessary skills they may switch over to other jobs as they may find more lucrative opportunities.

INTRODUCTION TO LABOUR LAWS

In society regulations are the basis of steady growth, the governing factors, ensuring that everything occurs in conformity with the plan and policy adopted, the instructions issued and the principles established. They pinpoint the weakness and errors so that they may be rectified and their recurrence may be prevented. They operate on everything – people, objects and actions. Thus, a regulation is a process by which we may check whether or not plans are being adhered to, whether the environment is saved from pollution whether law and order is maintained or not, whether the interests of the workers are safeguarded or not, whether the small entrepreneurs are getting the raw materials or not, and whether there are any deviations for which a corrective action needs to be taken.

Objective

The basic objective behind the whole process of regulations is to ensure that the results of operation conform as closely as possible to established standards of goods, specified procedures, or instructions. The small-scale industry has to develop as an important segment of society, as such it has to adhere to the rules of the land, i.e., it has to be subjected to the various regulations. Regulations governing the small-scale industry are of two types: *Protective* and *Promotional.* Protective regulations are in the nature of various safeguards, while promotional regulations are in the nature of giving a push to the small-scale industry, i.e., they are growth-oriented.

Type of Controls

Government controls or regulations assumes several forms. The controls are grouped into formal and informal, direct and indirect, promotional and regulatory and inducive and coercive controls.

Formal and Informal Controls: Formal controls are usually those emanating from legislation, as for example, the Industries (Development and Regulation) Act, 1951, the Companies Act, 1956, and the Monopolies and Restrictive Trade Practices Act, 1969. Formal controls are very powerful and when we think of government control over business, we generally mean formal controls. Informal controls refer to the controls which various groups impose upon themselves out of need and custom. Business firms in various lines of activity develop conventions, informal, agreements, and accepted ways of doing things that have important regulative implications.

Direct and Indirect Controls: When government fixes prices of certain products or services, it is an example of direct control. The administered price policy of the Government of India is a direct control measure. The variation of corporate income tax to influence economic activity is an indirect control measure. Businessmen prefer indirect controls to direct regulations.

(a) Government regulations designed to make competition work, the MRTP Act, for example;

(b) Government competition with business firms as a means of setting standards of competition; or

(c) Direct government ownership and operation to supplement competition.

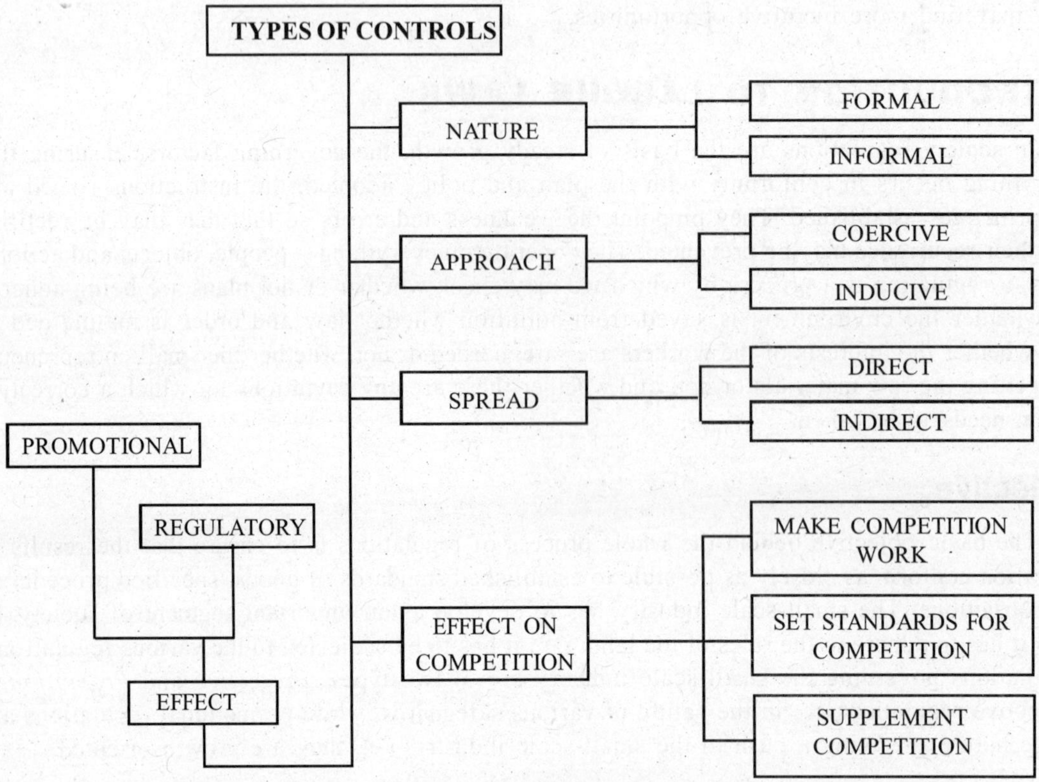

Fig. 13.1: Classification of Regulatory Measures

Promotional and Regulatory Controls: Promotional measures are of a positive nature, and include such activities as expansion of public sector establishment and operation of development banks, revival of sick units, encouragement to small-scale units, removal of regional imbalances, provision of incentives and subsidies and export promotion.

Regulatory measures ensure orderly development of industries with the least wastages of resources. Regulatory measures include direct controls like the Industries (Development and Regulation) Act, the Monopolies and Restrictive Trade Practices Act, the Companies Act, the Foreign Exchange Regulation Act, and price and distribution controls, labour laws, and indirect controls like monetary policy and fiscal policy.

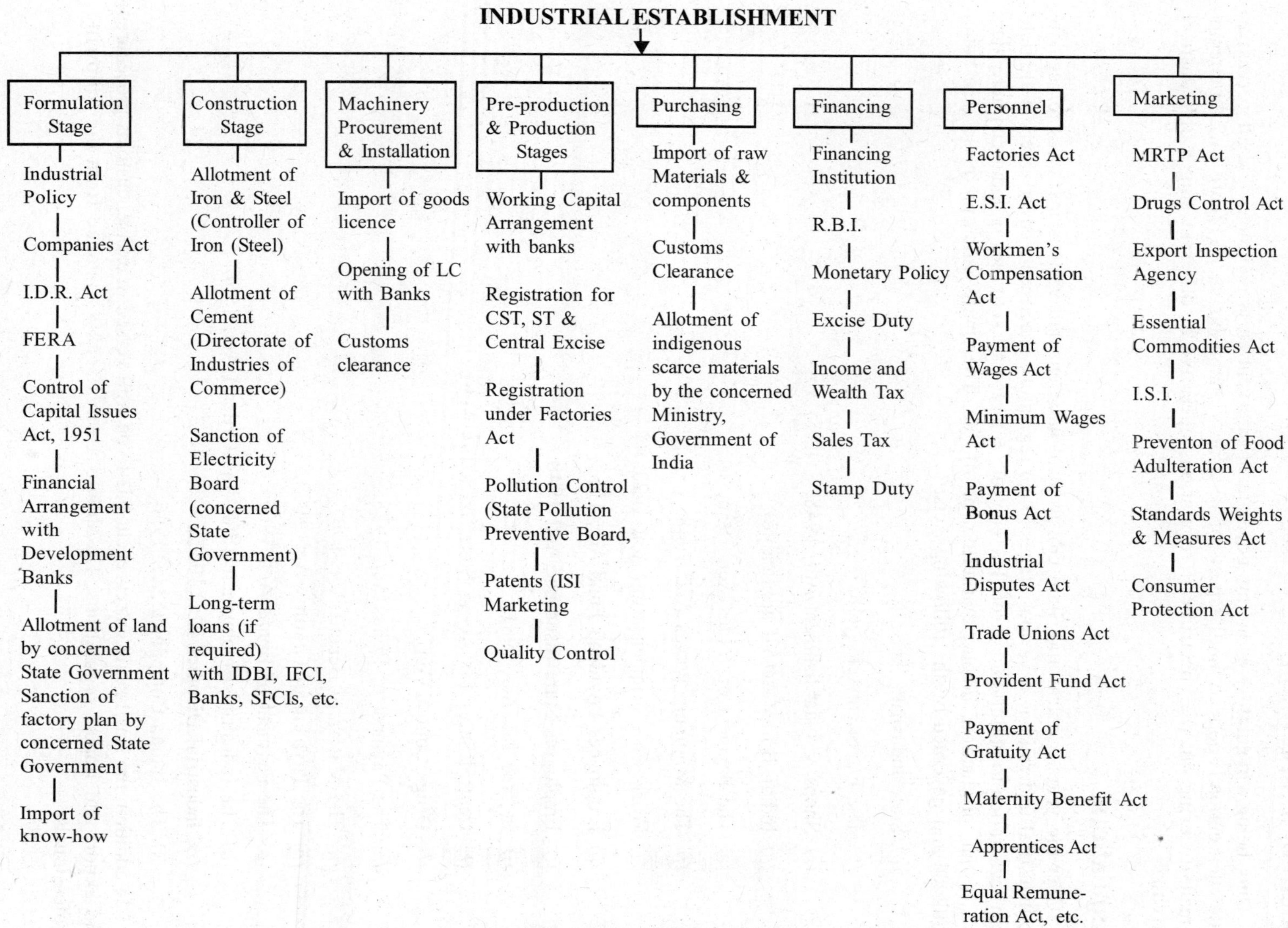

Fig. 13.2: Spectrum of Regulatory Control

Extent of Intervention

Ours being a regulatory economy, government intervention is enormous and all pervasive. State intervention is noticed in all aspects of a business establishment. In Figure 13.2 an attempt is made to bring out the spectrum of regulations operative at different stages of industrial activities.

Regulations

Over the years, Central and State Government have enacted various measures to regulate the industrial undertaking at various stages. Such regulatory enactments cover a very wide field from registration to pollution control. The controls embrace all activities of industrial activities, *viz.*, layout, production, labour, marketing, profit, etc. The small-scale enterprises are being regulated and governed by the following Acts:

(a) State Industries Acts;

(b) The Factories Act, 1948;

(c) Shops & Establishment Act, 1948;

(d) Indian Boiler Act (if applicable);

(e) The Payment of Wages Act, 1936;

(f) The Minimum Wages Act, 1948;

(g) Workmen's Compensation Act, 1923;

(h) Employees Povidend Fund Act, 1952;

(i) Employees State Insurance Act, 1948;

(j) Income Tax Act, 1981;

(k) Central Sales Tax Act & State Sales Tax Acts;

(l) Drugs Control Act;

(m) The Payment of Bonus Act, 1978;

(n) The Maternity Benefit Act, 1961.

(o) The Payment of Gratuity Act, 1972.

(p) The Payment of Bonus Act, 1965.

(q) The Industrial Employment (Standing Orders) Act, 1956;

(r) Industrial Disputes Act, 1947.

(s) The Indian Companies Act, 1956.

In addition, the small-scale entrepreneur has to be well versed in excise, customs procedures and export and import regulations. He should always seek assistance from the following professionals:

(a) Inspecting Staff of Government;

(b) Labour Consultants;

(c) Financial Consultants.

(d) Legal Consultants

(e) Income-tax Consultants

(f) Excise and Customs Consultants

(g) Exports & Imports Consultants

The salient features of the regulations governing the SSIs industries are summarised below:

1. Industrial Development (Regulation) Act

The IDR Act is an instrument in the hands of the Government for the control and direction of private sector industrial investment through the mechanism of the industrial licensing system, which enables in to exert pressure on the applications in a variety of ways. Conceptually, the Government ought to direct further industrial investment in such product-lines which would better serve the overall national interest and in such geographical areas which need it the most.

It is a complicated, time-consuming and costly exercise to acquire an industrial licence. Sometimes, it takes before it can be obtained. Obviously, it cannot be the intention of the Government to extend this procedure to the small-scale sector because it would be impossible to implement. A small unit needs the recommendations of an agency to prepare an application for an industrial licence.

The agency is responsible for checking the veracity of what the applicant says in his application.

In recent years, there has been quite a clamour from various associations of SSIs for their legislative protection. August 1971, the Small-Scale Industries Board, at its 29th meeting, had recommended to the Government to set up a committee to examine the feasibility of enacting suitable legislation for the development of SSIs. Always eager to form committees, the Government speedily acceded to the recommendation of the board and constituted a committee in January 1972 under the chairmanship of Mr. A.R. Bhat to draft a legislation for this sector. It was, moreover, required to identify specific areas where legislation was considered necessary and to submit drafts for the purpose.

In its report submitted in August 1972, the Bhat Committee prepared a total of five draft legislations for the Government's approval. They were: The Small Industries Development Act, while included a definition of the small-scale industry; the Restricted Parternership Act; the Small Industries Reservation Act; the Small-scale Ancillary Industries Act; and the Public Stores Purchase and Disposal Act for Small Industries.

The committee has quoted extensively from similar legislative enactments in the USA and Japan. However, though well over nine years have passed since the recommendations were submitted to it, the Government has not been able to take any decision on them, perhaps because it has reservations on the desirability of enacting such legislation. If this is so, it should come out in the open and share its viewpoint with others.

The small-scale sector in this country is an important sector, for it is capable of meeting the consumer goods needs of the community. It is, therefore, only fair that the government should keep the interests of the community uppermost in time, the small-scale sector must fulfil social and moral obligations if it desires protection against large houses, it should, on its part, safeguard the interests of millions of those who depend on it for their livelihood.

2. Factories Act, 1948

(i) Definition of a Factory: Section 2 (m) of the Act defines a factory as any place, wherein ten or more persons are working and in which manufacturing process is carried on with the aid of the appropriate power machinery and infrastructure. Premises in which power is not used come under the term of a factory if twenty or more persons are working in them. This definition brings a greater number of places under the purview of this Act that was the case under the Act of 1934.

(ii) Employment of Children: The Act fixes the maximum age of persons who can enter a factory for work at 14 years. It prohibits the employment of children up to the age of 13.

The Act further lays down that a qualified surgeon must certify that a person has completed the age of 14. Such certificates must be obtained by a factory manager and must be available for inspection by a factory inspector.

(iii) Hours of Work for Children: The Act reduces the hours of work for children between the ages of 14-17 from 5 hours a day to 4 hours a day. It also prohibits children from doing night shift.

(iv) Hours of Work for Adult Female and Male Workers: The Act prohibits employment of women in factories between 6 p.m. to 7 a.m. It reduces ten hours of work for adult men and women workers from 54 to 48 per week and from 9 hours to 8 hours a day.

The Act also lays down that the eight hours of work will be spread over a period of not more than 10 hours. Further, it provides that no worker shall work for more than 5 hours before he has had an interval or rest of at least half an hour. Lastly, the Act lays down that those workers who are made to work for more than 8 hours a day or 48 hours a week shall be paid for the extra hours at the rate of twice their ordinary rates of wages.

(v) Cleanliness: The Act lays down that every factory shall be kept clean and free from effluvia arising from any drain, privy or other nuisance. Accumulation of dirt and refuse shall be removed daily from the floor and the benches of workrooms, from staircases and passages, and disposed of in a suitable manner.

The floor of every workroom in the factory shall be cleaned once a week.

All inside walls, ceilings and partitions shall be white-washed at least once in fourteen months; if they are painted or varnished, they shall be repainted or revarnished once in five years.

Effective arrangements shall be made in every factory for the disposal of wastes arising out of the manufacturing processes carried on therein.

(vi) Ventilation and Temperature: Effective and suitable provision shall be made in every factory for securing and maintaining in every workroom adequate ventilation by the circulation of fresh air and the maintenance of such temperature as will secure therein reasonable conditions of comfort for those working there. Where excessively high temperatures are necessary for technical reasons, adequate measures shall be taken by the management to protect the workers from such temperatures.

The State Government may prescribe a standard of adequate ventilation and reasonable temperature for any factory or class of factories and can suggest ways and means for reducing excessively high temperatures.

In any factory, where dust or fumes injurious to the health of workers arise in any manufacturing process, effective measures shall be taken to prevent their inhalation or accumulation in any workroom.

(vii) Artificial Humidification: In factories where humidity is artificially increased, the State Government may:

(a) Prescribe standards of humidification;

(b) Regulation methods used for humidification;

(c) Direct prescribed tests for determining humidity, and directing that such tests are carried out — their results recorded; and

(d) Prescribe methods to be adopted for securing adequate ventilation and cooling of the air in those rooms where artificial humidity is introduced.

Water used for the purpose of humidification shall be such as has been certified by the municipal authorities as fit for drinking.

(viii) Overcrowding: To prevent overcrowding in a factory, the Act lays down that, in factories built before the passing of this Act, there shall be a space of at least 350 cubic feet per worker and in factories built after the Act came into force, it shall be at least 500 cubic feet. To arrive at these figures, a height above 14 feet shall not be taken into consideration. In accordance with this rule, the Chief Inspector of Factories will communicate each factory manager the maximum number of workers that may be employed on any premises. He has, however, the power to exempt any factory or workroom from this rule, if he is satisfied that its observance of this rule is not necessary in the interest of the workers employed therein.

(ix) Lighting: It is the duty of the management of a factory to maintain sufficient suitable lighting, natural or artificial or both, in a factory and in all the workrooms.

All glazed windows and sky-lights shall be kept clean on both the inner and outer surfaces, and effective measures shall be taken for the prevention of glare and formation of any shadows which may cause eye-strain or create a risk of accidents.

The State Government may make rules as to what is sufficient and suitable lighting, for a factory or a class of factories.

(x) Drinking Water: In every factory, effective arrangements shall be made to provide at suitable points conveniently situated for all workers employed, therein, a sufficient supply of wholesome drinking water.

In every factory, where more than 253 workers are ordinarily employed, provision shall be made for cool drinking water during the hot weather.

(xi) Toilets: In every factory, sufficient toilets shall be provided at places which are conveniently situated and are easily accessible to workers at all times while they are at the factory.

The State Government may prescribe the number of toilets to be provided in any factory in proportion to the number of male and female workers employed therein.

(xii) Provision of Spittoons: In every factory, there shall be sufficient number of spittoons in convenient places and they shall all be maintained in a clean and hygienic condition.

(xiii) Safety Provisions: According to the Act of 1934, a factory manager could afford to wait till an Inspector of Factories gave instructions as to what ought to be done to ensure the safety of workers. The Act of 1948 has placed the responsibility for safety matters on the shoulders of the owner or the manager of a factory. He must comply with all the safety provisions without waiting for the inspector's instructions.

Secondly, the Act places legal responsibility on the management for the maintenance and use of safety guards. It is its duty to supervise the use of these guards by the workers.

The specific provisions for safety are as follows: In every factory, all dangerous parts of all machines, such as the moving parts of prime movers, flywheels, electric generators, motors, rotary converters, etc., shall be securely fenced by safety guards of substantial construction which shall be kept in position while the parts of machines are in motion.

(xiv) Dangerous Fumes: Adequate provision shall be made in a factory where dangerous fumes are present in any chamber, tank, pipe, etc., for egress of such fumes.

(xv) Explosive Gases, Dust, Fume: If, in any factory, the manufacturing process raises dust, gas, fume or vapour which is likely to explode on ignition, all measures shall be taken to prevent any such explosion by:

(a) Providing an effective enclosure of the plant or machinery used in the process,

or

(b) The removal or prevention of accumulation of such dust, gas or fumes.

(xvi) Safety of Factory Buildings and Machinery: If it appears to the inspector that any building or part of factory is in such a condition that if it is dangerous to human life or safety, he may serve on the manager of the factory an order in writing specifying the measures that should be adopted and the specific date by which they should be carried out to ensure the safety of the building or factory. He may also serve an order to the manager, prohibiting its use until proper repairs or alternations have been carried out.

(xvii) Welfare Provisions:

(a) *Facilities for Washing:* In every factory, adequate and suitable facilities for washing shall be provided and maintained for the workers. Adequately screened facilities for washing shall be provided for male and female workers separately. Such facilities shall be conveniently accessible and shall be kept clean.

(b) *Storing and Drying Clothes:* The State Government may require any factory or class of factories to make provision therein of suitable places for keeping clothes not worn during working hours and for drying wet clothing.

(c) *Facilities for Sitting:* In every factory, suitable arrangement for sitting shall be provided and maintained for all workers obliged to work in a standing position in order that they may take advantage of rest in the course of their work.

(d) *First-aid Appliances:* First-aid boxes, equipped with the prescribed contents, which will readily accessible during all working hours, shall be provided and maintained in every factory. The number of such boxes shall not be less than one for every one hundred and fifty workers.

(xviii) Penalties for Breach of Provisions of the Act: For any contravention of the Act, the occupier and the manager of a factory shall each be guilty of an offence and be punishable with imprisonment for a term not exceeding three months or with a fine up to ₹ 500 or with both.

If any person, who has been convicted of any offence punishable under the provisions of this Act, is again found to be guilty of an offence involving contravention of the same provision within a period of two years from the date of conviction will undergo imprisonment up to six months or with a fine up to ₹ 1,000 or with both. This Act, for the time, provides that if any worker contravenes any provision of this Act or any rules or orders, such as the use of safety guards, etc., he shall be punishable with fine up to ₹ 20.

India's ratification of International Labour Convention No. 90 prohibiting the employment of young persons in factories at night necessitated an amendment of the relevant sections of the Factories Act, 1948. This was achieved by passing an Amendment Act in April 1954. This Act added a new chapter on "Annual Leave with Wages" to the Factories Act, 1948. It lays down a period of 240 days as the minimum attendance necessary during a calendar year to qualify for leave with wages. It also prohibits employment of young persons on cleaning, lubricating or adjusting any prime mover or transmission machinery while it is in motion, if such work exposes them to a risk of injury.

3. Income Tax Act

The tax concessions provided in the Income Tax Act for SSIs of minor significance. Under Section 80 HHA, which came into effect from the assessment year 1978-79, an assessment is entitled to a deduction in respect of profits and gains derived from a new small-scale industrial undertaking set up in any area at the rate of 20 per cent for the first ten assessment years. One of the conditions is that the unit should have commenced its manufacturing activity after September 30, 1977. This concession is discriminatory, for there is no justification for denying the benefit to those units which commenced manufacturing activity before September 30, 1977.

Moreover, the units in urban areas have been neglected. Unless we have correct statistics of the proportion of small-scale units in rural areas to those in urban areas and the proportion of the tax collected from rural units to the tax collected from urban ones, the significance of such a discriminatory tax concession cannot be evaluated.

Another incentive is the investment allowance under Section 32 A of the Act, under which a small-scale unit is entitled to a deduction at the rate of 25 per cent of the cost of plant and machinery installed after March 31, 1976. This allowance is capital-oriented, whereas most of the small-scale units are capital saving and labour-oriented.

At present, there is no Central Government definition of the term *Small-scale Industrial Undertaking* – a fact which indicates how unimportant these undertakings are in the eyes of the tax department. According to the definitions given under Section 32 A and 80 HHA, the term is used to mean an industrial undertaking whose aggregate value of machinery and plant – other than tools, jigs, dies and mould – installed on the last day of the previous year for the purpose of the business of the undertaking, does not exceed ₹ 10 lakh. In Section 58A of the Companies Act, however, the term is defined as any industrial undertaking registered with the Directorate of Industries or the Directorate of Small-scale Industries.

4. The Industrial Employment (Standing Orders) Act, 1946

The absence of standing orders clearly defining the rights and obligations of the employer and the workers in respect of recruitment, discharge, disciplinary action, holidays, leave, etc., was one of the most frequent causes of friction between management and workers. On the recommendations of the Tripartite Labour Conference held in 1943, 1944, 1945 the Government of India passed the Industrial Employment (Standing Orders) Act in 1946. This Act provides for the farming of standing orders in all establishment employing 100 or more persons. It requires employers to submit within six months of enactment of the law standing orders covering the classification of workmen (permanent, temporary, etc.), the manner of intimating to them their hours of work, holidays, pay-days and wage rates, the procedure to be followed while applying for leave and holidays, the termination of employment of notice of discharge and for disciplinary action. In pursuance of this Act, the Central Government published the Central rules in 1946 which were applicable to Commissioner's provinces and to the undertakings under the Central Government. Its lead was promptly followed by all State Governments. In Maharashtra State, it has been made applicable to establishments in which fifty or more persons are employed.

5. The Indian Trade Unions Act, 1926

The experience of the working of the system of free enterprise in the industrial field revealed that though theoretically both the employers and workers were free to enter into a contract and to agree upon the wages to be paid and received, in point of fact, for various reasons, this freedom did not benefit the workers in any way. Firstly, the commodity that a worker has to sell is highly perishable in the sense that if he refuses to work on a particular day because the wages offered are low, he cannot store up his labour of that day to be used the next day. This compels him to accept work even if the wages offered are unsatisfactory. Secondly, as his income is very low, he is not able to accumulate any savings on which he can fall back if and when he refuses to work. The consequences can be quite drastic. These two factors compel a worker to accept low wages and so the theoretical freedom of contract is not of much use to him. Lastly, the fact that a worker is a small-scale seller and the employer is a large-scale buyer reduces his bargaining power to a very great extent. It is possible for the employer to refuse the wage which a worker demands because it is possible for him to engage somebody else who is willing to work on lower wage. It is, however, relatively difficult for a worker to find an alternative employer who would pay him the wage he demands.

His weak bargaining position thus compels him to accept whatever wages are offered to him.

Rules of Trade Union: The rules of a union contain the following provisions:

(a) the name,

(b) the objectives for which it has been established,

(c) the purpose for which its general funds will be applicable,

(d) maintenance of the list of members for inspection by officers and members of the units,

(e) the admission of ordinary members who shall be persons engaged in the industry with which the union is connected and also the admission of honorary members to form the executive of the union,

(f) the conditions under which fines or forfeiture may be imposed on them,

(g) the manner in which any rule shall be amended, altered or rescinded,

(h) the manner in which the members of the executive and other officers of the union shall be appointed and removed,

(i) the safe custody of the funds of the union, the audit of accounts and inspection of the account books by the officers and members, and lastly,

(j) the manner in which the union will be dissolved.

Rights of Registered Trade Unions: A registered trade union has the following right:

(a) To collect membership fees on the premises of the factory without interference from the management;

(b) To put up notices of the meetings of the union and of the other activities of the union on the premises of the factory;

(c) To use the general funds for specific purposes;

(d) To raise funds for political purposes at the option of the members;

(e) To conduct a strike if called for by peaceful methods;

(f) To be exempted from the provisions of Section 120B, sub-section (2) of the Indian Penal Code if the members conduct a peaceful strike;

(g) To appoint outsiders in a number which is not more than one-half of the total number of office-bearers to the executive of the union; and

(h) To send to the Registrar, every year, an audited statement of receipts and expenditure.

6. The Payment of Wages Act, 1936

The payment of wages to factory workers in a particular form and at regular intervals without any unauthorised deductions is the objective of this Act.

Scope of the Act: The provisions of the Act are applicable to workers engaged in factories as defined by the Factories Act of 1948, and to persons employed on any railway by contractor or sub-contractor. The State Government may, after giving three months notice of its intention of doing so by a notification in the *Official Gazette*, extent the provisions of this Act to any class of persons employed in any industrial establishment. The provisions of this Act are applicable to those persons whose wages do not exceed ₹ 400 per month.

The Date of Payment of Wages: The wages of every person employed in a factory, industrial establishment, or a railway, where less than 1,000 persons are employed, shall be paid before the expiry of the seventh day after the completion of wage period, generally a month; the wages for a month, for example, shall be paid before the seventh day of the next month. In the factories in which more than 1,000 persons are employed, the wages shall be paid before the expiry of the tenth day of the next month. The wages of a person whose services have been terminated shall be paid on the next working day after such termination. The payment of wages shall be made on a working day.

The wage ceiling for the applicability of the Act has been increased through amendment from ₹ 1600/- to ₹ 6500/- per month w.e.f. 09.11.2005 and further to ₹ 10,000/- per month through notification w.e.f. 08.08.2007.

Authorised Deductions: The Act authorises the employer to make deductions from wages in the wake of:

(a) fines,

(b) absence from duty,

(c) damage to or loss of goods or money, where such damage or loss is due to the negligence or default on the part of the employee,

(d) housing accommodation supplied by the employer, and

(e) such amenities and services supplied by the employer as the State Government may authorise.

In the case of fines:

(i) It shall be imposed for those acts of commission and omission which the employer, with the approval of the State Government, may have specified by notice to his employees.

(ii) It shall be imposed on any employee unless he has been given an opportunity to show cause why the fine should not be imposed.

(iii) No fine shall be imposed on persons below the age of fifteen.

(iv) A fine imposed on any employee in any wage period should be according to the wages payable to him for the period.

(v) The fine so imposed shall be recovered in instalments or after the expiry of sixty days from the day on which it was imposed.

(vi) The fine and the actual amount recovered shall be recorded in a separate register in the prescribed form which will be utilised only for purposes beneficial to the

employees and as are approved by the prescribed authority. Applications for the recovery of fines, or of deductions not authorised under the Act, for delay in payment of wages shall be presented within six months of the date on which such fines were imposed or deductions were made or wages were due.

7. The Workmen's Compensation Act, 1923

Within the installation of machinery operated by motive power, the number of accidents in factories have increased considerably. Many times, worker have met with accidents, resulting in physical impairment and death working on machines in factories. This meant the loss of earnings for their immediate family. From a purely humanitarian point of view, it would be natural to expect that employers should give some compensation to such workers or their dependants. Further, even on economic grounds, it could be argued that the amount of compensation is a legitimate element of the cost of production under the factory system and, therefore, neither society nor employers should grudge to pay it in these critical situations. Some enlightened employers did pay compensation to their employees when they suffered accidents; but a large majority was not willing to accept this responsibility. The workers, however, could not claim compensation as a matter of right; and even when compensation was paid, there was bound to be an honest difference of opinion between an employer and an employee as regards the fairness of the amount paid. In order to provide some bases for a statutory claim for compensation to be paid to the disabled factory worker, Workmen's Compensation Acts have been passed in almost all the countries.

The following are the provisions of the Indian Workmen's Compensation Act:

Employer's liability for compensation: If a personal injury is caused to a worker by an accident arising out of and in the course of his employment, his employer shall be liable to any compensation in accordance with the provisions of this Act.

When employer is not liable: The employer, however, shall not be liable if:

(a) the injury results in a partial or total disablement of the worker for less than three days;

(b) if the injury can be directly attributed to the worker having been under the influence of drink or drugs; or

(c) if the injury can be directly attributed to the wilful disobedience by the worker of an order expressly given; or

(d) to the wilful removal or disregard by the worker of any safety guard or other device which he knew to have been provided for the purpose of securing his safety.

Occupational Diseases: If a worker engaged in any employment which involves the handling of wool, hair bristles or animal carcasses or loading or unloading of such merchandise, or in processes carried on in compressed air, or in processes which involve the use of lead or tetrayethyl or in processes involving exposure to nitrous fumes, contracts diseases like anthrax, compressed air illness, lead poisoning, or poisoning by nitrous fumes respectively; or when engaged continuously for not less than six months in any employment specified in Part B of Schedule III, contracts any disease specified in this schedule as an occupational disease, the contracting of such a disease shall be regarded as an injury by accident and shall be deemed to have arisen out of and in the employment. The State Government in the case of employments specified in Part C of the schedule, may make additions to the list of employments in Schedule III and specify the corresponding diseases after giving three months' notice in the *Gazette.*

Types of Injuries: Injuries under this Act have been classified into the following categories:

(1) Death,

(2) Permanent total disablement,

(3) Permanent partial disablement, and

(4) Temporary disablement, partial or total.

Amount of Compensation: The Act provides for compensation for these categories of injuries in Schedules I to IV.

Medical Examination: A worker who has given notice of an accident shall submit himself to a medical examination, if the employer insists on it by a qualified medical practitioner and free of charge. Similarly, a worker who is in receipt of half-monthly payments under this Act shall submit himself to such medical examination from time-to-time.

If a worker refuses to submit himself to such a medical examination without sufficient cause, his right to compensation shall be suspended.

8. The Employees State Insurance Act, 1948

Experience in the working of the Workmen's Compensation Act of 1923 revealed that the benefits conferred by it upon factory workers in many cases, did not reach them. This was due to various reasons. Firstly, a claim for compensation for injury had to be failed in an ordinary court of law and the lack of finance often made it impossible for a worker to file such a suit and fight it out. Secondly, armed with expert legal advice, it was often possible for an employer to prove that the accident either did not arise out of and in the course of employment or that it was due to the worker concerned being under the influence of drink or drug at the time of the accident, or that it was due to his negligence or his disobedience of safety rules. In such conditions, workers were generally unwilling to go to court of law, and preferred to accept whatever compensation employers chose to pay out of a sense of pity or charity. The Employees' State Insurance Act of 1948 was framed to prevent such victimisation of the worker by the employer.

Contributions: Every person, who is employed for wages in or in connection with the work of a factory or establishment to which this Act applies, shall be insured. All the insured workers, except those who earn wages of less than one rupee per day, shall pay their contributions to the Employees' State Insurance Corporation at the rates specified in the First Schedule to the Act. The employers shall pay their contributions at the rates specified in the above schedule.

Distribution of Benefits under the Act: The insured persons or as the case may be, their dependants shall be entitled to the following benefits, namely:

(a) Sickness benefits: Periodical payments to any insured person in case of his sickness certified by a duly appointed medical practitioner;

(b) Maternity benefits: Periodical payments: in case of confinement to an insured woman certified to be eligible for such payment by an authority specified in this behalf by the regulations;

(c) Disablement benefits: Periodical payments to an insured person suffering from disablement as a result of an injury sustained in the course of his employment;

(d) Dependants' benefits: Periodical payments to such dependants of an insured person who dies as a result of an injury sustained in the course of his employment; and

(e) Medical benefits: Medical treatment for an attendance on an insured person.

The Corporation may at the request of Government of India, extend medical benefits to the family of the insured person. Accordingly, these benefits have been so executed from 1st January, 1962.

A person who is in receipt of sickness or disablement benefits, must observe the following conditions:

(a) He shall remain under medical treatment at dispensary, hospital, clinic or other institution provided under this Act and shall carry-out the instructions of the medical officer or medical attendant in charge thereof;

(b) He shall not, while under treatment, do anything which might retard or prejudice his chances of recovery;

(c) He shall not leave the area in which medical treatment provided under this Act is being given without the permission of the medical officer or such other authority as may be specified in this behalf under the rules framed for this purposes; and

(d) He shall allow himself to be examined by any duly appointed medical officer or any other person authorised by Corporation in this behalf.

Penalties: If a person makes a false statement for the purpose of causing any increase in payment or benefit or for the purpose of causing any payment or benefit to be made where no payment or benefit is authorised, or for the purpose of avoiding any payment to be made by himself, he shall be punishable with imprisonment for a term up to three months or with fine up to ₹ 500 or with both.

If any person fails to pay any contribution which he is liable to pay, or deducts from the wages of an employee the whole or any part of the employee's contribution, or reduces the wages or any privileges or benefits admissible to an employee, dismisses, discharges, reduces or otherwise punishes an employee in contravention of Section 73, or files or refuses to submit any return required by the regulations or make a false return, or obstructs any inspector or other official of the Corporation in the discharge of his duties, or is guilty of contravention of, and non-compliance with, any of the requirements of this Act, he shall be punishable with imprisonment up to a period of three months or with fine up to ₹ 500 or with both.

9. The Maternity Benefit Act, 1961

The Maternity Benefit Act, 1961 regulates the employment of women in factories, mines, the circus industry, plantations and shops or establishments employing 10 or more persons except the employees who are covered under the Employees State Insurance (ESI) for certain periods before and after child birth and provides for maternity and other benefits.

10. The Payment of Bonus Act, 1965

The Payment of Bonus Act, 1965 provides for payment of bonus to employees of factories and establishments employing 20 or more persons. An Ordinance has been promulgated on 27.10.2007 to enhance the eligibility limit from ₹ 3500/- to ₹ 10,000/- per month, calculation ceiling increased from 2500/- to ₹ 3500/- and to make employees employed through contractors on building operations eligible for payment of bonus under the Payment of Bonus Act, 1965 w.e.f. 01.04.2006.

11. The Industrial Disputes Act, 1947

Industrial disputes, strikes and lockouts were not very common occurrences in India till 1914. It was, however, during the Great War of 1914-18 that the strike came to be regarded as an ordinary weapon of industrial warfare. During the war, while the cost of living went on rising, the wages did not keep pace with it. This gave rise to serious discontent among industrial workers and led to a series of strikes, notably in the textile industry in Bombay, in the post-war period. In addition to low wages, there were many other causes which were partly responsible for the outbreak of strikes during this period. The more important of these were long hours of work, bad conditions, insanitary housing conditions, absence of any provision till 1922 for compensation for injuries sustained in the course of employment, absence till 1925 of the right to form a trade union, ill-treatment of workmen by foremen or other mill officials, etc.

The important provisions of the Industrial Disputes Act of 1947 are:

(i) If any industrial dispute exists or is apprehended, the appropriate Government may, by order in writing: *(a)* refer the dispute to a board of promoting a settlement thereof; or *(b)* refer any matter appearing to be connected with or relevant to the dispute to a court of inquiry; or *(c)* refer the dispute to a tribunal for arbitration.

(ii) If either of the parties to a dispute or both of them apply to the Government to refer a dispute to board, court or tribunal, the appropriate Government, if satisfied that the person applying represents majority of each party, shall make the reference accordingly.

(iii) If a dispute has been referred to a board or a tribunal, the Government may prohibit the continuance of any strike or lockout in connection with such a dispute.

(iv) A settlement arrived at in the course of conciliation under the Act, or an award which is declared by the Government as binding on all the parties for at least six months.

(v) An award declared by a Government shall come into operation on such date as may be specified by the Government and shall remain in operation for a period for one year, or a shorter period, if so fixed by the Government.

(vi) Workers employed in public utility industries shall not go on a strike and the employers in such industries shall not resort to lockouts.

(a) without giving a fourteen days' notice and before the period of notice expires; or

(b) during the pendency of conciliation proceedings.

(vii) Workers employed in any industrial establishment shall not go on strike -

(a) During the pendency of conciliation proceeding; or

(b) During the pendency of proceeding before a labour court, tribunal or national tribunal; or

(c) During a period in which a settlement or award is in operation.

A strike or a lockout in contravention of any these provisions, shall be illegal.

No person shall knowingly expend or apply any money in direct furtherance or support of any illegal strike or lockout.

Penalties: Any worker who commences, continues or acts in furtherance of an illegal strike shall be punishable with imprisonment up to one month or with fine up to ₹ 50 or both.

12. The Employees Provident Fund Act, 1952

The Act provides for the institution of a contributory provident fund in establishment in which 20 or more persons are employed. The contribution, which shall be paid by the employer to the fund, shall be $8^1/_3$ per cent of the basic wage and the dearness allowance payable to each employee, while the employee's contribution shall be equal to the contribution payable by the employer.

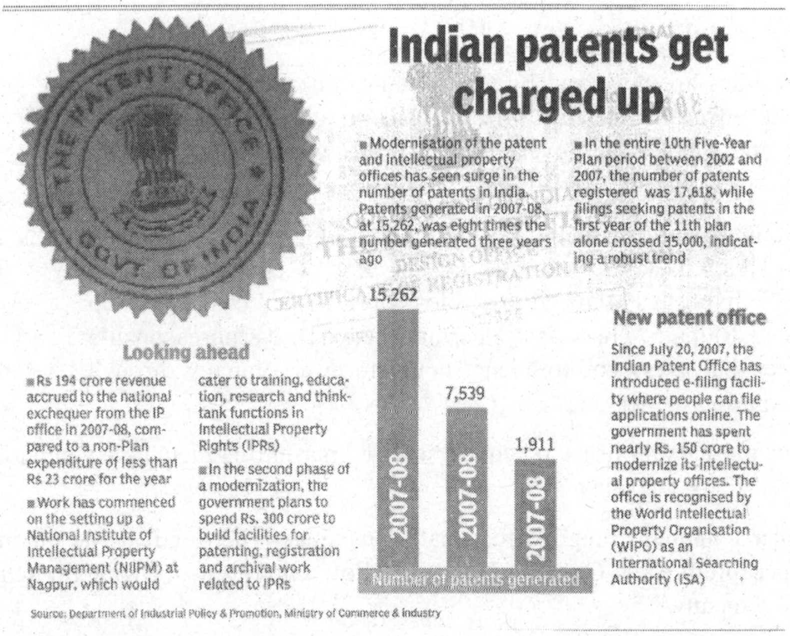
Indian patents get charged up

■ Modernisation of the patent and intellectual property offices has seen surge in the number of patents in India. Patents generated in 2007-08, at 15,262, was eight times the number generated three years ago

■ In the entire 10th Five-Year Plan period between 2002 and 2007, the number of patents registered was 17,618, while filings seeking patents in the first year of the 11th plan alone crossed 35,000, indicating a robust trend

Looking ahead

■ Rs 194 crore revenue accrued to the national exchequer from the IP office in 2007-08, compared to a non-Plan expenditure of less than Rs 23 crore for the year

■ Work has commenced on the setting up a National Institute of Intellectual Property Management (NIIPM) at Nagpur, which would cater to training, education, research and think-tank functions in Intellectual Property Rights (IPRs)

■ In the second phase of a modernization, the government plans to spend Rs. 300 crore to build facilities for patenting, registration and archival work related to IPRs

New patent office

Since July 20, 2007, the Indian Patent Office has introduced e-filing facility where people can file applications online. The government has spent nearly Rs. 150 crore to modernize its intellectual property offices. The office is recognised by the World Intellectual Property Organisation (WIPO) as an International Searching Authority (ISA)

Source: Department of Industrial Policy & Promotion, Ministry of Commerce & Industry

13. The Indian Boilers Act, 1923

An owner of a boiler shall not use it or permit to be used.

(a) unless it has been registered in accordance with the provisions of this Act;

(b) in the case of a boiler transferred from one State to another, until the transfer has been reported in the prescribed manner;

(c) unless certificate or provisional order authorising the use of the boiler is obtained under this Act;

(d) at a pressure higher than the maximum pressure recorded in such certificate or provisional order;

(e) unless the boiler is in charge of a person holding a certificate of competency.

Procedure: The owner of a boiler may apply to the inspector to have the boiler registered. Every such application shall be accompanied by the prescribed fee. He shall examine the boiler and submit a report to the Chief Inspector in the prescribed form.

The permit is a "must" for boilers.

14. The Indian Electricity Act, 1910

The Act relates to the supply and use of electricity energy.

Issue of Licence: A State Government may, on an application made in the prescribed form and on the payment of the prescribed fee, grant a licence to supply energy in any specified area and also to lay electric supply lines for the transmission of energy.

15. The Indian Companies Act, 1956

Indian companies are governed by the archaic Indian Companies Act, 1956, which has been amended 25 times. To make starting and running business easier and simpler the government is working the replace it with a new Act. The key points in the Bill are:

- Provisions that allow for the setting up of a One Person Company (OPC). This will help entrepreneurs start up as a company without facing the liabilities attached to a sole proprietorship or partnership firm. Says Rajpal: "This is an important proposal. It's unreasonable to expect that every entrepreneur should form a company through an association of persons".
- To allow partnership firms to acquire scale by permitting them to have up to 100 partners, compared to just 20 now.
- A simpler compliance regime for small companies. There will be no minimum floor for paid-up capital. Says Gupta: "This will allow entrepreneurs with limited resources to form a company."
- To broad base the talent pool available to companies. Companies will be allowed to have a minimum of only one Director resident in India. This will replace the present stipulation that requires all Whole-time Directors and the Managing Director of a company to be Indian residents.

- Greater flexibility in structuring ownership. The restrictions on the number of subsidiaries that a company can have will be done away with, subject to disclosure of their relationships and transactions/dealings between them. Consolidation of accounts, though, will be mandatory.
- A revised framework for regulation of insolvency, and completion of rehabilitation, winding up and liquidation of companies in a time-bound manner.
- The Bill stresses on self-regulation with disclosures and accountability and substitution of government control over internal corporate processes by empowering shareholders.
- It also proposes to scrap shares with differential voting rights. This will reverse the decision by the Department of Company Affairs in 2001 to allow Indian companies to issue shares with differential voting rights if it has distributable profits for the preceding three financial years.

CONCLUSION

Rules and regulations governing Small-scale Enterprises act as a governor ensuring steady growth of the industry as well as the environment (ecosystem) and the labour force. It ensures both healthy growth and rapid growth. The basic objective of these rules and regulations scale is to ensure that the results of operations confirm as closely as possible to established standards of goods, specified procedures or instruction. The need for rules and regulations are meant to put these SSIs small-scale industries on the successful track.

They are the directions for excellence, growth and development and, regulation is a monitoring mechanism of rules. Since, small-scale enterprise is concerned with land, environment, goods, people and consumer, rules and regulations have been formulated to safeguard these varied interests. If there is greater awareness among the entrepreneurs, these rules and regulations have minimum effect and disturbance. Thus, ensure steady and rapid growth of SSIs, develop new products and markets, produce quality goods, promote healthy development of human resources. More importantly, small industries are located nearer to the natural resources and human resources. They do not pollute or degrade the ecosystem, intimidate and exploit labour and cheat the consumer on all counts. They are, therefore, the basic component of the SSIs. They are like the lamp post which direct the growth of this sector on a firm ground.

ANNEXURE - I

Applicability of Various Labour Acts

204. A table indicating the factories or establishments to which various Labour Acts are applicable is given below to enable the entrepreneur to know the Acts applicable to his enterprise:

Name of the Act	*Factories or establishments to which applicable*	*Remarks*
Apprenticeship Act, 1961	—	Apprenticeship Adviser shall give a notice in writing to the employer. It
Contract Labour (Regulation and Abolition) Act, 1970	Where contract labour is permitted.	is permitted if work is intermitent or of sporadic nature.
	Establishment or contractors who employ or had employed 20 or more workers on any day in preceding 12 months.	Principal employer/contractor is required to seek registration/licence.
Employees Provident Fund and Family Pension Fund Act, 1952	Factories employing 20 or more persons and those industries which are specified in the Schedule.	Employer required to furnish particulars to Regional Commissioner within 15 days of the application of the Act to his establishment. Those employees are eligible to become members whose wages do not exceed ₹ 1,000 per month.
Employees State Insurance Act, 1948	Factories employing 20 or more persons, except specified seasonal factories.	
Employment Exchange (Compulsory Notification of Vacancies) Act, 1959	Establishments where ordinarily 25 or more persons are employed.	Vacancies are to be notified to local Employment Exchange one week before the date on which interview/test is to take place.
Employment of Children Act, 1938	Workshops engaged in specified processes; these processes are 10 in number.	Employment of children in these processes is prohibited. Child is defined as one who hs not completed his 14th year.
Equal Remuneration Act, 1976		Act enjoins every employer to pay equal remuneration to men and women workers.
Factories Act, 1948	Factories where 10 or more workers with the aid of power or 20 or more workers with out aid of power are working or were working on any day in preceding twelve months and where manufacturing process is carried on.	Occupier is expected to obtain prior permission for construction of factory permises and seek licence for the factory.

		Act is applicable to other places where manufacturing process is carried on, even though number of workers is less than 10 or 20, if so notified by the State Government.
Industrial Disputes Act, 1947	Any business, trade, undertaking, manufacture or calling of employer and includes any handicraft, or industrial occupation.	It deals with procedures for settlement of disputes and stipulates compensation for lay-off, retrenchment and closure of establishments.
Industrial Employment (Standing Order) Act, 1961	Industrial establishments employing one hundred or more workmen.	Standing Orders relating to classification of workmen, terms and conditions of services, etc. are to be got approved from certifying officers.
Maternity Benefit Act, 1961	Factories where 10 or more workers with aid of power or 20 or more workers without aid of power are/were working, mines and plantations or other establishments notified by the State Government.	Act is not applicable to any factory or establishment to which Employees State Insurance Act applies. A women is entitled to maternity benefit at the rate of average daily wages for 12 weeks (6 weeks before and 6 weeks after delivery) if she has worked for 160 days in 12 preceding months.
Minimum Wages Act, 1948	Certain specified employments or processes.	State Governments have fixed minimum wages for skilled, unskilled, manual and clerical workers, and have specified other conditions of service. Payment of Wages Act, 1936 is also applicable to these specified employments and processes.
Payment of Bonus Act, 1965	Factories where 10 more more workers with aid of power or 20 or more workers without aid of power are/were working; and establishments employing 20 or more persons.	A minimum bonus 8.33% of the salary or wages earned or ₹ 10, whichever is higher, is payable even if the establishment has made no profits. Maximum amount of bonus payable is 20 per cent of the salary or wage earned. Newly set up establishments are exempted from payment of bonus till they start deriving profit or for 5 years from their estalishment, whichever is earlier.
Payment of Gratuity Act, 1972	Factories where 10 or more workers with aid of power or 20 or more workers without aid of power are/were working; and mines or plantation, and shops or	An employer is required to furnish particulars to the controlling authority when Act becomes applicable, notify any change or closure of establishment.

	establishments employing 10 or more persons.	Gratuity is payable, after an employee has rendered five years of continuous service, at the rate of 15 days of wages for year's service, subject to a maximum of 20 month's wages.
Payment of Wages Act, 1936	Factories where 10 or more workers with aid of power or 20 or more workers without aid of power are/were working; other industrial establishments as are specified; specified employments included in the Schedule to Minimum Wages Act.	This Act seeks to regulate timely payment of wages in respect of persons, whose wages average less than ₹ 1,000 a month.
Sales Promotion (Conditions of Service) Act, 1976 Shops and Establishments Act of State Goverments Workmen's Compensation Act, 1923	Establishments engaged in Pharmaceutical industry. Shops, commercial establishments, residental hotels, restaurant, eating houses, etc. Certain specified employments.	Act is not applicable to such under-taking which are covered under Factories Act, 1948. Compensation is payable to workmen, whose monthly wages do not exceed ₹ 1,000 for injury by accident or occupational disease.

CHAPTER 14

SICKNESS IN SMALL-SCALE INDUSTRIES – REASONS AND REMEDIES

"Small units are more prone to failure and sickness than the medium and large-scale industries. A unit on sick bed itself a proof of the state of affairs in that business. Inability to function properly, leads to eventual failure of business. A business which has failed is considered to be a closed unit. A closed unit is one in which there are no production activities and there are no major recurring liabilities of salaries and wages. A sick unit on the other hand is one which is making losses, defaulting on the repayment of loans and payments to creditors. A sick unit is one which fails to generate internal surplus, on a continuing basis, to meet its obligations."

INTRODUCTION

Rapid industrial growth has brought in its wake incidence of sickness in the industrial sector including small-scale industries.

Sickness in industrial units is a gradual process and does not develop suddenly. In the initial stages, it gets reflected in the form of defects and mistakes in the unit's functional areas like production, finance and management. Later it is observed in the form of symptoms like irregular or unsatisfactory turnover in the account, slow and unsatisfactory movement of stocks, decline in production, sales and profitability frequent violation of terms and conditions and asking for additional grants.

Definition

The term *industrial sickness* has been defined in a number of ways and its concept lacks uniformity. A sick industrial unit may be defined as one when it fails to generate surplus on a continuous basis and depends on frequent infusion of external funds for its survival.

According to the Reserve Bank of India (RBI), and S.I. unit should be considered so if it has "incurred cash loss in the previous accounting year and is likely to continue to incur cash loss in the current accounting year, and has an erosion on account of cumulative cash losses to the extent of 50 per cent of those of its net worth."

A unit is likely to continue to incur cash losses for the current year as well as the following year and which has imbalance in its financial structure such as current ratio of less than 1:1 and worsening debt-equity ratio. According to ICICI "a sick industry is one whose financial viability is threatened by adverse factors present and continuing. The adverse factor might relate to management, market fiscal burden, labour relations or any other. When the impact of factors reaches a point where a company begins to incur cash losses leading to erosion of its funds, there is threat to its financial stability."

The sick industrial companies (special provision) Act, 1985 identifies sickness in terms of cash losses for two consecutive financial years and accumulated losses equalling or exceeding the net worth of the company at the end of the second financial year.

The definition of sick SSI units has been modified as under: "A small-scale industrial unit should be considered as sick if it has, at the end of any accounting year, accumulated losses equal to or exceeding 50 per cent of its peak net worth in the immediately preceding five accounting years" (Bihar Chambers of Commerce, Sep. 1989).

An analysis of all the definitions given above indicate that sickness, more or less, has a perfect positive correlation with profitability. Profitability alone can generate cash surpluses for an industrial unit to meet its various obligations to the creditors like financial institutions, the government and others.

Causes of Sickness

A. Internal Causes

(1) Planning

(a) Technical feasibility

Inadequate technical know-how
Locational disadvantage
Outdated production process

(b) Economic viability

High cost of inputs
Break-even point too high
Uneconomic size of project
Underestimation of financial requirements
Unduly large investment in fixed assets
Overestimation of demand.

(2) Implementation

Cost overruns resulting from delays in getting licences and sanctions, etc.
Inadequate mobilisation of finance.

(3) Production

(a) Production management

Inappropriate product-mix
Poor quality control
Poor capacity utilisation
High cost of production
Poor inventory management
Inadequate maintenance and replacement
Lack of timely and adequate modernisation, etc.
High wastage

(b) *Labour management*

Excessively high wage structure
Inefficient handling of labour problems
Excessive manpower
Poor labour productivity
Poor labour relations
Lack of trained skilled labour or technically competent personnel

(c) *Marketing management*

Dependence on a single customer or a limited number of customers/single or a limited number of products
Poor sales realisation
Defective pricing policy
Booking of large orders at fixed prices in an inflationary market
Weak market organisation
Lack of market feedback and market research
Lack of knowledge of marketing techniques
Unscrupulous sales/purchase practices

(d) *Financial management*

The road to business is paved with bad financial decisions. More often, the entrepreneur's financial mismanagement is responsible for a host of problems.
Poor resources management and financial planning
Faulty costing
Minimal capital
Liberal dividend policy
General financial indiscipline and application of funds for unauthorised purposes
Poor liquidity
Deficiency of funds
Overtrading
Unfavourable gearing or keeping adverse debt-equity ratio
Inadequate working capital
Absence of cost consciousness
Lack of effective collection machinery
Poor cash control
No plan "B" in sight
Throwing IT around
Delaying Debt
Borrowing Blind
Leaving lenders out
Thin reserves
Underestimation of expenses like import and transport costs
Excessive investment in infrastructure
Ignoring the lender like SIDBI

(e) *Administrative management*

Overcentralisation
Lack of professionalism

Lack of feedback to management (Management Information System)
Lack of controls
Lack of timely diversification
Excessive expenditure on R&D

Dividend loyalties (where the same management has interest in more than one unit, cases are known where promoters of limited companies who also own private ownership firms tend to look after the interests of the latter, often at the cost of the former)

Dissension within the management
Incompetent management
Dishonest management

B. External Causes

(a) *Infrastructural bottlenecks*
Non-availability of irregular supply of critical raw materials or other inputs
Chronic power shortage
Transport bottlenecks

(b) *Financial bottlenecks*
Non-availability of adequate finance

(c) *Government controls and policies, etc.*
Government price controls
Fiscal duties
Abrupt change in Government policies

Procedural delays on the part of the financial/licensing/other controlling or regulating authorities (Banks, Reserve Bank of India, financial institutions, Government departments, licensing authorities, Monopolies and Restrictive Trade Practices Board, etc.)

(d) *Market constraints*
Market saturation
Revolutionary technological advances rendering one's products obsolete

(e) *Extraneous factors*
Natural calamities
Political situation (domestic as well as international)
War
Sympathetic strikes
Multiplicity of labour unions.

Management Deficiency

It could be said that management deficiency is one of the biggest reasons for poor performance and sickness of small-scale units. The new entrants in the fields of small industries in many cases did not have any prior training or background in management of their enterprises and were adverse to innovations and changes. In the beginning of our industrial development era, this problem was not so critical but with growing sophistication and modernisation of market-requirements for the items produced by the small-scale sector, it has become very important for small entrepreneurs to employ modern methods of management, be it in the field of advanced technology or marketing.

Recent experiences have proved that entrepreneurship is not only an inborn gift, but it could also be cultivated through application and training. American Universities and colleges offering courses in starting and managing a small enterprise. The Carnegie Mellon University of USA is one of the prominent universities offering entrepreneurial training courses. In our country, similar entrepreneurship development training, programmes are organised by organisations, *viz.,* Centre for Development of Entrepreneurs, Gandhi Nagar (Gujarat), Small Industries Extension Training Institutes, Hyderabad, and other units of the Small Industries Development Organisation. The Centre for Development of Entrepreneurs has trained over 6,000 entrepreneurs till recently, out of which around 3,000 are running their own units successfully. The Small Industries Development Organisation has also been helpful in motivating a good number of entrepreneurs of the first generation. Recently, the Government of India has also established a National Institute for Entrepreneurship and Small Business at New Delhi which would shortly start its own programmes.

Finance

Financial inadequacy is also reported to be one of the most important causes leading to sickness of small-scale units. Undoubtedly, the Government has extended a number of incentives for the growth of small industries and some people feel that these have had negative effect on the small industries. Some others feel that in order to obtain more and more finance and concessions, the small entrepreneur often runs from one agency to another and consequently, cannot concentrate on his industry. There have also been reports that some of these incentives have been misused. However, the discussion here is related to small industries who have genuinely suffered for want of adequate and timely financing facilities. It is well-known that a committee set-up by the Government of India under the Chairmanship of Prof. A. M. Khusro, Ex-member, Planning Commission is already looking into the financing/credit problems/needs of small-scale industries and it is hoped that a separate Apex Financing Institution for small industries might be recommended. In addition, a separate legislation to protect the genuine interests of small-scale industries, including tiny and ancillary sector, is under consideration of the Government. It could also be expected that the Apex Financing Institution or Bank solely devoted to meet the credit needs of small industries in the country would bring out some hitherto unknown difficulties of the sector and come out with remedial measures to improve health of the weaker small units. The Bank may also provide expertise in guiding small entrepreneurs in their financial management problems and offer preventive assistance to them in case where sickness is anticipated.

Technology

Notable technological innovations and changes are taking place in industrially advanced countries of the world and small-scale industries in those countries are also correspondingly responding by upgrading their technology. For example, use of computers is being made in the design and production of individual components in job shops at costs comparable with costs of mass produced techniques. This has meaningful implications for a country like India, where at present a large number of small and ancillary industries are competing with large industries in a number of common product areas. While fiscal incentives given to small-scale industries are, indeed, of help, the ultimate answer will, of course lie in the small-scale industries upgrading and updating their own technology and skills to meet the stringent within the country and by importers abroad. Small units will have to be technologically modern and price-wise competitive to play a significant role and keep their place in the total industrial structure of the country. In this task, technocrat-entrepreneurs particularly, may have to play a leading role.

There is a misconception in some quarters that modernisation and upgradation of technology necessarily involves costly equipment and labour reduction. While the initial investment cost in modern plant facilities may be somewhat higher, the investment would ultimately result in long-term benefits to economy through higher and consistent quality and higher productivity achievements. Modern technology also need not necessarily mean adopting automation in every case. In case of small industries, the process of modernisation and upgradation of technology could be undertaken in phases depending upon the resources available with the units. Modernisation would, of course need higher and better skills to operate, maintain and run modern plant facilities to get the maximum productivity. While this might mean less demand for uneducated and unskilled personnel, it would on the other hand create opportunities for many skilled and educated operators, technicians and engineers in modern small industries.

Marketing

The last but not the least, the important factor causing sickness is the small industries' inability to market their products in a systematic way. It is well known that small-scale industries are mostly one man show or a family business and professional marketing is often not practised in such units. However, it may also be stated that during the last decade and a half, some of the progressive small-scale industries have also realised the need for scientific marketing methods and have therefore organised their own marketing networks on regional and national basis. This is true in some cases of manufacturers of domestic electrical appliances where these small-scale industries have a national network and a chain of distributors and retailers. Some of the large marketing organisations have also been helpful in undertaking the field of the products of small-scale industries mostly in the field of domestic electrical appliances. Such contacts have been educative for small industries in learning marketing techniques from their large-scale partners. In this context, it may be admitted that concept of forming consortia of small industries to share the marketing efforts has not been very successful and effective. A view is often expressed that marketing is purely an entrepreneurial function and the Government should only provide necessary training and other facilities with the financing institutions providing necessary financial help in initiating market surveys and other allied marketing activities.

In this context, it may also be stated that the Government has been quite responsive to the marketing needs of small-scale entrepreneurs producing a variety of items and has reserved over 800 items to be procured exclusively from small-scale sector under the Central Government Store Purchase Programme implemented by the DGS&D. In addition, instructions have been issued to the public sector enterprises and purchasing organisations of the Central Government to provide price preference to the products of the small-scale industries, wherever they compete with large scale manufacturers against tenders floated by the purchasing organisations. While the above measures are indeed helpful in providing some sort of marketing assurance to small-scale industries, this meets only a small part of small industries production. For a bulk of their production the small industries have necessarily to depend upon their own initiative, drive and innovations. It is here that training programme in modern methods of marketing will be helpful to small industries in upgrading their marketing technology on modern lines.

Constraints in Modernisation

While the need for upgradation of technology and modernisation of production processes and marketing methods is appreciated by small-scale industries, there are certain constraints experienced in bringing about the desired level of modernisation in a definite limited time. These constraints may briefly be stated as follows:

Investment Limits

A view is very often expressed by number of responsible people in various quarters that modernisation cannot be brought out by small-scale industries within the present investment limits of ₹ 3 crore in the case of small-scale industries and ₹ 3 crore in the case of small-scale ancillary units. The investment level of tiny sector has been raised to ₹ 25 lakh with effect from 07.02.97. An opposite view is also expressed that since more than 90 per cent of small units have an investment in the plant and equipment of less than ₹ 5 lakhs any increase in the investment limits would only benefit a very small percentage of small-scale units. Since both points of view have their own merits, the whole question would need to be studied in greater depth to weigh the pros and cons of bringing in an increase in the investment limits of the small-scale industries.

Pace of Change in Technology

Due to increase in R&D activities, undertaken by industries in the advanced countries, technological changes of far reaching importance are taking place rapidly and small-scale industries often find it extremely difficult to keep pace with these changes. Even in case of foreign technical collaboration from abroad into this country, only such technologies are given which have become partly out-moded in the collaborating countries. Many examples of this type are not difficult to seek in the field of electronics, electrical, automobiles, components, etc. This rapidly changing technology in certain industries in developed countries like USA, Japan, UK and West Germany have often forced them to vacate certain areas of production in favour of developing countries where the cost of labour element is still less. The investment dynamics in the field of electronics have resulted in a large number of US and European countries establishing a part of their manufacturing processing facilities in far eastern countries like Malaysia, Taiwan, Korea, Indonesia and Thailand. Even in these countries there has not been any marked transfer of technology or technology upgradation in the small-scale sector. It has also been experienced in these countries that in most cases, the foreign collaborators have not bothered to upgrade the technology of small or medium sector units. The situation in India is perhaps not totally different.

Technology Vs. Employment

One of the biggest constraints felt in upgrading the technology through automation is the fear that it might result in reduction of labour required. Since employment generation is one of the basic objectives for growth of small-scale industries in India, any proposal to induct modern technology, which would ultimately result in loss in employment, is not likely to be received with favour. Here also perhaps such industrial activities could be identified where modernisation would not necessarily mean automation resulting in reduction in overall employment in small-industries.

For example, in the field of electronic industry, the technological upgradation, which is continuously taking place, is also providing lot of scope for horizontal growth of ancillary, as well as assembly based industries in small-scale sector providing thereby increasing scope of employment. It is one of the major industries where small industries are thriving. New technologies are also coming in the field of automobiles an area where the scope of ancillarisation is considered to be of a very high order. Instead of replacing labour from the Small-scale sector, the input of technology will provide more employment in the ancillary and auxiliary sectors in these groups of industries.

Inadequate Availability of Inputs

Another factor which restricts the pace of modernisation is the non-availability of necessary financial, technical, raw material and other inputs needed by small-scale industries for modernisation. Also many small-scale industries would find it difficult to pay the cost of new technology individually and therefore, it would be necessary to identify and design an effective mechanism for import of modern technology in selected fields and delivering them to the needy small-scale industries. There could be several ways for transfer of technology imported from abroad and the large-scale industries in the private sector have to play a very important role in acting as carriers of technology from foreign countries to the small sector in India. An alternative may be to identify a Government Organisation to negotiate and buy appropriate modern technology in selected areas of development and industrial production.

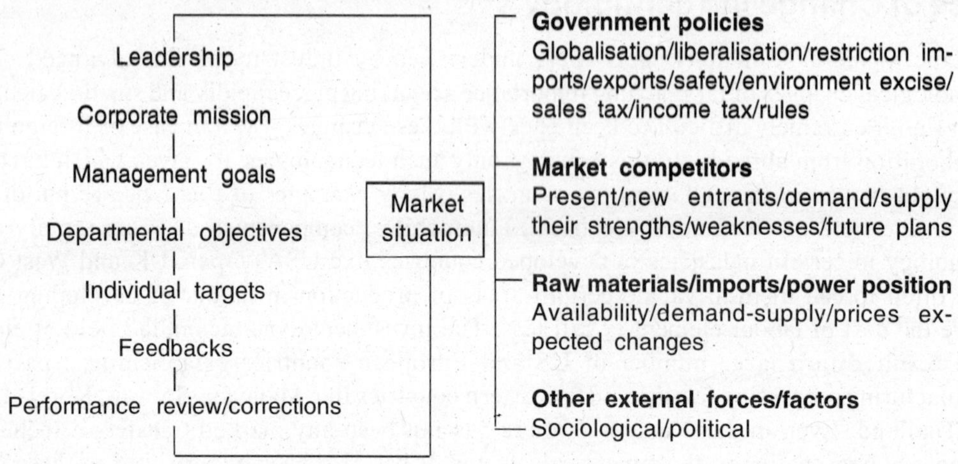

The tougher the market situation, the greater is the tension on the link chain and the organisational factors.

Fig. 14.1: Organisational Stress

Diagnosis

The normal diagnosis to find out the reasons for sickness starts from a series of interviews with people across the organisational structure. The major purpose of the interviews is to have a detailed insight into the working of the organisation, its strengths and weaknesses, the market situation and also the changes expected over a period of time. The following seven steps will enable a proper diagnosis of the organisational sickness:

(1) Interview people across the organisational structure (including workers) and the subsidiary structure of unions, suppliers, customers — to have a general feel of the problems that lead to the sickness.

(2) Hold fact finding sessions with individuals/groups in the middle/senior management level — to list the known/possible factors contributing to the sickness.

(3) Hold discussions with departmental/divisional heads to assess the nature and depth of the departmental problems (production, quality, conduct of business/routine activities in various departments.)

(4) Set up feedback/monitoring/audit control systems to periodically assess the performance, deviations and the needed corrections.

(5) Implement the use of modern management tools, techniques, information technology (cost control, TQM, JIT, inventory control, budgetary control...), to improve the bottom line.

(6) Plug the loopholes and make up the present deficiencies to achieve optimal production, high productivity, improved efficiencies, lower cost of resources, lower consumption factors and finally better realisations.

(7) Adopt business process reengineering in an effort to do the "Right Things" effectively and to achieve major breakthroughs in costs, quality and profits. This will help in planning expansions, closing unprofitable units and diversifications.

National Company Law Tribunal (NCLT)

It seems that steps to stem the rot in corporate assets in India are being held hostage to vested interest of a profession. The proposal to set up a National Company Law Tribunal (NCLT) which is supposed to take up the job of the BIFR and the company courts — financial restructuring and liquidation of corporate entities — has been caught in legal entanglements for long.

A recent World Bank study said liquidation of assets created in India could fetch the investor a return of just 16 cents against one dollar invested, whereas the average return is 65-70 cents in Japan and 35-40 cents in most European countries. It takes about 12 years to liquidate a company in India. In contrast, most developed countries are able to complete the process in 1-3 years.

The Irani Committee on new company law had recommended privatisation of the insolvency process which is now handled by a few overburdened "company courts" (designated high courts) and official liquidators, who often lack domain knowledge. It is crucial that during the liquidation process, the assets are protected from deterioration to enable their efficient redeployment and distribution. The proposed National Company Law Tribunal promises to address most of these issues, but the formation of the tribunal itself has created a row and is stuck in the Supreme Court. The NCLT would handle both restructuring and winding up of companies. It could pave way for a new insolvency system which is professional and responsive to the market realities.

The new Companies Act is expected to have a separate chapter to deal with insolvency. The idea is to engage professionals in the management and valuation of assets, special audits investigation etc., and also equip the adjudicator (the tribunal) with domain expertise.

At the other end of the scale, the SICA provisions are often abused by the promoter to seek protection and moratorium from recovery proceedings. Due to the delays in dissolution of the company which require the sanction of a few overburdened "company courts", an enormous chunk of the corporate assets in India lies dormant.

THE KEY FEATURES OF SICB *VIS-A-VIS* SICA

Features	*New SICB 1997*	*Old SICA 1985*
Definition of sickness	Debt default for four or more quarters in any two successive years to banks, FIs or any other secured creditors	Net worth erosion: i.e., accumulated losses having wiped away paid-up capital plus reserves
Reference to BIFR	Voluntary or optional in case of debt default, but mandatory if net worth has been eroded by 50 per cent from peak net worth (in last four years)	Mandatory
Role of BIFR	Of the nature of a mediator or facilitator	Like a court
Decision-Making	Three well-defined time-bound stages before BIFR, failing which liquidation	No time limits Average time for decision making almost two years
Appellate authority (AAIFR)	To be dissolved. No order or scheme of BIFR shall be appealed against and no Civil Court will have the jurisdiction to grant an injunction or stay	Appeal against BIFR orders could be made to AAIFR and also high courts
Rights of secured creditors	To vote on scheme, which would deemed to be passed if there is assent from secured creditors representing 75 per cent of the value of secured debt	*De jure,* to vote a scheme under Section 19(2). *De facto,* had to often acquiesce to BIFR and AAIFR decisions

Revival Plan

In short, the diagnosis will be a SWOT analysis of the organisation describing the Strengths, Weaknesses, Opportunities and Threats. This analysis will lead us to a meaningful revival plan and will also help in determining the right tools, techniques and remedies to be adopted. It may be emphasised that the revival plan has to be time-bound to achieve the expected changes and results.

The method of planning, defining the objectives and setting up of Targets, etc., is the subject of a separate chapter, not dealt herewith. However, the seven steps for the Revival Plan are given below:

(1) Finalise the goals/objectives/targets for performance at all levels to meet the organisation's mission.

(2) Issue policy guidelines on major aspects that affect the image of the company in public and the work culture inside the organisation.

(3) Initiate the preparation of detailed system manuals for the maintenance, budgets, costs, distribution, transportation, purchase, marketing inventory, personnel, etc.

(4) Analyse past reports on production, quality, costs, performance, accounts receivables, etc., and the connected financial and audit reports — to get an overall idea of the present working systems and results.

(5) Meet senior executives from marketing/finance/personnel/materials/secretarial/legal departments and (if possible) with competitors — to assess the external situations (Government policies, competitor's activities, raw materials position, union-political-social factors.)

(6) Brainstorm with a select group — to get creative ideas for improvement.

(7) Appraise the Board about the diagnosis and request them to spell out a clear "Mission" of the Company.

These measures would bring about cost-effective functioning of production units.

Institutional Mechanisms

Pursuant to the enactment of the Sick Industrial Companies (Special Provisions) Act, 1985, a Board for Industrial and Financial Reconstruction (BIFR) was set up in May 1987 under the administrative control of Ministry of Finance.

The BIFR has power to prepare rehabilitation schemes for revival of sick industrial companies in consultation with the agencies concerned. Till March 31, 1998, BIFR has received 3,148 references. The Board has sanctioned rehabilitation schemes for 625 units, recommended winding up for 579 units and declared 200 units no longer sick.

A sick industrial company has to report its sickness to the BIFR, once its accumulated losses at the end of financial year exceed 50 per cent of the peak net worth attained during the period of four years immediately preceding the financial year. BIFR provides a forum where the agencies concerned are brought together for analysing, diagnosing and evolving a reasoned decision for revival, or otherwise of the sick industrial unit. The agencies concerned are:

(i) Sick industrial unit

(ii) State Government

(iii) Banks and financial institutions

(iv) The concerned Departments of the Central Government.

SICA has invested BIFR with the following powers:

(i) Potential sickness has to be reported to BIFR;

(ii) Mismanagement of industrial units by any person can be looked into by BIFR and, the BIFR may direct that person to restore the losses; and

(iii) BIFR can initiate changes in management, amalgamation of the sick industrial company with any other healthy company, sale or lease of a part, or whole of the industrial unit, or any other preventive/remedial measures.

Remedial Measures

(1) Early detection of sickness, it was generally felt, could go a long way in initiating remedial measures for restoring potential sick units to health. Need was stressed for the establishment of a proper management information system for providing early warning signals from within.

(2) Financial institutions and banks should initiate necessary corrective action for sick or prone-to-sickness units based on diagnostic studies. In case of growing sickness, they should also consider assumption of management responsibility where they are confident of restoring a unit to health.

(3) Wherever possible, attempts should be made to restore sick units to financial health. However, where the judgement is that a sick unit cannot be retrieved, it should be allowed to be wound up. The divestment of a sick unit, if desired by an industrial group, for handing it over to someone else with the requisite experience of running such a unit should be allowed expeditiously so that it can be restored to health before the situation gets out of control.

(4) Excessive concern overunemployment resulting from the closure of a sick unit is unwarranted. This can be taken care of through other measures, such as the setting up of a national fund for the purpose and strengthening of the facilities for retraining of workers.

(5) The proposal to set up a special institution — the Board for Financial and Industrial Reconstruction — appears to be a sound one. It should play the role of a single window clearing agency. However, the Board should not be asked to go merely by mechanical indicators to determine sickness in industry. For instance, the criterion of erosion in net worth for determining the seriousness of sickness, although it does indicate that everything is not well with a unit, is not meaningful. Erosion could take place by internal as well as external factors. There is, therefore, no justification for punishing management for erosion in net worth if it is caused by factors beyond its control.

(6) Similarly, the proposal visualising that the management of a unit that has lost net worth in entirety will not be allowed to manage that unit any more, needs to be reconsidered. Before branding the management as a bad one, all the aspects of the case ought to be examined.

(7) The proposal that managements responsible for mismanagement should not be allowed assistance from financial institutions even for new ventures, too, needs rethinking.

(8) Nothing will do greater damage to the development of the spirit of entrepreneurship in the community than the fear that one is likely to be punished for sickness which is not of one's own market but is the result of lapses committed elsewhere.

(9) It is important that in any scheme of reconstruction of a sick unit, all the stakeholders bear sacrifices on equitable and just basis.

(10) The important criterion for takeover of a sick unit by another company should be whether the company taking over the sick unit has skill, technology and finance to save it. Considerations on MRTP/FERA accounts should not come in the way.

(11) There is need for a fresh look at Section 72-A of Income Tax Act to remove the inhibition caused to companies taking over sick units by insistence on the part of income Tax authorities for prior full implementation of the revival schemes before tax benefits can accrue.

(12) Debt-equity ratio ought to be realistic. Fiscal policy, too, requires rationalisation.

(13) Incentives should be provided to professional managers helping in reviving sick units.

(14) Treatment of capital-intensive units prone to sickness has to be on a different footing than tackling of sickness in industry in general.

CONCLUSION

Sickness in industry, especially in the small-scale sector in particular is a cause for concern. The banks, financial institution and the Government should address to redressal strategies for these sick units. Revival of sick units should be taken on a priority basis.

Even when detailed project reports are prepared, inexperienced entrepreneurs may 'build' sickness into their units from the conception stage itself. For example, they may opt for an improper location, employ inadequately experienced consultants, choose inappropriate technology, underestimate the fixed and operational costs involved in the manufacture of their products, and embark on a project without a proper market survey.

Given the general spread of sickness in the small-scale sector, it seems that government agencies have not properly scrutinized project proposals. In fact, T. Ragupati, a faculty member of the Industrial Development Department, Small Industries Extension Training Institute, Hyderabad, places the blame squarely on government agencies.

"The sickness among new small-scale units is attributable to their indiscriminate promotion by government agencies in order to achieve employment targets fixed under Plan programmes. During the Fifth Plan, and in later years, there was an increased emphasis on providing job opportunities by developing small-scale and tiny units. It resulted in hastliy prepared and implemented programmes for the promotion of these units.

"Campaigns were undertaken by the promotional agencies to select unemployed educated and technically qualified persons as entrepreneurs in promoting small industries. Financial agencies like banks were subjected to pressures to finance without adequate evaluation of the projects. This appears to be the principal factor for the ever-rising incidence of sickness among newly promoted industries, particularly in backward areas."

In the present context, the only healthy way is to nurse these millions of small units for overall progress. This is nosier said than done, due to wide gap in enlightened managers. Our employment scenario does not compel the management graduates to serve these units, at least for some initial period, neither do the owners show an openness for such managerial interaction.

A possible alternative is to counsel these units, without hurting the sentiments of the owner at the very first stage. After some success is achieved, trust is built and confidence is created, one can slowly advance and undertake further reform process, always holding the flag as an external catalyst. This will evidently be time-consuming, but expected to be result yielding at slow pace.

While conceptualising and designing the coverage of business consultancy for small and medium scale industries, one essentially needs to consider the totality of its dimension, for understanding, acceptance and application by such clientele. Piecemeal advice may not serve their purpose. The idea is to offer turnkey solutions and induce things to happen. Psychological barrier may hinder the process initially, but once the link is established, demand will cross every hurdle.

Analysing the scope of such total counselling, welcome across three principal areas, for need based steering:

- Technical aspects related to present or proposed activity.
- Managerial functions in isolation and integration.
- Commercial proceedings, with applicable rules and regulations.

Once again, it will require lot of expertise and exposures to plan and extend counselling on all these areas, preferably from a single window. For this, pooling of resources will be necessary. A tall order indeed, but there seems to be no short cut.

The empirical studies show that by adopting better practices, right technology, new work culture and professional management, small-scale industries can improve their health and elevate from smaller status. In the process improve the health of the industry as well as of the economy.

In the current rising wave of economic growth and liberalisation and in the absence of systematic market research, capacities far in excess of demand have been set up in many industries. Thus, in addition to some of the old and obsolete industries, many relatively new investments have either turned sick or have shutdown. The Government has taken several imaginative measures to revive many of these. The Board for Industrial Finance and Reconstruction (BIFR) was created to expedite revival schemes.

The Indian economy and the business environment, currently undergoing important structural changes, will grow faster than ever and will encounter myriad complexities of a free enterprise system. The private sector, which had always clamoured for freedom to conduct its affairs, is now face-to-face with the realities of standing more or less on its own. We had not realised that change would be upon us as fast as it has.

Business now has an opportunity to transform individuals and organisations into vibrant and competitive entities. Industries which cannot generate surplus can neither have any place in our country nor can they achieve the goal of a more egalitarian society. It is through productive endeavours and mutual co-operation of those engaged in industry and agriculture, that the larger issues of population control, unemployment and poverty alleviation can be effectively tackled.

The era of mutual distrust, Government controls and disruptive trade union movements must, under these changing circumstances, recede into the background. Our economy to get progressively drawn into the sphere of a new international trade and export will have to grow faster.

•

15 INCENTIVES AND SUBSIDIES

CHAPTER

INTRODUCTION

Entrepreneurs in India are offered a number of incentives with their strategic contributions to economic development. Firstly, they facilitate the decentralisation of economic power by encouraging prospective entrepreneurs to take up industrial ventures and assist in the dispersal of industries over India's geographical area. Secondly, they facilitate the transformation of a traditional technology, which is characterised by low skill, low productivity and low wages, into a modern technology, subsequently characterised by improved skills, high productivity, rising wages and a higher standard of living. They serve as a catalyst to start a dynamic process of development. They also influence the location of enterprises and contribute to regional distribution and development.

The Ford Foundation Team, which visited India in 1953-54, suggested a positive programme for the development of modern SSIs. Based on the recommendations of this team, the Government provided a broad infrastructural and institutional set-up for the accelerated growth of these industries.

In the present chapter, an attempt has been made to indicate the assistance and the incentives which are available from the Government.

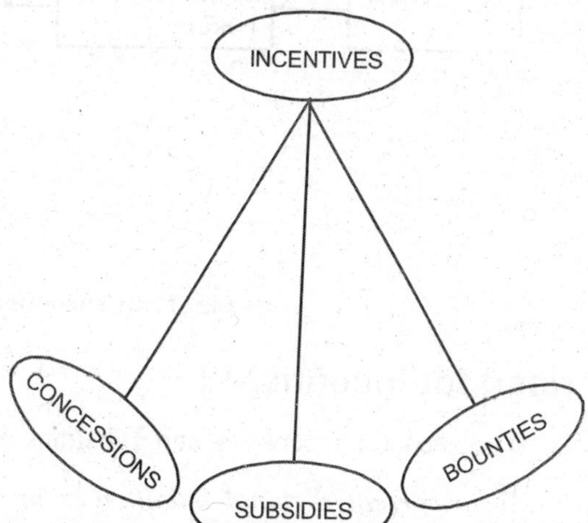

Fig. 15.1: Pattern of Incentives

Incentives

The term 'incentive' means encouraging productivity. It is motivational force which makes an entrepreneur take a right decision and act upon it. Broadly, incentives include concessions, subsidies and bounties. Economic incentives — both financial and non-financial — push an entrepreneur towards decisive decision and action.

Subsidy

'Subsidy' denotes a single lump sum which is given by a Government to an entrepreneur to cover the cost. The term *'bounty' denotes* a bonus or financial aid given to an industry to help it to compete with other units in the country or in a foreign-market. The objective of incentives is to motivate an entrepreneur to set up a new venture in the larger interest of the nation and the society.

Controversies on the Efficacy of Incentives and Subsidies

Often one comes across an intellectual controversy over the good or evil or nil effect of incentive programmes. According to one criticism, the argument proceeds, of course, with empirical evidence and other pure measurement approaches, that incentive schemes would ultimately deteriorate into useless tax give-aways, would only cause other States to reciprocate with the result that industry locations would be affected by those lures and would cause the financial position of the exchequer seriously impaired. While this argument may be true, the industrial development schemes have been with use for more than three decades. As against this view, there are study results establishing the economic significance of the impact of incentive programmes. We also find, to our surprise, the fast-growing, information on the reappraisal of the *'legitimacy'* of the regional economic industrial policy with incentive schemes.

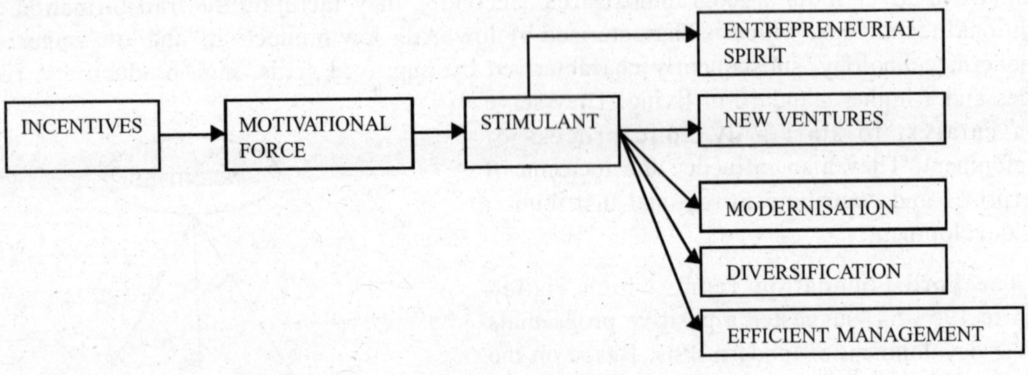

Fig. 15.2: Incentives as a Motivational Force

Need for Incentives

The need for incentives and subsidies arise for the following reasons:

1. *To correct regional imbalances in development:* The usual package of incentives and concessions has been available in backward as well as developed districts. It has been, however, the experience, of industrial administration, department of industries, district level officers, development corporations, etc., that what is lacking in the backward districts is the overall existing environmental growth. One of the ways is to identify pockets of savings of different activity groups like traders, businessmen, agriculturists, professionals, etc., and provide them with relevant information as well as suitable incentives to offset the disadvantages prevailing

in such places. Industrial policy uses incentives both to correct the market imperfections and to accelerate the process of industrialisation so as to drive the forces of supply and demand reach the equilibrium level. Such a policy then aims at inducing some entrepreneurs or sections of the community (e.g., technicians) to locate their industrial units in areas selected by Government rather than that of their own choice. Regional balances can also lead to effective utilisation of regional resources, removal of disparities in income and levels of living and contribute to a more integrated society.

2. *To promote entrepreneurship by removing economic constraints:* As for the economic constraints, the new entrants in the field face many impediments on account of inadequate infrastructures. The new entrepreneur suffers because of distances separating central administrative organs from entrepreneurs and their projects, deficiency of various supporting services such as market intelligence, entrepreneurial guidance and training, technical consultancy and merchant banking facilities, lack of an institutional mechanism to provide full-time management personnel complementary to that of the new entrepreneurs, and finally, from insufficient orientation of the promotional institutions, barring a few exceptions, at the State level to the needs of new entrepreneurs.

The various incentives normally aim at mitigating some or all of the problems by several means. Industrial estates, industrial complexes, industrial nucleus, etc., availability of power, concessional finance, capital investment subsidy, transport subsidy, etc., are all but a few examples of incentives to solve constraints impeding the emergence of entrepreneurs in industry.

3. *To provide competitive strength, survival and growth:* Some of the incentives are concerned with the establishment of industries while others are concerned with the survival and growth of industries. Several incentives are confined to the first few years of the establishment of the unit while a few of them are made available over a long period. Instance may be cited of the reservation policy for SSIs due to which a small firm can hope to compete in the market to which entry by larger units is barred. If these units are already established and are brought under the reservation policy later, it will be a case of incentive to support its competitive strength. For a new comer, the reservation is an incentive to enter the industry itself. A price preference improves its competitive strength.

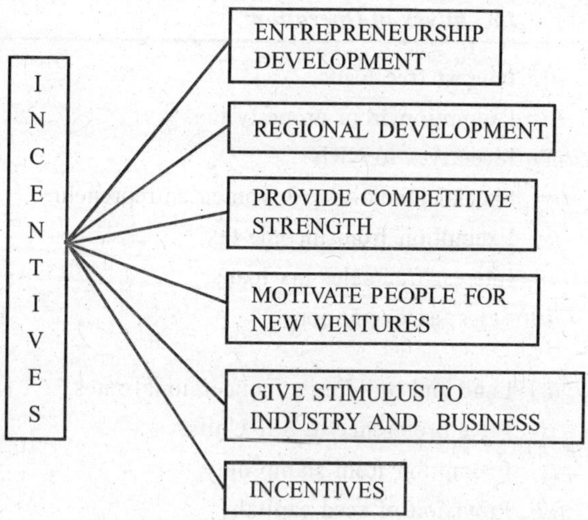

Fig. 15.3: Objectives of Incentives

Incentives Strategy

1. Subsidy for purchase of know-khow	—	Varies from 50 per cent to 100 per cent of cost
2. Entrepreneur Training	—	Free with stipend for SC/ST and women entrepreneurs
3. Developed land	—	At subsidised cost, on hire-purchase/outright purchase basis
4. Factory shed	—	In industrial estates subject to availability
5. Machinery	—	On hire-purchase/lease
6. Seed capital loan (Margin Money Loan)	—	To start industries
7. Central Investment Subsidy	—	At the rate of 25 per cent varies from ₹ 10 lakh to ₹ 50 lakh
8. State Investment Subsidy	—	10 per cent to 15 per cent
9. Tax Exemption	—	Excise and sales-tax exemption from stamp duty and concessional registration changes
10. Establishment Grant	—	In some cases
11. Stamp Duty	—	Exempted

Thus, a creative and shrewd entrepreneur can set-up a small-scale industry and/ or industries without putting a single pie of his own and even capital out of it. Some successful entrepreneurs have built their own industrial empire, acquired status and power.

Schemes of Incentives and Subsidies in Operation

Incentives in Operation	*Subsidies in Operation*
(i) Interest free loans,	*(i)* Export/Import subsidies and bounties,
(ii) Exemption from property tax,	*(ii)* Subsidy for R&D works,
(iii) Incentives to NRIs,	*(iii)* Capital investment subsidy,
(iv) Special incentives to women entrepreneurs,	*(iv)* Transport subsidy,
(v) Exemption from income-tax,	*(v)* Interest subsidy,
(vi) Interest-free sales tax loans,	*(vi)* Subsidy for power generations,
(vii) Sales tax exemptions,	*(vii)* Subsidies to artisans and traditional industries including handlooms,
(viii) Land and building at concessional rates,	*(viii)* Subsidy for buying test equipment,
(ix) Price preference to SSI Units,	*(ix)* Subsidy for industrial housing,
(x) Exemption from stamp duty,	*(x)* Subsidy/assistance for technical consultancy
(xi) Provision of seed capital,	*(xi)* Subsidising the cost of market studies/ feasibility studies or reports.
(xii) Allotment of developed/constructed sheds,	*(xii)* Subsidised consultancy services
(xiii) Allotment of controlled or subsidised raw materials	*(xiii)* Subsidy for market studies
(xiv) Concessional water	*(xiv)* Subsidy for quality standards
(xv) Special facilities for import of raw materials	
(xvi) Taxation benefits	
(xvii) Excise concessions	

The Assistance Programme

Some of the important measures of assistance now available for the entrepreneurs in the industrial sector are:

(i) Technical assistance through industrial extension service;
(ii) Assistance for obtaining raw materials;
(iii) Cash assistance;
(iv) Supply of machinery on hire-purchase basis;
(v) Marketing assistance;
(vi) Assistance to small entrepreneurs;
(vii) Rural industries projects;
(viii) Seed capital assistance;
(ix) Concessional finance assistance;
(x) Technology assistance;
(xi) Pollution control.

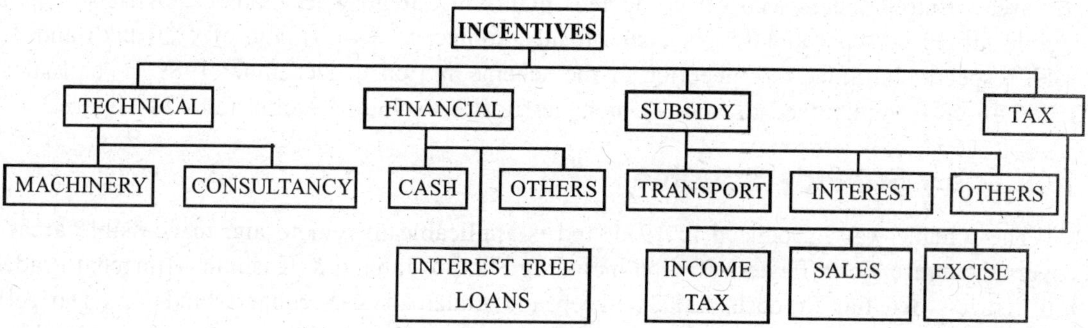

Fig. 15.4: Types of Incentives

In order to promote industrialisation of the country as a whole and to remove disparities in levels of development between different regions, the Central Government is operating three major schemes, *viz.*, central investment subsidy scheme, transport-subsidy scheme and central assistance scheme for infrastructural development in no-industry districts.

Advantages of Incentives and Subsidies

(a) They act as a motivational force which makes the prospective entrepreneurs to enter into manufacturing line.

(b) They encourage the entrepreneurs to start industries in backward areas;

(c) By providing subsidies and incentives the Government can:

(i) Bring industrial development uniformly in all regions.
(ii) Develop more new entrepreneurs which leads to entrepreneurial development.
(iii) Increase the ability of entrepreneurs to face competition successfully.
(iv) Reduce the overall problems of small-scale entrepreneurs.

Problems of Incentives and Subsidies

- Empirical studies reveal that the incentives and subsidies are being highly misused.
- Incentives and subsidies turned out to be grounds for dishonesty.
- They have given scope for favouritism and rampant corruption.
- They have become the seeds of unethical business practices.
- Resulted in financial drain on the exchequer.
- The real objective of providing incentives, subsidies and assistance is hardly achieved.

Central Investment Subsidy Scheme

This was introduced in 1971, and has been modified from time-to-time. The scheme is for encouraging setting up of industries in centrally notified backward areas. For setting up industries in Category "A" backward areas, subsidy is allowed at the rate of 25 per cent subject to a maximum of ₹ 25lakh (enhanced to ₹ 50 lakh for setting up electronics industry in hilly districts). It is 15 per cent and 10 per cent subject to a maximum of ₹ 1.5 lakh and ₹ 10 lakh for category 'B' and 'C' districts respectively. MRTP/FERA companies are not eligible for subsidy in Category 'C' areas. Entrepreneurs who set up nucleus plants in Category 'B' and 'C' districts/areas are legible for 20 per cent and 15 per cent subsidy, subject to a maximum of ₹ 20 lakh and ₹ 15 lakh respectively. Since the inception of the scheme and up to December 1989, a total sum of ₹ 855.46 crore reimbursed to States/Union Territories excluding Delhi and Chandigarh.

Transport Subsidy Scheme

The scheme was introduced in 1971 and is applicable to remote and inaccessible areas. It covers the entire North Eastern Region including Sikkim, Jammu & Kashmir, Himachal Pradesh, hill districts of Uttar Pradesh, Lakshadweep and Andaman & Nicobar Islands and Darjeeling District of West Bengal. Identified promotional institutions which transact business on behalf of small, village and cottage industries are also eligible for transport subsidy. Transport subsidy is paid on the transport costs of industrial raw materials which are brought into and finished goods which are taken out of these areas to identified rail heads/ports. In the North Eastern region, subsidy is available at the rate of 90% and for Himachal Pradesh, hill districts of Uttar Pradesh and Darjeeling District of West Bengal, it is 75 per cent. It is also available at the rate of 90 per cent for movement of raw materials within the N.E. region and at the rate of 50 per cent for movement of finished goods in this region from one state to another state. For airlifting of electronic components/products from Kolkata airport to the airport nearest to the locations of the industrial units in this region subsidy is allowed at the rate of 75 per cent and *vice versa*.

Central Assistance for Infrastructural Development in No-industry Districts under the Old Scheme

To assist State Governments in taking up infrastructural development in one or two identified growth centers in each no-industry district, the Centre gives financial assistance which is limited to one-third of the total cost of infrastructural development, .subject to a maximum of ₹ 2 crore per district. Two types of patterns have been laid down for the purpose:

Pattern I

₹ 2 crore as subsidy from the Central Government.

₹ 2 crore as share of the State Government.

₹ 2 crore as loan from IDBI on concessional terms.

Pattern II

₹ 2 crore as subsidy from the Central Government.

₹ 4 crore as share of the State Government.

₹ 5 crore as loan from IDBI on concessional terms after the shares of State and Centre are spent.

For States in the N.E. region, the scheme has been further liberalised. In a total project of ₹ 4 crore, the Centre's shares would be 50%, i.e., ₹ 2 crore per district and the State Governments have the option to fund the balance of ₹ 2 crore either from their own funds or by raising a loan from IDBI. Construction of sheds, subject to a ceiling of 25% of the total cost, has been allowed in the case of this region only.

So far, 51 growth centres in 44 districts of the States of Rajasthan, Orissa, Karnataka, U.P., Bihar, Maharashtra, West Bengal, Tripura, Nagaland, A.P., and Mizoram have been approved by the Government for development of infrastructural facilities. A sum of ₹ 15.42 crore has been released for creating infrastructural facilities in the States of Rajasthan, Orissa, U.P., Karnataka, M.P., Maharashtra, Mizoram, Bihar and West Bengal till December 1988.

Reservation/ De-reservation of Products for Manufacture in the Small-scale Sector

With a view to providing to the SSI opportunities for technological upgradation, promotion of exports and economies of scale, items reserved for exclusive manufacture by the SSI have been dereserved from time-to-time. The dereservation process involves extensive consultation with all the stakeholders, including the SSI associations and various Ministries/Departments concerned and the Planning Commission. As per the provisions of the I (D&R) Act, an Advisory Committee has been constituted which recommends reservation/dereservation of items from time-to-time. The Advisory Committee makes its recommendations on the basis of the laid down procedure in the I (D&R) Act, 1951 which relates to the economy of scale, the level of employment, the possibility of encouraging and diffusing entrepreneurship in industry, the prevention of concentration of economic power to the detriment of the common interest and any other issue which the Committee may think fit. The Advisory Committee has met 26 times so far. The last meeting of the Committee was held on 24th October, 2006. During the year 2006-07, 180 items reserved for manufacture in small-scale industries have been deserved. As on date, there are 326 items reserved for exclusive manufacture in small-scale sector.

CONCLUSION

Besides incentives and subsidies given by the Centre, the State Governments too offer fiscal and monetary incentives and subsidies help entrepreneurs setting up their industries in the States to overcome certain disadvantages. The entrepreneurs are attracted to some State for their package of incentives and subsidies. The foremost incentive is a stable government with excellent law and order situation followed by availability of disciplined, dedicated and skilled labour force. However, states do attract industries by giving incentives in regard to sales tax, octroi, and subsidised loan. These incentives have helped in large measure in attracting entrepreneurs to set up industries — and accelerate the process of industrialisation. State incentives and subsidies have helped entrepreneurs to locate their projects and industrialise the State on a firm foundation. The innovations of these incentives and subsidies indicate their adaptability and the vital role they have been playing in the process of industrial development, spanning rural and urban, backward and non-backward and organised and unorganised, large, medium and small sectors of the economy — each sector needing different approaches, strategies, skills and techniques.

16

CHAPTER

Institutional Support to Small-scale Industries

INTRODUCTION

Industrialisation is widely recognised as one of the important means to usher in economic and social transformation in the developing countries, albeit there are controversies about the weightage to be given to industrialisation as an element of the development mix. The industrial revolution which enabled the advanced countries of today to take-off to economic prosperity has given us quite a few lessons in development. However, the nature and problems of industrialisation of the developing countries are not the same as the historial experience of the developed economies. The developing nations, in general, are confronted with strungling competition from industrialised countries, fast depleting resource base, falling productivity and rising costs in certain sectors, inter-sectoral conflicts within the economy and so on. Yet, industrialisation, hard the task as it is, indispensable for survival and growth.

Industrialisation is essential not only for generation of employment and achieving industrial self-sufficiency but also for the accelerated development of agriculture and other sectors through the backward and forward linkages. Industrialisation can also play a role in improving the balance of trade of a nation. The social impact of industralisation are of no less significance. Industrialisation, of course, brings with it a number of economic, social, ecological and even political problems.

Industrial development depends on the entrepreneurs, capital, human resources, infrastructure, geographic and climatic factors, agricultural development, market, technology, innovation, natural resources, and Government policies and programmes. In the developing countries, the Government plays the entrepreneurial role.

In the developing countries, where the infrastructural facilities for development are inadequate and entrepreneurial activities are scarce, the promotional role of the government assumes special significance. The State will have to assume direct responsibility to build up and strengthen the necessary development infrastructures such as power, transport, finance, marketing, institutions for training and guidance and other promotional activities, etc.

The promotional role of the State also encompasses the provision of various fiscal, monetary and other incentives, including measures to cover certain risks, for the development of certain industries in the core sector of the economy. More importantly, the Government builds up a sound institutional infrastructure and fosters entrepreneurship and thus accelerates the process of industrialisation on an ongoing basis.

A Catalytic Agent

An entrepreneur is one of the important segments of economic growth. Basically, an entrepreneur is a person who is responsible for setting up a business or an enterprise. In fact, he is one who has the initiative, skill for innovation and who looks for high achievements. He is a catalytic agent of change and works who looks for high achievements. He is a catalytic agent of change and works for the good of people. He puts up new grainfield projects that actually creates wealth, opens up employment opportunities and fosters other sectors.

The entrepreneur brings in overall change through innovation for the maximum social good. Human values remain sacred and inspires him to serve the society. He has firm belief in social betterment and he carries out this responsibility with conviction. In the process, he accelerates personal, economic as well as human development. The entrepreneur is a visionary and an integrated man with outstanding leadership qualities. With a desire to excel, the entrepreneur gives top priority to Research and Development. He always works for the well-being of the society. More importantly, entrepreneurial activities encompass all fields/sectors and foster a spirit of enterprise for the welfare of mankind.

Thus, emerges the notion of the "genius entrepreneur" whose success is in a large measure caused by his unswerving dedication to setting high goals and to reaching for them. He has vision on which he bases his own objectives and sets his own goals. And he does this not simply on the basis of last year's results plus some growth factor, but on the basis of his own perception, of his own capabilities and to satisfy his own needs.

Among other distingushing attributes of entrepreneurship are a willingness to assume risk; a sense of acquisitiveness or uncreasing curiosity; insight into the relationship between concepts, objectives, needs; and needs satisfaction; sound judgement as to what is central and peripheral to attaining his objectives, initative and creativity; problem-solving ability; ability to marshall resources needed to achieve his objectives and goals; and the administrative ability to organize those resources to accomplish his goals and satisfy his minor needs.

Importance in Development

Entrepreneurial development is a subject that has assumed great importance and is bound to be one of the dominant topics of discussion during the decades to come. This is as it should be in the context of rapid industrialisation in India. But to create an atmosphere of spontaneous will to co-operate is not all that easy. Resistance to change can be resolved by involving people in the process. The remedy lies in fostering an entrepreneurial spirit among the prople.

An entrepreneur is one of the most important as well as significant inputs in the economic development of a country or of a region within a country. Entrepreneurial competence makes all the difference to the rate of economic growth. The need for a broad-based entrepreneurial class in India arises from the need to speed up the process activating the factors of production, dispersal of economic activities, creating employment opportunities — all of which are capable of leading to higher rate of economic growth. It is now well recognised that entrepreneurs can be developed through appropriately designed entrepreneurship development programmes.

Institutional Support

The scale and scope of operations of entrepreneurs and the far-reaching developments in the economic climate have brought to the fore, importance of institutional assistance at various levels. In fact, the success of entrepreneurship depends solely on the well-established institutional set-up.

The instititions fostering entrepreneurial development can be classified into: *(i)* Promotional, *(ii)* Financial, *(iii)* Technical, *(iv)* Marketing, *(v)* Training, *(vi)* Others, and *(vii)* Associations.

They are as follows:

A. Promotional

1. Directorate of Industries of State Governments.
2. The Small Industries Development Organisation.
3. The State Small Industries Corporation.
4. The State Industrial and Investment Corporations.
5. The Industrial Development Corporations.
6. The Electronic Corporations.
7. Udyog Mitra.
8. The State Development Corporations.
9. The National Small Industries Corporation.
10. The Small-scale Industries Board.
11. The National Industrial Development Corporation.
12. The National Productivity Council.
13. The State Electricity Boards.
14. The Indian Bureau of Standards.
15. The District Industries Centres.
16. The State Industrial Development Corporations.
17. The WTO cell.
18. Coir Board.
19. District Industries Centres.

B. Financial

1. The State Financial Corporations.
2. The Industrial Finance Corporation of India.

3. Commercial Banks.
4. The Life Insurance Corporation of India.
5. The General Insurance Coporation of India/Insurance Companies
6. The Unit Trust of India.
7. The Small Industries Development Bank of India.
8. Mutual Funds.
9. Leasing Companies.
10. The Risk Capital Foundation.
11. The National Bank for Agriculture and Rural Development.
12. The Khadi and Village Industries Commission.
13. Stock Exchanges.
14. Venture Capital Finance.
15. The Housing Development Finance Corporation Ltd.
16. The Shipping Credit and Investment Company of India.
17. The World Bank.
18. The Housing and Urban Development Corporation Ltd.

C. Technical

1. The Industrial and Technical Consultancy Organisation.
2. The Controller or General Patents, Designs and Trademarks.
3. Pollution Control Boards.
4. The Central Institute of Tool Design.
5. The Institute for Design for Electrical Measuring Instruments.
6. The National Institute of Design.
7. The Technology Development and Information Company of India Ltd.
8. The Products and Process Development Centres.

D. Marketing

1. The Indian Investment Centres.
2. The Export Promotion Councils.
3. Commodity Boards.
4. Bhandars — Retail Shops.
5. Export Houses.
6. The Indian Institute of Packaging.
7. The Export Inspection Council.
8. The Jute Corporation of India.
9. The State Trading Corporation of India.
10. The Minerals and Metals Trading Corporations of India.

11. The Export-Import Bank of India.
12. The Indian Institute of Foreign Trade.
13. Export Credit Guarantee Corporation of India Ltd.

E. Training

1. The Centre for Entrepreneurship Development.
2. The Entrepreneurship Development Institute of India.
3. The Management Development Institute.
4. The Institute of Management.
5. Institute of Entrepreneurship Development.
6. The National Institute for Entrepreneurship and Small Business Development.
7. The Science and Technology Entrepreneurship Parks.
8. The National Institute of Small Industry Extension Training.
9. Universities — Commerce Faculty.
10. The Integrated Training Centre (Industrial).
11. Industrial Training Institutes.
12. Polytechniques.
13. Training of Rural Youth for Self-employment.
14. The Indian Institute of Entrepreneurship.
15. EDPs of SIDBI.
16. The National Institute of Fashion Technology.
17. The Central Footwear Training Institute, Agra.

F. Others

1. The Bureau of Industrial Costs and Prices.
2. The Indian Council of Arbitration.
3. The Credit Rating Information Services of India Ltd.
4. The OTC Exchange of India.

G. Associations

1. The National Alliance of Young Entrepreneur.
2. The Association of Women Entrepreneurs of Karnataka.
3. The Coimbatore District Small-scale Industries Association.
4. Industrial Associations.
5. Merchant Chambers.
6. Industry and Trade Associations.
7. Consideration of Indian Industries.
8. Federation of Indian Chamber of Commerce and Industry.

9. PHD Chamber of Commerce and Industry.
10. Associated Chambers of Commerce and Industry of India.
11. Federation of Indian Export Organisation.
12. The World Association for Small and Medium Enterprises.
13. Federation of Associations of Small Industries of India.
14. Consortium of Women Entrepreneurs of India.
15. Laghu Udyog Bharati.
16. Indian Council of Small Industries.
17. Federation of Tiny and Small Industries of India.
18. Federation of Indian Micro and Small and Medium Enterprises.
19. National Association of Software and Service Companies.
20. Association of Lady Entrepreneurs of Andhra Pradesh.

H. Research Institutes

1. The Central Manufacturing Technology Institute.
2. The Central Pulp and Paper Research Institute.
3. The National Council for Cement and Building Materials.
4. Automotive Research Association of India.
5. Indian Rubber Manufacturers Research Association.
6. The National Institute of Design.
7. The Quality Council of India.
8. The Central Leather Research Institute.
9. The Council of Scientific and Industrial Research (CSIR).
10. Centre for Development of Stones.
11. Electronics Service & Training Centre (ESTC), Ramnagar, Uttarkhand.
12. The Institute for Design of Electrical Measuring Instruments (IDEM), Mumbai.
13. Process-cum-product Development Centre, Meerut.
14. Centre for the Development of Glass Industry, Firozabad.
15. Process and Product Development Centre, Agra.
16. Central Institute of Tool Design, Hyderabad.

The success of industrialization to a great extent, goes to these institutions. The role of the various institutions set up, especially to foster the growth of industries in general and small enterprises in particular is quite unique. In this chapter, an attempt has been made to have an overview of the institutions fostering the development of small enterprises and rapid growth of entrepreneurship in India.

The development of small-scale industries is primarily the responsibility of the State Government; but in consideration of the fact that various questions and issues involved in the programme of development of the small industries have an all-India character and can be efficiently considered and tackled at the national level, and also because of the scale on which

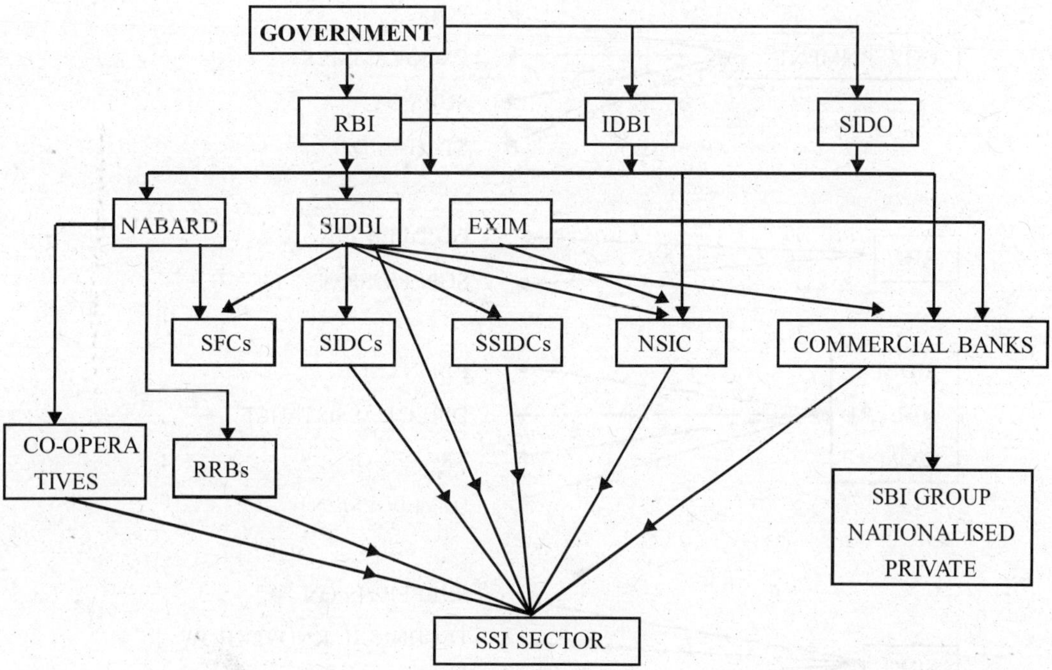

Fig. 16.1: Institutional Framework for the Flow of Financial Assistance to the SSI Sector

efforts were required to be made to tackle the problems, it was considered desirable by the Central Government to assume responsibility for planning and co-ordinating the basic programme of development. With this end in view, an All-India Board, known as the Small-scale Industries Board, was set-up in November 1954, charged with the responsibility of overall planning, co-ordination and development of small-scale industries in the country. The Board is composed of Central and State Government officials, representatives of various institutions, financing bodies, the Federation of Small-scale Industries Associations and a number of non-officials representing trade, industry and other interests. The meetings of the Board are held by rotation in each State, usually once every six months. This, no doubt, helps the members to acquire first-hand knowledge of developments in every state, besides drawing their attention to the particular problems of local industries. The Board discusses questions connected with credit facilities, supply of raw materials, revision of the definition of small-scale industries for the purposes of assistance programmes, dispersal of industries; it reviews the programme of implementation and formulates new directives for a further growth of the small industry sector. Although the Board functions in an advisory capacity, its decisions are given very great importance by the Government.

SMALL INDUSTRIES DEVELOPMENT ORGANISATION (SIDO)

SIDO is created for development of various small-scale units in different areas. SIDO is a subordinate office of department of SSI and ARI. It is a nodal agency for identifying the needs of SSI units coordinating and monitoring the policies and programmes for promotion of the small industries. It undertakes various programmes of training, consultancy, evaluation for needs of SSI and development of industrial estates. All these functions are taken care with 27 offices, 31 SISI (Small Industries Service Institute) 31 extension centers of SISI and 7 centers related to production and process development.

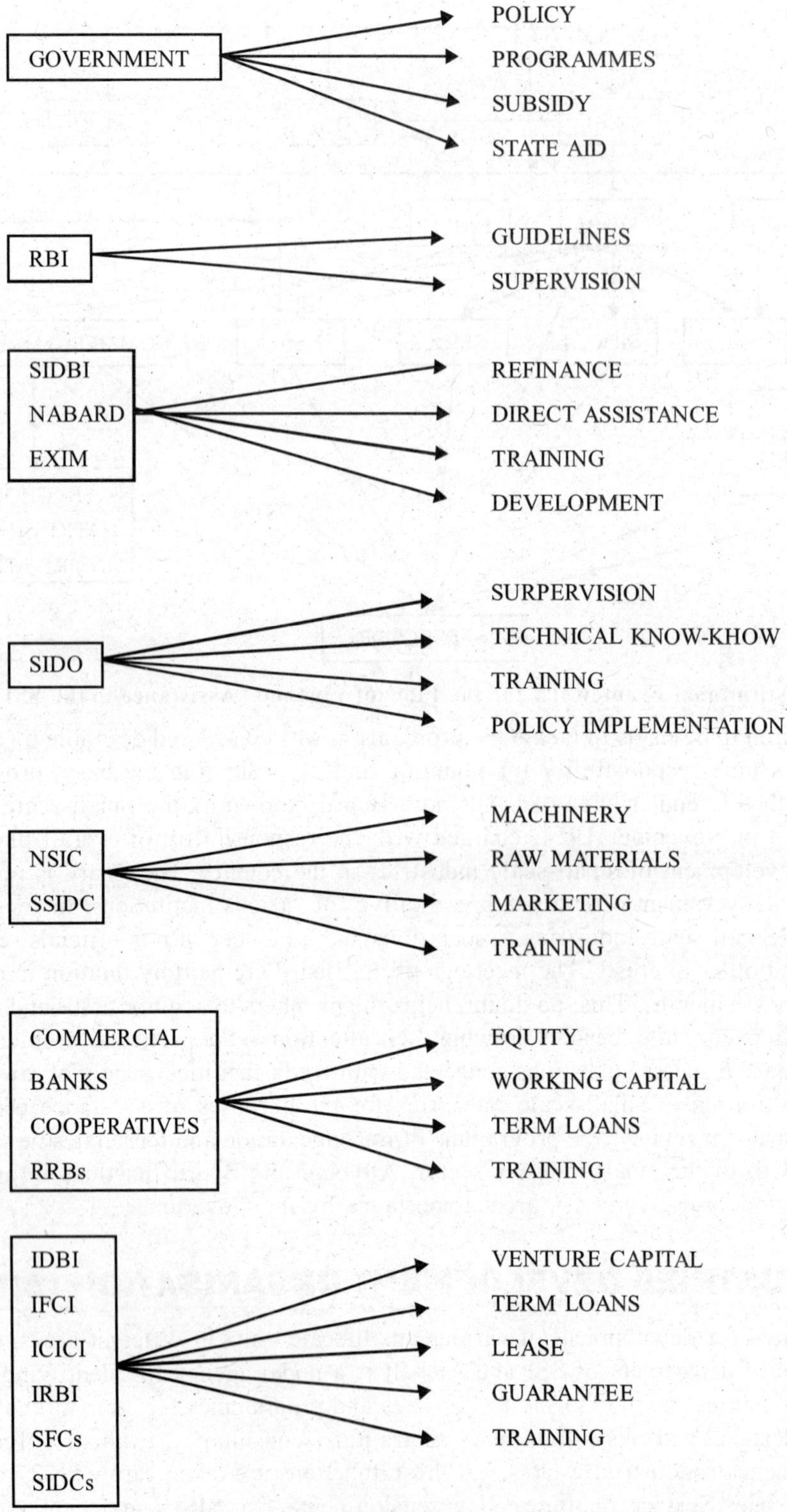

Fig. 16.2: Type of Finance Provided by Different Institutions

The activities of SIDO are divided into three categories as follows:

(a) Coordination activities of SIDO:

(1) To coordinate various programmes and policies of various state governments pertaining to small industries.

(2) To maintain relation with central industry ministry, planning commission, state level industries ministry and financial institutions.

(3) Implement and coordinate in the development of industrial estates.

(b) Industrial development activities of SIDO:

(1) Develop import substitutions for components and products based on the data available for various volumes-wise and value-wise imports.

(2) To give essential support and guidance for the development of ancillary units.

(3) To provide guidance to SSI units in terms of costing market competition and to encourage them to participate in the government stores and purchase tenders.

(4) To recommend the central government for reserving certain items to produce at SSI level only.

(c) Management activities of SIDO:

(1) To provide training, development and consultancy services to SSI to develop their competitive strength.

(2) To provide marketing assistance to various SSI units.

(3) To assist SSI units in selection of plant and machinery, location, layout design and appropriate process.

(4) To help them get updated in various information related to the small-scale industries activities.

SMALL INDUSTRIES SERVICE INSTITUTES (SISI)

The small industries service institutes have been set up in state capitals and other places all over the country to provide consultancy and training to small entrepreneurs both existing and prospective.

The main functions of SISI include:

(1) To serve as interface between central and state government.

(2) To render technical support services.

(3) To conduct entrepreneurship development programmes.

(4) To initiate promotional programmes.

SISIs also render assistance in the following areas:

- Economic consultancy/information/EDP consultancy.
- Trade and market information.
- Project profiles.
- State industrial potential surveys.
- District industrial potential surveys.
- Modernisation and in-plant studies.
- Workshop facilities.
- Training in various trade/activities.

DISTRICT INDUSTRIES CENTERS (DIC)

The District Industries Centres (DICs) programme was started in 1978 with a view to provide integrated administrative framework at the district level for promotion of small-scale industries in rural areas. The DICs are envisaged as a single window interacting agency at the district level providing service and support to small entrepreneurs under a single roof. DICs are the implementing arm of the Central and State Governments of the various schemes and programmes. Registration of small industries is done at the district industries centre and PMRY (Pradhan Mantri Rojgar Yojana) is also implemented by DIC. The organizational structure of DICs consists of General Manager, Functional Managers and Project Managers to provide technical services in the areas relevant to the needs of the district concerned. Management of DIC is done by the State Government.

The main functions of DIC are:

(1) To prepare and keep model project profiles for reference of the entrepreneurs.

(2) To prepare action plan to implement the schemes effectively already identified.

(3) To undertake industrial potential survey and to identify the types of feasible ventures which can be taken up in ISB sector, i.e., industrial sector, service sector and business sector.

(4) To guide entrepreneurs in matters relating to selecting the most appropriate machinery and equipment, sources of it supply and procedure for importing machineries.

(5) To provide guidance for appropriate loan amount and documentation.

(6) To assist entrepreneurs for availing land and shed equipment and tools, furniture and fixtures.

(7) To appraise the worthiness of the project-proposals received from entrepreneurs.

(8) To help the entrepreneurs in obtaining required licenses/permits/clearance.

(9) To assist the entrepreneurs in marketing their products and assess the possibilities of ancillarization.

(10) To conduct product development work appropriate to small industry.

(11) To help the entrepreneurs in clarifying their doubts about the matters of operation of bank accounts, submission of monthly, quarterly and annual returns to government departments.

(12) To conduct artisan training programme.

(13) To act as the nodal agency for the district for implementing PMRY (Prime Minister Rojgar Yojana).

(14) To function as the technical consultant of DRDA in administering IRDP and TRYSEM programme.

(15) To help the specialized training organisations to conduct entrepreneur development programmes.

In fine DICs function as the torch-bearer to the beneficiaries/entrepreneurs in setting up and running the business enterprise right from the concept to commissioning. So the role of DICs in enterprise building and developing small-scale sector is of much significance.

INDIAN INSTITUTE OF ENTREPRENEURSHIP

With an aim to undertake training, research and consultancy activities in small and micro-enterprises focusing on entrepreneurship development, the Indian Institute of Entrepreneurship (IIE) was established in the year 1993 in Guwahati by the erstwhile Ministry of Industry (now the Ministry of Micro, Small and Medium Enterprises), Government of India as an autonomous national institute. The institute began operating from April 1994 with the North East Council (NEC), Governments of Assam, Arunachal Pradesh and Nagaland and SIDBI as its other stakeholders.

The policy direction and guidance to the institute is provided by its Board of Management whose Chairman is the Secretary to Government of India, Ministry of Micro, Small and Medium Enterprises (MSME). The Governing Council of the institute is headed by Chairman, NEC and the Executive Committee is headed by the Secretary, Ministry of MSME, Government of India.

Objectives

- To organise and conduct training for entrepreneurship development.
- To evolve strategies and methodologies for different target groups and locations and conduct field tests.
- To identify training needs and offer training programmers to Government and non-Government organizations engaged in promoting and supporting entrepreneurship.

- To document and disseminate information needed for policy formulation and implementation related to self-employment.
- To identify, design and conduct training programmes for existing entrepreneurs.
- To prepare and publish literature related to entrepreneurship and industrial development.
- To organise seminars, workshops and conferences for providing a forum for interaction and exchange of views by various agencies and entrepreneurs.
- To conduct research for generating knowledge to accelerate the process of entrepreneurship development.
- To act as a catalyst for development of elf-employment/entrepreneurship, industry/business.
- To evolve, design and help in the utilisation of various media for creating entrepreneurship.

Activities

The activities of the institute include identification of training needs, designing and organizing programmers both for development functionaries and entrepreneurs; evolving effective training strategies and methodologies for different target groups and locations; organize seminars, workshops and conferences for providing for interaction and exchange of views by various agencies and entrepreneurs; undertaking research on entrepreneurship development, documenting and disseminating information needed for policy formulation and implementation on self-employment and entrepreneurship.

The institute acts as a catalyst for entrepreneurship development by creating an environment for entrepreneurship in the support system, developing new entrepreneurship, helping in the growth of existing entrepreneurs and propagation of entrepreneurial education.

NATIONAL SMALL INDUSTRIES CORPORATION LTD.

The National Small Industries Corporation Ltd., (NSIC) was set-up by the Government of India in 1955 with the objective of promoting and developing small-scale industries in the country. Various activities undertaken by NSIC include supply of indigenous and imported machines on easy hire-purchase and lease terms, marketing of the products of small industries on consortia basis, export marketing of small industries products, developing export worthiness of small-scale units, enlistment of small-scale units for participation in Government stores purchase programme development and modernisation of preto types of machines, equipment and tools supply and distribution of indigenous and imported raw materials, training in various tools technical trades and co-operation with other developing countries in setting-up of small-scale projects on turnkey basis.

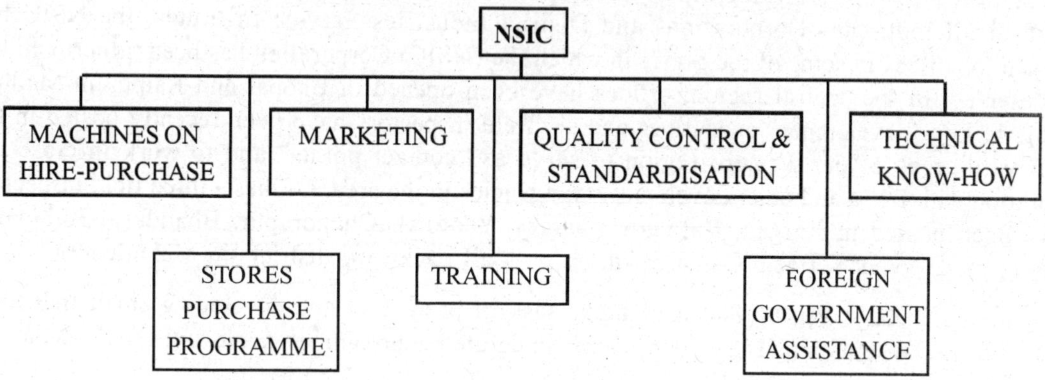

Fig. 16.3: Activities of National Small Industries Corporation (NSIC)

Formerly, the Corporation had four subsidiary corporations at Delhi, Mumbai, Kolkata and Chennai. However, since 1961, all the subsidiary corporations have been amalgamated with the main Corporation, and three branch offices have been set-up at Mumbai, Kolkata and Chennai. The Delhi subsidiary corporation has been merged with the parent Corporation, and its work is looked after by a separate Delhi cell set-up in it. The National Small Industries Corporation provides a complete package of financial assistance and support in the following areas:

- Supply of both indigenous and imported machines on easy hire-purchase terms. Special concessional terms have been introduced for units promoted by entrepreneurs from weaker sections of the society, women entrepreneurs, ex-servicemen and those units located in the backward areas.
- Marketing of small industries products within the country.
- Export of small industries products and developing export worthiness of small-scale units.
- Enlisting competent units and facilitating their participation in Government Stores purchase programme.
- Developing prototypes of machines, equipment and tools which are then passed on to small-scale units for commercial production:

- Technical training in several industrial trades, with a view to create technical culture in the young entrepreneurs.
- Development and upgradation of technology and implementation of modernisation programmes.
- Supply and distribution of indigenous and improved raw materials.
- Supply of both indigenous and imported machines on easy lease terms to existing units for diversification and modernisation.
- Providing of common facilities through Prototype Development & Training Centres.
- Setting-up Small-scale industries in other developing countries on turnkey basis.

With a view to giving a fillip to development efforts and to supplement the activities of State Small Industries Corporations and District Industries Service Institutes, the NSIC has opened its offices in some of the States in which the (NSIC) Corporation has been hitherto under-represented. In the central region, offices have been opened in Bhopal and Raipur in Madhya Pradesh. Four development executives and six field inspectors have been recently posted in the backward areas of the Western region to serve as "contact points" and to work in close co-operation with DICs and other developmental agencies in the area. Of these, three field inspectors have been posted in Raigad, Ratnagiri, Satara, Yeotmal, Chandrapur, Bhandara, Buldhana, Aurangabad, Nanded, Beed, Osmanabad, etc., — all backward districts in Maharashtra.

The NSIC has taken up the challenging task of promoting and developing small industries almost from the scratch and has adopted an "integrated approach" to achieve its socio-economic

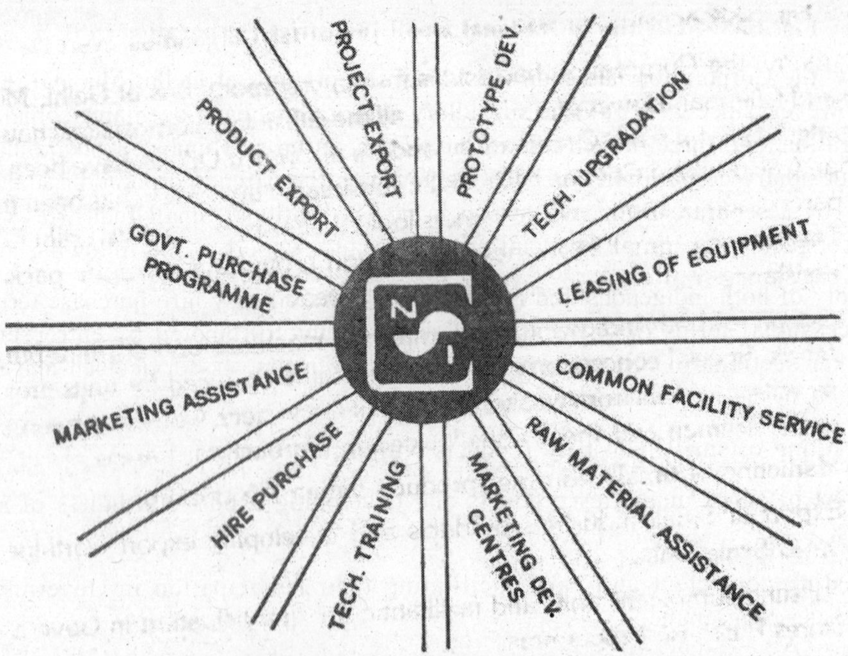

Fig. 16.4: A Unique Package of Assistance for Small Entrepreneurs

objectives. It has created a proper "industrial" atmosphere and has infused confidence in the small entrepreneurs to prepare schemes for the manufacture of products or identify the balancing equipment for purposes of modernisation and or diversification. The small unit, because it is small, is always short of resources. The NSIC, therefore, supplies machinery and equipment, marketing inputs and technical support to small units. And so the seedling comes up as – a "factory" which provides jobs for the unemployed or underemployed.

Over the years and particularly during this decade, the NSIC, with its deliberate and concentrated efforts, has developed an unsurpassed reputation of an effective and efficient nodal agency for providing assistance to the vibrant small-scale sector. All these years, through its dynamic approach and the package of assistance, it has been significantly contributing to the development of entrepreneurs, building up of strong industrial base, spreading of technical culture, promoting balanced regional growth, development of rural and backward areas, etc., as well as in employment generation, in all parts of the country.

STATE INDUSTRIAL DEVELOPMENT CORPORATIONS

The State Industrial Development Corporations (SIDCs) were established under the Company Act, 1956 in the sixties and early seventies' as wholly-owned State Government undertakings for promotion and development of medium and large industries. SIDCs act as catalysts for industrial development and provide impetus to further investment in their respective States. SIDCs provide assistance by way of term loans, underwriting and direct subscription to shares/ debentures and guarantees. They undertake a variety of promotional activities such as preparation of feasibility reports, industrial potential surveys, entrepreneurship development programmes and developing industrial areas/estates. SIDCs are also involved in setting up of medium and large industrial projects in the joint sector in collaboration with private entrepreneurs or as wholly-owned subsidiaries. The SIDCs activities have now widened to include equipment leasing, providing tax benefits under State Government's Package Scheme of Incentives, merchant banking services and setting-up of mutual funds. Some of the SIDCs also offer a package of developmental services such as technical guidance, assistance in plant location and co-ordination with other agencies.

Of the 28 SIDCs operating in the country, nine are twin-function. SDICs functioning also as SFCs to provide assistance to small-scale units as well as act as promotional agencies. The twin-function SIDCs are in Arunachal Pradesh, Manipur, Meghalaya, Mizoram, Nagaland, Tripura, Goa, Pondicherry and Sikkim. Seven SIDCs are also involved in infrastructure development and other extensions, services for the small sector.

The SIDCs are agent of IDBI and SIDBI for operating its seed capital scheme. Under the scheme, equity type assistance is provided to deserving first generation entrepreneurs who possess necessary skills but lack adequate resources required towards promoters' contribution.

The major functions of these Corporations include:

- Providing risk capital to entrepreneurs by way of equity participation and seed capital assistance;

- Grant of financial assistance to industrial units by way of loans, guarantees and of late, lease finance by some Corporations;
- Administering incentive schemes of Central/State Governments;
- Promotional activities such as identification of project ideas through industrial potential surveys, preparation of feasibility reports, selection and training of entrepreneurs; and
- Developing industrial areas/estates by providing infrastructure facilities.

Since the actual range of activities being undertaken by individual SIDC depends upon the specific responsibilities entrusted by the respective State Union Territory, there is considerable diversity in activities among the different SIDCs.

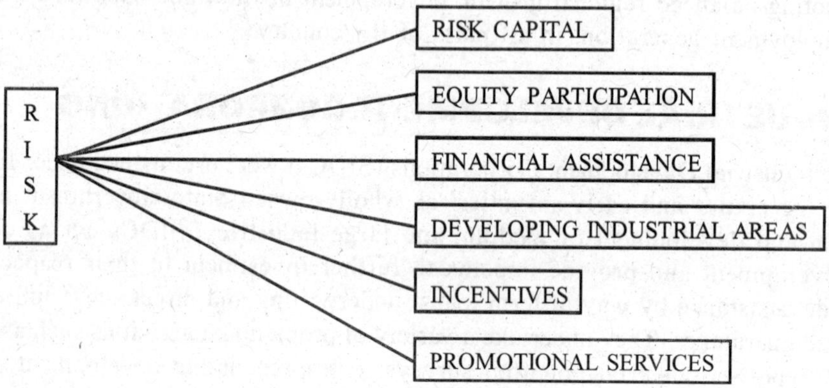

Fig. 16.5 : Functions of SIDCs

STATE SMALL INDUSTRIES DEVELOPMENT CORPORATIONS

The State Small Industries Development Corporations (SSIDCs) established under the Companies Act, 1956, are State Government undertakings, responsible for catering to the needs of the small, tiny and cottage industries in the Statel/Union Territories under their justification. SSIDCs enjoy operational flexibility and can undertake a variety of activities for development of the small sector. As at present, 18 SSIDCs are in operation.

Some of the important activities undertaken by SSIDCs includes: *(i)* procurement and distribution of scarce raw materials, *(ii)* supply of machinery on hire-purchase basis, *(iii)* providing assistance for marketing of the products of small-scale units, *(iv)* construction of industrial estates/sheds, providing allied infrastructure facilities and their maintenance, *(v)* extending seed capital assistance on behalf of the State Governments, and *(vi)* providing management assistance to production units.

A change in the role of SSIDCs has been prompted by the new Industrial Policy. SSIDCs are gearing up to change themselves from raw material distributors to organisations that will take care of various aspects of small industry development, especially marketing. SSIDCs would, thus, help the tiny and small industries increase their market share. The new policy calls for establishment of counselling and common testing facilities and provision of a mechanism to allow corporation of the latest technology in the small sector. SSIDCs are also planning to set-up centres for display of/and information dissemination on SSI products, and for providing small office spaces for SSIs in need.

Information for the analysis/discussion that follows, pertains to 11 SSIDCs located in Andhra Pradesh, Assam, Bihar, Goa, Gujarat, Jammu & Kashmir, Himachal Pradesh, Kerala, Punjab, Rajasthan and Tamil Nadu.

STATE FINANCIAL CORPORATIONS

State Financial Corporations (SFCs), operating at the State-level, form an integral part of the development financing system in the country. They function with the objective of financing and promoting small and medium enterprises for achieving balanced regional socio-economic growth, catalysing higher investment, generating greater employment opportunities and widening the ownership base of industry.

At present, there are 18 SFCs in the country, 17 of which were set up under the SFCs Act, 1951. Tamil Nadu Industrial Investment Corporation.Ltd., set up in 1949 under the Companies Act as Madras Industrial Investment Corporation also functions as a full-fledged SFC. SFCs extend financial assistance to industrial units by way of term loans, direct subscription to equity/ debentures, guarantees, and discounting of bills of exchange. SFCs operate a number of schemes of refinance and equity type of assistance formulated by IDBI/SIDBI which include schemes for artisans, special target groups like SC/ST, women, ex-servicemen, physically handicapped, etc., and for transport operators, setting up hotels, tourism-related activities, hospitals and nursing homes, etc. Over the years, the SFCs have extended their activities and coverage of assistance.

Concerns Eligible for Assistance

Industrial concerns eligible for financial accommodation under the State Financial Corporation Act, 1951 are those which are engaged in the following activities: *(a)* Manufacture of goods; *(b)* preservation of goods; *(c)* processing of goods; *(d)* mining; *(e)* generation of distribution of electricity or any other form of power; *(f)* hotel industry; *(g)* transport of passenger or goods by road or by water or by air; *(h)* maintenance, repair, testing or servicing of machinery of any description of vehicles or vessels or motor boats or, trawlers or tractors; *(i)* assembling, repairing or packing any article with the aid of machinery or power; *(j)* the development of any contiguous area of land as an industrial estate; *(k)* fishing or providing shore facilities for fishing or maintenance thereof; *(l)* providing special or technical knowledge or other services for the promotion of industrial growth.

SFCs extend financial assistance to industrial units by way of term loans, direct subscription to equity/debentures, guarantees and discounting of bills of exchange. SFCs operate a number of schemes of refinance and equity type of assistance formulated by IDBI/SIDBI which include schemes for artisans, social target groups like SC/ST, women, ex-servicemen, physically handicapped, etc., and for transport operators, setting up hotels, tourism-related activities, hospitals and nursing homes, etc.

Objectives and Functions

- The main function is to provide term loans for the acquisition of land, building, plant and machinery, pre-ops and other assets.
- Promotion of self-employment.
- To encourage new and technically/professionally qualified women entrepreneurs in setting up industrial projects.
- To finance expansion, modernisation and upgradation of technology in the existing units.
- To provide financial assistance for the rehabilitation of sick units financed by the Delhi Financial Corporation.

The outstanding bank credit to small-scale industries increased by 22.0 per cent to ₹ 43,508 crore on March 31, 1998, whereas credit to medium and large industries increased by 14.5 per cent to ₹ 1,17,530 crore. The medium and large industries claimed 73.0 per cent of the total outstanding credit to industrial sector as on March 31, 1998. Industries which accounted for bulk of the outstanding credit as on March 31, 1998 were engineering (14.2 per cent), textiles (13.1 per cent) and chemicals, dyes, paints, etc. (11.3 per cent).

Table 16.1 Industry-wise Deployment of Gross Banks Credit

(₹ crore)

Industry	*Outstanding as on*		
	March 18, 1994	*March 29, 1996*	*March 27, 1998*
Engineering	17,127	25,621	22,833
Chemicals, dyes, paints, etc.	10,034	16,450	18,120
Textiles	10,128	15,999	21,071
Iron & Steel	4,528	8,482	15,767
Other metals & metal products	3,199	3,977	5,193
Gems & Jewellery	1,975	2,785	3,530
Total (including others)	80,482	1,24,937	1,61,038

DIRECTORATE OF INDUSTRIES OF THE STATE GOVERNMENTS

It should be mentioned here that the small-scale industries sector is a State subject under the Indian Constitution and, as such, the primary responsibility for all executive action in regard to its development and the implementation of the programme of assistance to it is that of the State Government. The work relating to the development of industries in general and small-scale industries in particular is looked after by the Directorate of Industries in each State and in each Union Territory. There are 22 such Directorates all over the country. Each organisation is staffed with administrative and technical officers at the State Headquarters and by a District Industries Officer, with appropriate supporting staff, in each District. The State Directorates run various training schemes, production schemes and common facilities schemes. They also provide facilities of developed industrial land and built-up factory sheds in industrial estates, allocate quotas of scarce raw materials, certify import requirements and organise industrial co-operatives. Their functions are varied and have growth with the development and diversification of the small industries sector. Each State Director of Industries is assisted by an Additional Directors or a Joint Director and a number of Deputy Directors, Assistant Directors and Technical Officers in charge of specific fields of activities. At the district level, the work is looked after by the District Industries Officer or the Assistant Director of Industries. He is assisted by one or two inspectors, depending upon the quantum of work and the industrial importance of the district. The district industries staff looks after not only the small-scale industries programme but also other programmes, e.g., handicrafts, village industries, etc. In a number of states there are at the block level, Extension Officers for industries to act as liaison officers between the District Industries Office and the field.

The Directorate of cottage and small-scale industries provides a wide variety of assistance. The details are given below:

General Assistance

1. Entrepreneurial Development Programmes
2. Industrial Accommodation
3. Priority on Telephone and Power
4. Supply of Machinery on Hire Purchase
5. Scarce raw materials
6. Recommendation for import
7. Research grant and Award of Prizes
8. Modernisation.

Marketing Assistance

9. Export and Marketing assistance
10. Reservation of items for State Government purchase
11. Single point registration of NSIC
12. Earnest money exemption
13. 15 per cent price preference
14. Quality marking.

Financial Assistance

15. Loan under BSAI Act
16. Central/State Investment Subsidy
17. Subsidy towards fees of consultants
18. Subsidy on rent for sheds/land
19. 25 per cent subsidy on captive generation sets
20. 20 per cent subsidy on HT/LT powerline
21. 30 per cent subsidy on power bill
22. 3 per cent interest subsidy on working capital
23. 25 per cent interest subsidy on term loan
24. Rebate on handicrafts raw materials units
25. 15 per cent subsidy on new employment
26. Subsidy on stamp duty/registration
27. Return of Octroi/Entry Tax
28. Sales Tax exemption and loan
29. 5 per cent extra subsidy for Scheduled Castes/Scheduled Tribes
30. Margin Money Loan
31. 20 per cent margin money to sick units.

For Cottage Section

32. Rebate/grant/loan to Khadi and Village Industries
33. Financial assistance for tools/implements
34. Rebate on handicrafts/khadi
35. Training, common facilities, design development
36. Financial assistance to Co-operatives
37. Rural artisans programme/IRDP.

SMALL INDUSTRY EXTENSION TRAINING INSTITUTE (SIETI)

The Small Industry Extension Training Institute (SIETI), Hyderabad, was set-up as an autonomous body in 1962 and was registered under the Societies Registration Act. It is engaged mainly in training Central and State Government officers who are entrusted with the responsibility of implementing the small industry development programmes. The Institute conducts courses in industrial management and area development techniques. It also conducts intensive courses in certain aspects of industrial management — in production management, financial management, cost accounting, etc. The Institute undertakes research in fields which are related to development of small industries.

SMALL-SCALE INDUSTRIES BOARD (SSIB)

The Government of India invited in 1953, an international team of experts sponsored by the Ford Foundation to study the problems of small-scale industries for the purpose of recommending a programme of development in view of their importance in the national economy. The recommendations of the team fall under three categories, *viz.*, *(a)* those relating to the provision of technical know-how and knowledge of business methods and management; *(b)* those that bear on the financial assistance to be provided in the form of credit facilities; and *(c)* those that are concerned with other forms of aid and services, such as assistance in securing Government contracts, market facilities and research and supply of modern machine tools on easy instalment terms. Among the many steps the Central Government took in pursuance of these recommendations was the setting-up of the Small-Scale Industries Board in November 1954 to advise it on the programme and work of the different agencies looking after the development of small-scale industries in the country.

Set-up

The Board has at present 50 members, including representatives of the Central and State Governments, the Reserve Bank of India and the State Bank of India, non-officials, etc.

The Union Minister for Industries is the Chairman of the Board. Besides co-ordinating the activities of the National Small Industries, Corporation and the Small Industries, which have been set-up by Government to assist in the executing of policies bearing on the development of small industries, the Board reviews at its periodical meetings the work of the various development agencies, discusses such weaknesses as may be located in planning or execution, and offers advice on modifications or improvements. A Standing Committee of the Board was set-up in 1957, which meets at least once in two months. The Committee, as recently reconstituted, consists of 10 members, including the Union Minister for industries, who is its Chairman. For implementing the recommendations and policies laid down by the Small-scale Industries Board a separate officer of the rank of Joint Secretary (with the designation of Development Commissioner for Small-scale Industry) has been appointed in the Ministry of Commerce and Industry. The activities of the National Small Industries Corporation and the Small Industries Service Institute are controlled by him.

Similar Boards have also been established in all the States except Kerala, West Bengal and Madhya Pradesh. In Kerala, the State Co-ordination Committee for Small-scale Industries discusses all matters relating to these industries. A high power Small-Scale Industries and Handicrafts Co-ordination Committee has been set-up in West Bengal. The Joint Development Commissioners of Directors of Small Industries Service Institutes have been appointed as members of the State Board in Tamil Nadu, Bihar, Odisha, Punjab, Andhra Pradesh, Assam, Maharashtra and Karnataka.

Activities of the Board

The Small-scale Industries Board is concerned with the development of industrial undertakings which have capital investment of less than ₹ 5 lakh and which employ less than

50 persons per shift when using power and less than 100 persons per shift when not using power. Match-manufacturing cooperative societies, tailoring co-operative societies and sports-goods manufacturing units are, however, considered to be small-scale undertakings irrespective of the number of workers employed in them, provided that the capital investment in these units does not exceed ₹ 5 lakhs. These Boards, however do not cover such village industries as wool, handmade paper, palm gur, Khandsari sugar, rice husking, oil pressing by ghanies, bee-keeping, etc., and certain other industries like handloom, khadi, handicrafts, coir and silk for which separate All-India Boards have been constituted.

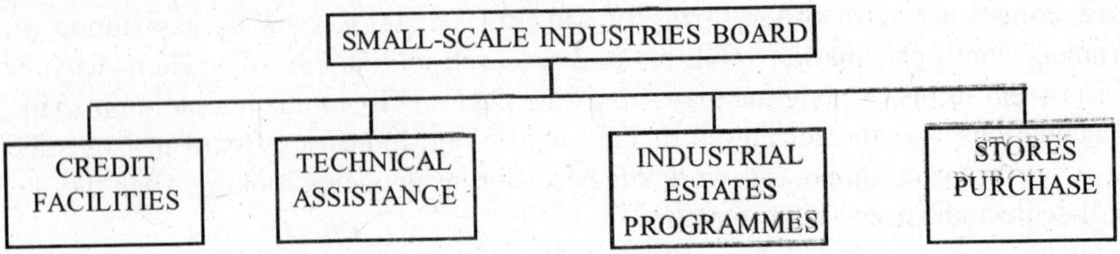

Fig. 16.6: Small-Scale Industries Board (SSIB)

The Small-scale Industries Board and its Standing Committees have examined a large number of problems faced by small-scale industries and have taken decisions regarding the action to be taken by various agencies: Central and State Governments, National Small Industries Corporation, Small Industries Service Institutes, etc. Some of the more important decisions taken by the Board are briefly set out in the following paragraphs:

Credit Facilities: The question of providing adequate credit to small industries on liberal terms has been under the consideration of the Board for a long time. The terms and conditions under which loans were sanctioned under the "Liberalised Scheme" evolved by Government in June 1955 have since been further liberalised, with the result that it is now possible for small industrialists in most States to get loans up to ₹1,000 on personal bond; up to ₹ 5,000 by offering one or more sureties, and above ₹ 5,000 against the security of land, buildings, plant, machinery, stocks and other assets (including the assets to be created out of the loan) up to 75 per cent of the value of the assets offered as security. The concessional rate of interest payable by industrial co-operatives is 2 $^1/_2$ per cent for amount up to ₹ 2 lakhs, while for others, it is 3 per cent for amount up to ₹ 50,000.

In 1991, some measures were taken to increase the flow of funds, particularly to village, cottage, tiny and small-scale units, at specified rates of interest. These measures are:

(a) Bank credit to artisans, village and cottage industries and small-scale industries in the tiny sector would be treated as composite term loan for equipment or working capital or both, up to ₹ 25,000, with a repayment period of 7 to 10 years or more.

(b) The rate of interest on term loans has been uniformly brought to 15 per cent.

(c) On the credit for working capital above ₹ 25,000 but less than ₹ 100 lakhs granted to artisans, village and cottage industries and small-scale industries in the tiny sector, the rate of interest would not exceed 12 $^1/_2$ per cent per annum.

(d) Simplified interview-cum-appraisal form for small units would be available.

(e) Applications for would-be available small loans will be disposed of within a period of 30 days at the district level.

(f) To get over the difficulty of delayed payments, the RBI has issued instructions that the accounts of the creditors should be bifurcated to show the dues of the SSI units and those remaining unpaid for over 120 days. Banks have been advised to fix separate credit limits for purchases made from small-scale units.

INDUSTRIAL DEVELOPMENT BANK OF INDIA (IDBI)

The Industrial Development Bank of India (IDBI) was established on 1st July, 1964 as a wholly-owned subsidiary of the Reserve Bank of India under the IDBI Act, 1964. With the recent enactment of the Public Financial Institutions Laws (Amendment) Act, 1975, the entire issued capital of the IDBI (₹ 50 crores) held by the Reserve Bank of India will stand transferred to and vest in the Central Government. In accordance with the provisions of this Act, the IDBI has become the principal financial institution for co-ordinating, in conformity with national priorities, the working of institutions engaged in financing, promoting or developing industries.

The IDBI's statute enables it to have a considerable operational flexibility. It can finance all types of industrial concerns engaged or to be engaged in the manufacture, processing or preservation of goods; or in mining, transport, generation and distribution of power; or in fishing, providing shore facilities for fishing; or in the hotel industry; or in the maintenance repair, testing or servicing of machinery or vehicles or vessels or motor boats or trailers or tractors. There are no restrictive provisions in the IDBI Act regarding the nature and type of security to be obtained from the assisted concerns. Also, no upper or lower limit for assistance to any concern or of the size of concern itself has been prescribed though, for operational reasons, certain criteria are generally kept in view.

Management and Organisation

The direction and management of the IDBI's affairs are vested in a Board of Directors. Apart from its Head Office in Mumbai, the IDBI has three Regional Offices in Kolkata, Chennai and New Delhi. Besides, it has twelve branch offices at Ahmedabad, Bangalore, Bhopal, Bhubaneshwar, Chandigarh, Cochin, Gauwahati, Hyderabad, Jaipur, Jammu, Kanpur and Patna, which function as initial contact points between the IDBI and the local industrialists, entrepreneurs and various State and other agencies concerned with industrial progress.

A special fund, called as the Development Assistance Fund, has been set-up in the IDBI under its statute for assisting, with the prior approval of the Central Government, specially deserving projects to which banks and other financial institutions are not likely to advance the requisite finance in ordinary course of business. This assistance includes:

(i) Direct assistance;

(ii) Refinance of industrial loans;

(iii) Bills rediscount assistance;

(iv) Export finance; and

(v) Subscription to shares and bonds of financial institutions.

SMALL INDUSTRIES DEVELOPMENT BANK OF INDIA (SIDBI)

The idea of setting up Small Industries Development Bank of India (SIDBI), in response to a long-standing demand from the small-scale sector as an apex-level national institution for promotion, financing and development of industries in the small-scale sector, embodied an opportunity to set up a proactive, responsive and forward looking institution to serve the current and emerging needs of small-scale industries in the country. As a precursor to the setting up of the new institution, the Small Industries Development Fund was created by Industrial Development Bank of India (IDBI) in 1986 exclusively for refinancing, bills rediscounting and equity support to the small-scale sector. The outstanding portfolio of the order of ₹ 4,200 crore from IDBI was transferred to SIDBI in March 1990. SIDBI started off from a strong base: percentage of IDBI, backing of a special statute – the Small Industries Development Bank of India Act of 1989, a large capital base of ₹ 450 crore, availability of experienced manpower endowed with development banking skills carved out of IDBI's professional staff and ready availability of a vast network of institutional infrastructure and enduring financial linkages with State Financial Corporations (SFCs), commercial banks and other institutions; all these augured well for the growth of the nascent institution. SIDBI became operational on April 2, 1990.

The Environment

Indian economy has been in transition for most part of the last five years: the industrial policy, fiscal policy, public sector policy, foreign investment policy, trade policy and monetary and credit policies have been in various stages of liberalisation. Decontrol, deregulation and delicensing have given enormous scope for private initiative and market forces to come to play. New relationships within and between different sectors in the economy are being evolved; the small-scale sector has been an important constituent of such a liberalisation in the country, Government of India formulated a set of new policies aimed at harnessing the potential of the small-scale sector in August 1991 – a-year-and-half after the establishment of SIDBI. The prescriptions of the policy focused at removal of impediments affecting the growth of small-scale sector together with consolidation of the strengths, in the context of the emerging economic order. SIDBI has been refining its strategies and business policies in alignment with the policy changes which have been taking place at the national level.

Operational Strategy

Stepping up of flow of credit to the units in the small-scale sector through direct and indirect financing mechanisms and ensuring speedy disbursement have remained the main plank of the operational strategy of SIDBI. Over the years, the share of direct assistance in the total assistance has steadily gone up.

The new schemes designed and implemented were directed at filling the gaps in the existing credit delivery system focussing on new target groups and activities. These are targeted at addressing some of the major problems of SSIs, in areas such as marketing, infrastructure development, delayed realisation of bills, ancillarisation, obsolescence of technology, quality improvement, export financing and venture capital assistance. The terms of assistance under various schemes have been substantially liberalised based on an ongoing review process. The procedures have been simplified with gradual decentralisation and progressive delegation of powers aimed at higher levels of operational efficiency and better customer service.

To mitigate the difficulties faced by SSIs on account of delayed payments, two factoring companies, *viz.*, SBI Factors and Commercial Services Pvt. Ltd., and Canbank Factors Ltd., have been established with SIDBI as a partner with 20 per cent shareholding, SIDBI has enlarged the list of institutions eligible for refinance in order to widen its reach. It enrolled itself as an institutional member of Over The Counter Exchange of India (OTCEI). This facilitates SSIs to access capital market through the route of OTCEI in raising resources in a cost-effective manner. SIDBI has also been granted the status of Category I Merchant Banker by Securities and Exchange Board of India. SIDBI extends resource support to Non-banking Finance Companies by way of lines of credit against their assistance to units in the small-scale sector by way of leasing, hire-purchase and bought-out deals.

The operational priorities of SIDBI, therefore, were to build up a financial portfolio reflecting a high order of health and strength based on quality or assets. SIDBI maintains an organisational structure which is lean, functional and capable of adapting to the state-of-the-art technology to remain efficient and competitive. The strength of SIDBI is reflected in the quality of its portfolio; over 97 per cent of its portfolio consists of standard assets. SIDBI has obtained a high investment grade rating 'AAA' by The Credit Rating Information Services of India Ltd., for its unsecured bonds. There has been consistent growth in the gross income and profits of SIDBI in the last five years. Though of a modest scale, SIDBI has been transferring to IDBI surplus of its profits after appropriations as return on capital. SIDBI is one of the development financial institutions in the country with a high capital adequacy ratio. It is a matter of satisfaction that in respect of resource mobilisation efforts during the last five years, leading international aid giving and lending agencies have lent considerable resource support to SIDBI. There has been a significant shift in approach with regard to the working relationship with commercial banks. Besides using the branch network of banks to reach ultimate beneficiaries, SIDBI now focuses on a collaborative effort so as to facilitate timely flow of credit both by way of term loans and working capital to the small-scale units. To reinforce such a relationship on a lasting basis. Memoranda of Understanding have been signed by SIDBI with many leading banks.

Growing Operations

From a predominantly refinancing and bills rediscounting institution, SIDBI has emerged as a major purveyor of a wide variety of financial services to the small-scale sector. At present, financial assistance being provided by SIDBI covers direct equity participation, equity type loan on soft terms, term loan, working capital — both rupee finance and foreign currencies, bills discounting, venture capital support and different forms of resource support to banks and other institutions. The proportion of direct assistance in the total portfolio of SIDBI has increased significantly.

Support Services

Over the years, the scope of promotional and developmental activities has been enlarged to encompass several new activities. Technology adoption, technology exchange, transfer and upgradation, quality promotion, enlarging marketing capabilities-both domestic and international, entrepreneurship development, management development, environment management, rural industrialisation, support to self-help groups, information dissemination through publication of project profiles for tiny and hi-tech small industrial units are now covered under promotional and developmental services. In such activities, SIDBI operates in collaboration with voluntary organisations, non-government organisations, technology firms, consultancy organisations and multilateral international agencies to enhance the level of overall impact of such activities on the sector.

The Impact

The overall economic impact of SIDBI's operations during the last five years has been in terms of cumulative investment catalysed of the order of ₹ 34,380 crore and fresh employment opportunities for about 86 lakh persons. The visible impact of promotional and developmental activities of SIDBI in select clusters of SSIs such as lock, leather, glass, brass and ready-made garments has been noticeable with commensurate improvement in overall productivity, product quality levels and process standards in such clusters. Significant achievements have made in these spheres will be buttressed with new initiatives in the years to come.

KHADI AND VILLAGE INDUSTRIES COMMISSION (KVIC)

The Khadi & Village Industries Commission established by an Act of Parliament is a statutory organisation engaged in promoting and developing khadi and village industries for providing employment opportunities in the rural areas and thereby strengthening the rural economy. It took over the activities from the erstwhile All India Khadi Village Industries Board on 1st April, 1957. The KVIC has been identified as one of the major organisations in decentralised sector for generating non-farm employment opportunities in the rural areas at low per capita investment.

Main Objectives

- The social objective of providing employment in rural areas;
- The economic objective of producing saleable articles; and
- The wider objective of creating self-reliance amongst the people and building up a strong rural community spirit.

Functions

The functions of KVIC as prescribed under the KVIC Act, 1956 (No. 61 of 1956) and Rules made thereunder are as follows:

(i) to plan and organize training of persons employed or desirous of seeking employed employment in khadi and village industries;

(ii) to build up reserves of raw materials and implements and supply them to persons engaged or likely to be engaged in production of handspun yarn or khadi or village industries at such rates as the Commission may decide;

(iii) to encourage and assist in the creation of common service facilities for the processing of raw materials or semi-finished goods and for otherwise facilitating production and marketing or khadi or products of village industries;

(iv) to promote the sale of marketing or khadi or products of village industries or handicrafts and for this purpose forge links with established marketing agencies wherever necessary and feasible;

(v) to encourage and promote research in the technology used in khadi and village industries, including the use of non-conventional energy and electric power with a view to increasing productivity, eliminating drudgery and otherwise enhancing their competitive capacity and to arrange for dissemination of salient results obtained from such research;

(vi) to undertake directly or through other agencies studies of the problem of khadi or village industries;

(vii) to provide financial assistance to institutions or persons engaged in the development and operation of khadi or village industries and guide them through supply of designs, prototypes and other technical information for the purpose of producing goods and services for which there is effective demand in the opinion of the Commission;

(viii) to undertake experiments of pilot projects which in the opinion of the Commission are necessary for the development of khadi and village industries;

(ix) to establish and maintain separate organisations for the purpose of carrying out any or all of the above matters; to promote and encourage co-operative efforts among the manufacturers of khadi or persons engaged in village industries;

(x) to ensure genuineness and to set up standards of quality and ensure that products of khadi and village industries do conform to the said standards, including issue of certificates or letters or recognition to the concerned persons; and

(xi) to carry-out any other matter incidental to the above.

Organisational Set-up

The Central Office of the KVIC is at Mumbai with one Zonal Office at Guwahati and 29 State Offices. Functional directorates have been constituted to co-ordinate the functions like training, marketing, accounts, khadi, economic research, Rural Employment Generation Programme (REGP), etc.

KVIC also undertakes training activities through its 43 departmental and non-departmental training centres (NDTCs). Marketing is taken up through its 12 departmentally run Khadi Gramodyog Bhawans and 7,050 institutional sales outlets located in different parts of the country. Six Central Silver Plants provide quality raw material to khadi institutions.

Implementing Agencies

Khadi and Village Industries (KVI) programmes are implemented through 5,549 registered institutions, cooperative societies, 33 State/Union Territories (UTs) Khadi and Village Industries Boards (KVIBs) and 27 public sector banks, regional rural banks and a few selected co-operative banks.

The khadi programme is implemented through institutions registered either with the KVIC or the State KVIBs.

In the case of village industries, the KVIC implements the Rural Employment Generation Programme (REGP).

Grouping of Industries

While the khadi programme comprises handspun and handwoven cotton, woollen, muslin and silk varieties, the village industries programmes have been classified into seven broad groups. These are:

(i) Mineral Based Industry;

(ii) Forest Based Industry;

(iii) Agro and Rural Industry;

(iv) Polymer and Chemical Based Industry;

(v) Rural Engineering and Bio-technology;

(vi) Handmade Paper and Fibre Industry;

(vii) Service Industry.

Industries connected with meat (slaughter), i.e., processing, canning and/or serving items made therefrom, production/manufacturing or sale of intoxicant items like beedi/pan/cigar/cigarette, etc., any hotel or dhaba or sales outlet serving liquor, preparation/producing tobacco as raw materials, tapping of toddy for sale, manufacturing of polythene carry bags of less than 20 microns thickness and manufacturing of carry bags or containers made of recycled plastics for storing, carrying, dispensing or packaging of food-stuff, etc., are not assisted under KVI programme as these are either not eco-friendly or against the ideology and ethos of Mahatma Gandhi.

Budgetary Support to KVIC

The Government of India through the Ministry of Agro and Rural Industries provides funds to KVIC for undertaking its various activities under Plan and Non-plan heads.

These funds are provided primarily by way of grants and loans and in turn KVIC re-allocates them to implementing agencies, namely the State KVIBs, institutions registered under the Societies Registration Act, 1860, and co-operative societies registered under the Co-operative Acts of the State Governments- implementing banks, etc. The Commission's administrative expenditure including pension payment, is met out of Non-plan Government Budgetary Support.

The details of funds provided from Budgetary Source (both under Plan and Non-plan) during the Tenth Plan are as under:

Year	Budget Allocation (RE)		Fund Released	
	Plan	***Non-plan***	***Plan***	***Non-plan***
2002-2003	394.67	84.87	340.55	83.36
2003-2004	444.75	83.75	423.60	63.70
2004-2005	462.00	84.91	460.99	83.90
2005-2006	560.82	84.82	558.56	84.76
2006-2007	592.93	84.82	463.59	55.26

Released as on 31st Dec., 2006.

Physical Performance of the KVI Sector

The KVI sector recorded an improved performance during 2005-06 in comparison to the previous year. The total KVI production stood at ₹ 12,383.84 crore (khadi – ₹ 468.30 crore and VI – ₹ 11,915.54 crore) in 2005-2006 as against ₹ 10,920.43 crore (khadi – ₹ 461.51 crore and VI – ₹ 10,458.89 crore) in 2004-2005, reflecting an increase of 13.40 per cent. Similarly, sales of KVI products increased to ₹ 15,276.02 crore (khadi – ₹ 628.69 crore and VI ₹ 14,647.33 crore) as compared to ₹ 13,105.19 crore (khadi – ₹ 617.84 and VI-₹ 12,487.35 crore), registering a growth of 16.56 per cent during 2005-06.

The total cumulative employment in the KVI sector is estimated to have increased to 82.77 lakh (8.68 lakh in khadi and 74.09 lakh in VI) in 2005-2006 as against the previous year's level of 76.78 lakh (8.64 lakh in khadi and 68.14 lakh in VI), registering a growth of 7.80 per cent.

The total KVI production during 2006-07 (up to December 2006) is estimated at ₹ 10,325 crore (₹ 339.50 crore in khadi and ₹ 9,985.50 in VI) as compared to ₹ 7,639 crore (₹ 322.13 crore in khadi and ₹ 7,315.80 in VI) in 2005-06 (up to December 2005), registering an overall growth of 35.16 per cent. Sales increased to to ₹ 12,347.70 crore (₹ 438.60 crore in kahdi and ₹ 11,909.10 crore in VI) in 2006-07 (up to Dec. 2006) as compared with ₹ 9,040.37 crore (₹ 415.04 crore in khadi and ₹ 8, 625.33 crore in VI) during the corresponding period of 2005-06 reflecting a growth of 36.60 per cent.

Total employment in KVI sector is estimated to have increased to 85.22 lakh (8.77 lakh in khadi and 76.45 lakh in VI) in 2006-2007 (up to December 2006 as compared to 79.71 lakh persons during the corresponding period of 2005-06, registering a growth of 6.91 per cent.

Major Schemes being Implemented by KVIC

1. Rural Employment Generation Programme (REGP)
2. Interest Subsidy Eligibility Certification (ISEC) Scheme
3. Rebate Scheme
4. Product Development, Design Intervention and Packaging (PRODIP).
5. Rural Industries Service Centres (RISC)
6. Janashree Bima Yojana (KBY)
7. Quality Control in Khadi
8. Exhibitions
9. Government Supply
10. Research and Development
11. Rural Industrial Consultancy Service (RICS)
12. Setting up of raw material godowns
13. People Education Programme (PEP)
14. Credit Guarantee Trust Fund for Small Industries (CGTSI).
15. System for Programme Analysis and Reporting for KVIC (SPARK)
16. Scheme for enhancement of productivity and competitiveness of khadi industry and artisans.

COMMERCIAL BANKS

The Indian commercial banking system consists of 297 scheduled banks. As on June 30, 2000, the total number of branches of SCBs was 65,340 of which 32,771 were in rural areas.

Lending is an important strategy of banking. Lending sets in motion a chain of economic activities, both direct and indirect, and fosters new services, which are conducive to accelerated socio-economic growth.

Commercial banks have been in the forefront in fostering the growth of small-scale industries. Apart from finance, they provide a package of ancillary services to small-scale industry both in urban and rural areas.

Commercial banks provide working capital, venture capital medium, long-term financial assistance and export credit to new and existing small industries for construction of factory buildings, purchase of machinery, raw materials, marketing and advances in four-forms, *viz.*, cash credits, overdrafts, loans and packing credit. Loans are also extended for setting up industrial estates.

The banks have been opening specialised small-scale industries branches to enable them to provide financial assistance at the single point. The SSI specialised branches were already functioning in 23 of the 85 identified districts with high concentration of small units.

Commercial banks play an important role in extension of financial assistance particularly for meeting the working capital requirements of the sector. As per the extant policy, the SSI sector is accorded priority status for grant of loans. The position of balance outstanding by Public Sector Banks (PSBs), Foreign banks and private sector banks.

The RBI has listed the following short comings of banks. The major short comings relate to lack of appropriate discretionary powers with officers, delay in sanctions of limits and completion of formalities and not computing working capital limits in accordance with RBI guidelines. The corrective action by the banks will improve flow of credit to the small-scale sector.

Commercial banks and assistance to small-scale industry is quite unique in the coming years, banks' operations will be attuned to the priorities of small-scale industries and will seek to coverage their assistance to the maximum extent possible. Banks participation in the growth of small-scale industry has been meaningful and fruitful.

TECHNICAL CONSULTANCY ORGANISATIONS

A network of Technical Consultancy Organisations (TCOs) was set-up in seventies and eighties by IDBI, IFCI, and ICICI in association with state-level financial/development institutions and commercial banks with the objective of making available under a single roof inexpensive consultancy services to small and medium-scale industry and new entrepreneurs. At present, there are 17 TCOs in the country, some of which cover more than one state. In addition, Technical Consultancy Services Organisation of Karnataka, functions for Karnataka.

TCOs render consultancy services to individual entrepreneurs, Government departments and agencies, various State-level development/financial institutions, commercial banks and other institutions in their promotional tasks for industrial development. Initially, the major trust of TCO's activities was in the area of pre-investment studies. However, over the years, TCOs have diversified their consultancy services. Their services now encompass areas of project consultancy, management, market and export consultancy. Project consultancy covers identifying industrial potential through area studies/surveys, preparing project profiles, feasibility reports, pre-investment studies, identifying potential entrepreneurs and providing them with technical and management assistance. Management consultancy includes project supervision and where necessary, rendering technical and administrative assistance. It also includes undertaking diagnostic studies of sick units for rehabilitation purposes. Under their market consultancy services, TCOs undertake market research and surveys for specific products. Their export consultancy services include assignments for export-oriented projects based on modern technology. TCOs also undertake assignments on turnkey basis, and take up energy audit and energy conservation assignments.